MEDICAL BRIEFS

A DICTIONARY OF REALTIME BRIEFS FOR COURT REPORTERS

VOLUME 2 – PREFIXES & SUFFIXES

compiled by
Laurie Boucke

WHITE BOUCKE
PUBLISHING
LAFAYETTE, COLORADO

First Published July 1998
Reprinted January 2001, September 2003

Printed in USA

ISBN 1-888580-02-X

Library of Congress Cataloging-in-Publication Data

Boucke, Laurie.
Medical briefs : a dictionary of realtime briefs for court reporters / compiled by Laurie Boucke.
p. cm.
ISBN 1-888580-02-X (set)
Includes bibliographic references (p.).
Contents: Vol 1. Main dictionary -- v. 2 Prefixes & suffixes.
1. Medical shorthand--Dictionaries. 2. Stenotyp. 3. Law Reporters. I. Title.
R728.8.B67 1998 98-8417
653'.18--dc21 CIP

WHITE BOUCKE PUBLISHING
PO BOX 400, LAFAYETTE, CO 80026, USA
www.white-boucke.com

INTRODUCTION

GENERAL

Volume 2 of this machine stenographer's medical dictionary contains lists of prefixes, suffixes and other combining forms in the following order:

Prefixes, alphabetical by English.
Prefixes, alphabetical by steno.
Suffixes, alphabetical by English.
Suffixes, alphabetical by steno.

The "PREFIXES BY STENO" and "SUFFIXES BY STENO" sections allow you to:

- View, study and/or memorize steno outlines in proximity to alphabetically related outlines.
- Serve as an *aide-mémoire* for occasions where you remember a steno outline but cannot recall the English translation.
- Eliminate confusion when viewing words with multiple steno entries in the main dictionary.
- Eliminate conflicts.
- Provide ideas for you to form your own briefs.

PREFIXES

The "PREFIXES BY ENGLISH" section provides suggestions for the following:

- For one-stroke outlines, an initial letter is given (H– for *"hypo"*), to be included in a single-stroke outline, such as HOIPG for *"hypoglycemia."*
- For two-stroke outlines, a prefix is given (HOIP for *"hypo"*), to be followed by a suffix: HOIP/GLAEM for *"hypoglycemia."*

Stand-alone words versus prefixes. Where a stand-alone word and a prefix are the same in English, high frequency prefixes are usually given a separate steno outline, e.g., use KRIFT for the prefix *"cyst"* and KR*IS for the stand-alone word *"cyst."*

Where possible, stand-alone words and prefixes with the same English definiton are given similar steno outlines, e.g., use KHOE for the word *"echo"* and KHO for the prefix *"echo."*

Prefix entries marked with an obelisk. When a prefix has one or just a few entries in one form and many entries in a closely related form, an obelisk (†) form of the prefix can be used. In the example of the prefixes *"ped"* and *"pedio,"* the prefix *"pedio"* appears only once in this dictionary whereas the prefix *"ped"* has many entries. Some reporters may prefer to use the same steno prefix for both, as no conflicts will be created, but a minor adjustment will need to be made. If PED is defined as *"ped~"* then PED/FOEB will translate as *"pedphobia."* In order to obtain the correct English translation, define PED/FOEB as *"pediophobia."* This entry appears as PED/FOEB† in the main dictionary.

In most situations where a prefix is marked with an obelisk, a second prefix outline without an obelisk is provided for the same prefix, e.g., both PLU and PLUR† can be used for the prefix *"pleur."* For further information on obelisks, see "OBELISKS & ASTERISKS" (page v).

SUFFIXES

All steno suffixes are written in one stroke. The suffix listings include the following:

- Regular medical suffixes as found in medical dictionaries and textbooks (e.g., *"itis"*)
- Words used as suffixes (e.g., *"vascularization"*)
- Word parts used as suffixes (e.g., *"vasology"*)
- Compacted compound suffixes (e.g., *"cholangiocystoduodenostomy"*)

Compacted compound suffixes. Compacted compound suffixes are used. For example, the one-stroke steno suffix KLAOJ fuses four separate building blocks (*chol* + *angio* + *jejuno* + *stomy*) and potentially nine syllables and nine steno strokes. Note that in addition to being used as a suffix (e.g., H–PG/KLAOJ for *"hepaticocholangiojejunostomy"*), KLAOJ is also used for the stand-alone word *"cholangiojejunostomy."*

Stand-alone words versus suffixes. In the example *"hypercholesteremia"* (HAOIRP/KLAOERM), enter *"cholesteremia"* into your dictionary as a stand-alone word (that is, without a preceding "delete space command" to make it a suffix). When used as a suffix, the preceding prefix plus its "delete space command" will join the two parts into one word. Use KLAOERM for *"cholesteremia"* and HAOIRP/KLAOERM for *"hypercholesteremia."*

Suffix Variations. The following suffix variations are provided:

- Suffixes beginning with and without the combining vowel *"o,"* e.g., *"tomy"* and *"otomy."*
- Suffixes involving a variety of other combining letters:

  "emesis" and *"temesis"*
  "logist," "ologist" and *"tologist"*
  "metry," "ometry" and *"imetry"*

- Antonyms such as *"kinesis"* and *"akinesis."*
- Closely related suffixes such as *"anacinesis"* and *"anakinesis."*

Suffix variations are identified by a "*see also*" note in the "SUFFIXES BY ENGLISH" section, referring you to related forms of the suffix in question, e.g., "metry (*see also* ometry *and* imetry)."

UNWANTED DOUBLE-VOWEL RESOLUTION

When a prefix ends with the letter *"o"* and a suffix begins with an *"o,"* it is usually necessary to eliminate one of the letters. In such situations, two different prefixes and/or suffixes are provided, allowing you to "mix and match" according to your preference.

In the example *"angiosis,"* the main generic building blocks are JO + OESZ, where JO is the outline for the prefix *"angio"* and OESZ is the outline for the suffix *"osis."* This combination would give *"angi**oo**sis"* unless the entire outline JO/OESZ is entered as *"angiosis"* in your medical CAT dictionary.

For those who prefer to build words from a prefix and suffix (and not enter a two-stoke outline in your medical CAT dictionary), a selection can be made from the following medical building blocks:

> The prefix JI for *"angi"* can be combined with suffix OESZ for *"osis."*
> The prefix JO for *"angio"* can be combined with suffix SIS for *"sis."*

Both of the above examples create the term *angiosis.*

See "Suffix Variations" (page iv) and "MEDICAL BUILDING BLOCKS" (Introduction to Volume 1) for further information on this topic.

OBELISKS & ASTERISKS

As in Volume 1, obelisks (†) and asterisks (*) are used for specific purposes:

- An obelisk indicates that a two-stroke steno outline must be entered into your medical dictionary in order to translate correctly. In most cases, an obelisk appears where one letter needs to be adjusted.
- The asterisk has four main uses:

  Avoid conflicts.
  Relate two similar suffixes to each other.
  Form a different letter (combination) or sound.
  Distinguish a full word from its hyphenated version.

Expanded information regarding the use of obelisks and asterisks can be found in the Introduction to Volume 1.

PREFIXES
(BY ENGLISH)

A

Prefix or Combining Form	1 stroke	2 strokes
a	A–, –A–	AI/
ab	B–	AB/
abdomino	A–, B–	AOMD/
acantho	K–	KAO*NT/
acephalo	SF–	SFOEL/
achillo	K–	KLOL/
acid	SD–	SID/, SD*ID/
acido	SD–	SDOE/
acin	S–	SNAN/
acne	A–	AENK/
acro	K–, KR–	AORK/
acromio	K–, KR–	KMAO/
actino	T–	AONGT/
ad	D–	AD/
aden	D–	DWEN/
adeno	D–	DWON/
adenoma	D–	DWOEM/
adip	DW–	DW*IP/
adipo	DW–	DWIP/
adipos	DW–	DWIPS/
adren	DR–	DR–N/, DR*EN/
adreno	DR–	DRAOEN/
aero	A–, R–	RO/, A*ER/

after	A–, F–	A*FR/
agglutin	GL–	GLAONT/
agglutino	GL–	GLAOT/
aggluto	GL–	GLOUT/
albumin	B–	BAOUM/
albumino	B–	BAOM/
aldosterono	DR–	DROEFT/
algio	J–	AOJ/
algo	G–	AOG/
all	L–	AUL/
allo	L–	LO/
alveo	A–, V–	AVL/, OFL/
alveolo	A–, V–	OEFL/
ambi	A–, B–	KBAM/
ambly	A–, BL–	KBLIM/
amnio	A–, O–, N–	OIM/
amphi	A–, F–	FIMP/
ampho	A–, F–	FOEMP/
amygdalo	M–	MIGD/
amylo	L–, Y–	LYAM/
amyo	M–	MYAO/
an	N–	AN/
ana	N–	NA/
anatomico	T–	TAOMG/
andro	D–	DROE/
angei (*see* angi)		
angi	J–	JI/
angino	J–	JOIG/
angio	J–	JO/
angioma	J–	JAOM/
aniso	N–	AOINZ/
ankylo	A–	ANK/
ano	A–	AOUN/
ant	A–	ANT/
ante	A–	AENT/
antero	A–	AORNT/
anthraco	A–, TH–	THRAK/
anti	A–	AOINT/
anti- (*hyphenated*)	A–	AO*INT/
antro	A–, T–	TRANT/
aort	A–, AO–	TAORT/
aortico	A–, AO–	TORKT/
aorto	A–, AO–	TOERT/
ap	A–, P–	AP/
api	A–	AOIP/

apico	A–	AOIPG/
apo	A–, P–	PO/
append	P–	PAEND/
appendico	P–	PAEKD/
aqua	KW–	KWAU/
arachno	R–, WR–	RAOK/
arachnoid	R–, WR–	RAFPD/, WRAFPD/
arch	A–	AUFP/
archi	A–	OIFP/
arter	A–, TR–	TRER/
arteri	A–, TR–	TRAOER/
arterial- (*hyphenated*)	A–, TR–	AERLT/
arterio	A–, TR–	TROER/
arteriolo	A–, TR–	TROERL/
arthr	T–, TH–	A*RT/
arthro	T–, TH–	AO*RT/
arytenoid	O–	OIRND/
asthen	S–, TH–	STHEN/
astheno	S–, TH–	STHOEN/
astragalo	S–	SGO/
astro	ST–	STRA*S/
ataxia	T–	TA*X/, TWAX/
atelo	T–	TLAT/
athero	A–, TH–	THUR/
atrio	A–, TR–	TRAO/
attico	A–, T–	AEKT/
audio	A–, AU–	AOD/
auriculo	A–, AU–	AORKL/
auto	A–, AU–	AOUT/
auxo	KP–	UX/
axillo	A–, KP–	OXL/
axio	A–, KP–	AOIX/
axo	KP–	OEX/
axon	KP–	KPAON/

B

bacter	B–	BAERKT/
bacteri	B–	BRE/
bacterio	B–	BOEK/
balano	B–, BL–	BOENL/
baro	B–, BR–	BRAO/
bary	B–	BA*R/
basi	B–	BAEZ/

basio	B–	BOEZ/
bathy	B–	BO*IT/
bi	B–	B*I/
bili	B–	BLI/
bin	B–	BIN/
bio	B–	BO/
bis	B–	BIS/
blast	BL–	BLA*S/, BLAFT/
blasto	BL–	BLAO*S/, BLAOFT/
blastoma	BL–	BLOEM/
blenn	BL–	BL–N/
blenno	BL–	BLEN/
blephar	BL–	BLAUF/, BL*EF/
blepharo	BL–	BLEF/
brachio	B–, BR–	BRAOFP/
brachy	B–, BR–	BROIFP/
brady	B–, BR–	BROID/
branchio	BR–	BRAONG/
bronchi	B–, BR–	BRAOEK/
bronchio	B–, BR–	BROIK/
broncho	B–, BR–	BRONK/
bucco	B–	BOK/
bulbo	B–	BAOBL/
burso	B–	BAORS/

C

caco	K–	KWAOK/
calcaneo	K–	KAEN/
calci	K–, KR–	KRALS/
cantho	K–, TH–	THOEKT/
capillar	K–, KP–	KPLAR/
capillario	K–, KP–	KPLAOR/
capsulo	K–, KP–	KPOEL/
carcino	K–, SK–	KARZ/
carcinogen	K–, SK–, SG–	SGEN/, KRING/, SKROG/
carinoma	K–, SK–	SKROEM/, SGROEM/
cardi	K–	KRAURD/
cardio	K–	KRAUR/
carp	K–	KARP/
carpo	K–	KAORP/
cata	K–	KAT/
ceco	S–	SAO*EK/, SK–K/

celio	S–	SLE/
celo	S–	SLAOEL/
cement	S–	SEMT/
cemento	S–	SMAONT/
cen	S–, KR–	KRAOEN/
ceno	S–, KR–	KROE/
centro	S–, KR–	STROE/
cephal	SF–	SFAL/
cephalo	SF–	SFAOL/
cerebello	S–	SBLOE/
cerebro	S–	SBROE/
cervico	S–	SERK/, SIFRB/
cheil	K–	KHAOI/
cheilo	K–	KHOI/
cheir	K–	KH*IR/
cheiro	K–	KHIR/
chemo	K–, KH–	KMOE/
chloro	K–, KL–	KLAUR/
chol	K–, KH–	KHOEL/
cholangio	K–, KL–	KLAONG/
chole	K–, KH–	KHOIL/
cholecyst	K–, KH–	KH*IS/
cholecysto	K–, KH–	KHAO*S/
choledoch	K–, KH–	KHOLD/
choledocho	K–, KH–	KHOELD/
cholera	K–	KLER/, KLOER/
cholesterin	K–, KL–	KLERN/
cholestero	K–, KL–	KLOEF/
cholesterol	K–, KL–	KLES/, KL*ES/
cholesterolo	K–, KL–	KLOEFL/
cholo	K–, KH–	KHO*EL/
chondr	K–	KHAUND/
chondro	K–	KHOEND/
choreo	KH–, KR–	KHAOE/
chorio	KH–, KR–	KROIR/
choroido	KR–	KWOID/
chromato	KR–, KM–	KMAT/
chromo	K–, KR–	KMO/
chrono	K–, KR–	KRON/
chyl	K–	KAOI/
chylo	K–	KLAOI/
cilio	S–	SLO*/
cine	S–	SNE/
cineto (*see* kineto)		
cleido	KL–	KLOED/

clino	K–, KL–	KLAO*IN/
co	K–	KOE/
coagulo	K–, KW–	KWAOG/
cocco	K–	KOK/
coccy	K–, S–	SKAOEX/
coccygo	K–, S–	SKOEG/
cochleo	K–	KOEKL/
col	K–	KOL/
coleo	K–	KLE/
coli	K–	KLAOE/
collagen	K–, KL–	KAUJ/
collageno	K–, KL–	KLAUJ/
colo	K–	KOEL/
colon	K–, KL–	KLON/
colono	K–, KL–	KLAUN/
colostr	K–, KL–	KLAO*S/
colostro	K–, KL–	KLO*ES/
colp	K–	KLOP/
colpo	K–	KLOEP/
condylo	K–	KONLD/
condyloma	K–	KMOEN/
contra	K–, KR–	KRAUNT/
contra- (*hyphenated*)	K–, KR–	KRA*UNT/
copro	K–, KR–	KROERP/
cor	K–	KOR/
cord	K–	KORD/
cordo	K–	KO*RD/
core	K–	KOER/
corneo	K–	KOERN/
cortico	K–	KOERK/
cost	K–	KO*S/
costi	K–	KAO*ES/
costo	K–	KAO*S/
counter	K–	KOURN/
cox	K–	KOX/
coxo	K–	KO*X/
cranio	K–, KR–	KROIN/
crico	K–, KR–	KRAOIK/
cricoid	K–, KR–	KROIKD/
cry	K–	KRAOI/, KRAO*I/
crymo	K–	KRAO*IM/
cryo	K–	KRO/
crypt	K–, KR–	KRIPT/
crypto	K–, KR–	KROIPT/
cuneo	K–	KAOUN/

cyan	S–	SY–N/, SYA*N/
cyano	S–	SYOEN/
cyber	S–	SAOIRB/
cyclo	S–, SK–	SKLO/
cyst	S–, K–	KRIFT/
cysti	S–, K–	KRAOEFT/
cystico	S–, K–	KRAOEFK/
cystin	S–, K–	STYIN/
cysto	S–, K–	KROIFT/
cyto	S–	STAOIT/

D

dacry	D–	DAK/
dacryo	D–	DOEK/
dactyl	D–	DAKL/
dactylo	D–	DOKL/
de	D–	DE/
deciduo	D–, SD–	SDWO/
den	D–	DEN/
dent	D–	DENT/
dentin	D–	DWINT/
dentino	D–	DWOENT/
dento	D–	DWOEN/
derm	D–	DERM/
derma	D–	DAERM/
dermat	D–	D–RMT/
dermato	D–	DAERMT/
dermo	D–	DOERM/
desm	SD–	SD–FM/
desmo	SD–	SDEFM/
deuter	D–	DAORT/
deutero	D–	DOERT/
dextro	D–	DROEX/
di	D–	D*I/
dia	D–	DY/
diabeto	D–	DOEBT/
diaphano	D–	DOEFN/
diaphragm	D–	DAOIRM/, DAOIFRM/
diastemato	D–, SD–	SDYAMT/
diplo	D–	DLO/
dipso	D–	DOPS/
dis	D–, SD–	DIS/
disc	D–	D–FK, D*IFK/

disco	D–, SD–	SDO/
disto	D–	D*IS/
dolicho	D–, DL–	DLOEK/
dorsi	D–	DORZ/
dorso	D–	DOERZ/
drepano	D–	DRAN/
duodeno	D–, DW–	DWU/
dynamo	D–, DM–	DMO/
dys	D–	DYS/

E

ec	K–	EK/
eccentro	KP–	KPRO/
ecchondro	KP–	KPAUND/
ecchym	KM–	KPEM/
echin	E–, KP–	KHEN/
echino	E–, KP–	KHOEN/
echo	K–	KHO/
eco	K–	AOEK/
ecto	K–	OEKT/
ectro	K–	ERKT/
elasto	L–	LAEFT/
electro	L–	TROE/
eleo	L–	EL/
embol	KB–	KBOL/
embolo	KB–	KBLO/
embryo	KB–	KBRE/
embryon	KB–	KBRON/
en	N–	EN/
encephal	SN–	SNAFL/
encephalo	SN–	SNAOFL/
endo	D–	DOE/, N–D/
endocrino	K–	KROEN/, KR*EN/
enter	SPW–	SPW*/
entero	SPW–	SPW/
ento	SPW–	ENT/
eosino	Y–	SNEN/
ep	EP–	*EP/
ependymo	P–	PAOMD/
epi	E–, P–	EP/
epidermo	D–	ERP/
epididymo	Y–	YOPD/
epilepto	L–	LOIPT/

epiphysio	SF–	SFIPS/
epiplo	P–	PLOIP/
episio	P–	PIS/
epithelio	P–	P*ET/
ereth	E–	*IRT/
erg	E–	*ERG/
ergo	E–	YERG/
ergot	E–	ERGT/
eroto	E–	ERT/
erythr	R–	Y*ERT/
erythro	R–	YO*ERT/
eschar	SKH–	SKHAR/
eso	S–	ES/, EZ/
esophag	S–, SF–	SFOJ/
esophago	S–, SF–	SFOG/
esthesio	S–, ST–	STHOES/
ethmoid	TH–	THOIMD/
ethyl	E–, T–	*ELT/
etio	TL–	TYO/
eu	Y–	AOU/
eury	Y–	YUR/
ex	KP–	EX/
excito	KP–	KPOE/
exo	KP–	KPO/
extero	KP–	KPROE/
extra	KP–	STRA/
extra- (*hyphenated*)	KP–	STRA*/

F

facio	F–	FAIRB/
false- (*hyphenated*)	F–	FALZ/
fascio	F–	FOERB/
femoro	F–	FRO/
feto	F–	FAO*ET/
fibrillo	F–, FR–	FROBL/
fibrin	F–	FRIN/
fibrino	F–	FRIB/
fibro	F–	FRAOIB/
fibroma	F–	FROEB/
fistulo	F–	FLAO/
flavo	F–, FL–	FLAIV/
fluor	F–, FL–	FL–R/
fluoro	F–, FL–	FLOER/

Prefix	Stroke begins	Brief
follicul	F–, FL–	FLOKL/
folliculo	F–, FL–	FLOEK/
freno	F–, FR–	FRAOEN/
frigo	F–, FR–	FRIG/
frigor	F–, FR–	FRIRG/
fronto	F–, FR–	FROENT/
fructo	F–, FR–	FRAOKT/
fuso	F–	FAOUS/

G

Prefix	Stroke begins	Brief
galact	GL–	GLAK/
galacto	GL–	GLAOK/
galvano	G–	GAVN/
gameto	G–	GOEMT/
gangli	G–, GL–	GLING/
ganglio	G–, GL–	GLANG/
gaster	G–	GAFRT/
gastr	G–	GAFT/
gastro	G–	GA*S/
genito	G–, J–	GONT/
geno	G–, J–	J*EN/
genu	G–, J–	JU/
geo	G–, J–	JOE/
germ	G–, J–	JERM/
gero	G–, J–	GRO/
geronto	G–, J–	GRONT/
giganto	G–, J–	JAOIG/
gingiv	J–	JIJ/, JIVN/
gingivo	J–	JAOV/
gingly	J–	JINL/
gleno	GL–	GLEN/
glio	GL–	GLAOI/
glom	GL–	GLOM/
glomerulo	GL–	GLORL/
gloss	GL–	GLOSZ/
glosso	GL–	GLOES/
gluco	GL–	GLOUK/
glucos	GL–	GLOUKS/
glyco	GL–	GLOIK/
glycos	GL–	GLOIKS/
gnath	N–, G–	NA*T/
gnatho	N–, G–	NAO*T/
gon	G–	G–N/

gonad	G–	GOEND/
gonado	G–	GOND/
gone	G–	GON/
gonio	G–	GO*I/
gono	G–	GAUN/
gony	G–	GY/, G*N/
granulo	G–	GRUNL/
grapho	G–	GRAUF/
gyn	G–	GAO*IN/
gyne	G–	GY–N/
gyneco	G–	GEK/
gyno	G–	GAOIN/
gyro	G–, J–	GAOR/

H

hem	H–	H*EM/
hema	H–	HAEM/
hemangio	H–	HAO/
hemat	H–	H*EMT/
hemati	H–	H*IMT/
hematin	H–	HENT/
hemato	H–	HEMT/
hemeral	H–	HA*ERM/
hemi	H–	H–M/
hemo	H–	HEM/
hepat	H–	H*P/
hepatic	H–	HAEPG/
hepatico	H–	H–PG/
hepato	H–	H–P/
heredo	H–	H–RD/
herm	H–	H–RM/
hernio	H–	H–RN/
heter	H–	H*ET/
hetero	H–	HET/
hidr	H–	H*IR/
hidro	H–	HO*IR/
his	H–	HIS/
histamin	H–	HIFM/
histio	H–	H–FT/
histo	H–	HOFT/
holo	H–	HOL/
homeo	H–	HO*EM/
homo	H–	HOM/, HO*M/

hormono	H–	HORM/
humero	H–	HOURM/
hy	H–	HAO*I/
hyal	H–	HYAL/, HYAOIL/
hyalin	H–	HIN/
hyalo	H–	HYOEL/
hydatid	H–	HAOITD/
hydr	H–	HIR/
hydro	H–	HOIR/
hygro	H–	HAOIG/
hymen	H–	HAO*IM/
hymeno	H–	HO*IM/
hyo	H–	HYO/, HO*I/
hyp	H–	HAO*IP/
hyper	H–	HAOIRP/
hypn	H–	H*N/, HY–P/
hypno	H–	H–N/, HYIP/
hypo	H–	HOIP/
hypsi	H–, Y–	YIPS/
hypso	H–, Y–	YOPS/
hyster	H–	HIFR/, H*IS/†
hystero	H–	H*IS/

I

iatro	Y–	YAOIRT/
ichthyo	TH–	THAOE/
ictero	Y–	YOERKT/
ideo	Y–	YOED/
idio	Y–	YO*D/, DYI/
igni	G–	*IG/
ileo	Y–	YIL/
ileoceco	Y–	YILG/
ilio	Y–	YOIL/
immuno	M–, KB–	MUN/
in	N–	IN/
incud	K–	INGD/
incudo	K–	AONGD/
infra	F–	FRA/
infra- (*hyphenated*)	F–	FRA*/
infundibul	N–	NAOUFL/
infundibulo	N–	NOEFL/
inguino	G–	GAOUN/
ino	N–	NO*/

insulin	SL–	SLIN/
insulino	SL–	SLOIN/
insulo	SL–	SUL/
inter	SPW–	SPWR/
intercosto	SPW–	SPWO*ES/
intero	SPW–	SPWRO/
intra	SPW–	SPWRA/
intra- (*hyphenated*)	SPW–	SPWRA*/
intro	SPW–	SPWOR/
intus	SPW–	SPWUZ/
ion	Y–	AOIN/
iono	Y–	YOEN/
ionto	Y–	YOENT/
irid	Y–, IR–	IRD/
irido	Y–, IR–	OIRD/
isch	SH–, SKH–	SKH/
ischi	SH–, SKH–	SKHI/
ischia	SH–, SKH–	SKHA/
ischio	SH–, SKH–	SKHO/
ischo	SK–	SKHOE/
iso	S–	SHO/, SO*/
isthm	S–	STHIM/
isthmo	S–	STHOM/
ithy	STH–	*IT/

J

jejun	J–	JAOEJ/
jejuno	J–	JAOJ/
juxta	J–	JUXT/
juxta- (*hyphenated*)	J–	JAUXT/

K

karyo	K–	KRAU/
kata (*see* cata)		
kerat	K–	KERT/
kerato	K–	KOERT/
keto	K–	KAOET/
keton	K–	KWON/
kilo	K–	KL–/
kin	K–	KIN/

kine	K–	K*IN/
kinesi	K–	KINZ/
kinesio	K–	KENZ/
kineto	K–	KWOINT/
klepto	KL–	KL–PT/
koilo	K–	KLOILG/
kymo	K–	KMAOI/
kypho	K–	KOIF/
kysth	K–	K*IT/, K*ITS/
kyto (*see* cyto)		

L

labyrinth	R–	R*INT/
lacrimo	L–	LAORMG/
lact	L–	LAKT/
lacti	L–	LAOEKT/
lacto	L–	LOEKT/
lalo	L–	LAOL/
lamina	L–	LAM/
lapar	L–	L–RP/
laparo	L–	LARP/
laryng	L–	LAENG/
laryngo	L–	LAERNG/
latero	L–	LAORT/
leio	L–	LO*I/
lenti	L–	LE/, L*INT/
lenticulo	L–	LAOKL/
lentigin	L–	LIJT/
lepto	L–	LEP/
leuc (*see* leuk)		
leuco (*see also* leuko)	L–	LAO*K/
leuk	L–	LAO*UK/
leukemo	L–	LAO*UM/
leuko (*see also* leuco)	L–	LAOUK/
levo	L–	LOEV/
lien	L–	LAO*EN/
lieno	L–	LAO*IN/
linguo	L–	LOUNG/
lip	L–	LIP/
lipo	L–	LOIP/
lipoid	L–	POID/
lipoma	L–	LOEMP/
lith	L–	L*IT/

litho	L–	LOET/
lochio	L–	LOEFP/
log	L–	LOG/
logad	L–	LAOGD/
logo	L–	LOEG/
lord	L–	LORD/
lordo	L–	LAORD/, LO*RD/
lumbo	L–	LOUB/
lymph	Y–	YOIMP/
lympha	Y–	YAMP/
lymphat	Y–	YAMPT/
lympho	Y–	YOMP/
lymphoid	Y–	YOID/
lymphoma	Y–	YOEM/
lyo	L–	LOI/

M

macr	M–	M–RK/
macro	M–	MAK/
maculo	M–	MAKL/
mamm	M–	MA*M/
mammill	M–	M*IL/
mammo	M–	MAOM/
mast	M–	MA*S/
masto	M–	MAO*S/
mastoid	M–	MOITD/
maxillo	M–	MOXL/
mazo	M–	MAOS/
meat	M–	MAET/
meato	M–	MOET/
mechano	M–	MAEFP/
medi	M–	MED/
mediastino	M–	MAOEFT/
medico	M–	MOEKD/
medio	M–	MOD/, M*D/
medullo	M–	MAOLD/
meg	M–	M*EG/
mega	M–	MEG/
megal	M–	MA*EG/
megalo	M–	MAOLG/
meio	M–	MO*E/
mel	M–	M*L/
melan	M–	ML–N/

Prefix	Initial	Steno
melano	M–	MLOEN/
melanoma	M–	MLAEM/
melit	M–	MLIT/
melo	M–	MO*IL/
mening	M–, J–	MIJ/, MENG/
meninge	M–, J–	MOIJ/, MENG/†
meningeo	M–, J–	MOEJ/, MENG/†
meningio	M–, J–	MAOJ/, MENG/†
meningo	M–, J–	MOEG/
menisc	M–	M–FK/, MIFK/
menisco	M–	MOFK/
meno	M–	M*EN/
mero	M–	MROE/
mes	M–	MES/
mesio	M–	MAO*EZ/
meso	M–	MEZ/
mesoderm	M–	MERMS/, MERMD/
met	M–	MET/
meta	M–	M*ET/
metabol	M–	MOBT/
meteor	M–	MYOR/
meteoro	M–	MYAOER/
meth	M–	M*ET/ †
methyl	M–	MY*L/
metr	M–	MRAOET/
metro	M–	MROET/
micr	M–	MIRK/
micro	M–	MORK/
mid	M–	MID/
milli	M–	ML–L/
milliampere- (*hyphenated*)	M–	MA*EMP/
mono	M–	MAUN/
mono- (*hyphenated*)	M–	MA*UN/
morphin	M–	MOFRN/
morpho	M–	MOFR/
muci	M–	MAOUZ/
mucin	M–	MAOUNZ/
mucino	M–	MAONZ/
muco	M–	MOUK/
mucor	M–	MAORK/
multi	M–	MULT/
musculo	M–	MAOFL/
my	M–	MI/
myco	M–	MYOEK/, MY–K/
myel	M–, Y–	MAO*IL/

myelin	M–	MAOINL/
myelino	M–	MAONL/
myelo	M–, Y–	MOIL/
myeloblast	Y–, M–	YAFT/
myeloma	M–, Y–	YOL/
myo	M–	MAOI/
myomo	M–	MO*IM/
myop	M–	MO*P/
myos	M–	MAO*IS/
myringo	M–	MRING/
mytho	M–	MO*IT/
myx	M–	M*IX/
myxedema	M–	MAOEMD/
myxo	M–	MOIX/

N

nano	N–	NA*N/
narco	N–	NARK/
naso	N–	NAS/
necr	N–	N*ERK/
necro	N–	N*EK/
neo	N–	NO*E/
nephr	F–, N–	N*EF/
nephro	F–, N–	NEF/
neur	N–	NUR/
neuri	N–	N*UR/
neuro	N–	NOUR/
neuro- (*hyphenated*)	N–	NO*UR/
neurode	N–	NOURD/
neurolept	N–	NLEPT/
neutr	N–	NRUT/
neutro	N–	NRAOT/
nevo	N–	N–V/
noci	N–	NO*S/
noct	N–	NOKT/
non	N–	NON/
non- (*hyphenated*)	N–	NO*N/
norm	N–	NORM/
normo	N–	NO*RM/
noso	N–	NO*EZ/
nucleo	N–, K–	NAOULG/
nulli	N–	NO*IL/
nyct	N–	N*IKT/

nycto	N–	NAOKT/
nymph	N–	NIMP/
nympho	N–	NOMP/

O

o	O–	O/
occipito	S–	SOPT/, SAOPT/
occluso	K–	KLAOUZ/
ochlo	O–, KL–	OKL/
ochro	O–, K–	OEFP/
octa	O–	AUKT/
octi	O–	O*KT/
octo	O–	O*KT/†
oculo	O–, K–	OEKL/
odont	D–	DAO*NT/, DAONT/†
odonto	D–	DAONT/
odor	D–	DOR/†
odori	D–	DOIR/
odyn	D–	DYN/†
odyno	D–	DYN/
oiko	O–	OIK/
olecran	L–	L*EK/
oleo	O–	OEL/
olfact	O–, F–	OEFKT/
olig	O–, GL–	GLIG/
oligo	O–, GL–	GLOG/
om	O–	O*M/
oment	M–	MAONT/
omento	M–	MOENT/
omo	O–	OM/
omphal	O–, F–	OMP/
omphalo	O–, F–	OEMP/
on	O–	ON/
onco	O–	AUNG/
oneir	O–	O*IRN/, OIRN/†
oneiro	O–	OIRN/
onomato	O–	AOMT/
onto	O–	OENT/, O*NT/
onych	O–	ONK/
onycho	O–	OENK/
oo	O–	AO/
oophor	F–	AOF/
oophoro	F–	AOFR/

ophthalm	F–	OFLT/
ophthalmo	F–	OEFLT/
opistho	P–	P*ITS/
opt	T–	OPT/
optico	T–	AOPGT/
opto	T–	AOPT/
orbit	O–	ORBT/
orbito	O–	OIRB/
orch	O–, KH–	O*RK/, ORK/[†]
orchi	O–, KH–	ORK/
orchid	O–, KH–	O*RKD/, ORKD/[†]
orchido	O–, KH–	ORKD/
orchio	O–, KH–	OERK/
organ	O–, G–	GORN/
organo	O–, G–	GAORN/
oro	O–	O*R/
orrho	O–, R–	WROE/
orth	O–, TH–	O*RT/
ortho	O–, TH–	O*ERT/
oscheo	SK–	SKHE/
oscillo	S–	SKHIL/
osm	S–	SM–/
osmo	S–	SMO/
oss	S–	AUSZ/
osseo	S–	AOS/
ossi	S–	AOSZ/
ossicul	S–	AOULS/
ost	S–	A*US/
oste	S–	AUTS/
osteo	S–, TW–	AUS/
osteoma	TW–	TWOEM/
ot	T–, Y–	YOET
oto	T–	OET/
ovar	O–	AOVR/
ovari	AO–, V–	AOV/
ovario	O–	OIV/
over	O–, V–	OVR/
ovi	V–	V*I/
ovo	V–	VO*/
oxy	KP–	OIX/
oxygen	SH–	SHEN/

P

pachy	P–	PA*K/
palat	P–	PALT/
palato	P–	PAOLT/
paleo	P–	PA*EL/
pali	P–	PLAU/†
palin	P–	PLAUN/
pall	P–	PLAU/
pallid	P–	PL–D/
pallido	P–	PLOED/
pan	P–	PAN/
pancreat	P–	PRANG/
pancreatico	P–	PRAOKT/
pancreato	P–	PRAT/
pancreo	P–	PRAOENG/
pannicul	P–	P–NL/
pant	P–	PANT/
panto	P–	PAONT/
papill	P–	PLAP/
papillo	P–	PLAOP/
papulo	P–, PL–	PLAO/
par	P–	PA*R/
para	P–	PAR/
para- (*hyphenated*)	P–	P–R/
paraffin	P–	PAEFR/, PAFRN/
parasit	P–	PAIRTS/
parieto	P–, PR–	PRAO/
parturi	P–	PRART/
parvo	P–	PAUFRB/
path	P–	PA*T/
patho	P–	PAO*T/
ped	P–	PAOED/, PED/
pedi	P–	PAOED/ †, PED/ †
pedicul	P–	PAOUKL/
pediculo	P–	PAOKL/
pedio	P–	PAOED/ †, PED/ †
pedion	P–	PAOEND/
pedo	P–	PAO*ED/, P*ED/
peduncul	P–	PAOULG/
pelvi	P–	PEV/
pelvio	P–	PAOV/
pelvo	P–	POEV/
pep	P–	PEP/

pepsin	P–	PEFN/, PEPZ/
pepto	P–	POPT/
per	P–	P*ER/
peri	P–	PRI/
perineo	P–	PIRN/
perio	P–	PROE/
perioste	P–, PR–	PRAUF/
periosteo	P–, PR–	PRAUFT/
periosto	P–, PR–	PRAU/
peritone	P–	PRO*EN/
peritoneo	P–	PROINT/
pero	P–	PAO*E/
petro	P–	PROET/
petrolat	P–	TROELT/
phaco	F–	FAO*K/
phago	F–	FOEG/
phak	F–	FA*K/
phall	F–	FAL/†
phallo	F–	FAL/
phanero	F–	FAERN/
pharma	F–	FA*URM/
pharmaco	F–	FARK/
pharyng	F–	FAIRNG/
pharyngo	F–	FAORNG/
phleb	FL–	FL*EB/
phlebo	FL–	FLEB/
phon	F–	FO*EN/ †
phono	F–	FO*EN/
phoro	F–	FROE/
phosphat	SF–	SFAT/
phospho	SF–	SFOE/
phosphor	SF–	SFOUR/
phot	F–	FO*T/, FOT/†
photo	F–	FOT/
phren	FR–	FREN/ †
phrenic	FR–	FRENG/
phrenico	FR–	FROINK/
phreno	FR–	FROEN/
physio	F–	FIZ/, FOIZ/
physo	F–	FAOIZ/
phyt	F–	PY–T/
phyto	F–	PYOET/
pigment	P–	PIMT/
pigmento	P–	PAOMT/
pili	P–	PLAO*E

pilo	P–	PLO*/
pimel	P–	PEM/, PEMP/
pin	P–	PIN/
pineal	P–	PAENL/
pinealo	P–	POENL/
placent	P–	PLAFNT/
placento	P–	PLAOFNT/
plagio	P–	PLOIJ/
plan	PL–	PLAN/
plano	P–	PLAON/
plant	PL–	PLANT/
plasm	PL–	PL–FM/
plasma	P–	PL–M/
plasmato	P–	PL–MT/, PLAOFMT/
plasmo	P–	PLAMZ/
platy	P–	PLALT/
pleio	P–	PLAOIL/
pleo	P–	PLOIL/
plesio	P–	PL–Z/
pleur	PL–	PLU/, PLUR/ †
pleuro	PL–	PLUR/
plex	PL–	PL*EX/
plexi	PL–	PLO*IX/
pluri	PL–	PLIR/
pneo	N–	NYO/
pneum	N–	N*UM/
pneuma	N–	NAUM/
pneumat	N–	NAO*MT/
pneumato	N–	NAOMT/
pneumo	N–	NAOM/
pneumon	N–	NO*EM/
pneumono	N–	NOEM/, NAO*UM/
pod	P–	POD/
podo	P–	POED/
poikilo	P–	POIKL/
polio	P–	PLOL/
pollen	P–	PLO*N/
poly	P–	POL/
polymer	P–	PLERM/
polyp	P–	PLIP/
por	P–	POR/
poro	P–	PO*ER/
porphyrin	P–	POEFR/, POFRN/
porto	P–	POERT/
poso	P–	POEZ/

post	P–	POEFT/
post- (*hyphenated*)	P–	PO*ES/
postero	P–	POEFRT/
posth	P–	PO*FT/
pre	P–	PRE/
presby	P–	PREBS/
presso	P–	PR–Z/
priap	P–	PRAIP/
pro	P–	PRO/
proct	P–	PROKT/
procto	P–	PROK/
proprio	P–	PROIP/
pros	P–	PROZ/
proso	P–	PRAOS/
prosop	P–	PRAOPS/
prosopo	P–	PROEPS/
prostat	P–	PRA*S/
prostatico	P–	PRAOK/
prostato	P–	PRO*S/
prostho	P–	PRO*ETS/
prot	P–	PRO*ET/†
protein	P–	PROIN/
proteo	P–	PRO*IT/
prothrombin	P–, TH–	THRAUB/
proto	P–	PRO*ET/
proxim	P–, KP–	PRIMX/, KPRIX/
proximo	P–, KP–	PROIMX/, KPROX/
pseud	S–	SWAOD/, SAO*D/
pseudo	S–	SWAO/, SAO*UD/
psych	S–, SK–	SAOIK/
psycho	S–, SK–	SKOE/
psychodo	S–, SK–	SKOED/
psychoto	S–, SK–	SKOEKT/
psychro	S–, SK–	SKRO*E/
pterygo	T–	TOERG/
ptyal	T–	TYAL/
ptyalo	T–	TYOEL/
pubo	P–	POB/
pudend	P–	PAOUND/
pulmo	PL–	PAOM/
pulmono	P–	PLOUM/
pulp	P–	POUP/, PL*UP/
pupillo	P–	PLOUP/
py	P–	PY/
pyc	P–	PY*K/

pyel	P–	PYEL/
pyelo	P–	PYOEL/
pykno	P–	PY–K/
pyle	PL–	PYAOIL/
pylor	PL–	PLOR/
pyloro	PL–	PLOER/
pyo	P–	PYO/
pyreto	P–, PR–	PYET/
pyrexio	PR–	PROEX/
pyro	P–	PAOIR/

Q

quadrant	KW-	KWARNT/, KWAERNT/
quadri	KW-	KWOD/

R

rachi	R–	RAIFP/
rachio	R–	ROFP/
radiculo	R–	RAOKL/
radio	R–	RAO/
re	R–	RE/
re- (*hyphenated*)	R–	R*E/
rect	R–	REKT/
recto	R–	ROEKT/
reflex	R–	R–FX/
reflexo	R–	ROFX/
refract	R–, FR–	FRAEK/
ren	R–	REN/
reni	R–	RIN/
reno	R–	RAOEN/
reticul	R–	RIKL/
reticulo	R–	RUKL/
retino	R–	RAONT/
retro	TR–, R–	TRO/
rhabdo	R–, WR–	WRABD/
rheo	R–, WR–	WRAOE/
rheum	R–, WR–	WRAOM/
rheuma	R–, WR–	RO*IM/, WROIM/
rhin	R–, WR–	WRAOIN/
rhino	R–, WR–	WROIN/

rhitid	R–, WR–	WRITD/
rhiz	R–	WRAOIZ/
rhizo	R–	WRAOIS/
rhodo	R–, WR–	WROED/
rhomb	R–, WR–	WROM/
rhombo	R–, WR–	WROEM/
rhonch	R–, WR–	RONG/
rhytid	R–, WR–	WROITD/
ribo	R–	RAOIB/
roentgen	R–	RENG/
roentgeno	R–	ROENG/
rubro	R–	RAOB/

S

sacchar	S–	SKA*FP/
saccharo	S–	SKAFP/
sacro	S–	SKRO/
salping	SP–	SP*ING/
salpingo	SP–	SPING/
sangui	S–	SGU/
sanguino	S–	SGOE/, SWOENG/
sapro	S–	SPRO/
sarc	S–	SA*RK/
sarco	S–	SARK/
sarcoma	S–	SKOEM/
scapho	SK–	SKAOF/
scapul	SK–	SKLUP/
scapulo	SK–	SKLOEP/
scat	SK–	SKAT/
scato	SK–	SK–T/
schisto	SK–	SKHIS/
schizo	SK–	SKIS/
scirrh	S–, SK–	SKHIR/
scirrho	S–, SK–	SKIR/, SKHOR/
scler	SK–	SKL*ER/
sclera	SK–	SKLAER/
sclero	SK–	SKLER/
sclerotico	SK–	SKLOEKT/
scolio	SK–	SKLOEL/
scopo	SK–	SKO*EP/
scoto	SK–	SKOET/
scotoma	SK–	SKAUMT/
scrofulo	SK–	SKROEFL/

sebo	S–	SAOEB/
secret	SK–	SKRET/
secreto	SK–	SK–RT/
self- (*hyphenated*)	S–, SF–	SEFL/
semeio	S–, SM–	SMAOI/
semi	S–	SMI/
semi- (*hyphenated*)	S–	SEM/
semino	S–	SMOE/
senso	S–	SOENS/
sensori	S–	SOIRS/
sept	S–	SPE/
septi	S–, SP–	SPI/
septico	S–, SP–	SPOE/
septo	S–	SPO/
sero	S–	SAO*ER/
sial	S–	SAOIL/
sialo	S–	SAOL/
sidero	S–,	SDRO/
sigmoid	S–, SM–	SMOID/
sigmoido	S–, SM–	SMOED/
silico	S–	SLO/
sinistro	S–, SN–	SNIRS/
sino	S–, SN–	SNOI/
sinus	S–, SN–	SNUS/
sito	S–	STO*/
skeleto	SK–	SKOELT/
socio	S–	S–RB/
soma	S–	SAOM/
somat	S–, SM–	SAMT/
somatico	S–, SM–	SMOIK/
somato	S–, SM–	SAOMT/
somn	S–	SAUM/
somni	S–, SM–	SOIM/
somno	S–, SM–	SNAUM/
sono	S–	SOEN/
spasm	SP–	SPAFM/
spasmo	SP–	SPAZ/
spectro	SP–	SPREK/
sperm	SP–	SPIRM/
sperma	SP–	SPARM/
spermat	SP–	SPARMT/
spermato	SP–	SPAORMT/
spermio	SP–	SPAORM/
spermo	SP–	SPOERM/
sphacel	S–	SFAFL/

sphacelo	S–	SFAOFL/
sphen	SF–	SFEN/
spheno	SF–	SFOIN/
sphenoid	SF–	SFO*ID/, SFOID/[†]
spher	SF–	SFIR/
sphero	SF–	SFOIR/
sphincter	SF–	SFING/, SFINGT/
sphinctero	SF–	SFONG/
sphingo	SF–	SFOEG/
sphygmo	SM–	SFIG/
spino	SP–	SPOIN/, SPAO*IN/
spirillo	S–, SP–	SPRIL/
spiro	SP–	SPOIR/
spirochet	SP–	SPAOIRK/
splanchn	SP–	SPLANG/
splanchno	SP–	SPLONG/
splen	SP–	SPLEN/
spleni	SP–	SPL*IN/
spleno	SP–	SPLON/
spondyl	S–, SP–	SPAUNL/
spondylo	S–, SP–	SPAONL/
spongio	S–, SP–	SPAOJ/
sporo	SP–	SPROE/
squamo	SK–	SKWOM/
stapedio	S–, ST–	STOEPD/
staphyl	S–	STAFL/
staphylo	S–	STAOFL/
stato	S–	STA*T/
steato	ST–	STAOET/
steno	ST–	ST–N/, SNO/
sterco	ST–	STOIRK/
stercoro	ST–	STROIK/
stereo	ST–	STER/
sterno	ST–	STOIRN/
stoma	ST–	STOEM/
stomat	ST–, SM–	STAMT/
stomato	ST–, SM–	STOEMT/
strepto	ST–	STROPT/
strio	ST–	STOIR/
strum	S–, ST–	STRUM/
stylo	ST–	STLO/
sub	S–	SUB/
sudo	S–	SAOD/
sudor	S–	SAORD/
super	S–	SPR–/

super- (*hyphenated*)	S–	SP–R/
supero	S–	SPRAO/
supra	S–, SP–	SPRA/
supra- (*hyphenated*)	S–, SP–	SAORP/
sym	S–	SIM/, SYM/
sympathetico	S–	STHOE/
sympathico	S–	SKPO/
sympatho	S–	STHO/
symphyseo	S–	SFES/
symphysio	S–	SFOES/
symptom	S–	STOM/
syn	S–	SIN/
synapto	S–	SNAOPT/
synarthro	S–, SN–	SNA*RT/
syndesm	S–	SD–M/
syndesmo	S–	SDOFM/
syngenesio	S–	SGAOES/
synovio	S–, SN–	SNOIV/
syphil	S–, SF–	SFLI/
syphilo	S–	SFLO/
syring	S–	SYING/
syringo	S–	SYONG/

T

tabo	T–	TBOE/
tachy	T–	TA*K/
talo	T–	TLAOL/, TAO*L/
talon	T–	TLAON/
tars	T–	TARS/
tarso	T–	TAORS/
tecto	T–	TWOEK/
tel	T–	T*EL/
tele	T–	TL*E/
teleo	T–	TAO*EL/
temporo	T–	TOERM/
ten	T–	TEN/
tend	T–	TEND/
tendo	T–	TOND/
teno	T–	T*EN/
tenon	T–	TAUN/
tenonto	T–	TA*UNT/
tephro	T–	TREF/
terato	T–	TAERT/

thalamo	T–, TH–	THAM/
thalasso	T–, TH–	THAOLS/
thanato	TH–	THAONT/
theco	TH–	THOIK/
thel	TH–	THAOEL/
therm	TH–	THERM/, TH–RM/
thermo	TH–	THORM/
thigmo	TH–	THOEMG/
thio	TH–	THOI/
thoraco	T–, TH–	THOERK/
thromb	T–, TH–	THRAUM/
thrombo	T–, TH–	THROM/
thym	T–, TH–	THAOIM/
thymo	T–, TH–	THAOM/
thyreo	T–, TH–	THOER/, THAO*ER/
thyro	T–, TH–	THOIR/
thyroid	T–, TH–	THROID/, THAOIRD/
thyroido	T–, TH–	THOERD/
tibio	T–	TOIB/
tono	T–	TAO*N/
tonsillo	T–	TAONL/
top	T–	TOP/
topo	T–	TO*P/
tox	T–	TO*X/
toxi	T–	TO*IX/
toxic	T–	TOK/
toxico	T–	TOIX/
toxin	T–	TOX/
toxo	T–	TOEX/
trabecul	TR–	TRABL/
trabeculo	TR–	TRAOBL/
trachel	TR–	TR–KL/
trachelo	TR–	TROEKL/
tracheo	TR–	TROIK/
tran	TR–	TRA*N/
trans	TR–	TRANS/
transverso	TR–	TROEFRS/
trauma	TR–	TRAUM/
traumato	TR–	TROEMT/
tri	T–	TRI/
trich	TR–	TRIFP/
trichin	TR–	TRINK/
trichino	TR–	TRONK/
tricho	TR–	TR*IK/
trigon	TR–	TRAOING/

trigono	TR–	TROIG/
troph	T–, TR–	TROFP/
tropho	T–, TR–	TROEFP/
trypano	TR–	TRAO*IP/
tuber	T–	TAOURB/
tubercul	T–	TOUBL/
tuberculo	T–	TOEBL/
tubero	T–	TRAOB/
tubo	T–	TOUB/
tubulo	T–	TOIBL/
tympan	T–, TW–	TIMP/
tympano	T–, TW–	TOMP/
typhl	T–	TIFL/
typhlo	T–	TOEFL/
typho	T–	TAOIF/

U

ul	U–	AOUL/
ulcer	U–	ULS/
ulcero	U–	URLS/
ule	U–	OUL/
ulno	U–	OUNL/
ulo	Y–, U–	YAOUL/
ultra	U–	URLT/
un	N–	UN/
under	N–	UNDZ/
uni	Y–	YOI/
ur	Y–	YAOU/, YOIR/
uranisco	Y–	YANS/
urano	Y–	YAORN/
urat	Y–	YOURT/
urea	Y–	YAOR/
ureo	Y–	YOR/
ureter	Y–	YERT/, AOURT/
uretero	Y–	YOERT/
urethr	AOUR–	YAO*ET/
urethra	Y–	AO*URT/
urethro	AOUR–	YO*ET/
uri	Y–	YIR/
uric	Y–	YAOURK/
urico	AOUR–, Y–	YURG/
uricos	AOUR–, Y–	YURGS/
urin	Y–	YIRN/

urino	Y-	YORN/
uro	Y-	AOUR/
urobilin	AOU-	AOURBL/
uter	Y-	YURT/
utero	Y-	YAORT/
utriculo	Y-	YAOUK/
uveo	AOU-	OUV/
uvula	Y-	YAOUV/
uvulo	Y-	YOEV/

V

vaccino	V-	VOIX/
vagin	V-	VAJ/
vagino	V-	VOEJ/
vago	V-	VAOG/
valvo	V-	VAOFL/
valvulo	V-	VOEVL/
varico	V-	VAURK/
vas	V-	VAS/
vasculo	V-	VUK/, VUFK/
vaso	V-	VAOS/
velo	V-	V*EL/
veno	V-	VAON/
venom	V-	VEM/
ventri	V-	VAOERNT/
ventriculo	V-	VAOUL/
ventro	V-	VOENT/
vertebro	V-	VAOB/
vesico	V-	VEFK/
vesicul	V-	VAOUKL/
vesiculo	V-	VUKL/
vestibulo	V-	VIB/
vibro	V-	VOERB/
viscero	V-	VOEFR/
visuo	V-	VAOZ/, VURB/
vivi	V-	VAOEV/
vomero	V-	V-RM/
vulvo	V-	VOIV/

X

xanth	Z–, KP–	ZANT/
xanthin	Z–, KP–	ZINT/, KP*INT/
xantho	Z–, KP–	ZOENT/
xen	Z–, KP–	ZEN/
xeno	Z–, KP–	Z–N/
xero	Z–, KP–	ZE/
xiphi	Z–, KP–	ZIF/, SIF/
xipho	Z–, KP–	ZOEF/
xiphoid	Z–, KP–	ZIFD/

Z

zonul	Z–	ZUL/
zoo	Z–	SAO/
zoster	Z–	ZORS/
zyg	Z–	ZY–G/
zygo	Z–	ZOEG/
zygomatico	Z–	ZMAK/, ZMAT/
zymo	Z–	ZMO/

PREFIXES
(BY STENO)

A

AB/ . . . . ab
AD/ . . . . ad
AEKT/ . . . . attico
AENK/ . . . . acne
AENT/ . . . . ante
A*ER/ . . . . aero
AERLT/ . . . . arterial- (*hyphenated*)
A*FR/ . . . . after
AI/ . . . . a
AN/ . . . . an
ANK/ . . . . ankylo
ANT/ . . . . ant
AO/ . . . . oo
AOD/ . . . . audio
AOEK/ . . . . eco
AOF/ . . . . oophor
AOFR/ . . . . oophoro
AOG/ . . . . algo
AOIN/ . . . . ion
AOINT/ . . . . anti
AO*INT/ . . . . anti- (*hyphenated*)
AOINZ/ . . . . aniso
AOIP/ . . . . api
AOIPG/ . . . . apico
AOIX/ . . . . axio
AOJ/ . . . . algio

AOMD/ . . . . abdomino
AOMT/ . . . . onomato
AONGD/ . . . . incudo
AONGT/ . . . . actino
AOPGT/ . . . . optico
AOPT/ . . . . opto
AORK/ . . . . acro
AORKL/ . . . . auriculo
AORNT/ . . . . antero
AO*RT/ . . . . arthro
AOS/ . . . . osseo
AOSZ/ . . . . ossi
AOU/ . . . . eu
AOUL/ . . . . ul
AOULS/ . . . . ossicul
AOUN/ . . . . ano
AOUR/ . . . . uro
AOURBL/ . . . . urobilin
AOURT/ . . . . ureter
AO*URT/ . . . . urethra
AOUT/ . . . . auto
AOV/ . . . . ovari
AOVR/ . . . . ovar
AP/ . . . . ap
A*RT/ . . . . arthr
AUFP/ . . . . arch
AUKT/ . . . . octa
AUL/ . . . . all
AUNG/ . . . . onco
AUS/ . . . . osteo
A*US/ . . . . ost
AUSZ/ . . . . oss
AUTS/ . . . . oste
AVL/ . . . . alveo

B

BAERKT/ . . . . bacter
BAEZ/ . . . . basi
BAOBL/ . . . . bulbo
BAOM/ . . . . albumino
BAORS/ . . . . burso
BAOUM/ . . . . albumin
BA*R/ . . . . bary

B*I/ . . . . bi
BIN/ . . . . bin
BIS/ . . . . bis
BLAFT/ . . . . blast
BLAOFT/ . . . . blasto
BLAO*S/ . . . . blasto
BLA*S/ . . . . blast
BLAUF/ . . . . blephar
BLEF/ . . . . blepharo
BL*EF/ . . . . blephar
BLEN/ . . . . blenno
BLI/ . . . . bili
BL-N/ . . . . blenn
BLOEM/ . . . . blastoma
BO/ . . . . bio
BOEK/ . . . . bacterio
BOENL/ . . . . balano
BOEZ/ . . . . basio
BO*IT/ . . . . bathy
BOK/ . . . . bucco
BRAO/ . . . . baro
BRAOEK/ . . . . bronchi
BRAOFP/ . . . . brachio
BRAONG/ . . . . branchio
BRE/ . . . . bacteri
BROID/ . . . . brady
BROIFP/ . . . . brachy
BROIK/ . . . . bronchio
BRONK/ . . . . broncho

D

DAERM/ . . . . derma
DAERMT/ . . . . dermato
DAK/ . . . . dacry
DAKL/ . . . . dactyl
DAOIFRM/ . . . . diaphragm
DAOIRM/ . . . . diaphragm
DAONT/ . . . . odonto
DAONT/ † . . . . odont
DAO*NT/ . . . . odont
DAORT/ . . . . deuter
DE/ . . . . de
DEN/ . . . . den

Steno	Prefix
DENT/	dent
DERM/	derm
D-FK/	disc
D*I/	di
D*IFK/	disc
DIS/	dis
D*IS/	disto
DLO/	diplo
DLOEK/	dolicho
DMO/	dynamo
DOE/	endo
DOEBT/	diabeto
DOEFN/	diaphano
DOEK/	dacryo
DOERM/	dermo
DOERT/	deutero
DOERZ/	dorso
DOIR/	odori
DOKL/	dactylo
DOPS/	dipso
DOR/ [†]	odor
DORZ/	dorsi
DRAN/	drepano
DRAOEN/	adreno
DR*EN/	adren
D-RMT/	dermat
DR-N/	adren
DROE/	andro
DROEFT/	aldosterono
DROEX/	dextro
DWEN/	aden
DWINT/	dentin
DWIP/	adipo
DW*IP/	adip
DWIPS/	adipos
DWOEM/	adenoma
DWOEN/	dento
DWOENT/	dentino
DWON/	adeno
DWU/	duodeno
DY/	dia
DYI/	idio
DYN/	odyno
DYN/ [†]	odyn
DYS/	dys

E

EK/ . . . . ec
EL/ . . . . eleo
*ELT/ . . . . ethyl
EN/ . . . . en
ENT/ . . . . ento
EP/ . . . . epi
*EP/ . . . . ep
*ERG/ . . . . erg
ERGT/ . . . . ergot
ERKT/ . . . . ectro
ERP/ . . . . epidermo
ERT/ . . . . eroto
ES/ . . . . eso
EX/ . . . . ex
EZ/ . . . . eso

F

FAERN/ . . . . phanero
FAIRB/ . . . . facio
FAIRNG/ . . . . pharyng
FA*K/ . . . . phak
FAL/ . . . . phallo
FAL/ † . . . . phall
FALZ/ . . . . false- (*hyphenated*)
FAO*ET/ . . . . feto
FAOIZ/ . . . . physo
FAO*K/ . . . . phaco
FAORNG/ . . . . pharyngo
FAOUS/ . . . . fuso
FARK/ . . . . pharmaco
FA*URM/ . . . . pharma
FIMP/ . . . . amphi
FIZ/ . . . . physio
FLAIV/ . . . . flavo
FLAO/ . . . . fistulo
FLEB/ . . . . phlebo
FL*EB/ . . . . phleb
FLOEK/ . . . . folliculo
FLOER/ . . . . fluoro
FLOKL/ . . . . follicul

FL–R/ . . . . fluor
FOEG/ . . . . phago
FOEMP/ . . . . ampho
FO*EN/ . . . . phono
FO*EN/ † . . . . phon
FOERB/ . . . . fascio
FOIZ/ . . . . physio
FOT/ . . . . photo
FOT/ † . . . . phot
FO*T/ . . . . phot
FRA/ . . . . infra
FRA*/ . . . . infra- (*hyphenated*)
FRAEK/ . . . . refract
FRAOEN/ . . . . freno
FRAOIB/ . . . . fibro
FRAOKT/ . . . . fructo
FREN/ † . . . . phren
FRENG/ . . . . phrenic
FRIB/ . . . . fibrino
FRIG/ . . . . frigo
FRIN/ . . . . fibrin
FRIRG/ . . . . frigor
FRO/ . . . . femoro
FROBL/ . . . . fibrillo
FROE/ . . . . phoro
FROEB/ . . . . fibroma
FROEN/ . . . . phreno
FROENT/ . . . . fronto
FROINK/ . . . . phrenico

G

GAFRT/ . . . . gaster
GAFT/ . . . . gastr
GAOIN/ . . . . gyno
GAO*IN/ . . . . gyn
GAOR/ . . . . gyro
GAORN/ . . . . organo
GAOUN/ . . . . inguino
GA*S/ . . . . gastro
GAUN/ . . . . gono
GAVN/ . . . . galvano
GEK/ . . . . gyneco
GLAK/ . . . . galact

GLANG/ . . . . ganglio
GLAOI/ . . . . glio
GLAOK/ . . . . galacto
GLAONT/ . . . . agglutin
GLAOT/. . . . . agglutino
GLEN/. . . . . gleno
GLIG/ . . . . olig
GLING/. . . . . gangli
GLOES/ . . . . glosso
GLOG/. . . . . oligo
GLOIK/ . . . . glyco
GLOIKS/ . . . . glycos
GLOM/ . . . . glom
GLORL/. . . . . glomerulo
GLOSZ/. . . . . gloss
GLOUK/ . . . . gluco
GLOUKS/. . . . . glucos
GLOUT/ . . . . aggluto
G–N/ . . . . gon
G*N/. . . . . gony
GOEMT/. . . . . gameto
GOEND/. . . . . gonad
GO*I/. . . . . gonio
GON/ . . . . gone
GOND/. . . . . gonado
GONT/. . . . . genito
GORN/ . . . . organ
GRAUF/ . . . . grapho
GRO/ . . . . gero
GRONT/. . . . . geronto
GRUNL/ . . . . granulo
GY/. . . . . gony
GY–N/. . . . . gyne

H

HAEM/ . . . . hema
HAEPG/ . . . . hepatic
HA*ERM/ . . . . hemeral
HAO/ . . . . hemangio
HAO*I/. . . . . hy
HAOIG/ . . . . hygro
HAO*IM/ . . . . hymen
HAO*IP/ . . . . hyp

Steno	Prefix
HAOIRP/	hyper
HAOITD/	hydatid
HEM/	hemo
H*EM/	hem
HEMT/	hemato
H*EMT/	hemat
HENT/	hematin
HET/	hetero
H*ET/	heter
H–FT/	histio
HIFM/	histamin
HIFR/	hyster
H*IMT/	hemati
HIN/	hyalin
HIR/	hydr
H*IR/	hidr
HIS/	his
H*IS/	hystero
H*IS/ †	hyster
H–M/	hemi
H–N/	hypno
H*N/	hypn
HO*EM/	homeo
HOFT/	histo
HO*I/	hyo
HO*IM/	hymeno
HOIP/	hypo
HOIR/	hydro
HO*IR/	hidro
HOL/	holo
HOM/	homo
HO*M/	homo
HORM/	hormono
HOURM/	humero
H–P/	hepato
H*P/	hepat
H–PG/	hepatico
H–RD/	heredo
H–RM/	herm
H–RN/	hernio
HYAL/	hyal
HYAOIL/	hyal
HYIP/	hypno
HYO/	hyo

HYOEL/ . . . . hyalo
HY–P/ . . . . hypn

I

*IG/ . . . . igni
IN/ . . . . in
INGD/ . . . . incud
IRD/ . . . . irid
*IRT/ . . . . ereth
*IT/ . . . . ithy

J

JAOEJ/ . . . . jejun
JAOIG/ . . . . giganto
JAOJ/ . . . . jejuno
JAOM/ . . . . angioma
JAOV/ . . . . gingivo
JAUXT/ . . . . juxta- (*hyphenated*)
J*EN/ . . . . geno
JERM/ . . . . germ
JI/ . . . . angi
JIJ/ . . . . gingiv
JINL/ . . . . gingly
JIVN/ . . . . gingiv
JO/ . . . . angio
JOE/ . . . . geo
JOIG/ . . . . angino
JU/ . . . . genu
JUXT/ . . . . juxta ~

K

KAEN/ . . . . calcaneo
KAO*ES/ . . . . costi
KAOET/ . . . . keto
KAOI/ . . . . chyl
KAO*NT/ . . . . acantho
KAORP/ . . . . carpo
KAO*S/ . . . . costo

KAOUN/ . . . . cuneo
KARP/ . . . . carp
KARZ/ . . . . carcino
KAT/ . . . . cata
KAUJ/ . . . . collagen
KBAM/ . . . . ambi
KBLIM/ . . . . ambly
KBLO/ . . . . embolo
KBOL/ . . . . embol
KBRE/ . . . . embryo
KBRON/ . . . . embryon
KENZ/ . . . . kinesio
KERT/ . . . . kerat
KHAOE/ . . . . choreo
KHAOI/ . . . . cheil
KHAO*S/ . . . . cholecysto
KHAUND/ . . . . chondr
KHEN/ . . . . echin
KHIR/ . . . . cheiro
KH*IR/ . . . . cheir
KH*IS/ . . . . cholecyst
KHO/ . . . . echo
KHOEL/ . . . . chol
KHO*EL/ . . . . cholo
KHOELD/ . . . . choledocho
KHOEN/ . . . . echino
KHOEND/ . . . . chondro
KHOI/ . . . . cheilo
KHOIL/ . . . . chole
KHOLD/ . . . . choledoch
KIN/ . . . . kin
K*IN/ . . . . kine
KINZ/ . . . . kinesi
K*IT/ . . . . kysth
K*ITS/ . . . . kysth
KL–/ . . . . kilo
KLAOE/ . . . . coli
KLAOI/ . . . . chylo
KLAO*IN/ . . . . clino
KLAONG/ . . . . cholangio
KLAO*S/ . . . . colostr
KLAOUZ/ . . . . occluso
KLAUJ/ . . . . collageno
KLAUN/ . . . . colono
KLAUR/ . . . . chloro

KLE/ . . . . coleo
KLER/. . . . . cholera
KLERN/ . . . . cholesterin
KLES/ . . . . cholesterol
KL*ES/ . . . . cholesterol
KLOED/ . . . . cleido
KLOEF/ . . . . cholestero
KLOEFL/ . . . . cholesterolo
KLOEP/. . . . . colpo
KLOER/ . . . . cholera
KLO*ES/ . . . . colostro
KLOILG/. . . . . koilo
KLOL/ . . . . achillo
KLON/ . . . . colon
KLOP/ . . . . colp
KL-PT/ . . . . klepto
KMAO/ . . . . acromio
KMAOI/ . . . . kymo
KMAT/ . . . . chromato
KMO/ . . . . chromo
KMOE/ . . . . chemo
KMOEN/ . . . . condyloma
KOE/. . . . . co
KOEKL/ . . . . cochleo
KOEL/. . . . . colo
KOER/ . . . . core
KOERK/ . . . . cortico
KOERN/ . . . . corneo
KOERT/. . . . . kerato
KOIF/. . . . . kypho
KOK/ . . . . coccco
KOL/ . . . . col
KONLD/. . . . . condylo
KOR/ . . . . cor
KORD/ . . . . cord
KO*RD/ . . . . cordo
KO*S/ . . . . cost
KOURN/. . . . . counter
KOX/ . . . . cox
KO*X/. . . . . coxo
KPAON/. . . . . axon
KPAUND/. . . . . ecchondro
KPEM/. . . . . ecchym
KP*INT/ . . . . xanthin
KPLAOR/ . . . . capillario

KPLAR/ . . . . capillar
KPO/ . . . . exo
KPOE/ . . . . excito
KPOEL/ . . . . capsulo
KPRIX/ . . . . proxim
KPRO/ . . . . eccentro
KPROE/ . . . . extero
KPROX/ . . . . proximo
KRALS/ . . . . calci
KRAOEFK/ . . . . cystico
KRAOEFT/ . . . . cysti
KRAOEN/ . . . . cen
KRAOI/ . . . . cry
KRAO*I/ . . . . cry
KRAOIK/ . . . . crico
KRAO*IM/ . . . . crymo
KRAU/ . . . . karyo
KRAUNT/ . . . . contra
KRA*UNT/ . . . . contra- (*hyphenated*)
KRAUR/ . . . . cardio
KRAURD/ . . . . cardi
KR*EN/ . . . . endocrino
KRIFT/ . . . . cyst
KRING/ . . . . carcinogen
KRIPT/ . . . . crypt
KRO/ . . . . cryo
KROE/ . . . . ceno
KROEN/ . . . . endocrino
KROERP/ . . . . copro
KROIFT/ . . . . cysto
KROIKD/ . . . . cricoid
KROIN/ . . . . cranio
KROIPT/ . . . . crypto
KROIR/ . . . . chorio
KRON/ . . . . chrono
KWAERNT/ . . . . quadrant
KWAOG/ . . . . coagulo
KWAOK/ . . . . caco
KWARNT/ . . . . quadrant
KWAU/ . . . . aqua
KWOD/ . . . . quadri
KWOID/ . . . . choroido
KWOINT/ . . . . kineto
KWON/ . . . . keton

L

LAEFT/	elasto
LAENG/	laryng
LAERNG/	laryngo
LAKT/	lact
LAM/	lamina
LAOEKT/	lacti
LAO*EN/	lien
LAOGD/	logad
LAO*IN/	lieno
LAO*K/	leuco
LAOKL/	lenticulo
LAOL/	lalo
LAORD/	lordo
LAORMG/	lacrimo
LAORT/	latero
LAOUK/	leuko
LAO*UK/	leuk
LAO*UM/	leukemo
LARP/	laparo
LE/	lenti
L*EK/	olecran
LEP/	lepto
LIJT/	lentigin
L*INT/	lenti
LIP/	lip
L*IT/	lith
LO/	allo
LOEFP/	lochio
LOEG/	logo
LOEKT/	lacto
LOEMP/	lipoma
LOET/	litho
LOEV/	levo
LOG/	log
LOI/	lyo
LO*I/	leio
LOIP/	lipo
LOIPT/	epilepto
LO*RD/	lordo
LORD/	lord
LOUB/	lumbo
LOUNG/	linguo

L–RP/ . . . . lapar
LYAM/ . . . . amylo

M

MAEFP/ . . . . mechano
MA*EG/ . . . . megal
MA*EMP/ . . . . milliampere (*hyphenated*)
MAET/ . . . . meat
MAK/ . . . . macro
MAKL/ . . . . maculo
MA*M/ . . . . mamm
MAOEFT/ . . . . mediastino
MAOEMD/ . . . . myxedema
MAO*EZ/ . . . . mesio
MAOFL/ . . . . musculo
MAOI/ . . . . myo
MAO*IL/ . . . . myel
MAOINL/ . . . . myelin
MAO*IS/ . . . . myos
MAOJ/ . . . . meningio
MAOLD/ . . . . medullo
MAOLG/ . . . . megalo
MAOM/ . . . . mammo
MAONL/ . . . . myelino
MAONT/ . . . . oment
MAONZ/ . . . . mucino
MAORK/ . . . . mucor
MAOS/ . . . . mazo
MAO*S/ . . . . masto
MAOUNZ/ . . . . mucin
MAOUZ/ . . . . muci
MA*S/ . . . . mast
MAUN/ . . . . mono
MA*UN/ . . . . mono- (*hyphenated*)
M*D/ . . . . medio
MED/ . . . . medi
MEG/ . . . . mega
M*EG/ . . . . meg
M*EN/ . . . . meno
MENG/ . . . . mening
MENG/ † . . . . meninge, meningeo, meningio
MERMD/ . . . . mesoderm
MERMS/ . . . . mesoderm

MES/ . . . . mes
MET/ . . . . met
M*ET/. . . . . meta
M*ET/ † . . . . meth
MEZ/ . . . . meso
M–FK/ . . . . menisc
MI/ . . . . my
MID/. . . . . mid
MIFK/. . . . . menisc
MIGD/. . . . . amygdalo
MIJ/. . . . . mening
M*IL/. . . . . mammill
MIRK/ . . . . micr
M*IX/ . . . . myx
M*L/. . . . . mel
MLAEM/. . . . . melanoma
MLIT/ . . . . melit
ML–L/. . . . . milli
ML–N/ . . . . melan
MLOEN/ . . . . melano
MOBT/ . . . . metabol
MOD/ . . . . medio
MO*E/. . . . . meio
MOEG/ . . . . meningo
MOEJ/ . . . . meningeo
MOEKD/. . . . . medico
MOENT/. . . . . omento
MOET/. . . . . meato
MOFK/ . . . . menisco
MOFR/. . . . . morpho
MOFRN/ . . . . morphin
MOIJ/. . . . . meninge
MOIL/ . . . . myelo
MO*IL/ . . . . melo
MO*IM/. . . . . myomo
MO*IT/. . . . . mytho
MOITD/. . . . . mastoid
MOIX/ . . . . myxo
MO*P/. . . . . myop
MORK/. . . . . micro
MOUK/. . . . . muco
MOXL/ . . . . maxillo
MRAOET/. . . . . metr
MRING/. . . . . myringo
M–RK/ . . . . macr

MROE/ . . . . mero
MROET/ . . . . metro
MULT/. . . . . multi
MUN/ . . . . immuno
MYAO/. . . . . amyo
MYAOER/ . . . . meteoro
MY–K/ . . . . myco
MY*L/ . . . . methyl
MYOEK/ . . . . myco
MYOR/. . . . . meteor

N

NA/. . . . . ana
NA*N/. . . . . nano
NAOKT/ . . . . nycto
NAOM/ . . . . pneumo
NAOMT/. . . . . pneumato
NAO*MT/. . . . . pneumat
NAO*T/ . . . . gnatho
NAOUFL/ . . . . infundibul
NAOULG/ . . . . nucleo
NAO*UM/ . . . . pneumono
NARK/ . . . . narco
NAS/. . . . . naso
NA*T/ . . . . gnath
NAUM/ . . . . pneuma
N–D/. . . . . endo
NEF/. . . . . nephro
N*EF/. . . . . nephr
N*EK/ . . . . necro
N*ERK/ . . . . necr
N*IKT/. . . . . nyct
NIMP/. . . . . nymph
NLEPT/ . . . . neurolept
NO*/ . . . . ino
NO*E/. . . . . neo
NOEFL/ . . . . infundibulo
NOEM/ . . . . pneumono
NO*EM/ . . . . pneumon
NO*EZ/ . . . . noso
NO*IL/ . . . . nulli
NOKT/ . . . . noct
NOMP/ . . . . nympho

NON/ . . . . non
NO*N/ . . . . non- (*hyphenated*)
NORM/ . . . . norm
NO*RM/ . . . . normo
NO*S/ . . . . noci
NOUR/ . . . . neuro
NO*UR/ . . . . neuro- (*hyphenated*)
NOURD/ . . . . neurode
NRAOT/ . . . . neutro
NRUT/. . . . . neutr
N*UM/ . . . . pneum
NUR/ . . . . neur
N*UR/. . . . . neuri
N-V/. . . . . nevo
NYO/. . . . . pneo

O

O/ . . . . o
OEFKT/ . . . . olfact
OEFL/. . . . . alveolo
OEFLT/ . . . . ophthalmo
OEFP/. . . . . ochro
OEKL/. . . . . oculo
OEKT/ . . . . ecto
OEL/. . . . . oleo
OEMP/ . . . . omphalo
OENK/ . . . . onycho
OENT/ . . . . onto
OERK/ . . . . orchio
O*ERT/. . . . . ortho
OET/ . . . . oto
OEX/. . . . . axo
OFL/ . . . . alveo
OFLT/ . . . . ophthalm
OIFP/. . . . . archi
OIK/. . . . . oiko
OIM/ . . . . amnio
OIRB/. . . . . orbito
OIRD/. . . . . irido
OIRN/ . . . . oneiro
OIRN/ † . . . . oneir
O*IRN/ . . . . oneir
OIRND/ . . . . arytenoid

Steno	Prefix
OIV/	ovario
OIX/	oxy
OKL/	ochlo
O*KT/ †	octo
O*KT/	octi
OM/	omo
O*M/	om
OMP/	omphal
ON/	on
ONK/	onych
O*NT/	onto
OPT/	opt
O*R/	oro
ORBT/	orbit
ORK/	orchi
ORK/ †	orch
O*RK/	orch
ORKD/	orchido
ORKD/ †	orchid
O*RKD/	orchid
O*RT/	orth
OUL/	ule
OUNL/	ulno
OUV/	uveo
OVR/	over
OXL/	axillo

P

Steno	Prefix
PAEFR/	paraffin
PAEKD/	appendico
PA*EL/	paleo
PAEND/	append
PAENL/	pineal
PAFRN/	paraffin
PAIRTS/	parasit
PA*K/	pachy
PALT/	palat
PAN/	pan
PANT/	pant
PAO*E/	pero
PAOED/	ped
PAOED/ †	pedi, pedio
PAO*ED/	pedo

PAOEND/ . . . . pedion
PAOIR/. . . . . pyro
PAOKL/ . . . . pediculo
PAOLT/ . . . . palato
PAOM/ . . . . pulmo
PAOMD/ . . . . ependymo
PAOMT/ . . . . pigmento
PAONT/ . . . . panto
PAO*T/ . . . . patho
PAOUKL/ . . . . pedicul
PAOULG/. . . . . peduncul
PAOUND/. . . . . pudend
PAOV/ . . . . pelvio
PAR/ . . . . para
PA*R/ . . . . par
PA*T/ . . . . path
PAUFRB/ . . . . parvo
PED/ . . . . ped
PED/ † . . . . pedi, pedio
P*ED/ . . . . pedo
PEFN/ . . . . pepsin
PEM/ . . . . pimel
PEMP/. . . . . pimel
PEP/ . . . . pep
PEPZ/ . . . . pepsin
P*ER/ . . . . per
P*ET/. . . . . epithelio
PEV/ . . . . pelvi
PIMT/ . . . . pigment
PIN/. . . . . pin
PIRN/. . . . . perineo
PIS/ . . . . episio
P*ITS/. . . . . opistho
PLAFNT/ . . . . placent
PLALT/ . . . . platy
PLAMZ/ . . . . plasmo
PLAN/ . . . . plan
PLANT/ . . . . plant
PLAO/. . . . . papulo
PLAO*E . . . . pili
PLAOFMT/. . . . . plasmato
PLAOFNT/ . . . . placento
PLAOIL/. . . . . pleio
PLAON/ . . . . plano
PLAOP/ . . . . papillo

PLAP/ . . . . papill
PLAU/ . . . . pall
PLAU/ † . . . . pali
PLAUN/ . . . . palin
PL–D/ . . . . pallid
PLERM/ . . . . polymer
PL*EX/ . . . . plex
PL–FM/ . . . . plasm
PLIP/ . . . . polyp
PLIR/ . . . . pluri
PL–M/ . . . . plasma
PL–MT/ . . . . plasmato
PLO*/ . . . . pilo
PLOED/ . . . . pallido
PLOER/ . . . . pyloro
PLOIJ/ . . . . plagio
PLOIL/ . . . . pleo
PLOIP/ . . . . epiplo
PLO*IX/ . . . . plexi
PLOL/ . . . . polio
PLO*N/ . . . . pollen
PLOR/ . . . . pylor
PLOUM/ . . . . pulmono
PLOUP/ . . . . pupillo
PLU/ . . . . pleur
PLUR/ . . . . pleuro
PLUR/ † . . . . pleur
PL–Z/ . . . . plesio
P–NL/ . . . . pannicul
PO/ . . . . apo
POB/ . . . . pubo
POD/ . . . . pod
POED/ . . . . podo
POEFR/ . . . . porphyrin
POEFRT/ . . . . postero
POEFT/ . . . . post
POENL/ . . . . pinealo
PO*ER/ . . . . poro
POERT/ . . . . porto
PO*ES/ . . . . post- (*hyphenated*)
POEV/ . . . . pelvo
POEZ/ . . . . poso
POFRN/ . . . . porphyrin
PO*FT/ . . . . posth
POID/ . . . . lipoid

Steno	Prefix
POIKL/	poikilo
POL/	poly
POPT/	pepto
POR/	por
P–R/	para- (*hyphenated*)
PRAIP/	priap
PRANG/	pancreat
PRAO/	parieto
PRAOENG/	pancreo
PRAOK/	prostatico
PRAOKT/	pancreatico
PRAOPS/	prosop
PRAOS/	proso
PRART/	parturi
PRA*S/	prostat
PRAT/	pancreato
PRAU/	periosto
PRAUF/	perioste
PRAUFT/	periosteo
PRE/	pre
PREBS/	presby
PRI/	peri
PRIMX/	proxim
PRO/	pro
PROE/	perio
PRO*EN/	peritone
PROEPS/	prosopo
PROET/	petro
PRO*ET/	proto
PRO*ET/ †	prot
PRO*ETS/	prostho
PROEX/	pyrexio
PROIMX/	proximo
PROIN/	protein
PROINT/	peritoneo
PROIP/	proprio
PRO*IT/	proteo
PROK/	procto
PROKT/	proct
PRO*S/	prostato
PROZ/	pros
PR–Z/	presso
PY/	py
PYAOIL/	pyle
PYEL/	pyel

PYET/ . . . . pyreto
PY–K/ . . . . pykno
PY*K/ . . . . pyc
PYO/ . . . . pyo
PYOEL/ . . . . pyelo
PYOET/ . . . . phyto
PY–T/ . . . . phyt

R

RAFPD/ . . . . arachnoid
RAIFP/ . . . . rachi
RAO/ . . . . radio
RAOEN/ . . . . reno
RAOIB/ . . . . ribo
RAOK/ . . . . arachno
RAOKL/ . . . . radiculo
RAONT/ . . . . retino
RE/ . . . . re
R*E/ . . . . re- (*hyphenated*)
REKT/ . . . . rect
REN/ . . . . ren
RENG/ . . . . roentgen
R–FX/ . . . . reflex
RIKL/ . . . . reticul
RIN/ . . . . reni
R*INT/ . . . . labyrinth
RO/ . . . . aero
ROEKT/ . . . . recto
ROENG/ . . . . roentgeno
ROFP/ . . . . rachio
ROFX/ . . . . reflexo
RO*IM/ . . . . rheuma
RONG/ . . . . rhonch
RUKL/ . . . . reticulo

S

SAMT/ . . . . somat
SAO/ . . . . zoo
SAOD/ . . . . sudo
SAO*D/ . . . . pseud

SAOEB/ . . . . sebo
SAO*EK/ . . . . ceco
SAO*ER/ . . . . sero
SAOIK/ . . . . psych
SAOIL/ . . . . sial
SAOIRB/ . . . . cyber
SAOL/ . . . . sialo
SAOM/ . . . . soma
SAOMT/ . . . . somato
SAOPT/ . . . . occipito
SAORD/ . . . . sudor
SAORP/ . . . . supra- (*hyphenated*)
SAO*UD/ . . . . pseudo
SARK/ . . . . sarco
SA*RK/ . . . . sarc
SAUM/ . . . . somn
SBLOE/ . . . . cerebello
SBROE/ . . . . cerebro
SDEFM/ . . . . desmo
SD-FM/ . . . . desm
SD*ID/ . . . . acid
SD-M/ . . . . syndesm
SDO/ . . . . disco
SDOE/ . . . . acido
SDOFM/ . . . . syndesmo
SDRO/ . . . . sidero
SDWO/ . . . . deciduo
SDYAMT/ . . . . diastemato
SEFL/ . . . . self- (*hyphenated*)
SEM/ . . . . semi- (*hyphenated*)
SEMT/ . . . . cement
SERK/ . . . . cervico
SFAFL/ . . . . sphacel
SFAL/ . . . . cephal
SFAOFL/ . . . . sphacelo
SFAOL/ . . . . cephalo
SFAT/ . . . . phosphat
SFEN/ . . . . sphen
SFES/ . . . . symphyseo
SFIG/ . . . . sphygmo
SFING/ . . . . sphincter
SFINGT/ . . . . sphincter
SFIPS/ . . . . epiphysio
SFIR/ . . . . spher
SFLI/ . . . . syphil

SFLO/. . . . . syphilo
SFOE/ . . . . phospho
SFOEG/ . . . . sphingo
SFOEL/ . . . . acephalo
SFOES/ . . . . symphysio
SFOG/ . . . . esophago
SFOID/ † . . . . sphenoid
SFO*ID/. . . . . sphenoid
SFOIN/ . . . . spheno
SFOIR/ . . . . sphero
SFOJ/. . . . . esophag
SFONG/ . . . . sphinctero
SFOUR/ . . . . phosphor
SGAOES/ . . . . syngenesio
SGEN/. . . . . carcinogen
SGO/. . . . . astragalo
SGOE/ . . . . sanguino
SGROEM/. . . . . carcinoma
SGU/. . . . . sangui
SHEN/ . . . . oxygen
SHO/ . . . . iso
SID/ . . . . acid
SIF/. . . . . xiphi
SIFRB/ . . . . cervico
SIM/. . . . . sym
SIN/ . . . . syn
SKAFP/ . . . . saccharo
SKA*FP/ . . . . sacchar
SKAOEX/ . . . . coccy
SKAOF/ . . . . scapho
SKAT/ . . . . scat
SKAUMT/ . . . . scotoma
SKH/ . . . . isch
SKHA/ . . . . ischia
SKHAR/. . . . . eschar
SKHE/ . . . . oscheo
SKHI/. . . . . ischi
SKHIL/. . . . . oscillo
SKHIR/ . . . . scirrh
SKHIS/ . . . . schisto
SKHO/ . . . . ischio
SKHOE/. . . . . ischo
SKHOR/ . . . . scirrho
SKIR/ . . . . scirrho
SKIS . . . . schizo

Steno	Prefix
SK-K/	ceco
SKLAER/	sclera
SKLER/	sclero
SKL*ER/	scler
SKLO/	cyclo
SKLOEKT/	sclerotico
SKLOEL/	scolio
SKLOEP/	scapulo
SKLUP/	scapul
SKOE/	psycho
SKOED/	psychodo
SKOEG/	coccygo
SKOEKT/	psychoto
SKOELT/	skeleto
SKOEM/	sarcoma
SKO*EP/	scopo
SKOET/	scoto
SKPO/	sympathico
SKRET/	secret
SKRO/	sacro
SKRO*E/	psychro
SKROEFL/	scrofulo
SKROEM/	carcinoma
SKROG/	carcinogen
SK-RT/	secreto
SK-T/	scato
SKWOM/	squamo
SLAOEL/	celo
SLE/	celio
SLIN/	insulin
SLO/	silico
SLO*/	cilio
SLOIN/	insulino
SM-/	osm
SMAOI/	semeio
SMAONT/	cemento
SMI/	semi
SMO/	osmo
SMOE/	semino
SMOED/	sigmoido
SMOID/	sigmoid
SMOIK/	somatico
SNAFL/	encephal
SNAN/	acin
SNAOFL/	encephalo

SNAOPT/ . . . . synapto
SNA*RT/ . . . . synarthro
SNAUM/ . . . . somno
SNE/ . . . . cine
SNEN/ . . . . eosino
SNIRS/ . . . . sinistro
SNO/ . . . . steno
SNOI/ . . . . sino
SNOIV/ . . . . synovio
SNUS/ . . . . sinus
SO*/ . . . . iso
SOEN/ . . . . sono
SOENS/ . . . . senso
SOIM/ . . . . somni
SOIRS/ . . . . sensori
SOPT/ . . . . occipito
SPAFM/ . . . . spasm
SPAO*IN/ . . . . spino
SPAOIRK/ . . . . spirochet
SPAOJ/ . . . . spongio
SPAONL/ . . . . spondylo
SPAORM/ . . . . spermio
SPAORMT/ . . . . spermato
SPARM/ . . . . sperma
SPARMT/ . . . . spermat
SPAUNL/ . . . . spondyl
SPAZ/ . . . . spasmo
SPE/ . . . . sept
SPI/ . . . . septi
SPING/ . . . . salpingo
SP*ING/ . . . . salping
SPIRM/ . . . . sperm
SPLANG/ . . . . splanchn
SPLEN/ . . . . splen
SPL*IN/ . . . . spleni
SPLON/ . . . . spleno
SPLONG/ . . . . splanchno
SPO/ . . . . septo
SPOE/ . . . . septico
SPOERM/ . . . . spermo
SPOIN/ . . . . spino
SPOIR/ . . . . spiro
SPR–/ . . . . super
SP–R/ . . . . super- (*hyphenated*)
SPRA/ . . . . supra

SPRAO/ . . . . supero
SPREK/ . . . . spectro
SPRIL/. . . . . spirillo
SPRO/ . . . . sapro
SPROE/. . . . . sporo
SPW/ . . . . entero
SPW*/ . . . . enter
SPWO*ES/ . . . . intercosto
SPWOR/. . . . . intro
SPWR/. . . . . inter
SPWRA/. . . . . intra
SPWRA*/. . . . . intra- (*hyphenated*)
SPWRO/. . . . . intero
SPWUZ/ . . . . intus
S-RB/. . . . . socio
STAFL/. . . . . staphyl
STAMT/ . . . . stomat
STAOET/ . . . . steato
STAOFL/. . . . . staphylo
STAOIT/. . . . . cyto
STA*T/. . . . . stato
STER/ . . . . stereo
STHEN/. . . . . asthen
STHIM/. . . . . isthm
STHO/ . . . . sympatho
STHOE/ . . . . sympathetico
STHOEN/. . . . . astheno
STHOES/ . . . . esthesio
STHOM/ . . . . isthmo
STLO/ . . . . stylo
ST-N/ . . . . steno
STO*/. . . . . sito
STOEM/. . . . . stoma
STOEMT/ . . . . stomato
STOEPD/ . . . . stapedio
STOIR/. . . . . strio
STOIRK/ . . . . sterco
STOIRN/ . . . . sterno
STOM/ . . . . symptom
STRA/. . . . . extra
STRA*/. . . . . extra- (*hyphenated*)
STRA*S/. . . . . astro
STROE/ . . . . centro
STROIK/ . . . . stercoro
STROPT/ . . . . strepto

STRUM/ . . . . strum
STYIN/. . . . . cystin
SUB/ . . . . sub
SUL/ . . . . insulo
SWAO/ . . . . pseudo
SWAOD/ . . . . pseud
SWOENG/ . . . . sanguino
SYA*N/. . . . . cyan
SYING/ . . . . syring
SYM/ . . . . sym
SY-N/ . . . . cyan
SYOEN/ . . . . cyano
SYONG/ . . . . syringo

T

TAERT/ . . . . terato
TA*K/ . . . . tachy
TAO*EL/ . . . . teleo
TAOIF/. . . . . typho
TAO*L/. . . . . talo
TAOMG/ . . . . anatomico
TAO*N/. . . . . tono
TAONL/ . . . . tonsillo
TAORS/. . . . . tarso
TAORT/ . . . . aort
TAOURB/ . . . . tuber
TARS/. . . . . tars
TAUN/ . . . . tenon
TA*UNT/. . . . . tenonto
TA*X/ . . . . ataxia
TBOE/ . . . . tabo
T*EL/ . . . . tel
TEN/ . . . . ten
T*EN/ . . . . teno
TEND/ . . . . tend
THAM/ . . . . thalamo
THAOE/ . . . . ichthyo
THAOEL/. . . . . thel
THAO*ER/. . . . . thyreo
THAOIM/. . . . . thym
THAOIRD/. . . . . thyroid
THAOLS/ . . . . thalasso
THAOM/ . . . . thymo

Steno	Prefix
THAONT/	thanato
THERM/	therm
THOEKT/	cantho
THOEMG/	thigmo
THOER/	thyreo
THOERD/	thyroido
THOERK/	thoraco
THOI/	thio
THOIK/	theco
THOIMD/	ethmoid
THOIR/	thyro
THORM/	thermo
THRAK/	anthraco
THRAUB/	prothrombin
THRAUM/	thromb
TH-RM/	therm
THROID/	thyroid
THROM/	thrombo
THUR/	athero
TIFL/	typhl
TIMP/	tympan
TLAOL/	talo
TLAON/	talon
TLAT/	atelo
TL*E/	tele
TOEBL/	tuberculo
TOEFL/	typhlo
TOERG/	pterygo
TOERM/	temporo
TOERT/	aorto
TOEX/	toxo
TOIB/	tibio
TOIBL/	tubulo
TOIX/	toxico
TO*IX/	toxi
TOK/	toxic
TOMP/	tympano
TOND/	tendo
TOP/	top
TO*P/	topo
TORKT/	aortico
TOUB/	tubo
TOUBL/	tubercul
TOX/	toxin
TO*X/	tox

TRABL/ . . . . trabecul
TRA*N/ . . . . tran
TRANS/. . . . . trans
TRANT/. . . . . antro
TRAO/ . . . . atrio
TRAOB/. . . . . tubero
TRAOBL/ . . . . trabeculo
TRAOER/. . . . . arteri
TRAOING/ . . . . trigon
TRAO*IP/ . . . . trypano
TRAUM/ . . . . trauma
TREF/ . . . . tephro
TRER/ . . . . arter
TRI/ . . . . tri
TRIFP/ . . . . trich
TR*IK/ . . . . tricho
TRINK/ . . . . trichin
TR–KL/ . . . . trachel
TRO/ . . . . retro
TROE/. . . . . electro
TROEFP/ . . . . tropho
TROEFRS/ . . . . transverso
TROEKL/ . . . . trachelo
TROELT/ . . . . petrolat
TROEMT/. . . . . traumato
TROER/. . . . . arterio
TROERL/ . . . . arteriolo
TROFP/. . . . . troph
TROIG/. . . . . trigono
TROIK/. . . . . tracheo
TRONK/ . . . . trichino
TWAX/ . . . . ataxia
TWOEK/ . . . . tecto
TWOEM/ . . . . osteoma
TYAL/ . . . . ptyal
TYO/. . . . . etio
TYOEL/ . . . . ptyalo

U

ULS/ . . . . ulcer
UN/ . . . . un
UNDZ/ . . . . under
URLS/ . . . . ulcero

URLT/ . . . . ultra
UX/. . . . . auxo

V

VAJ/ . . . . vagin
VAOB/ . . . . vertebro
VAOERNT/ . . . . ventri
VAOEV/. vivi
VAOFL/. . . . . valvo
VAOG/ . . . . vago
VAON/ . . . . veno
VAOS/. . . . . vaso
VAOUKL/. . . . . vesicul
VAOUL/ . . . . ventriculo
VAOZ/ . . . . visuo
VAS/. . . . . vas
VAURK/. . . . . varico
VEFK/ . . . . vesico
V*EL/. . . . . velo
VEM/ . . . . venom
V*I/. . . . . ovi
VIB/. . . . . vestibulo
VO*/ . . . . ovo
VOEFR/ . . . . viscero
VOEJ/. . . . . vagino
VOENT/. . . . . ventro
VOERB/. . . . . vibro
VOEVL/ . . . . valvulo
VOIV/. . . . . vulvo
VOIX/ . . . . vaccino
V-RM/. . . . . vomero
VUFK/. . . . . vasculo
VUK/. . . . . vasculo
VUKL/. . . . . vesiculo
VURB/ . . . . visuo

W

WRABD/ . . . . rhabdo
WRAFPD/ . . . . arachnoid
WRAOE/. . . . . rheo

WRAOIN/ . . . . rhin
WRAOIS/ . . . . rhizo
WRAOIZ . . . . rhiz
WRAOM/ . . . . rheum
WRITD/ . . . . rhitid
WROE/ . . . . orrho
WROED/ . . . . rhodo
WROEM/ . . . . rhombo
WROIM/ . . . . rheuma
WROIN/ . . . . rhino
WROITD/ . . . . rhytid
WROM/ . . . . rhomb

Y

YAFT/ . . . . myeloblast
YAMP/ . . . . lympha
YAMPT/ . . . . lymphat
YANS/ . . . . uranisco
YAO*ET/ . . . . urethr
YAOIRT/ . . . . iatro
YAOR/ . . . . urea
YAORN/ . . . . urano
YAORT/ . . . . utero
YAOU/ . . . . ur
YAOUK/ . . . . utriculo
YAOUL/ . . . . ulo
YAOURK/ . . . . uric
YAOUV/ . . . . uvula
YERG/ . . . . ergo
YERT/ . . . . ureter
Y*ERT/ . . . . erythr
YIL/ . . . . ileo
YILG/ . . . . ileoceco
YIPS/ . . . . hypsi
YIR/ . . . . uri
YIRN/ . . . . urin
YO*D/ . . . . idio
YOED/ . . . . ideo
YOEM/ . . . . lymphoma
YOEN/ . . . . iono
YOENT/ . . . . ionto
YOERKT/ . . . . ictero
YOERT/ . . . . uretero

Steno	Prefix
YO*ERT/	erythro
YOET	ot
YO*ET/	urethro
YOEV/	uvulo
YOI/	uni
YOID/	lymphoid
YOIL/	ilio
YOIMP/	lymph
YOIR/	ur
YOL/	myeloma
YOMP/	lympho
YOPD/	epididymo
YOPS/	hypso
YOR/	ureo
YORN/	urino
YOURT/	urat
YUR/	eury
YURG/	urico
YURGS/	uricos
YURT/	uter

Z

Steno	Prefix
ZANT/	xanth
ZE/	xero
ZEN/	xen
ZIF/	xiphi
ZIFD/	xiphoid
ZINT/	xanthin
ZMAK/	zygomatico
ZMAT/	zygomatico
ZMO/	zymo
Z–N/	xeno
ZOEF/	xipho
ZOEG/	zygo
ZOENT/	xantho
ZORS	zoster
ZUL/	zonul
ZY–G/	zyg

SUFFIXES (BY ENGLISH)

A

abdominal . . . . . /ABL
abdominoperitoneal . . . . . /BIRNL
abduction . . . . . /DBUX
ability . . . . . /–BLT
ablation . . . . . /BLAGS
ablative . . . . . /BLAV
able . . . . . /–BL, /AIBL
abortal . . . . . /BAORLT
abrader . . . . . /BRAERD
abrasion . . . . . /BRAEGS
abscess . . . . . /ABZ
absorb . . . . . /SORB
absorption . . . . . /SORBGS
acanthocytosis . . . . . /KA*NTS, /KAO*TS
acanthoma . . . . . /KO*ENT
acanthosis . . . . . /KO*ETS
acardius . . . . . /KRAUD
acariasis (*see also* cariasis) . . . . . /KROIS
accelerator . . . . . /SLOR
accelerin . . . . . /SL*ERN
access . . . . . /KRES, /KREF
accessory . . . . . /KRERS
accommodation . . . . . /KOJ
acephalus . . . . . /SFLAS
acetabular . . . . . /TBLAR
acetate . . . . . /STAE

achiever . . . . /KHAOEVR
achondroplasia . . . . /KHAIPZ, /KHA*IPS, /KHA*EPZ
achromatic . . . . /KRO*MT
achromatopsia . . . . /KROPT
acid . . . . /SD*ID, /SID
acidaminuria . . . . /SDAOUR
acidemia . . . . /SDAEM
acidify . . . . /SDAOIF
acidimeter . . . . /SDIRMT
acidity . . . . /SDIT
acidometer . . . . /SDOERMT
acidosis . . . . /SDOES
acids . . . . /SIDZ, /SDIDZ, /SD*IDZ
aciduria . . . . /SDOUR
acinal . . . . /SNA*L
acinar . . . . /SNAUR
acinous . . . . /SNUZ
acme . . . . /AEK
acousia . . . . /KWAOUZ, /KWAOUS
acousis . . . . /KWOUS, /KWOUSZ
acousma . . . . /KWAOUM
acoustic . . . . /KAO*US, /KAOUFT
acoustics . . . . /KAO*USZ, /KAOUFTS
acrasia . . . . /KRAISZ
acratia . . . . /KRAIRB
acria (*see also* akria) . . . . /KRAI
acromegaly . . . . /KRAELG
acromial . . . . /KROIL
acrosome . . . . /SKROM
acrosomia . . . . /SKRAOM
act . . . . /AK, /AKT
actinic . . . . /ANGT
actinomycin . . . . /TAOIFM
actinomycosis . . . . /TYOESZ
action . . . . /AX
activate . . . . /TWAET
activated . . . . /TWAETD
activation . . . . /TWAEGS
activator . . . . /TWAERT
active . . . . /TIV, /TIF
activity . . . . /TIVT, /TIFT
acuity . . . . /KWAO*UT
acupuncture . . . . /KWAOUP
acusia . . . . /KWAOS
acusis (*see also* akusis) . . . . /KWAOSZ, /KWAOUSZ

acute . . . . /KWAOUT
ad . . . . /A*D
adaptation . . . . /DAPGS
adductor . . . . /DRUK
adelphus . . . . /DEFLS
aden . . . . /DW*EN
adenalgia . . . . /DWALG
adenectasis . . . . /DWAISZ
adenectomy . . . . /DWEKT
adenia . . . . /DWAOEN, /DWAOE
adenic . . . . /DENK, /DWENK
adenitis . . . . /DWENTS
adenocarcinoma . . . . /DWROEM
adenocele . . . . /DWAOEL
adenocyst . . . . /DW*IS
adenocystoma . . . . /DWAUMT
adenogram . . . . /DWRAM
adenography . . . . /DWAEF
adenoid . . . . /DWOI
adenoidal . . . . /DWOIL
adenoidectomy . . . . /DWOIKT
adenoleukopoiesis . . . . /DLOIPS
adenolymphitis . . . . /DWIMT, /DWIMTS
adenoma . . . . /DWOEM
adenomatosis . . . . /DWOEMTS
adenoncus . . . . /DWONG
adenopathy . . . . /DWO*P, /DWO*PT
adenoscirrhus . . . . /DIRS
adenosis . . . . /DWOESZ
adenosus . . . . /DWUS
adenotomy . . . . /DWOT
adenotropic . . . . /DWOEPK
adenous . . . . /DWOUS
adenovarix . . . . /DWAIRX
adequacy . . . . /KWATS
adequate . . . . /KWAT
adipose . . . . /DWOES
adiposis . . . . /DWOEPSZ
adiposity . . . . /DWOPT
adipsia . . . . /DWOIPS
adjuvant . . . . /JAOUVT
admission . . . . /DMIGS, /MOIGS, /M*IGS
adolescence . . . . /DLENS
adolescent . . . . /DLENT
adrenal . . . . /DRAOENL

adrenalism . . . . /DRAOEFM
adrenergic . . . . /DRERJ
adrenocorticalism . . . . /DROFM
adrenocorticism . . . . /DRIFM
adsorbent . . . . /DOERBT
adsorption . . . . /DOERBGS, /DOERPGS, /SOERPGS
adventitial . . . . /TAOERBL
adynamic . . . . /DWAMG
ae . . . . /AE
aeration . . . . /AIRGS
aerobe . . . . /RO*EB
aerocele . . . . /AOERLS
aeroperitoneum . . . . /PAORM
aerophagy . . . . /AIRJ
aerophil . . . . /A*IRP
aerophile . . . . /AOIRL
aerophilic . . . . /AIRLG
aerosol . . . . /AERZ
aerotherapy . . . . /THOIRP
affective . . . . /FAEVK
affectivity . . . . /FAEVT
afferent . . . . /AEFRNT
affinity . . . . /AIFNT
aganactesis . . . . /GAKT, /GAKTS
agent . . . . /J–
agents . . . . /J–S
ageusia . . . . /GAOUS, /GAOUZ
agglutinable . . . . /GLIBL
agglutination (*see also* gglutination) . . . . /GLAOUNGS, /GLUNGS
agglutinative . . . . /GLAOUV
agglutinin (*see also* gglutinin) . . . . /GLAOUT
agglutinogen . . . . /GLAOUJ
agglutinoid . . . . /GLOIND, /GLAOTD
aggregate . . . . /AEGT
agmia . . . . /MA*G
agnosia . . . . /GOENZ
agnosis . . . . /GAONSZ
agogatresia . . . . /GRAOEZ
agogic . . . . /GOJ
agogue (*see also* gogue) . . . . /GOEG, /GO*G, /GA*UG
agogy . . . . /GOEJ
agonal . . . . /GONL
agra . . . . /GRAG
agral . . . . /GRA*L
agraphia . . . . /GRAOIF

agric	/GR*IK
agrous	/GROUS
akinesia (*see also* kinesia)	/KWAEN
akinesis (*see also* kinesis)	/KWAENZ
akria (*see also* acria)	/KRA*I
akusis (*see also* acusis)	/KAOSZ
al	/AL
albinism	/BAOIFM
albumin	/BAOUM
albuminemia	/BAOUN
albuminimeter	/BAOUMT
albuminmetry	/BAOURMT
albuminosis	/BOESZ
albuminous	/BAOUMS
albuminuria	/BAOURM
albuminuric	/BLURK
albumoid	/BOIMD
albumorrhea	/BRAOE
albumose	/BOES
albumosuria	/BAOUR
alcohol	/KHOL
alcoholism	/KHOFM
aldehyde	/HALD
aldosteronemia	/DRAEM
aldosteronism	/DOEFM
aldosteronuria	/DAOUR
ale	/A*EL
algesia	/JAOELS
algesic	/JAOELG
algetic	/JAOEKT
algia	/ALG
algic	/AKL
algiform	/JAULG, /JO*RM
alienitis	/YAENTS
alimentation	/LAOEMGS
alimentosis	/LOEMTS
alis	/AELZ
alkalescence	/KLAENSZ
alkaline	/KLAIN
alkalinity	/KLINT
allantoic	/LOINK
allantoinuria	/LAOURNT
allantois	/LOINT
allele	/LAO*EL
allelic	/LAOELG

allergen . . . . /LAERN
allergenic . . . . /LERG
allergic . . . . /LERJ
allergies . . . . /L–RJS
allergization . . . . /L–RGS
allergosis . . . . /LERJS
allergosorbent . . . . /LORNT, /LOERNT
allergy . . . . /L–RJ
allocortex . . . . /LOERX
alloplasia . . . . /LAIPZ
alope . . . . /LAO*P
alopecia . . . . /PAOERB
alopia . . . . /LOEP
alum . . . . /LA*UM
alveolar . . . . /AEVL
alveolitis . . . . /AOIVLT, /AOIVLTS
alveolography . . . . /AEFLG
amaurosis . . . . /MAURSZ
amaurotic . . . . /MAURKT
ambient . . . . /KBINT
amblyopia . . . . /BLOEP, /BLOIP
ambulation . . . . /BLAIGS
ambulic . . . . /BLAFMG, /BAOUK
ambulism . . . . /BLAFM
amebiasis . . . . /MAOIBZ
amebimeter . . . . /BIRMT
ameboid . . . . /MOIBD
ameloblastoma . . . . /MOBL
amidase . . . . /AIMDZ, /AEMDZ
amide . . . . /AOIMD
amine . . . . /A*EM
aminoacidemia . . . . /SDAOEM
aminoaciduria . . . . /SDAOURM
aminos . . . . /AOEMS, /AO*EMS
ammeter . . . . /A*RMT
ammonemia . . . . /NAOEM
ammoniac . . . . /AOMG
ammonuria . . . . /NAO*UR
amnesia . . . . /NAOEMZ, /ZHA
amnion . . . . /NYON
amnionitis . . . . /AOIMT, /AOIMTS
amnios . . . . /NYOZ
amniotic . . . . /OIKT
amorphic . . . . /MAOFRK
amorphous . . . . /MAUFS

amorphus . . . . /MUFS
ampere . . . . /AEMP
amphetamine . . . . /FET, /FA*ET
ampullary . . . . /RAIMPL
amputation . . . . /KBA*IGS, /KBAIX
amygdalitis. . . . . /MIGTS
amylase. . . . . /YAES
amylasemia . . . . /YAEMS
amylasemic. . . . . /YAEMG
amyloidosis. . . . . /YOLD, /YOLDZ, /YLOIDZ
amyosthenia . . . . /YAOEMS, /YAOENS
amyosthenic . . . . /YENK, /YENG
an . . . . /AN
anabolic . . . . /NOBLG
anabrosis . . . . /BROENSZ
anacinesia (*see also* anakinesia) . . . . /KAENS
anacinesis (*see also* anakinesis) . . . . /KAENZ
anacusia . . . . /NAOUZ
anacusis . . . . /NAOUSZ
anagenesis. . . . . /NAEJS
anakinesia (*see also* anacinesia) . . . . /KA*ENS, /KINS
anakinesis (*see also* anacinesis) . . . . /KAENSZ
anal . . . . /AINL
analeptic . . . . /NAEPT
analgesia . . . . /JAOEZ
analgesic . . . . /JAOEFK
analosis . . . . /OESZ, /OINLS
analysis . . . . /NALZ
-analysis . . . . /NA*LZ
analyst . . . . /NALTS
analytic. . . . . /NILT
analyzer. . . . . /NARLS
anamorph . . . . /NAOF
anaphylactic . . . . /FLINGT
anaphylaxis . . . . /FLANXZ
anaphysis . . . . /FOINSZ
anastomosis . . . . /NA*S, /SNOS, /SMOS
anastrophe . . . . /SNAOFT
anatomical . . . . /NAEMG
anatomies . . . . /NAEMTS
anatomist. . . . . /NIMS
anatomists . . . . /NIMSZ
anatomy . . . . /NAEMT
anconeus . . . . /KOINZ
andrism . . . . /DRAFM

androgen . . . . . /DROEG
android . . . . . /DRAOND
andromorphism . . . . . /DROUFM
andromorphous . . . . . /DROUFS
androsterone . . . . . /DROENT
anemia . . . . . /NOIM
anemic . . . . . /NO*IK
anemometer . . . . . /MA*EMT
anencephaly . . . . . /SNAEFL
aneresis . . . . . /NAERSZ
anesthesia . . . . . /THAOERB, /STHAOEZ, /AEN
anesthetic . . . . . /THET
aneurysm . . . . . /NURM
aneurysmoplasty . . . . . /NURPTS
aneurysmorrhaphy . . . . . /NURMZ
angeitis . . . . . /JOITS
angial . . . . . /JAOIL
angiectases . . . . . /JAESZ
angiectasia . . . . . /JAIZ
angiectasis . . . . . /JAISZ
angiectatic . . . . . /JAEKT
angiectodes . . . . . /JOEDZ
angiectomy . . . . . /JIKT, /J*EKT
angiitis . . . . . /JAOETS
angina . . . . . /JAOIN
anginal . . . . . /JAOINL
angioadenography . . . . . /YAEFG
angioblast . . . . . /JA*S, /JAFT
angioblastoma . . . . . /JOM
angiocapillary . . . . . /JLAIR
angiocarcinoma . . . . . /JOERM
angiocholitis . . . . . /JAOILTS
angioendothelioblastoma . . . . . /JOEBL
angioendothelioma . . . . . /JOENL
angioenterostomy . . . . . /JAOFT
angiofibroma . . . . . /JOEFM
angiofibrosis . . . . . /JOEBSZ
angiogram . . . . . /JARM
angiography . . . . . /JAEF
angiology . . . . . /JAOLG
angioma . . . . . /JAOM
angiomatosis . . . . . /JAOMT
angiomatous . . . . . /JOUMT, /JOUMTS
angiomyomatosis . . . . . /JOIMTS
angion . . . . . /JA*UN, /JAON

angiopathic . . . . /JAOFK
angiopathy . . . . /JOPT
angiopericytoma . . . . /JAOIMT
angiophlebitis . . . . /JEB, /JEBT
angioplasia . . . . /JAEPZ
angioplasty . . . . /JAPT
angiosarcoma . . . . /JARK
angiosclerosis . . . . /JLOEZ
angioscopy . . . . /JOIP
angiosis . . . . /JOESZ
angiostomy . . . . /JAUFT
angiotic . . . . /JOKT
angiotomy . . . . /JAUT
angitic . . . . /JIGT
angitis . . . . /JAOITS
angium . . . . /J*UM
angiuria . . . . /J*UR
angle . . . . /AENL
-angle . . . . /A*ENL
angular . . . . /GLAUR
animation . . . . /NAEMGS, /NAIMGS
ankyloblepharon . . . . /AEFB
ankyloses . . . . /AINKSZ, /ANLS
ankylosis . . . . /AINKZ
annular . . . . /AOUNL
anomalous . . . . /AONLS
anomaly . . . . /AON
anope . . . . /NO*IP
anopia . . . . /NAOP
anopic . . . . /NAOPG
anopoiesis . . . . /NOIPSZ
anopoietic . . . . /NOIPGT
anopsia . . . . /NAOPS, /NOPS
anoptic . . . . /NAUPT, /NAO*PT
anosmia . . . . /NAUS
ansotomy . . . . /AONZ
ant . . . . /ANT
antagonist . . . . /TAEFT, /GAOIFT
anterior . . . . /AOR
anthracosis . . . . /THROEX
anthrax . . . . /THRAX
anthropic . . . . /THRAOPK
antibody . . . . /AEBD, /AOB, /AOBD
antigen . . . . /AEJ
antigenic . . . . /AENG, /ANG

antigens . . . . . /AEJS
antisepsis . . . . . /SAEPS, /SAEPSZ
antiserum . . . . . /SAERM
antitoxin . . . . . /AOX, /AONX
-antitoxin . . . . . /AONKS
antral . . . . . /TRANL
antritis . . . . . /TRITS
antrostomy . . . . . /TRAONTS
antrotomy . . . . . /TRAONT
ants . . . . . /ANTS
anxiety . . . . . /ZAOI
aortic . . . . . /AORKT
aortic bodies . . . . . /AORBS
aortitis . . . . . /AORTS
aortography . . . . . /AORG
aperture . . . . . /AFPT
-aperture . . . . . /AEFPT
apex . . . . . /AEPX
aphasia . . . . . /FAES
aphasic . . . . . /FAEFK
aphasis . . . . . /FA*ESZ, /FASZ
apheresis . . . . . /FRASZ
aphia . . . . . /AIF
aphic . . . . . /AFK
aphrodisia . . . . . /FRAOES
aphrodisiac . . . . . /FRAOEDZ
aphrodism . . . . . /FRIFM
aphrodite . . . . . /FRAOITD
aphroditism . . . . . /FRIFMT
apical . . . . . /APG
aplasia . . . . . /AIPZ, /APLS
apnea . . . . . /PAEP, /A*EP
apneic . . . . . /PAEPG, /A*EPG
apochromat . . . . . /POFPT
apochromatic . . . . . /POFMT
apocleisis . . . . . /PLAOIKSZ
apokleisis . . . . . /PLAOIKS
aponeurotic . . . . . /PAOURK, /PAOURKT
apophyseal (*see also* -apophysial) . . . . . /PAEFL
apophyses . . . . . /PAOEF
apophysial (*see also* -apophyseal) . . . . . /POFL
apophysis . . . . . /POF
apophysitis . . . . . /PAOIFT
apoplectic . . . . . /PLAOKT
apoplexy . . . . . /PLAOX

aporia (*see also* -poria) . . . . /PO*UR
apostasis . . . . /PA*US
apostema . . . . /PAOEFT, /PAO*ES
apparent . . . . /PAERNT
appendectomy . . . . /PENGD
appendicitis . . . . /PAETS
appendicular . . . . /PLAERP
appendix . . . . /PAEX
apraxia . . . . /PRAX
apt . . . . /APT
aptation . . . . /APGS
aqueous . . . . /KWAES
ar . . . . /A*R
arachnoid . . . . /RAFPD, /WRAFPD
arachnoiditis . . . . /ROIFPT
arche . . . . /AFP
architectonic . . . . /TWONG
architectonics . . . . /TWONGS
architectural . . . . /AERKL
architecture . . . . /AERK
archy . . . . /O*IFP, /AOIFP
arctia . . . . /A*RKT
arcuate . . . . /AURKT
are . . . . /R–, /A*IR
areolar . . . . /RAORL
ares . . . . /A*IRS
argyria . . . . /JAOERJ
argyrism . . . . /JIFM
argyrosis . . . . /JAURJ
argyrum . . . . /JIRM
arousal . . . . /ROULS
arrhythmia . . . . /WRA*IT
arrhythmic . . . . /WRAIFK, /WRIFK
ars . . . . /ARZ
arterial . . . . /AERL
arteriectasia . . . . /TRAES
arteriodialysis . . . . /TRALS
arteriography . . . . /AEFG
arteriole . . . . /ARLT, /TAOERL
arteriotony . . . . /TROERN
arteritis . . . . /TRAERTS
arthria . . . . /A*URT
arthric . . . . /THRARK, /THRAURK
arthritic . . . . /THRIKT
-arthritic . . . . /THROIKT

arthritica . . . . . /THRAIKT
arthritis . . . . . /THRITS
arthritism . . . . . /TLIFM
arthrocace . . . . . /THROKZ
arthrodia . . . . . /THROED
arthrodial . . . . . /THROELD
arthrogram . . . . . /THRAM
arthrography . . . . . /THROG
arthroisis . . . . . /THROIS
arthrolysis . . . . . /THROLS
arthromeningitis . . . . . /TOIT
arthron . . . . . /THRAUN
arthropathy . . . . . /THROPT
arthroplasty . . . . . /THRAPT
arthros . . . . . /A*RTS
arthroses . . . . . /THREZ, /THRESZ
arthrosis . . . . . /THROESZ, /THROEZ
arthrotomy . . . . . /THROT
arthrus . . . . . /THRAUS
articular . . . . . /TLAUR
articulate . . . . . /TLAET, /TARK
articulation . . . . . /TARX, /TLAEGS
arytenoid . . . . . /OIRND
arytenoideus . . . . . /OIRNDZ
ascorbic . . . . . /SKOB
ase . . . . . /AIZ
ases . . . . . /AISZ
asmus . . . . . /SMAS
asphyxia . . . . . /SFAX
assay . . . . . /SA*I
assimilable . . . . . /SMIBL
assimilate . . . . . /SMILT
assimilation . . . . . /SMILGS
association . . . . . /SOERBGS
aster . . . . . /A*RS
asthenia (*see also* sthenia) . . . . . /THAOEN
asthenic (*see also* sthenic) . . . . . /THENK
asthma . . . . . /SMAZ
asthmatic . . . . . /SMAKT
astragalar . . . . . /SGLAR
astragaloid . . . . . /SGLOID
astringent . . . . . /STRIJT
astrocytoma . . . . . /STROEMT
astronautics . . . . . /STRAUKS
asynergia . . . . . /SNARJ

ataxia	/TA*X, /TWAX
ataxic	/TWOIKT
ataxy	/YAX, /TWOIX
ate	/AET
ated	/AETD
atelectasis	/TLAEX
atelia	/TAOEL
atherogenic	/THURG
atheroma	/THO*EM
athetoid	/THOID
athetosis	/TO*ET
athresis	/THRAOEZ
atic	/A*KT
atics	/A*KTS
ation	/AIGS
atism	/TAFM
atlas	/TLATS
atloid	/TLOD, /TLO*ID
atloidean	/TLOND, /TLOIND
atom	/TOUM
atomic	/TAUMG
atonia	/TWAON, /TYAON
atony	/TWO*EN, /TYOEN
atresia	/TRAOEZ
atrial	/TRAL
atrics	/YATS
atriostomy	/AO*S
atrophia	/TRAOF
atrophic	/TROFK
atrophy	/TROF
atropine	/TRAOEFN
atry	/YA*RT
attach	/TAFP
attachment	/TAFMT
atticotomy	/TOIMT
atypical	/TWOIP
auchenitis	/AUFPTS
auchenotomy	/AUFPT
audible	/AUBL
audient	/DYENT
auditory	/AORD
augiaphobia	/JAOB
augmentation	/A*UGS
augmentive	/AUVGT
aural	/AURL

aurale . . . . /A*URL
auricular . . . . /AURKL
auricularis . . . . /AURKLS
auriculovertebral . . . . /AIVL
auscultation . . . . /SKWAOLGS
authenticity. . . . . /THINT
autogram . . . . /AOUGT
autograph . . . . /GRAOF
autography . . . . /GROIF
autoimmune . . . . /AO*UM
autonomic. . . . . /AOUK
autoplasty . . . . /PLAO*S
autotroph. . . . . /TRAOFT
autotrophic . . . . /TRAOFG
auxe. . . . . /A*UX
auxesis . . . . /AOEKS
auxis . . . . /AUKZ
availability. . . . . /VAIBLT
avitaminosis . . . . /AOIVMT, /AOIVMTS
avulsion . . . . /WULGS
axial . . . . /AXL, /SKWIL
axillary. . . . . /ARXL, /ZAIRL
axiogingival . . . . /KPINL
axis . . . . /SKWIS
axitis . . . . /SKWAOITS
axoid . . . . /KPOID
axon. . . . . /KPAON
axonal. . . . . /KPAONL
axone . . . . /KPOEN
axonic . . . . /KPAONK, /KPONK
axonography . . . . /KPAONG
azotemia . . . . /ZOET
azoturia . . . . /ZAOUR

B

bacillary. . . . . /SBAFL
bacillemia . . . . /SBLAOEM
bacilli. . . . . /SBIL, /SBLIBL, /SBAOI
bacillosis . . . . /SBAFLS
bacilluria. . . . . /SBLUR, /SBLAOUR
bacillus . . . . /SBLUS
bacteri. . . . . /BARKT
bacteria . . . . /BAKT, /BAEKT

bacteriaceae . . . . /BAOES
bacterial . . . . /BARL, /BAOERL
bacteriosis . . . . /BROES
bacteriotherapy . . . . /BAERP
bacterium . . . . /BAOERM
balance . . . . /BAL
balancing . . . . /BALG
ballism . . . . /BLIM
ballismus . . . . /BLIMS
band . . . . /BAND
bang . . . . /BANG
bank . . . . /BANK
bar . . . . /BAR
barbital . . . . /BARBT, /BARBL
barbiturate . . . . /BRIFP
barbiturates . . . . /BRIFPS
barbituric . . . . /BAOURK
barbituric acid . . . . /BAOURKD
baria . . . . /BAOR
baric . . . . /BA*RK, /BR*IK
barism . . . . /BAFRM, /BRIFM
baropathy . . . . /BARPT
basal . . . . /BAILZ
base . . . . /BAIS
basia . . . . /BAIZ
basial . . . . /BAELZ
basic . . . . /BAIFK
basilar . . . . /BALZ
basioglossus . . . . /BLAIS
basis . . . . /BAZ
basophilic . . . . /BIFLG
behavioral . . . . /BAIVRL, /BAIFRL
bevel . . . . /BEVL
bezoar . . . . /BAOEZ
biasis . . . . /BAOISZ
bicarbonate . . . . /BARP
bicarbonatemia . . . . /BREM
bicipital . . . . /BIPT
bifemoral . . . . /BEFRL, /BIFRL, /BAOFRL
bilia . . . . /BLA
biliary . . . . /BLIR
bilin . . . . /BL*IN
bilinemia . . . . /BLAO*EM
bilinicterus . . . . /BLIKT
bilinogen . . . . /BAOILG

bilinuria . . . . /BLAOURN
bilious . . . . /BLUS
bilirubin . . . . /BLAOB, /BLAOUN
bilirubinemia . . . . /BLAOEB
bilirubinogen . . . . /BLAOJ
binocular . . . . /BAUKL, /BOKL
biodynamics . . . . /BAOMGS
biogenesis . . . . /BENSZ
biologic . . . . /BL–J
biological . . . . /BLAL
biologist . . . . /BOLT, /BOLGT
biologists . . . . /BOLTS, /BOLGTS
biology . . . . /BOLG
bion . . . . /BAOIN
bionic . . . . /BOINK
biont . . . . /BAOINT, /BONT
bionts . . . . /BAOINTS, /BONTS
biophobia . . . . /BOEB
bioscope . . . . /BOEP
bioscopy . . . . /BOEPG
biosis . . . . /BOISZ
biotaxes . . . . /BEKTS
biotaxis . . . . /BAOKTS
biote . . . . /BYOIT
biotic . . . . /BOIT
biotics . . . . /BOITS
biotin . . . . /BOINT
biotism . . . . /BOIFM
birth . . . . /B*IRT
bite . . . . /BAOIT
bium . . . . /BOIM
bladder . . . . /BLAD, /BLARD
bladders . . . . /BLADZ, /BLARDZ
blast . . . . /BLA*S, /BLAFT
blastema . . . . /BLAOEMT
blastemia . . . . /BLEFT
blastemic . . . . /BLEK
blastic . . . . /BLAFK
blastoid . . . . /BLOID
blastoma . . . . /BLOEM
blastomas . . . . /BLOEMS
blastomata . . . . /BLAMT
blastomatosis . . . . /BLOEMT
blastomycosis . . . . /BLAOIKS
blastomyoma . . . . /BLOIM

blastopenia . . . . . /BLAOEPT
blastosis . . . . . /BLOESZ
blastotic . . . . . /BLOFKT
blasts . . . . . /BLA*SZ, /BLAFTS
blastula . . . . . /BLAOUL
bleach . . . . . /BLAOEFP
blennia . . . . . /BL*EN
blennorrhea . . . . . /BLAOER
blepharia . . . . . /BLAEF
blepharic . . . . . /BLAEFK
blepharism . . . . . /BLEFM
blepharon . . . . . /BLEFRN, /BLEFN
blepharopterygium . . . . . /BLEJ
blephary . . . . . /BLOIF
blepsia . . . . . /BLEPS
blepsis . . . . . /BLEPSZ
block . . . . . /BLOK
blood test . . . . . /BLUT, /BL*ES
blot . . . . . /BLOT
blotting . . . . . /BLOGT
bodies . . . . . /BODZ
body . . . . . /BOD
bole . . . . . /BO*EL
bolia . . . . . /BAO*L
bolism . . . . . /BLOEFM
bolometer . . . . . /BOERLT
boly . . . . . /BL*E
boma . . . . . /BO*EM
borate . . . . . /BAORT
boric acid . . . . . /BOERKD
born . . . . . /BORN
borreliosis . . . . . /BRAELS, /BAORLS, /BOERLS
bothrion . . . . . /BROIN
bothritis . . . . . /BRO*IT
boulia . . . . . /BAOL
bound . . . . . /BOUN
box . . . . . /BOX
brachia . . . . . /BRAIFP
brachial . . . . . /BRAIFPL, /BRAIKL
brachiocephalia . . . . . /BRAFL
brachium . . . . . /BROIM
brachius . . . . . /BRAFPZ
brachycephalic . . . . . /BREFK
brachycephaly . . . . . /BREFL
brachydactylia . . . . . /BRIKL

brachydactyly . . . . . . /BRAKD
bradia . . . . . . /BRAID
brain . . . . . . /BRAIN
branchial . . . . . . /BRANG
bregmatic . . . . . . /BREGT
brenner . . . . . . /BRERN
bromate . . . . . . /BROEMT
bromated . . . . . . /BROEMTD
bromic . . . . . . /BROM
bromide . . . . . . /BRAOIMD
bromidrosis . . . . . . /BROEMD
bromous . . . . . . /BROUMS
bromous acid . . . . . . /BROUMD
bronchial . . . . . . /BRONLG
bronchiectasis . . . . . . /BRAESZ
bronchiolar . . . . . . /BRAORL, /BROERNL
bronchiolitis . . . . . . /BRAOTS
bronchitis . . . . . . /BRONTS, /BRAOITS
bronchomegaly . . . . . . /BRELG
bronchoscopy . . . . . . /BROIP
bronchotomy . . . . . . /BRONGT
bubonocele . . . . . . /BAOUBS
buccal . . . . . . /BAOKL
buccoaxial . . . . . . /BAOXL
bucco-occlusal . . . . . . /BLAOL
buccopulpal . . . . . . /BOUP
bulbar . . . . . . /BLAURB
bulbia . . . . . . /BL*IB
bulbic . . . . . . /BOUK
bulbospinal . . . . . . /BAOINL
bulbous . . . . . . /BLOUBS
bulbus . . . . . . /BLUBS
bulge . . . . . . /BULG
bulia . . . . . . /BAOUL
bulic . . . . . . /BAOULG
bullous . . . . . . /BLOULS
bursal . . . . . . /BURLS
bursitis . . . . . . /BURTS, /BAOIRTS
butane . . . . . . /BAINT
byon . . . . . . /BYO*N, /BYAUN

C

cace . . . . . /KA*IS
cachectic . . . . . /KAEFPT
cachexia . . . . . /KAEFP
cadence . . . . . /KAINDZ
cadent . . . . . /KAINT
cairograph . . . . . /KRAOIF
cal . . . . . /KAL
calary . . . . . /KLAIR
calate . . . . . /KL–T
calated . . . . . /KL–TD
calation . . . . . /KL–GZ
calcaneal . . . . . /KLAENL
calcanean. . . . . . /KLA*ERN
calcaneobursitis . . . . . /KBURTS, /KBAOIRTS
calcarine . . . . . /KARKL
calcemia . . . . . /KLAOEMS
calcemic . . . . . /KLAOEMGS
calcia . . . . . /KALZ
calcic . . . . . /KALG
calcification . . . . . /KAFLGS
calcin . . . . . /SKLAN
calcinemia . . . . . /KOIMS, /KAO*EMS
calcinosis. . . . . . /KALSZ
calcinuria . . . . . /KLAOURN
calcipectic . . . . . /KLEPGT
calcipexy . . . . . /KLEPX
calcium . . . . . /KALS
calciuria . . . . . /KLAOUR
calculous . . . . . /KLOUZ
calculus . . . . . /KL–S
calcuria . . . . . /KLURK
calent . . . . . /KAILT
caliceal (*see also* calyceal) . . . . . /KLAOEL
calicostomy. . . . . . /KLAOMT
caliectasis . . . . . /KLAEKT
calix. . . . . . /KAILX
call . . . . . /KAUL
caloric. . . . . . /KLAORK
calorie. . . . . . /KLAOR
calyceal (*see also* caliceal) . . . . . /KLIL
calycosis . . . . . /KLOEKSZ
calyx . . . . . /KAILGS

cameral . . . /KAERL
camerate . . . /KMAIRT
camnosis (*see also* kamnosis) . . . /KOEMSZ
campimeter . . . /KPAOERMT
campsia . . . /KAMS, /KAMPZ
campsis . . . /KAMSZ, /KAMZ
campsodynia . . . /KPIN
canal . . . /KANL
canales . . . /KAENLS
canalicular . . . /KLIRKL
canaliculitis . . . /KLIKTS
canalis . . . /KAINLS
canalization . . . /KANLGS
cancellous . . . /KLEF
cancer . . . /KAERN
cancerous . . . /KAERNZ
canities . . . /KAOERBS
canthal . . . /THAUNL
canthectomy . . . /KAEKT, /THA*EKT
canthic . . . /TH*IK
canthosis . . . /THOEKTS
canthus . . . /THUKS
capillaris . . . /KPLIRS
capillary . . . /KPLAIR
capitate . . . /KPOIT
capitates . . . /KPOITS
capitulate . . . /KPIFP
capitulation . . . /KPIFPGS
capnia . . . /KP–N
capnic . . . /KP–K
capsectomy . . . /SKAPT
capsid . . . /KAPDZ
capsular . . . /KPURL, /KPAOURL, /KP–FRL
capsulation . . . /KPAFLGS
capsule . . . /KP–FL, /KPAOUL
capsulitis . . . /KPLAOIT
capsulization . . . /KPAOULGS, /KP–FLGS
carbia . . . /KRAUB
carbon . . . /KBON
carbonate . . . /KBONT, /KBAENT
carboxylic acid . . . /KBOKLD
carcinogen . . . /SGEN, /KRING, /SKROG
carcinogenesis . . . /SGENSZ
carcinogenic . . . /SGENG
carcinoma . . . /SKROEM

cardectomy . . . /K*EKT
cardia . . . /KAUR, /KAURD
cardiac . . . /KAURK
cardial . . . /KARL, /KA*URL
cardian . . . /KRAURN
cardic . . . /KRAURKD
cardicentesis . . . /KRAO*ETS
cardiectomy . . . /KREKT
cardii . . . /KAOIRD
cardinal . . . /KARNLD
cardiocentesis . . . /KRAOETS, /KENTS
cardiogram . . . /KR–M, /KAURMG
cardiograph . . . /KRAF
cardiographic . . . /KRAFK
cardiography . . . /KRAOEF, /KROG
cardiokinetic . . . /KRENGT
cardiolysis . . . /KARLS
cardiomediastinitis . . . /KRAOINTS
cardiomyotomy . . . /KRAURMT
cardiopathy . . . /KAURPT
cardioperitoneal . . . /KIRNL
cardiopexy . . . /KAURPX
cardiophone . . . /KRO*EN
cardiophonograph . . . /KRAOF
cardiophrenic . . . /KREFN
cardioplasty . . . /KAURP
cardioplegia . . . /KAURJ
cardiopleural . . . /KPLERL
cardiorrhaphy . . . /KRAEF
cardioscope . . . /KROEP
cardiosis . . . /KWOES
cardiostomy . . . /KRO*S
cardiosymphysis . . . /KRIMPS
cardiotomy . . . /KMAOE
carditic . . . /KRAURKT
carditis . . . /KAOITS
cardium . . . /KAURMD
cardius . . . /KRUDZ
cardosis . . . /KAURDZ
cardotomy . . . /KAURTD
care . . . /KAIR
cariasis (*see also* acariasis) . . . /KRAOSZ
carotic . . . /KROKD
carotid . . . /KROTD
carp . . . /KARP

carpal . . . . /KARPL
carpectomy . . . . /KPEK, /KRAEPT
carpi . . . . /KPAOI
carpophalangeal . . . . /KPAENL
carpus . . . . /KARPS
carteresis . . . . /KRAOERTS
cartilage . . . . /KLART, /KARLT
cartilaginous . . . . /KLAJS
cartilago . . . . /KLAGT
caruncular . . . . /KRURNG
carynosis . . . . /KOIRNSZ
caryoblast (*see also* karyoblast) . . . . /KBAO*FT
caryocyte (*see also* karyocyte) . . . . /KRAO*T
caryon (*see also* karyon) . . . . /KRA*UN
caryosis . . . . /KRARSZ
caryote (*see also* karyote) . . . . /KRO*ET
caryotic (*see also* karyotic) . . . . /KRAO*KT
cast . . . . /KA*S
castration . . . . /KRAIFGS
catabasis . . . . /KBAISZ
catabolic . . . . /KBLOK
catabolism . . . . /KBLOFM
catalepsy . . . . /KLEP
catalysis . . . . /KAULTS
catalyst . . . . /KLIS
catalytic . . . . /KLAKT
catalyze . . . . /KL–Z
catalyzer . . . . /KLAOIRS
cataphoria . . . . /KPOIR
cataract . . . . /KAKT
catarctic . . . . /KRARKT
catarrh . . . . /KRAR
catarrhal . . . . /KRARL
catarxis . . . . /KRARX
cate . . . . /KAET
catharsis . . . . /THAURS
cathartic . . . . /THAURKT
catheresis . . . . /KRAO*ET, /KRAO*ESZ
cathereti c . . . . /KR*ET, /KRERKT
catheter . . . . /THERT
catheterism . . . . /THEFM
catheterization . . . . /THERGS
cation . . . . /KAEGS
caudad . . . . /KA*UD
caudal . . . . /KAUD, /KA*ULD

caudate . . . . /KAID
caulia . . . . /KLAUL
causal . . . . /KAUFL
cauterectomy . . . . /KRAUKT
cauterization . . . . /KA*UGS, /KA*URGS
cautery . . . . /KA*URT, /KRAUT
cava . . . . /KAV
caval . . . . /KAVL
cavernosus . . . . /KOEVRNS
cavernous . . . . /KAVRNS, /KAFRNS
cavitary . . . . /KAVRT
cavogram . . . . /KAVG
cavography . . . . /KRAEVG
ccipital (*see also* occipital) . . . . /SAUPT, /SO*IPT
cclusal (*see also* occlusal *and* clusal) . . . . /KLULZ
cecal . . . . /SAOEKL
cecitis . . . . /SAOETSZ
cecostomy . . . . /SKOS, /SKO*S
cectomy . . . . /S*EKT
cecum . . . . /SKAOEK, /SK*UM
cele (*see also* coele *and* coel) . . . . /KRAOEL
celectomy . . . . /KRAOEKT
celia (*see also* coelia) . . . . /SLAE
celiac . . . . /SLAEK
celial . . . . /SL*IL
celialgia . . . . /KRAOEJ
celic . . . . /KRAOEKL
celidosis (*see also* kelidosis) . . . . /SLOEDZ
celiocentesis . . . . /SLENTS
celiotomy . . . . /SLOMT
celitis . . . . /KRAOELTS, /SLAOETS
cell . . . . /KREL
celled . . . . /KRELD
cellular . . . . /SLER
cellularity . . . . /SLAERT
cellulitis . . . . /SLAOITS, /SL–TS
cellulose . . . . /KROELS, /SLOEZ
celom . . . . /SL*EM
celorraphy . . . . /SLAOEF
celoschisis . . . . /SLISZ
celous . . . . /SLOUZ
cemental . . . . /SMAENL
cementitis . . . . /SMAOINTS
cementoclasia . . . . /SKLAIZ
cementosis . . . . /SAOEMTS

cementum . . . . /SMUM
cenesthesia . . . . /KRAOENS
cenosis . . . . /SNO*EZ
centesis . . . . /STAOESZ, /SENTS
centetic . . . . /SENGT
centive . . . . /SNEVT
central . . . . /STRAL
centric . . . . /STRENK
centricity . . . . /STREFNT, /STREFRNT
centrifugation . . . . /STRUFGS, /STRIFGS
centrifuge . . . . /STRAOUJ
centriole . . . . /STRO*EL
centrism . . . . /STRIFM
centrum . . . . /SNUM, /STR*UM
centrums . . . . /SNUMS, /STRUMS
cephalalgia . . . . /SFALG
cephalalgic . . . . /SFAKL
cephalia . . . . /SFLAL
cephaliasis . . . . /SFLAOIS
cephalic . . . . /SFEK
cephalics . . . . /SFEKZ
cephalies . . . . /SFLAOES
cephalism . . . . /SFIFM
cephalisms . . . . /SFIFMS
cephalitis . . . . /SFAOIT
cephalization . . . . /SFELGS
cephalocele . . . . /SFAOEL
cephalodynia . . . . /SFIND
cephalography . . . . /SFRAEF
cephalogyric . . . . /SFAOIK
cephaloid . . . . /SEFLD
cephaloma . . . . /SFOEM
cephalometry . . . . /SFORMT
cephalon . . . . /SFLAON
cephalopathy . . . . /SFA*T, /SFA*ET
cephalopolysyndactyly . . . . /SFAOEP
cephalorrhachidian . . . . /SFAFP, /SFRIFP
cephaloscope . . . . /SFOEP
cephalosis . . . . /SFLOES
cephalosyndactylia . . . . /SFAOEKL
cephalosyndactyly . . . . /SFIKL
cephalotome . . . . /SFOM
cephalotomy . . . . /SFOT
cephalous . . . . /SFOUS
cephalpelvimetry . . . . /SFEVMT

cephalus . . . /SFLUS, /SFUS
cephaly . . . /SFLAOE
ceps . . . /S*EPS
ception . . . /S*EPGS
ceptive . . . /SEVPT
ceptor . . . /SERPT
ceptors . . . /SERPTS
cerastism . . . /KRAFM
ceratitis (*see also* keratitis) . . . /KRERTS
ceratosis (*see also* keratosis) . . . /KRO*ETS
ceratous . . . /SERTS
cercosis . . . /SKOEFS
cere . . . /KRER
cerebellar . . . /SBLAR
cerebellum . . . /SBLUM
cerebration . . . /SBRAEGS
cerebritis . . . /SBRAOITS
cerebrorenal . . . /SBRAENL
cerebrorenal syndrome . . . /SBRAENLD
cerebroside . . . /SBRAOID
cerebrum . . . /SBRUM
cerosis . . . /SAOERSZ
cervical . . . /SR–FL, /SR–VL
cervicalis . . . /SR–VLS
cervicitis . . . /SEFRBT, /SEFRBTS
cervix . . . /SR–FX, /SR–VX
cession . . . /S*EGS
chalasia . . . /KHALS
chalasis . . . /KHALSZ
chalazia . . . /KLAERB
chancre . . . /SHANG
change . . . /KHAING, /KHAIJ
charge . . . /KHARJ
cheilia (*see also* chylia) . . . /KHAO*IL
cheiloplasty . . . /KAOIP
cheiloscope . . . /KHAOIP
cheiral . . . /KHOIRL, /KHAO*IRL
cheiria (*see also* chiria) . . . /KHAO*IR
chemical . . . /KHEM
chemist . . . /KM*ES, /KMEFT
chemistries . . . /KHEMSZ
chemistry . . . /KHEMZ
chemists . . . /KM*ESZ, /KMEFTS
chemotherapy . . . /KAOEM
chemy . . . /KHOIM

chesia . . . /KHAES
chetia . . . /KHAERB
chezia . . . /KHAEZ
chiasmatic . . . /KAOIFMT
chiasmic . . . /KAOIFMG
chilia . . . /KHO*IL
chiral . . . /KHAOIRL
chiria (*see also* cheiria) . . . /KHAOIR
chirurgic. . . /KHAOIRK
chirurgical. . . /KHIRLG, /KHAOIRLG
chirus. . . /KHIRS
chitin. . . /KAOINT
chloral . . . /KLOERL
chlorate. . . /KLAORT
chloremia . . . /KLAOEM
chloremic . . . /KLAO*EMG
chlorhydria . . . /KLAOIRD
chloric. . . /KLORK
chloridation . . . /KLOERGS
chloride . . . /KLOIRD
chloridemia . . . /KLAOEMD
chlorin. . . /KLORN
chlorinated. . . /KLORNTD
chlorination. . . /KLOIRNGS
chlorine . . . /KLOIRN
chlorite. . . /KLAOIT
chlorization. . . /KLOERZ
chlorophyll . . . /KLOF
chloropia . . . /KLAORP
chlorous . . . /KLOURZ
chloruration . . . /KLAOURGS
chloruria . . . /KLIR
cholagogue . . . /KHAUG
cholangeitis . . . /KLET, /KLETS
cholangiocystoduodenostomy . . . /KLIFD
cholangioduodenostomy. . . /KLOFT
cholangioenterostomy . . . /KLENT
cholangiogastrostomy . . . /KLAG
cholangiogram. . . /KLAORM
cholangiography . . . /KLAOFG
cholangiojejunostomy . . . /KLAOJ
cholangiostomy . . . /KLANG
cholangitis . . . /KLAOITS
cholate . . . /KLAIT, /KHAOLT
cholecyst . . . /KHIFT

cholecystectomy . . . /KHOIKT
cholecystis . . . /KHITS
cholecystitis . . . /KHOELT, /KHOELTS
cholecystocholedochectomy . . . /KHOEKT
cholecystography . . . /KHOEFG
cholecystokinin . . . /KHAOINS
-cholecystokinin . . . /KHAO*INS
cholecystostomy . . . /KHOS, /KHO*S
cholecystotomy . . . /KHOT, /KHO*T
choledochostomy . . . /KHOFPS
choledochotomy . . . /KHOFPT
choledochus . . . /KLED
cholera . . . /KLER, /KLOER
choleresis . . . /KLAOESZ
choleretic . . . /KLORKT
cholesteatoma . . . /KHOEMT
cholesteremia . . . /KLAOERM, /KLERMT
cholesteremic . . . /KLAOERMG
cholesterin . . . /KLERN
cholesterol . . . /KLES, /KL*ES
cholesterolemia . . . /KLOERM
cholesterolemic . . . /KLOERMG
cholesterolia . . . /KLOEL
cholia . . . /KHAOL
cholic . . . /KHOELG
cholic acid . . . /KHOELGD
choline . . . /KLEN
cholinergic . . . /KLIJ
cholinesterase . . . /KLA*ES
cholitis . . . /KHAOILT, /KHAOILTS
choluria . . . /KHOUR
chondral . . . /KAUND
chondrectomy . . . /KHAUKT
chondria . . . /KHORND
chondriac . . . /KHORNGD, /KHAK
chondriacal . . . /KHORNL
chondrial . . . /KAURND
chondriasis . . . /KHORNSZ
chondritis . . . /KHAOITS
chondrium . . . /KHORM
chondrodysplasia . . . /KHAIDZ
chondrodystrophia . . . /KHOF
chondrodystrophy . . . /KHOEF
chondrofibroma . . . /KHOEB
chondrofibrosarcoma . . . /KHOEFM

chondrogenesis . . . . /KHOENDZ
chondrolysis. . . . . /KHOLSZ
chondroma . . . . /KHOEM
chondromatosis . . . . /KHOEMTS
chondromyxoma . . . . /KHOIX
chondropathia . . . . /KHA*PT, /KHAO*PT
chondropathy . . . . /KHAEPT, /KHA*ET
chondroplasia . . . . /KPLAEZ
chondrosarcoma . . . . /KHOEMS
chondroscapularis. . . . . /KHAURPS
chondroseotomy . . . . /KHOTS
chondroses . . . . /KHOERSZ
chondrosis . . . . /KHOESZ
chondrosteosis . . . . /KHOEFS
chondrostosis. . . . . /KHOETS
chondrotomy . . . . /KHOET
chondrous . . . . /KHOUS
chord . . . . /KHORD
chordal . . . . /KHAORLD
chorditis . . . . /KHOITS
chordon . . . . /KHORN
chore . . . . /KHOER
chorea . . . . /KHAOR
choria . . . . /KHAUR
chorial. . . . . /KHORL
chorioidal . . . . /KRO*ILD
chorioiditis . . . . /KROIDZ
chorion . . . . /KHOERN
chorionic. . . . . /KHOERNG
chorioretinitis . . . . /KHERNT
chorism . . . . /KHIFM
choroid . . . . /KROID
choroidal . . . . /KROILD
choroidea . . . . /KHOID
choroiditis. . . . . /KROIDZ
chroia. . . . . /KRO*I
chroic . . . . /KHOIK
chroism. . . . . /KROEFM
chromasia . . . . /KMAIS, /KMAIZ
chromasy . . . . /KMAZ
chromat . . . . /KRAMT, /KHAMT
chromate . . . . /KAEM
chromatic . . . . /KROMT
chromatin . . . . /KROEMT
chromatinization . . . . /KRINGS

chromatism . . . . . /KMIFM
chromatization . . . . . /KROEMGS
chromatography . . . . . /KMOFG
chromatophil . . . . . /KROIF
chromatophile . . . . . /KRAOIFL
chromatophilia . . . . . /KRAOFL
chromatophilic . . . . . /KROIFK
chromatopsia . . . . . /KROEPT
chromatopsy . . . . . /KROPTS
chromatosis . . . . . /KROEMS, /KROEMSZ
chromatotic . . . . . /KMOK
chrome . . . . . /KROEM
chromemia . . . . . /KMAOEM
chromesthesia . . . . . /KROEMZ
chrometer . . . . . /KRAUMT
chromhidrosis . . . . . /KHOIZ
chromia . . . . . /KROM, /KRAO*M
chromic . . . . . /KROEMG
chromidrosis . . . . . /KROISZ
chromism . . . . . /KMOEFM
chromogen . . . . . /KROEJ
chromogenic . . . . . /KROENK
chromogenicity . . . . . /KROENGT, /KRIFNT
chromogens . . . . . /KROEJS
chromometer . . . . . /KROERMT
chromophil . . . . . /KMIF, /KROEFL
chromophile . . . . . /KMAOIF
chromophilia . . . . . /KMAOEFL
chromoprotein . . . . . /KHROIP
chromoscopy . . . . . /KROIPZ
chromosomal . . . . . /KMOEL, /SMOEL
chromosome . . . . . /SMOEM, /KMOEMS, /ZOEM
chromotrichia . . . . . /KHIFP
chromous . . . . . /KROMS
chromy . . . . . /KRO*IM
chronal . . . . . /KROINL
chronia . . . . . /KHOIN
chronic . . . . . /KRONK
chronism . . . . . /KRAUFM
chronograph . . . . . /KROEF
chronorrhea . . . . . /KRERN
chronoscope . . . . . /KHOEP
chronous . . . . . /KROUNZ
chrony . . . . . /KRO*IN
chroous . . . . . /KHOUZ

chrosis . . . . . /KROES
chrosy . . . . . /KRO*IS
chrous . . . . . /KROUZ
chthonography . . . . . /THOEG
chthonous . . . . . /KHOUNS
chute . . . . . /SHAOUT
chyle . . . . . /KAOIL
chylema . . . . . /KHAO*EM
chylia (*see also* cheilia) . . . . . /KHAOIL, /KAO*IL
chylomicronemia . . . . . /KMOEK
chylous . . . . . /KAOILS
chyluria . . . . . /KAOIRL
chyme . . . . . /KAOIM
chymia . . . . . /KHAO*IM
chysis (*see also* enchysis) . . . . . /KHISZ
cibal . . . . . /SAOIBL
cidal (*see also* icidal) . . . . . /SAOILD
cide (*see also* icide) . . . . . /SAO*ID
cidin . . . . . /SD*IN
cilia . . . . . /SLA
ciliary . . . . . /SLIR
cilium . . . . . /SL*UM
cillin . . . . . /SL*IN
cin . . . . . /S*IN
cineangiocardiography . . . . . /SKRAOEF, /SNAOEF
cineangiography . . . . . /SNAIFG, /JAEFG
cinefluorography . . . . . /SFLURG
cinematograph . . . . . /SGRAFT
cinematography . . . . . /SMAUG, /SNAUG
cinerea (*see also* cineria) . . . . . /SIRN, /SNAOERN
cineria (*see also* cinerea) . . . . . /SNIRN
cinesia . . . . . /SNAOES
cinesimeter . . . . . /SNAOEMT
cinesis . . . . . /SNAO*ESZ
cinesthesia (*see also* kinesthesia) . . . . . /SNEZ
cinesthetic . . . . . /SNEK
cinetic . . . . . /SNET
cinin (*see also* kinin) . . . . . /SN*IN
cins . . . . . /S*INS
cipital . . . . . /SPA*L
ciput . . . . . /SP*UT
circular . . . . . /SLAR
circulation . . . . . /SL-GS
circulatory . . . . . /SIRKT, /SLORT
cirrhosis . . . . . /SIRS, /KROEZ

cirsocele . . . . . /SIRZ
cision . . . . . /SIGS
cisternal . . . . . /STIRNL
cisternography . . . . . /STIRNG
cisternostomy . . . . . /STERNT
citraturia . . . . . /STRAOUR
citremia . . . . . /STRIM
citric . . . . . /KRIRK, /STR*IK
city (*see also* icity) . . . . . /STI
cladic . . . . . /KLAKD
cladism . . . . . /KLAFM
clamis . . . . . /KLAMZ
clasia . . . . . /KLAIZ
clasis (*see also* klasis *and* oclasis) . . . . . /KLAZ, /KLAISZ
class . . . . . /KLASZ
clast . . . . . /KLA*S
clastic (*see also* klastic *and* oclastic) . . . . . /KLAFT
clastoma . . . . . /KLOEM
clasty . . . . . /KLAS
clave . . . . . /KLAIV
clavian . . . . . /KLAIVN, /KLAIFN
clavicular . . . . . /KLAFRL, /KLAVRL
clavicularis . . . . . /KLIVRL, /KLIFRL
claviculars . . . . . /KLAFRLZ, /KLAVRLZ
clavius . . . . . /KLAIVS
cleidal . . . . . /KLAOILD
cleidodysostosis . . . . . /KLOEFSZ
cleidomastoid . . . . . /KLOITD
cleidomastoideus . . . . . /KLOITDZ, /KLOITSDZ
cleisis . . . . . /KLAOISZ
clepsia . . . . . /KLEPZ
clepsis . . . . . /KLEPSZ
clesis . . . . . /KLESZ
climacteric . . . . . /KMAKT
climatics . . . . . /KLOIMTS
climatologist . . . . . /KLIFMT
climatology . . . . . /KLIMG
clinal . . . . . /KLAOINL
clination . . . . . /KLINGS
clinic . . . . . /KLIN
clinical . . . . . /KLINL
clinoid . . . . . /KLO*I
clip . . . . . /KLIP
clisis . . . . . /KLOISZ
clitoris . . . . . /KLIT

clival . . . /KLIVL
clonal . . . /KLOENL
clonality . . . /KLOENLT
clonia . . . /KLAON
clonic . . . /KLONK
clonus . . . /KLUNS
closure . . . /KLO*UR
clotting . . . /KLOGT
clusal (*see also* occlusal *and* cclusal) . . . /KLUL
clusion (*see also* occlusion) . . . /KLOGS
clysis . . . /KLAOIS
clysmia . . . /KLAIMZ
clyster . . . /KLIFR
cnemia . . . /SNAO*EM
cnemial . . . /SNAO*EL
cnemic . . . /NAOEMG
cnemidion . . . /NAOEMD
cnemis . . . /NAOEMS
cnemism . . . /NAOEFMS
coagulability . . . /KWABLT
coagulable . . . /KWABL
coagulant . . . /KWANLT
coagulation . . . /KWAGS
coagulative . . . /KWAFT
coagulator . . . /KWARG
coagulin . . . /KWANG
coarctation . . . /KWARGS
cobalt . . . /KBAULT
coccal . . . /KAUKL
coccemia . . . /SKAEM
cocci . . . /SKOI
coccia . . . /SKAOX
coccic . . . /KOXZ, /SKAUK
coccicosis . . . /SKOEX
coccidal . . . /SKAO*ILD
coccidioidomycosis . . . /KMAOIKS
coccin . . . /SKOIN, /SK*IN
coccoid . . . /KOIKD, /KO*ID
coccolysin . . . /SKIFN, /SKOFN
coccolysis . . . /SKOLS
coccoma . . . /KMAUM
coccoses . . . /KAOEKS
coccosis . . . /KAUXZ
coccosuria . . . /SKAO*UR
coccus . . . /SKAUX, /KAUX, /KUS

coccygeal . . . /SKIJ
coccygeus . . . /SKIJS
coccypexia . . . /SKPEGS
coccypexy . . . /SKPEX
coccyx . . . /SKOX
cochleogram . . . /KLAERM
cochleograph . . . /KLAEF
cochleographic . . . /KLAEFK
cochleography . . . /KLAEFG
codone . . . /KWOEND
coel (*see also* cele *and* coele) . . . /KRAO*EL
coele (*see also* cele *and* coel) . . . /SLAOE, /KROEL
coelia (*see also* celia) . . . /SLAEL, /SLA*E
coelic . . . /KROEKL
coelom . . . /SLOM
coeloma . . . /SLAUM
coercible . . . /KWOEFBL
cogenic . . . /KOENG
cognition . . . /KOGS
cognitive . . . /KOV
coherence . . . /KWERNZ, /KW*ERNS
coherent . . . /KWERNT
coil . . . /KOIL
coimesis (*see also* koimesis) . . . /KROIMZ, /KROIMSZ
coital . . . /KOILT
coitus . . . /KOITS
colectomy . . . /KLEKT
colic . . . /KOKL
colitis . . . /KLOIT, /KLOITS
collagenous . . . /KAUJS
collateral . . . /KLARL
collation . . . /KLA*IGS
collic . . . /KLOKL, /K–KL
collicular . . . /KLARKL
collis . . . /K–LS
colloid . . . /KLOID
collusion . . . /KLAO*UGS
coloboma . . . /KLOEB, /KLAOB
cologastrostomy . . . /KLOEG
colon . . . /KLON
colonic . . . /KLONG
colonitis . . . /KLONT, /KLONTS
colonoscope . . . /KLO*EP
colonoscopy . . . /KLOIPS
colony . . . /KLOIN

colopexy . . . /KPEX
coloplasty . . . /KPLAOS, /KPLOS
coloplication . . . /KPLAOIGS
coloptosis . . . /KLOPT
coloration . . . /KLORGS
colorimeter . . . /KLORMT
colostomy . . . /KLOS, /KLO*S
colotomy . . . /KOLT, /KLOMT
colpectomy . . . /KLOPG
colpismus . . . /KPIZ
colpitis . . . /KLOIPT, /KLOIPTS
colpium . . . /KPUM
colpocele . . . /KPAOEL
colpometra . . . /KMAERT
colpoplasty . . . /KPLA*S
colpos (*see also* kolpos) . . . /KOLS
colposcope . . . /KLOEPS
colpotomy . . . /KOEPT
columnar . . . /KLAURM
coly . . . /KLAO*E
colysin . . . /KLIFN
coma . . . /KAOM, /KWOEM
comatose . . . /KWOEZ, /KWOEMT
comatous . . . /KWOUZ
combination . . . /KBAIGS
combustible . . . /KBUBL
comial . . . /KMAL
comma . . . /KMA
commata . . . /KMAOT
commensal . . . /KMENLS
commissural . . . /KMAOURL
communication . . . /KMUNGS
compatibility . . . /KPABLT
compatible . . . /KPABL
compensation . . . /KPENGS
competence . . . /KPES
competency . . . /KPAES
competent . . . /KPE
complement . . . /KPLEMT
complementary . . . /KPLERMT
complemented . . . /KPLEMTD
complementemia . . . /KPLAOEMT
complementemic . . . /KPLAOEMG
complex . . . /KPLEX
component . . . /KPOENT

components . . . . . /KPOENTS
composed . . . . . /KPOEFD
composition . . . . . /KPOGS, /KPOEGS
compound . . . . . /KPOUN
compress . . . . . /KPROS
compressible . . . . . /KPROFBL, /KPREFBL
compression . . . . . /KPROFGS
compressor . . . . . /KPROFR
compromised . . . . . /KM–D, /KPROMD
concave . . . . . /KWAEF, /KWAEV
concentration . . . . . /SKRAENGS
conceptive . . . . . /SKEVP
conchal . . . . . /KAONL
conchitis . . . . . /KAONGT, /KAONTS
conchous . . . . . /KUFPS
conditioned . . . . . /K–ND
conditioning . . . . . /K–NG
conductor . . . . . /KURKT
conductors . . . . . /KURKTS
condylalgia . . . . . /KLALG
condylar . . . . . /KRAUNL
condyle . . . . . /KAUNL
condyli . . . . . /KAOINLD
condylian . . . . . /KINLD
condylic . . . . . /KAUNG
condylitis . . . . . /KLOINTS
condyloid . . . . . /KOINL
condylous . . . . . /KOINLS
condylus . . . . . /KAUNLS
cone . . . . . /KOEN
congestive . . . . . /GEV
conglutinin . . . . . /GLONT
conia . . . . . /KAON, /KO*EN
conic . . . . . /KO*ENG
conid . . . . . /KOEND
conidium . . . . . /KMUMD
coniosis . . . . . /KOENS
conium . . . . . /KMUM
conization . . . . . /KOENGS
conjugant . . . . . /JAOUNG
conjugate . . . . . /JAOUG
conjunctival . . . . . /JIVL
conjunctivitis . . . . . /JIVT
connect . . . . . /KEK
connection . . . . . /KEX

connubial . . . /KAOBL
conscious . . . /KONS
consciously . . . /KONLS
consciousness . . . /KONSZ
conservative . . . /SKEFT
constitution . . . /KAOGS
constriction . . . /STRIX
constrictive . . . /STRIV, /STRIVK
constrictor . . . /STRIRK, /STRIRKT
contagious . . . /TAIJ
contaminate . . . /TAM
contaminated . . . /TAMD
contamination . . . /TAMGS, /TAJ
continence . . . /NENZ
continuous . . . /KOUS
contractility . . . /KRALT
contraction . . . /KRAX
contracture . . . /KROUR
control . . . /KROL
conule . . . /KAOUNL
conulid . . . /KAOUNLD
conus . . . /KUNS
conversion . . . /KWERGS
convert . . . /KWERT
convertin . . . /KWIRN
convex . . . /KWEX
convulsant . . . /KWUNT, /KWUVNT
convulsive . . . /KWUV
coordinate . . . /KAORD
coordination . . . /KAORNGS
cope . . . /KOEP
copia . . . /KO*EP
copic . . . /KOPG
copulation . . . /KOPGS, /KAUPGS
coracoid . . . /KRO*ID
cord . . . /KORD
cordal . . . /KAORLD
cordectomy . . . /KORKT
cordia . . . /KAO*RD
cordial . . . /KAO*RLD
cordialgia . . . /KAORLGD
corditis . . . /KRO*ITS
coria (*see also* koria) . . . /KRAO*R
coriasis . . . /KOERSZ
cormia . . . /KAORM

cormus . . . . . /KOERMS
corn . . . . . /KORN
cornate . . . . . /KROERNT
cornea. . . . . /KR–N
corneal . . . . . /KR–NL, /KOERNL
corneascleritis . . . . . /KLAOIRTS
corneosclerectomy . . . . . /KRERT
cornis . . . . . /KROERNS
cornous . . . . . /KOURNS
cornu . . . . . /KAOURN
cornuate . . . . . /KAOURNT
corona . . . . . /KRAON
coronal . . . . . /KRAONL
coronitis. . . . . /KROINT, /KROINTS
corporal . . . . . /KPORL
corporate. . . . . /KORPT
corporation . . . . . /KORPGS
corporeal . . . . . /KPAOERL
corporectomy . . . . . /KOERPT
corpuscular. . . . . /KPRUFL
correction . . . . . /KREX
cortex . . . . . /KOERX
cortical . . . . . /KOERLT
corticalism. . . . . /KOEFMT
corticectomy . . . . . /KROKT
corticism . . . . . /KOEFM
corticogram . . . . . /KOERG
corticography . . . . . /KRAEFG
corticohyperplasia . . . . . /KRAIPS
corticoid. . . . . /KOID
corticoidism . . . . . /KOIFM
corticomimetic . . . . . /KMIRMT
corticospinal . . . . . /KPAOINL
corticotrophic. . . . . /KROEFG
corticotropic . . . . . /KROEPG
corticotropin . . . . . /KROEFN, /KROEFRN
cortisone . . . . . /KOERTS
cosm . . . . . /KOFM
costal . . . . . /KOFL
costalgia. . . . . /KAFLG, /KAOFLG
costalis . . . . . /KOFLS
costals. . . . . /KOFLZ
costomy . . . . . /KMO*S
costosternal . . . . . /KAERNL
cotomy . . . . . /KO*T, /KMAUT

cotyloid . . . /KROITD
coulomb . . . /KLAOUM
couple . . . /KUPL
course . . . /KOURS
cowpox . . . /KOUPX
coxalgia . . . /SKAJ
coxitis . . . /SKAOIX
crania . . . /KRAN, /KRA*IN
cranial . . . /KRAINL
cranic . . . /KRAINK
craniectomy . . . /KRAIK
craniometry . . . /KRAOERMT
craniosis . . . /KROESZ
craniotomy . . . /KRAINT, /KRAOMT
cranitis . . . /KROITS
cranium . . . /KRAIRM
cranius . . . /KRAINZ
crasia . . . /KRAOS
create . . . /KRI
creatine . . . /KRAO*ENT, /KRA*ENT
creatinemia . . . /KRAO*EM
creation . . . /KRIGS
crepitant . . . /KREP
crepitation . . . /KRAEPGS
crescence . . . /KREFNS
cricothyroid . . . /KRAOIRD
cricothyrotomy . . . /KRAOIRMT
cricotomy . . . /KRAOIKT
crine . . . /KRIN
crinia . . . /KR*IN
crinic . . . /KRINK
crinin . . . /KRAOIN
crinism . . . /KRAOIFM
crinitis . . . /KRINTS
crinosis . . . /KRINSZ
crisia . . . /KR–Z
crisis . . . /KRAOISZ
crismus . . . /KRIMZ
crista . . . /KRA*S
cristal . . . /KRAFL
cristopathy . . . /KRO*T
crit . . . /KRIT
criterion . . . /KAOERN
critic . . . /KR–KT
critical . . . /KRIL

cross. . . . . /KROSZ
crotaphia . . . . . /KRAIFT
crotaphy . . . . . /KRAOFT
crotesis . . . . . /KRETS
crotic . . . . . /KROIKT
crotism . . . . . /KROIFM
crotous . . . . . /KROUTS
croup. . . . . /KROUP, /KRAOP
crural . . . . . /KRAOL, /KRURL
crureus . . . . . /KRURZ
cryal . . . . . /KRAO*IL
cryalgesia . . . . . /KRAOIL, /KRAOELS
cryesthesia . . . . . /KRAO*IT, /KRAOEZ
cryoscopy. . . . . /KRAOIP
cryotherapy . . . . . /KRAERP, /KRAEP, /KRAOIRP
crypsis . . . . . /KRIPZ, /KRIPSZ
cryptectomy . . . . . /KREPGT, /KRIPKT
cryptorchism . . . . . /KROFRM
cryptosis . . . . . /KROEPTS
cryptovirus . . . . . /KRAOIRS
crystal . . . . . /STLAL, /KRIFL
crystallin. . . . . /STLIN
crystalline . . . . . /STLAOEN
ctony . . . . . /KOEKT
cubital. . . . . /KAOUBLT
cular (*see also* ocular) . . . . . /O*KL
cularity (*see also* ocularity) . . . . . /OKLT
culture . . . . . /KOULT
cumbent . . . . . /KBUMT
cuneate . . . . . /KAENT
cuneiform . . . . . /KAOUFM
cuprein . . . . . /KAOURP
cupremia . . . . . /KPREM
cupriuria . . . . . /KPRAOUR
curable . . . . . /KAOURBL
curative . . . . . /KAOUVR, /KAOUVRT
curie . . . . . /KRAOE
curietherapy . . . . . /KAOURPT
current . . . . . /KURNT
cursive. . . . . /KUVS, /KUVRS
cursor . . . . . /KRORZ
curvation . . . . . /KUFRBGS
curvature . . . . . /KUFRBT
curve. . . . . /KUFRB
cusis . . . . . /KAO*UZ

cuspation . . . . /KUPGS
cuspid . . . . /SPID
cuspidal . . . . /SPALD
cuspidate . . . . /SPITD, /SPOIT
cusping . . . . /KUPGZ
cuss . . . . /KUSZ
cut . . . . /K*UT
cutaneostomy . . . . /KAOUNTS
cutaneous . . . . /KAOUTS
cuticle. . . . . /KAOULT
cuticular . . . . /KAOURLT
cution. . . . . /KAO*UGS
cutis . . . . /KWUTS, /KWAOUTS
cyamine . . . . /SMAOIN
cyanic . . . . /SYANG
cyanic acid . . . . /SYANGD
cyanide . . . . /KRAOIND
cyanin . . . . /SNIN
cyanine. . . . . /SNAOEN
cyanism . . . . /SYAFM
cyanogen . . . . /SYOENG, /SYA*EN
cyanogenic. . . . . /SYOENK, /SYAENG
cyanopia. . . . . /SNOIP
cyanopsia . . . . /SNOIPZ
cyanosis . . . . /SNOSZ
cyanotic . . . . /SNOKT, /SNAUT
cybernetics . . . . /SNAOIB, /SNAOIBT
cycle . . . . /SAOIKL
cyclectomy. . . . . /SKL*EKT
cyclic . . . . /SKLIK
cyclitis . . . . /SAOILTS, /SAOIKLT
cyclochoroiditis . . . . /SKLOIDZ
cycloduction . . . . /SKLOGS
cyclograph . . . . /SKLAF
cycloidal . . . . /SKLOIL, /SKLOIK
cyclophoria . . . . /SKLOIR
cyclosis . . . . /SKLOSZ
cyclotropia . . . . /SKLOIP
cyesis. . . . . /SAOIFSZ
cylinder . . . . /SLIND
cylindroid . . . . /SLOID
cyllosis . . . . /SLOISZ
cyphosis (*see also* kyphosis). . . . . /SFOEZ
cyrtosis. . . . . /SIRTSZ
cyst . . . . /KR*IS

cystadenoma . . . . /STAD
cystalgia . . . . /STALG, /STAJ
cystanastomosis . . . . /SNO*ES, /SNOEFT
cystectasia . . . . /STAIKT
cystectomy . . . . /STEKT
cystiasis . . . . /ST*ISZ
cystic . . . . /STIFK
cysticercosis. . . . . /STERKSZ
cystidotomy. . . . . /STOTD
cystine . . . . /STYAOEN
cystinuria . . . . /STYAOUR
cystis . . . . /STISZ
cystitis. . . . . /STAOITS
cystium . . . . /STYUM
cystivirus. . . . . STIVRS
cystoblennorrhea. . . . . /SBLEN
cystocele . . . . /KRAOELT
cystocleisis . . . . /SKLAOISZ
cystocolostomy . . . . /STLOS, /STLO*S
cystoduodenostomy. . . . . /SWOS, /SWO*S
cystogastrostomy . . . . /SGROFT
cystogram. . . . . /STRAM
cystography . . . . /STRAEF, /STAUG
cystojejunostomy . . . . /STOEJ
cystolithiasis . . . . /STLAO*ITS
cystoma. . . . . /STAOM
cystomeningocele . . . . /SMENG
cystometer . . . . /STAURMT
cystometrography . . . . /KRORMT
cystometry . . . . /STAORMT
cystomy . . . . /ST*IS
cystoneostomy . . . . /SNO*S
cystopexy . . . . /STEPGS
cystoplasty . . . . /SPLAS, /SPLA*S
cystoptosis. . . . . /STOEPTS
cystopyelitis . . . . /KPAOILT, /KPAOILTS
cystopyosis . . . . /SPOETS
cystorhinostenosis . . . . /STROESZ
cystorhinostomy. . . . . /STRO*S
cystorhinotomy. . . . . /KROIMT
cystorrhaphy . . . . /STOEF
cystoscope. . . . . /SKOEPT
cystoscopy . . . . /SKOIPT
cystosis. . . . . /STOES
cystostenosis . . . . /STOENSZ

cystostomosis . . . . . /STAOMTS
cystostomy . . . . . /STO*S, /STOFT
cystosyringotomy . . . . . /SGOT
cystosyrinx . . . . . /SAOIRNX
cystotome . . . . . /STAOMT
cystotomography . . . . . /STOEMG
cystotomy . . . . . /STAUT, /STOT
cystoureterocystotomy . . . . . /STAOURS
cystoureterotomy . . . . . /STAURT
cystourethrogram . . . . . /SAOURG
cytactic . . . . . /STAOIKT
cytal . . . . . /SAOILT
cytapheresis . . . . . /SAOEFSZ
cytaxia . . . . . /STAOIX
cytaxis . . . . . /STAOIXZ
cyte (*see also* ocyte) . . . . . /SOIT
cytemia . . . . . /SHOIM
cythemia . . . . . /STHAOEM
cytial . . . . . /SHIRBL
cytic . . . . . /SIKT, /STIKT, /STAOIK
cytioma . . . . . /STOIMT
cytoadherence . . . . . /STAOERNS
cytoblast . . . . . /SBLAS, /SBLA*S
cytoblastoma . . . . . /SBLOEM
cytocatheresis . . . . . /KRAO*ITS
cytochemistry . . . . . /STEMZ
cytoclasis . . . . . /STLAIZ, /STLAISZ
cytocrit . . . . . /SKRAOIT
cytogenesis . . . . . /STEJS, /STOJS
cytogenic . . . . . /STAOIG
cytogram . . . . . /SGRAM
cytoid . . . . . /SOITD
cytological . . . . . /STLAJ
cytology . . . . . /STOLG
cytolysin . . . . . /SLIFN
cytolysis . . . . . /STOLS, /STOLSZ
cytolytic . . . . . /STOIKL
cytoma . . . . . /SOEM, /SOEMT
cytomas . . . . . /SOEMZ, /SOEMTS
cytomata . . . . . /SAUMT
cytomatosis . . . . . /STOEMS
cytometer . . . . . /STORMT, /SAOIRMT
cytometry . . . . . /STAOERMT
cytoopsonin . . . . . /SNOPZ
cytopathia . . . . . /STA*IT

cytopathic . . . . /STPAFK
cytopathy . . . . /STA*ET
cytopenia . . . . /SPAOEN
cytophagia . . . . /SFAIJ
cytophagic . . . . /SFAIG
cytophagous . . . . /SFOUG
cytophagy . . . . /SOIFJ
cytopheresis . . . . /STRAOEFS
cytoplania . . . . /STLAIN
cytoplasmic . . . . /SPLAFMG
cytopoiesis . . . . /STOISZ
cytopoietic . . . . /STOIKT
cytorrhexis . . . . /STAOIRX
cytoschisis . . . . /STOKSZ
cytose . . . . /STOIZ
cytosis . . . . /STOESZ
cytotactic . . . . /STWAK
cytotaxia . . . . /STAEKZ
cytotaxis . . . . /STAEXZ
cytotherapy . . . . /STHERP
cytotic . . . . /STAUKT
cytotoxicity . . . . /STOFX
cytotoxin . . . . /STOIX
cytotripsis . . . . /STRIPSZ
cytotropic . . . . /STROPG
cytozoon . . . . /STAON
cytozoonosis . . . . /STAONSZ
cyturia . . . . /STUR, /SIRT

D

dacryolith . . . . /DLIT, /DL*IT
dactylia . . . . /DLAOEL
dactylic . . . . /DLAK
dactylism . . . . /DAFM, /DLAFM
dactylous . . . . /DLOUKS, /DUKLS
dactylus . . . . /DLUKZ, /DAKLS
dactyly . . . . /DLAOEK
dal . . . . /DA*L
dalton . . . . /DALT
deciduosis . . . . /SDWOESZ, /SDWOS
decision . . . . /SDIGS
decortication . . . . /DORX
dectic . . . . /D*IKT

dectoma. . . . . /DOIK
dectomy . . . . . /D*EKT
decussation. . . . . /DAOEX
deferentectomy . . . . . /D–FRNT
deferential . . . . . /DEFRNL
deferentitis. . . . . /DEFRNTS
deficiency. . . . . /DWAOERB
deficiency syndrome . . . . . /DWAOERBD
deficient . . . . . /DWIRBT
deficit . . . . . /SDEFT
deficits . . . . . /SDEFTS
degeneration. . . . . /JAIRGS, /DJAIGS
degenerative. . . . . /JAIV, /DJAIV
degradable . . . . . /DRAIBL
degradation . . . . . /DEGS
delic . . . . . /DEKL
delineation. . . . . /DLAEGS
delirium . . . . . /DLIRM, /DLUM
deltoid. . . . . /DLOID, /DELTD
dema (*see also* edema). . . . . /DA*EM
dementia. . . . . /DMERB
demia. . . . . /D*EM
demic . . . . . /DMIK, /D*EMG
dendrite . . . . . /DRAOIT
dendritic. . . . . /DROIKT
dendroglioma. . . . . /DLAUM, /DLOM
dendron . . . . . /DRON
dens . . . . . /DENZ
dense . . . . . /DENS
densimeter. . . . . /DIRMT
densitometer . . . . . /DERNTS
density . . . . . /D*ENS
dent . . . . . /DENT
dental . . . . . /DENL
dentale . . . . . /DAENL
dentes . . . . . /DAOENZ
dentia . . . . . /DERBS
dentin. . . . . /DWINT
dentinoma. . . . . /DOEMT
dentitis. . . . . /DINTS
dentium. . . . . /DERB
dentosis . . . . . /DENSZ
denture. . . . . /DAOURT
dependent. . . . . /DAENT
depolarization. . . . . /DOELGS

depolarizer . . . /DOERLT
depressant . . . /DRANT
depressive . . . /D–VP
depressor . . . /DR–P
derm . . . /DERM
derma . . . /DAERM
dermal . . . /DAERL
dermalization . . . /DAERLGS
dermals . . . /DAERLS
dermas . . . /DAERMS
dermatic . . . /DRAKT
dermatitis . . . /DERMT
dermatocele . . . /DMAOEL, /DAOELT
dermatoclysis . . . /DLAOIKS
dermatology . . . /DOLG
dermatome . . . /DMOEM
dermatomy . . . /DMAT
dermatoneurosis . . . /DOURMTS, /DNOURS
dermatoplasty . . . /DLA*S, /DLAFT
dermatopoikilosis . . . /DOIKLS
dermatoses . . . /DOIRMTS, /DOETSZ
dermatosis . . . /DOIRMT, /DMOESZ, /DOETS
dermatous . . . /DURMTS, /DMOUS
dermatrophia . . . /DRAOF
dermectasia . . . /DAEZ
dermia . . . /DA*ERM
dermiasis . . . /DERMSZ
dermic . . . /DERMG, /DIRMG
dermics . . . /DIRX, /DIRMGS
dermides . . . /DAOIDZ
dermidosis . . . /DERMDZ
dermis . . . /DERMS
dermitis . . . /DIRMTS
dermization . . . /DERMGS
dermoclysis . . . /DERKL
dermoid . . . /DMOID, /DROIMD
dermoidal . . . /DMOILD
dermolithiasis . . . /DLAO*ITS
dermoma . . . /DMAUM
dermoperiostosis . . . /DERPT
dermoplasty . . . /DERP
dermosis . . . /DERSZ, /DMOEZ
dermotropism . . . /DMOFM
deron . . . /DRO*N
desiccation . . . /SDAIX

desis . . . . . /DESZ
desma . . . . . /DMA
desmata . . . . . /DMAUT
desmia . . . . . /DMAOS
desmic . . . . . /DMEK
desmism . . . . . /DMIFM
desmitis . . . . . /SDAOIMT
desmium . . . . . /DMUM
desmodial . . . . . /DMOFL, /SDMOFL
desmos . . . . . /DOEMZ
desmoses . . . . . /DWAOEMS
desmosis . . . . . /SDOESZ, /DWOEMZ
desmosome . . . . . /SDOEM
desmotic . . . . . /SDOKT, /SDMOK
desmus . . . . . /SDUMS
destructive . . . . . /SDRUV
detection . . . . . /D*EGS
detector . . . . . /D-RK
determinant . . . . . /DAERNT
determination . . . . . /DERGS
deviation . . . . . /DWAIGS
dexterity . . . . . /DREXT
dextrin . . . . . /SDREX
dextrocardia . . . . . /DROEKD
dextrous . . . . . /DROUX
dia . . . . . /DAOE
diabetes . . . . . /DAOIB
diabetic . . . . . /DAOIBT
diaclast . . . . . /DYA*S
diadochokinesia . . . . . /DWAOED
diagnosis . . . . . /D-GS
diagnostic . . . . . /D-GT
diagnostics . . . . . /D-GTS
diagrammatic . . . . . /DRAMGT
diagraph . . . . . /DYAF
dial . . . . . /DAOIL
dialysis . . . . . /DAL
dialytic . . . . . /DLAOIKT
dialyzer . . . . . /DLAOIRS
diametric . . . . . /DAOIRKT, /DIRKT
diapedesis . . . . . /DAOEPS
diaphane . . . . . /DAOIFN
diaphanoscope . . . . . /SDOEP
diaphanoscopy . . . . . /SDOEPG
diaphany . . . . . /DAFN

diaphoresis . . . /DRAOSZ
diaphragm . . . /DAOIRM, /DAOIFRM
diaphragmatic . . . /DAOIFK
diarrheal . . . /DRAOEL
diarrheic . . . /DRAO*EK
diarthrosis . . . /DRO*ETS
diascope . . . /DWOEP
diascopy . . . /DWO*IP
diastalsis . . . /DAULS
diastase . . . /DAES
diastasis . . . /DAOIFT, /DAOIFTS
diastole . . . /SDOEL
diastolic . . . /SDLOK
diathermy . . . /DOIRM, /DO*IRM
diathesis . . . /DAO*IT
dic . . . /D*IK
dicliditis . . . /DIKL
dicrotic . . . /DROT
dicrotism . . . /DROFMT
dictiotomy . . . /DYOT
didymal . . . /DMAL
didymis . . . /DMIS
didymitis . . . /DOIMTS, /DMAOITS
didymus . . . /DMUS, /DOIMS
die . . . /DAOI
dieresis . . . /DAOIRS
dieretic . . . /DAOIRT
different . . . /DIFT
differentiate . . . /DAEFTD
differentiation . . . /DIFGS, /DAEFGS
diffusion . . . /DWAOUGS
digestible . . . /D–BL
digestion . . . /D–JS
digit . . . /DIJ
digita . . . /DAJT
digital . . . /DIJT
digitation . . . /DAIJS
dilatation . . . /DLIGS
dilating . . . /DLAIGT
dilation . . . /DLAIGS
dilative . . . /DLAIV
dilator . . . /DLAOIRT, /DLAIRT
dilution . . . /DILGS
dinia (*see also* odinia) . . . /D*N
diopter . . . /DWAOIP

dioptric . . . /DROPGT
diosis . . . /DAOISZ
diphtheria . . . /D*IPT
diphtheritic . . . /DERKT
diplegia . . . /DLAOEJ, /DPLAOEG
diploid . . . /DLOIP
diploidy . . . /DLOIPD
diplopia . . . /DLOEP
dipsia . . . /DIPZ
dipsic . . . /DIPGS
dipsomania . . . /DAOPS
directional . . . /DREXL
disc . . . /D*IFK, /D-FK
discharge . . . /DARJ
disciplinary . . . /SPLAIR
discoidal . . . /SDOILD
discus . . . /DISZ, /SDUS
disease . . . /D-Z
disjunction . . . /DWUNGS
disk . . . /DIFK
dislocation . . . /SLOEX
displacement . . . /SPLAIFMT
disposing . . . /SDPOEFG
disposition . . . /SPOGS, /SDPOGS
disruption . . . /DRUPGS
dissection . . . /SDEX
distal . . . /SDALT
distention . . . /STINGS, /ST*ENGS
distocclusal . . . /DLAOULS
distribution . . . /DRAOUGS, /DRAOUX
diuresis . . . /DREZ
diverticular . . . /DLUVR, /DLAVR
diverticulitis . . . /DLAOIVT, /DLAOIVTS
diverticulum . . . /DLUVM, /DIVRM
dochitis . . . /DOIFPT, /DOIFPTS
dochoplasty . . . /DOEPT
dochotomy . . . /DOFPT
dolichocolon . . . /DLON
dolichomelia . . . /DMAEL
dominance . . . /DOMS
dominant . . . /DAMT, /DO*MT
donesis . . . /DOENS
dont . . . /DA*UNT
dontal . . . /DONL
dontalgia . . . /DAULG

dontia (*see also* odontia) . . . /DONS, /DORB
dontiasis (*see also* odontiasis) . . . /DAOIRBS
dontic . . . /DONGT
dontics . . . /DONX, /DONTS
dontism . . . /DOFM
dontist . . . /DOFT, /DO*NT
dontitis (*see also* odontitis) . . . /DO*NTS, /DAOITS
dontium (*see also* odontium) . . . /DAOERB
dontologist . . . /DAUNLT
dontology . . . /DAUNL
dontolysis . . . /DOLS
dontoma (*see also* odontoma) . . . /DWO*M
dontosis . . . /DWOENTS
dontotropism . . . /DROEFM
dontous . . . /DOUNTS
dontropy . . . /DROEP
dontrypy . . . /DRIPT
dopa . . . /DAUP, /DAOP
dormital . . . /DAORMT
dormition . . . /DORMGS
dornase . . . /DORNZ
dorsad . . . /DAORD
dorsal . . . /DORLS
dosage . . . /DOEJ
dose . . . /DOES
dote . . . /DOET
drainage . . . /DRAIJ
drama . . . /DRAUM
drepanocytic . . . /DRAPG
drepanocytosis . . . /DROEPS
drive . . . /DRI
dromal . . . /DRO*EL
drome . . . /DROEM
drometer . . . /DRAUMT
dromia . . . /DRO*EM, /DRAO*M
dromic . . . /DROMG
dromous . . . /DROUMS
dromus . . . /DROMS
dromy . . . /DRO*IM
drosis (*see also* idrosis *and* hidrosis) . . . /DROSZ
drug . . . /DRUG
duct . . . /DUKT
ductal . . . /DUKL, /DAUKT
ductile . . . /DAOIKL
duction . . . /D*UX

ductitis . . . . . /DOIKT, /DOIKTS
ductor . . . . . /DURKT
ductors . . . . . /DURKTS
duodenal . . . . . /DWONL, /DWOLD
duodenectomy . . . . . /DWOKT
duodenitis . . . . . /DWOIT, /DWOITS
duodenoscopy . . . . . /DWOIP
duodenostomy . . . . . /DOS, /DO*S, /DWOS, /DWO*S
duodenum . . . . . /DWOD
duplicate . . . . . /DUP
duplication . . . . . /DUPGS
dural . . . . . /DRAL
duration . . . . . /DRAIGS, /DAOURGS
duric . . . . . /D*URK
durogram . . . . . /DAO*URM
durography . . . . . /DAOUFG
dynamia . . . . . /DWIM
dynamic . . . . . /DWAM
dynamics . . . . . /DWAMS
dynamogenic . . . . . /DMEJ
dynamograph . . . . . /DMOF
dynamometer . . . . . /DMOMT, /DAOINT
dynamometry . . . . . /DMERMT, /DMERT
dyne . . . . . /DAO*IN
dynia (*see also* odynia) . . . . . /DOIN, /D*IN
dynias (*see also* odynias) . . . . . /DOINS, /D*INS
dynic . . . . . /DOINK
dynics . . . . . /DOINKS
dyniotropism . . . . . /DOIFM
dyscrasia . . . . . /DRAIS
dyscrinia . . . . . /DYIN
dysenteric . . . . . /SDERK, /SDIRK
dysentery . . . . . /SDER
dysergia . . . . . /DERJ
dysesthesia . . . . . /SDAOEZ
dysgenesia . . . . . /DYENS, /DYENZ
dysgenesis . . . . . /DYENSZ
dyskinetic . . . . . /SKINGT, /SKENGT
dysleptic . . . . . /DLEPT, /DLEPGT
dysneuria . . . . . /DAOURN
dysodia . . . . . /SDOED
dysostosis . . . . . /SDOS
dyspepsia . . . . . /SPEPS
dysphoria . . . . . /SFAOR
dysplasia . . . . . /SDLAIS

dysplastic . . . . /SDLAS
dysplasty . . . . /SDLA*S
dysrhythmia . . . . /DR*IT
dystonia . . . . /SDOEN
dystony . . . . /SDOIN
dystrophia . . . . /SDRAOEF, /SDROF
dystrophic . . . . /SDROFK, /SDROEFK
dystrophy . . . . /SDROEF

E

ecbole . . . . /KBLOE
ecchysis . . . . /KHEXZ, /EFPSZ
eccrisia . . . . /KRIZ
eccrisis . . . . /KRISZ
eccritic . . . . /KRIKT, /KRIFKT
echoic . . . . /KHO*EK
echolalia . . . . /KLAIL
echoscopy . . . . /KHOIPG
eclampsia . . . . /KLAEMP
ecologist . . . . /KOELT
ecology . . . . /KOLG, /KOELG
economic . . . . /KMIK
economics . . . . /KMIKS
ecstasy . . . . /STAOE
ectad . . . . /KPAD
ectases . . . . /TAIZ
ectasia . . . . /TAIS
ectasic . . . . /TAIKSZ
ectasis . . . . /TAISZ
ectasy . . . . /TAEZ
ectatic . . . . /TAIKT
ectoblast . . . . /KBLAS
ectoderm . . . . /KPERM, /EKD
ectodermal . . . . /KPAERL
ectoiridectomy . . . . /TIRKT
ectoiridodialysis . . . . /TIRD
ectome . . . . /*EKT
ectomies . . . . /EKTS
ectomize . . . . /KMAOIZ, /TAOIZ
ectomized . . . . /TAOIFD
ectomizes . . . . /TAOIFS
ectomizing . . . . /TAOIFG
ectomopexy . . . . /KPOEX

ectomy . . . /EKT
ectopia . . . /TOEPT
ectopy . . . /TOIPT
ectothrix . . . /KHIX
ectromelia . . . /TROEM
ectropia . . . /TRO*P, /TRAOPT
ectropion . . . /TROEN
ectropium . . . /TROEMP
ectyposis . . . /KPOISZ
ed . . . /-D
edema (*see also* dema) . . . /D-M, /DAO*EM
edematoid . . . /DOID, /DOITD
edematous . . . /DOUMT, /DOUMS
education . . . /JAEGS
effect . . . /FEK
effector . . . /FERK
efferent . . . /EFRNT
efficient . . . /FIRB
ego . . . /GOE
eidosis . . . /AO*IDZ
eikonometer . . . /KAOIRMT
ejaculation . . . /JALGS
ejection . . . /J-GS
elasma . . . /ELZ, /LAEMS
elasmatosis . . . /LAEMZ
elasmoidea . . . /LOIMDZ
elastic . . . /LAFKT
elastin . . . /LAFN
elastosis . . . /LOEFTS
elcosis (*see also* helcosis) . . . /OEKLS
elcus . . . /EKLS
electric . . . /LEKT
electrical . . . /LAL, /LEKL
electricity . . . /LEFK
electrocardiogram . . . /AOEJD, /LAORM
electrocardiograph . . . /LAEF
electrocardiography . . . /OJD, /LOFG
electrode . . . /TROED
electroencephalography . . . /LAOFLG
electrolyte . . . /TROLT
electrolytemia . . . /TRAOEM
electrometer . . . /TROERMT
electron . . . /TRON
electronomic . . . /TROEMG
electrophoresis . . . /LAOEKSZ

electrophoretic . . . . . /LORKT
electrophysiologram . . . . . /FLAOM
electrophysiolograph . . . . . /FLAF
electrophysiolography . . . . . /FLOIF
element . . . . . /L–MT
elements . . . . . /L–MTS
elephantiasis . . . . . /EFLTS
elytrorrhaphy . . . . . /TROIR
embolectomy . . . . . /KBEKT
embolia . . . . . /KBAOL
embolic . . . . . /KBL*IK
embolism . . . . . /KBLIFM
embolus . . . . . /KBLUS
embryoma . . . . . /KBROEM
embryon . . . . . /KBROEN
embryonic . . . . . /KBRONG
embryony . . . . . /KBROIN
embryoplasia . . . . . /KBRAEZ
emesia . . . . . /AEMSZ
emesis . . . . . /EMS, /EMSZ
emetic . . . . . /AOEKT
emia . . . . . /AOEM
emic . . . . . /AOEMG
emization . . . . . /EMGS
emotivity . . . . . /MIVT
emphraxis (*see also* mphraxis) . . . . . /KBRAX
emphysema . . . . . /KBAOEM
employment . . . . . /PLOIMT
empyema . . . . . /PAIM
empyesis . . . . . /PAIMS
emulsification . . . . . /SMUFGS
enamel . . . . . /ENL
encephalia . . . . . /SNAEF
encephalic . . . . . /SNEFK
encephalitic . . . . . /SNIFK
encephalitis . . . . . /SNEFTS
encephalocele . . . . . /SNOEFL
encephalogram . . . . . /SNAM, /SNARM
encephalograph . . . . . /SNAFR
encephalography . . . . . /SNAEFG
encephalohypophyseal . . . . . /SNAUFL
encephalohypophysial . . . . . /SNOIFL
encephalomalacia . . . . . /SNAERB
encephalomeningitis . . . . . /SNAOIFTS
encephalomeningocele . . . . . /SNAOFM

encephalomeningomyelitis. . . . . /SNAOILT, /SNAOILTS
encephalomyelia . . . . /SNAOEL
encephalomyelitis . . . . /SNAOIMTS
encephalomyelogram . . . . /SNAMG
encephalomyelography . . . . /SNAOIFLG
encephalomyelopathy . . . . /SNOFL
encephalon . . . . /SNEFL
encephalopathy . . . . /SNA*ET
encephalos. . . . . /SNAOFLS
encephaloscope . . . . /SNOEP
encephalospinal. . . . . /SNAOINL
encephalotome . . . . /SNOEMT
encephalotomy. . . . . /SNOFT
encephalotropic . . . . /SNAOPK
encephalous. . . . . /SNOUFLS
encephalus . . . . /SNEFLS
encephaly . . . . /SNAOEFL
enchondroma . . . . /KHOERM
enchyma . . . . /ENK
enchymal . . . . /ENKL
enchyme . . . . /AOINK
enchymoma . . . . /KMO*EM
enchysis (*see also* chysis) . . . . /KHAOIZ
encleisis (*see also* enclisis) . . . . /KBLAOISZ
enclisis (*see also* encleisis) . . . . /KBLOISZ
endarterectomy . . . . /DAOKT
endemic . . . . /DWEMG
endocardial . . . . /NOERL, /DOERL
endocarditis . . . . /DROITS
endocrine. . . . . /KREN
endocrinism . . . . /KREFM
endocrinologies . . . . /KROENLS, /KROENGS
endocrinology . . . . /KROENL, /KROENG
endocrinopathy . . . . /KRA*EPT
endocrisia . . . . /KRENZ
endography . . . . /DOFG
endometritis . . . . /DRAOTS
endopathy . . . . /DOP
endoscope . . . . /SKROEP
endoscopy . . . . /SKROP
endosmosis. . . . . /DMOES
endothelial . . . . /TLAOEL
endothelial cell . . . . /TLEL
endothelial cells . . . . /TLELS
endothelioblastoma. . . . . /TBLOEM

endothelioma . . . . . /THOEM
endotheliomatosis . . . . . /THOIMTS
endotheliosarcoma . . . . . /DOERKL
endotheliosis . . . . . /TLAOELS
endothelium . . . . . /TLAOEM
energetic . . . . . /NERJT, /N-RJT
energetics . . . . . /NERJTS, /N-RJTS
energia . . . . . /NAERJ, /N*ERJ
engage . . . . . /GAEJ
engagement . . . . . /GAEMT
engineering . . . . . /JERG
engyophobia . . . . . /NOEFB
enhancement . . . . . /HAMT
enhancer . . . . . /HA*RNS
entad . . . . . /SPWAD
enteral . . . . . /SPWAERL
enteralgia . . . . . /SPWAL, /SPWALG
enteration . . . . . /SPWAIRGS
enterectomy . . . . . /SPWEKT
enteric . . . . . /SPWERK
enterics . . . . . /SPWERKZ
enteriolum . . . . . /SPWAORM
enteriopexy . . . . . /SPWAOPX
enteriorrhaphy . . . . . /SPWRAOF
enteriplication . . . . . /SPWLAOIGS
enteritis . . . . . /SPWAOIT, /SPWAOITS
enterium . . . . . /SPWREM
enteroanastomosis . . . . . /SPWAS, /SPWA*S
enterocele . . . . . /SPWAOEL
enterocolitis . . . . . /SPWLOIT, /SPWLOITS
enterocolostomy . . . . . /SPWLOS, /SPWLO*S
enterologist . . . . . /SPWOLT
enterology . . . . . /SPWOLG
enteron . . . . . /SPWRON
enterone . . . . . /SPWROEN
enteropathy . . . . . /SPWROP
enteroplasty . . . . . /SPWERPT
enteroptosis . . . . . /SPWOPT
enterorrhaphy . . . . . /SPWRAEF
enterostomy . . . . . /SPWOS, /SPWO*S
enterotomy . . . . . /SPWROT
entropium . . . . . /SPWROERP
entry . . . . . /SPWRI
environment . . . . . /VIRMT, /VAOIRMT
enzyme . . . . . /ZAOIM

eosinophil . . . . . . /YOEFL
eosinophilia . . . . . . /YAOEFL
eosinophilic . . . . . . /YOEFLG
ependymal . . . . . . /PA*EMD
ependymoma . . . . . . /PO*EMD
ephedrine . . . . . . /FERD, /FRIND
ephidrosis . . . . . . /DROEPSZ
epicondylar . . . . . . /PAURNL
epidemiology . . . . . . /EPLD
epidermal . . . . . . /DR–L
epidermic . . . . . . /DR–K
epidermitis . . . . . . /DAOIRTS
epidermoid . . . . . . /ERPD
epididymectomy . . . . . . /YIPD
epididymis . . . . . . /YEPD
epididymitis . . . . . . /YAOIMT, /YAOIMTS
epididymography . . . . . . /YOFG
epididymostomy . . . . . . /YOIPT
epigastrium . . . . . . /GREM
epiglottic . . . . . . /GLOPG
epiglottidean . . . . . . /GLOTD
epiglottideus . . . . . . /GLODZ
epilepsy . . . . . . /LEPS
epileptic . . . . . . /LEPG
epinephria . . . . . . /PREFRN
epinephrinemia . . . . . . /PROIM
epiphyseal . . . . . . /PAEFLS
epiphysial . . . . . . /PIFLS
epiphysis . . . . . . /PIFSZ
epiphysitis . . . . . . /POIFT
epiplocele . . . . . . /PLAOEL
epiploic . . . . . . /PLOIK
epithelia . . . . . . /PLA*E
epithelial . . . . . . /PLAL, /PLA*EL
epithelioma . . . . . . /PLOEM
epithelitis . . . . . . /THAOILTS, /PAOILTS
epithelium . . . . . . /PILT
epitrochlear . . . . . . /PRORKL
equilibrium . . . . . . /KLIB
equivalence . . . . . . /KWIVS, /KWIVNS
equivalent . . . . . . /KWIV
erection . . . . . . /AOERX
ereisis . . . . . . /AOIRSZ
eremia . . . . . . /AO*ERM
eresis . . . . . . /AOERZ

erethesia . . . /STHAOERS
erethism . . . /AIFM
ergasia . . . /GAIRZ
ergastic . . . /GAIRK
ergia . . . /ERJ
ergic . . . /ERK
ergy . . . /OIJ, /AOERJ
erism . . . /ERZ
erotic . . . /ROFT
eroticism . . . /ROFMT
erotism . . . /ROEFMT
eruption . . . /RUPGS
eruptive . . . /RUVPT
erysipelas . . . /RIPZ, /ERPZ
erysis . . . /AOERSZ
erythema . . . /AO*ERT
erythematous . . . /AOERMTS
erythrin . . . /Y*IRT
erythroblast . . . /RIFBT
erythroblastosis . . . /ROEBLS
erythrocyte . . . /RAO*IT
erythrocythemia . . . /RAO*ET
erythrocytic . . . /RIFKT
erythrodermia . . . /RA*ERM
erythroplasia . . . /YAEZ
erythrous . . . /RO*UTS
esis . . . /ESZ
esophageal . . . /SOFL
esophagitis . . . /SOFTS
esophagology . . . /SOFLG
esophagoplasty . . . /SFLA*S
esophagoscopy . . . /SOIPG
esophagostomy . . . /SAOFT
esophagus . . . /SOF, /SOFG
esophoria . . . /SFOR
ester . . . /ST*ES
esterase . . . /STRAES
esters . . . /ST*ESZ
esthesia (*see also* sthesia) . . . /STHAOES
esthesic . . . /STHAOEK
esthesiograph . . . /STHAOEFG
esthesiometer . . . /STHAOEMT
esthesioneuroma . . . /STHOERM
esthesis . . . /STHAOESZ
esthetic . . . /STHEKT

estimation . . . . /STIMGS
estrinemia . . . . /STR*EM
estrinism . . . . /STRIFN
estrogen . . . . /STREG
estrogenemia . . . . /STRAO*EM
estrogenic . . . . /STRINK
estrogenosis . . . . /STROJS
estrogenous . . . . /STROJ
estrous . . . . /EFRZ
estrum . . . . /EFRMS
estrus . . . . /EFRS
ether . . . . /AO*ET
ethics . . . . /THEX
ethmoid . . . . /THOIMD
ethmoidal . . . . /THOILD
ethmoidectomy . . . . /THOIKT
ethmoiditis . . . . /THOIMDZ
euploidy . . . . /YOIPD
eurynter . . . . /AOURNT
eurysis . . . . /YIRSZ
eurysm . . . . /AOUFM
eustachian . . . . /STAIRB, /YAOUGS
evacuation . . . . /VAEX
evolution . . . . /VOFLGS, /VAOULGS
evolutionism . . . . /VOUFM
evolutism . . . . /VOUFMT
exairesis (*see also* exeresis) . . . . /KPAERS
examination . . . . /KPAMGS, /KP–GS
exarthrosis . . . . /KPOEZ
excision . . . . /KPIGS
excitation . . . . /KPAOIGS
excitatory . . . . /KPOIRT
excitory . . . . /KPIRT
excretory . . . . /KPRAOERT
exeresis (*see also* exairesis) . . . . /KPERS
exertion . . . . /KPERGS
exfoliation . . . . /SFOELGS
existing . . . . /KPIFG, /KPIFGT
exophoria . . . . /KPOR
exoteric . . . . /KPERK
expiration . . . . /KPRAIGS
explexia . . . . /SPLAOERB
exploration . . . . /SPLOERGS
extended . . . . /STEND
extension . . . . /STENGS

external . . . . /KPERNL, /STERNL
extraction . . . . /STRAX
extractor . . . . /STRARK

F

face . . . . /FAIS
facial . . . . /FAIRBL
facialis . . . . /FAIRBLS
facient (*see also* ifacient) . . . . /FAIRBT
faciolingual . . . . /FLINL
faction (*see also* ifaction) . . . . /FWAX, /FA*X
factive (*see also* ifactive) . . . . /FAVK
factor . . . . /FAOK, /FAKT
factorial . . . . /FAOKL
familial . . . . /FLIL
family . . . . /FAEM
farad . . . . /FAURD
faradism . . . . /FAURDZ
faradization . . . . /FARGS
fascial . . . . /FARBL
fascialis . . . . /FAFLS, /FARBLZ
fascicular . . . . /FAURKL
fasciogram . . . . /FRAMG
fascitis . . . . /FARBTS
fast . . . . /FA*S
fat . . . . /FAT
fatty . . . . /FWAT
fauna . . . . /FA*UN
febrile . . . . /FRAOEBL, /FRAOIBL
fecia . . . . /FAOEZ
fection . . . . /F*EX
fective . . . . /FEVK
fecundation . . . . /FWUNGS
fecundity . . . . /FWUND
feedback . . . . /FAOEB
female . . . . /FAEL
femoral . . . . /FRAOL
femoroplasty . . . . /FRAPS, /FROEPT
femoropopliteal . . . . /FRAOEP
fenestria . . . . /FRAIFT
fensor . . . . /FORNS
ferient . . . . /FERNT
ferious . . . . /FAIRS

ferment . . . . . /FERMT
fermentation . . . . . /FERJ, /FERMGS
ferous (*see also* iferous) . . . . . /FERS
ferremia . . . . . /FAOEM
ferremic . . . . . /FAOEMG
ferric . . . . . /FAERK, /FRERK
ferricemia . . . . . /FAOEMS
ferrin . . . . . /FAIRN, /FEFRN
ferrism . . . . . /FAEFM
ferritin . . . . . /FAERT
fertile . . . . . /FERL
fertility . . . . . /FERLT
fetal . . . . . /FAOELT
fetation . . . . . /FAOEGTS
fetus . . . . . /FAOETS
fiber . . . . . /FAOIB
fiberscope . . . . . /FAOIP
fiberscopy . . . . . /FRAOIP
fibra . . . . . /FAOIRB
fibril . . . . . /FRIBL
fibrilla . . . . . /FLIRB
fibrillar . . . . . /FRIRBL
fibrillary . . . . . /FRAIRL, /FRAIRBL
fibrillatory . . . . . /FRIRBLT
fibrinogen . . . . . /FRING
fibrinogenemia . . . . . /FRAOEJ
fibrinolysin . . . . . /FIFRN, /FIFN
fibrinolysis . . . . . /FROLS
fibrinolytic . . . . . /FR*IKT
fibrinous . . . . . /FROUBS
fibroblast . . . . . /FBLAFT
fibroblastoma . . . . . /FLOEB
fibroid . . . . . /FROIBD, /FBROID
fibrolipoma . . . . . /FLOEMP
fibroma . . . . . /FROEB
fibromas . . . . . /FROEBS
fibromatoses . . . . . /FREMSZ
fibromatosis . . . . . /FROEMS, /FROEMSZ
fibromyoma . . . . . /FROIM
fibrosarcoma . . . . . /FRO*EM, /FRAUM
fibroscopy . . . . . /FROIP
fibrosis . . . . . /FROEBSZ
fibrositis . . . . . /FRAOIBS
fibrotic . . . . . /FROBT
fibrous . . . . . /FAOIBS

fibular . . . . /FLIBL
fic . . . . /F*IK
fication (*see also* ification) . . . . /F–X
fiche . . . . /FIFP
fid . . . . /F*ID
figure . . . . /FIG
figured . . . . /FIGD
filament . . . . /FLIMT
filamentous . . . . /FLOUMT, /FLOUMTS
filaments. . . . . /FLIMTS
filar . . . . /FLER
filaremia . . . . /FLAEM
filaria . . . . /FLA*ER
filarial . . . . /FLERL, /FLAIRL
filling . . . . /FILG
film . . . . /FIM
filter . . . . /FIRLT
filtrate . . . . /FRILT
filtration . . . . /FIRLGS
fissura . . . . /FURZ
fissural . . . . /FIRLZ
fissure . . . . /FIRZ
fistular . . . . /FLAR
fistulization . . . . /FLAOGS
fix . . . . /FIX
fixation. . . . . /FAIX
flagellate . . . . /FLAJ, /FLAIJ
flagellation . . . . /FLAIJS, /FLAEGS
flation. . . . . /FLA*IGS
flatulent . . . . /FLAFPT
flavin. . . . . /FLAIVN, /FLAIFN
flavine . . . . /FLEVN
flavonoid . . . . /FLOIVD
flavonoids . . . . /FLOIVDZ
flavous . . . . /FLAIVS
flect. . . . . /FL–KT
flection. . . . . /FL*EGS
fleur . . . . /FLIR
flexed . . . . /FLEKD
flexia . . . . /FLAEX
flexion . . . . /FL–X, /FLEFN, /FL*EX
flocculation . . . . /FLOKLGS
flocculent . . . . /FLONGT
flocculus . . . . /FLOKLZ, /FLUKL
flora . . . . /FLO*R

florescence . . . . . . /FLORNS
flow . . . . . . /FLOE
flowmeter . . . . . . /FLIRMT, /FLOIMT
fluctuating . . . . . . /FL*UG
fluctuation . . . . . . /FLUGS
fluence . . . . . . /FLUNZ
fluid . . . . . . /FLAOUD
fluorescein . . . . . . /FLAOZ
fluorescence . . . . . . /FLENS, /FLORS
fluorescent . . . . . . /FLENT, /FLES, /FLOR
fluorescin . . . . . . /FLINS
fluoric . . . . . . /FLORK
fluoride . . . . . . /FLAOURD, /FLOIRD
fluorogram . . . . . . /FLURM
fluorography . . . . . . /FLURG
fluorometer . . . . . . /FLORMT
fluoroscope . . . . . . /FLOERP
fluoroscopy . . . . . . /FLURP
fluorosis . . . . . . /FLURSZ
flutter . . . . . . /FLURT
fluvium . . . . . . /FLAOVM, /FLAOUVM
flux . . . . . . /FLUX
focal . . . . . . /FOEFL, /FOEKL
focusing . . . . . . /FOEFG
folding . . . . . . /FOLGD
folium . . . . . . /FL*UM
follicular . . . . . . /FLARK
folliculitis . . . . . . /FLARX
folliculoma . . . . . . /FLAUM
foot . . . . . . /FAOT
foramen . . . . . . /FRAEM
foramina . . . . . . /FAORM
forate . . . . . . /FROET
foration . . . . . . /FO*RGS
form (*see also* iform) . . . . . . /FORM, /FO*RM
formaldehyde . . . . . . /FLAOID
formation . . . . . . /FORMGS
formative . . . . . . /FOVT, /FOFRB
formic . . . . . . /FOERMG
forms (*see also* iforms) . . . . . . /FORMS, /FO*RMS
fracture . . . . . . /FRAK, /FRAKT, /FRAUR
fragment . . . . . . /FRAMT
fragous . . . . . . /FRUGS
frequency . . . . . . /FREKZ
friction . . . . . . /FRIGS

frigeration. . . . . /FRAEJ
frontal . . . . /FRONL
frontalis . . . . /FRONLS
fructokinase . . . . /FRUKTS, /FRAOINGS
fructose . . . . /FRAOUK, /FRAOUKT
fructosemia . . . . /FRAOEMZ
fugal . . . . /FAOUG
fuge . . . . /FAOUJ
fugic. . . . . /FAOUK
fugous . . . . /FAOUGZ
fulvin . . . . /FUVN
function . . . . /FUNGS
functional . . . . /FUNGLS
fundoscope . . . . /FOEPD
fungal. . . . . /FWUNL
furan . . . . /FRAOUN
furanose . . . . /FRAONS
furca . . . . /F*URK
furcate . . . . /FURKT
furcated. . . . . /FURKTD
furcation . . . . /FURGS
fusal . . . . /FAOUFL
fuscin . . . . /FUFS
fuscinosis . . . . /FAOURBS
fuse . . . . /FAOUZ
fusible . . . . /FAOUFBL
fusion. . . . . /FAOUGS
fy . . . . /F*I
fying . . . . /FAO*IG

G

gage . . . . /GAIG
gainer . . . . /GAIRN
gala . . . . /GL–
galactia . . . . /GLARB
galactic . . . . /GLAKT
galactocele. . . . . /GLAOEL
galactorrhea. . . . . /GLAOEK
galactoside . . . . /GLAKD
galactosides. . . . . /GLAKDZ
galactosis . . . . /GLOEKS
galactous . . . . /GLOUKT
galvanic. /GAVNG, /GLAVN, /GLAVNG

galvanism . . . /GAVM
galvanization . . . /GAVGS
galvanometer . . . /GOMT
game . . . /GAIM
gamentous . . . /GEMTS
gamete . . . /GAOEMT
gametic . . . /GEMT
gametocyte . . . /GAIMT
gametophyte . . . /GAOET
gamety . . . /GOIMT
gamist . . . /GAFMT
gamma . . . /GAM, /GMA
gammaglobulin . . . /GLAOBL, /GLA*UB
gammaglobulinemia . . . /GLAOEB
gamous . . . /GOUMS
gamus . . . /GUMZ
gamy . . . /GOIM, /GA*M
ganglial . . . /GLAUL
gangliitis . . . /GANTS, /GL–TS
ganglioma . . . /GLIM
ganglion . . . /GLAUN
ganglionic . . . /GLAUNG
ganglionitis . . . /GLAOINT, /GLAOINTS
ganglionosis . . . /GLAUNSZ
ganglitis . . . /GANGTS, /GLITS
gangrenous . . . /GRAENZ
gasia . . . /GAIZ
gasis . . . /GAISZ
gasserian . . . /GAERN
gaster . . . /GAFR
gastralgia . . . /GRALG
gastrectomy . . . /GEKT
gastria . . . /GRA*S
gastric . . . /GRIK
gastrin . . . /GRINS
gastrinemia . . . /GAOERM
gastritis . . . /GRAOIT, /GRAOITS
gastrium . . . /GRUM, /GRAOEM
gastrius . . . /GR*US
gastroanastomosis . . . /GOEMS
gastrocele . . . /GAOEL
gastroduodenoscopy . . . /GOIP
gastrogram . . . /GAFRM
gastrograph . . . /GROF
gastrography . . . /GROFG

gastromyotomy . . . . . /GAOIM
gastrone . . . . . /GRAON
gastrorrhaphy . . . . . /GRAEFP
gastroschisis . . . . . /GISZ, /GRISZ
gastroscope . . . . . /GOEP
gastroscopy . . . . . /GOIK
gastrostomosis . . . . . /GOEMZ
gastrostomy . . . . . /GOS, /GO*S, /GROFT
gastrotomy . . . . . /GAUT
gastrula. . . . . /GRAOULT
gastrulation . . . . . /GRAOULGS
gavage . . . . . /GAVJ
gee . . . . . /GAOE
gel . . . . . /GEL
gelatin . . . . . /GELT
gelosis . . . . . /JOELSZ
gemina . . . . . /G*EM
geminal. . . . . /JAEM
geminum . . . . . /JO*IM
geminus . . . . . /JEMS
gemmal. . . . . /JA*EM
gen (*see also* ogen) . . . . . /G*EN
genal . . . . . /GAO*ENL, /J-NL
genarian . . . . . /JAIRN
genase. . . . . /JAES
genases . . . . . /JAEZ
genate . . . . . /JAENT
gender . . . . . /JERND
gene. . . . . /GAOEN
geneic . . . . . /GAOEK
geneity . . . . . /GAOENT
geneization . . . . . /GAOENGS
geneous . . . . . /GENZ
generate . . . . . /JAIT
generated . . . . . /JAITD
generation . . . . . /JAIGS
generic . . . . . /GERK
genes . . . . . /GAOENS
genesia . . . . . /JAENZ
genesis (*see also* ogenesis) . . . . . /GENSZ, /JENSZ
genetic (*see also* ogenetic) . . . . . /GENT
genetical. . . . . /GANLT, /GEKL
geneticist . . . . . /JIFT
genetics (*see also* ogenetics) . . . . . /GENTS
genia . . . . . /JAOEN

genic (*see also* ogenic) . . . /GENG
genically . . . /JEKL
genicity (*see also* ogenicity) . . . /GINT
genics (*see also* ogenics) . . . /GENGS
genism . . . /JEFM
genital . . . /GAENL
genitalis . . . /GAILTS
genitalism . . . /GAEFM
genization . . . /GAENGS
genize . . . /JAOIF
genolysis . . . /GOLS
genolytic . . . /GIKT, /GLIKT
genosis . . . /GONSZ, /JONSZ
genote . . . /JOET
genous (*see also* ogenous) . . . /OJ, /J-NS
gens (*see also* ogens) . . . /G*ENS
genual . . . /GAOUL
genus . . . /GAOENZ
geny (*see also* ogeny) . . . /GOIN
geochemistry . . . /GEMZ
geography . . . /J-F
geria . . . /GAER
geriatrics . . . /GERTS
germinal . . . /JERL
germinoma . . . /GOERM
gerous . . . /JOURS
gerus . . . /GERZ
gesta . . . /JA*ES
gestate . . . /JEGT
gestation . . . /JEGS
gestational . . . /JELGS
geusesthesia . . . /GAOEZ
geusia . . . /GAOZ
geusic . . . /GAOX
geusis . . . /GAOESZ
geustia . . . /GAOTS
gglutination (*see also* agglutination) . . . /GLAO*UNGS, /GL*UNGS
gglutinin (*see also* agglutinin) . . . /GLAO*UT
gigantism . . . /JAOIFM
gingivae . . . /JAEV
gingival . . . /JAVL
glanders . . . /GLARND
glandula . . . /GLU
glandular . . . /GLAR
glandulitis . . . /GLANTS

glaucin . . . . . /GLAUS
glaucoma . . . . . /GLAUK
glenoid . . . . . /GLEND
glia . . . . . /GLA
gliacyte . . . . . /GLAT
glial . . . . . /GLAL
gliar . . . . . /GLIR
gliding . . . . . /GLAOIGD
glioblastoma . . . . . /GLOIB
gliocyte . . . . . /GLAOIT
gliocytoma . . . . . /GLOIM
glioma . . . . . /GLAUM, /GLO*EM
gliomas . . . . . /GLAUMS, /GLO*EMS
gliomatosis . . . . . /GLOEMT, /GLOEMTS
glioneuroma . . . . . /GLOERM
glioses . . . . . /GLOISZ
gliosis . . . . . /GLOESZ
globar . . . . . /GLORB
globin . . . . . /GLOEN, /GLUB
globinated . . . . . /GLOEND, /GLUBD, /GLAIBD
globinemia . . . . . /GLOEM
globininuric . . . . . /GLAOURK
globinocholia . . . . . /GLOEL
globinolysis . . . . . /GLOLS
globinometer . . . . . /GLORMT
globinometry . . . . . /GLOERMT
globinopathies . . . . . /GLOBT
globinopathy . . . . . /GLOBT
globinopepsia . . . . . /GLEPS
globinophilic . . . . . /GLIFG
globinous . . . . . /GLOBS
globinuria . . . . . /GLAOUR
globose . . . . . /GLOBZ, /GLO*EBS
globular . . . . . /GLAUBL
globulin . . . . . /GLOBL, /GLAOUB
globulinemia . . . . . /GLONL
globulinopathy . . . . . /GLO*PT
globulins . . . . . /GLOBLS, /GLAOUBS
globulinuria . . . . . /GLAOURB, /GLAOURN
globulose . . . . . /GLOEZ
globulosis . . . . . /GLOEBSZ
globus . . . . . /GLOEBZ
glomerator . . . . . /GLAERMT, /GLAIRMT
glomerular . . . . . /GLERL
glomerulus . . . . . /GLUS

glossa . . . . . . /GLOS
glossal . . . . . . /GLOFL
glossal nerve . . . . . . /GLEFRB, /GLEVRB
glossectomy . . . . . . /GLEKT
glossia . . . . . . /GLAOS
glossis . . . . . . /GLAOSZ
glossitis . . . . . . /GLAOITS
glossus . . . . . . /GLUSZ
glottic . . . . . . /GLOKT
glottid . . . . . . /GLAUTD, /GLO*TD
glottis . . . . . . /GLOTS
glucokinase . . . . . . /GLUKS
glucopenia . . . . . . /GLOUP
glucoprotein . . . . . . /GLOIN
glucose . . . . . . /GLAOUK
glucosidase . . . . . . /GLAOUKD
glucoside . . . . . . /GLAOKD
glucosometer . . . . . . /GLERT
glutamate . . . . . . /GLAEMT
glutamic acid . . . . . . /GLAOMD
glutamic aciduria . . . . . . /GLOURD
gluteal . . . . . . /GLAEL
gluteus . . . . . . /GLUTS
glycemia . . . . . . /GLAEM
glycemic . . . . . . /GLAEMG
glycemosis . . . . . . /GLAOISZ
glycerate . . . . . . /GLIFT, /GLIFRT
glyceric . . . . . . /GLAOERK
glyceride . . . . . . /GLIRD
glyceridemia . . . . . . /GLID
glyceridemic . . . . . . /GLIGD
glycerides . . . . . . /GLIRDZ
glycerol . . . . . . /GLOL
glycerolemia . . . . . . /GLEM
glycin . . . . . . /GLAOIZ
glycinemia . . . . . . /GLAOIS
glycinuria . . . . . . /GLAOURNS
glycoconjugate . . . . . . /GLAOIJ
glycogen . . . . . . /GLAOIK
glycogenolysis . . . . . . /GLOLSZ
glycolate . . . . . . /GLAEK
glycolic . . . . . . /GLOKL
glycolic acid . . . . . . /GLOKLD
glycopenia . . . . . . /GLAOEP
glycoplasmia . . . . . . /GLAOIMS

glycoprotein . . . . /GLAOIP
glycorrhachia . . . . /GLAIK
glycosemia . . . . /GLAOES
glycosuria . . . . /GLURS
glycosuric . . . . /GLOURK, /GL*URK
glyoxylemia . . . . /GLAOEMS, /GLAOEMX
glyphic . . . . /GLIK
glyphics . . . . /GLIX
gnathia . . . . /NO*IT
gnathic . . . . /NA*KT
gnathion . . . . /NAUN
gnathism . . . . /NAFMT
gnathous . . . . /NO*UTS
gnathus . . . . /N*UTS
gnomic . . . . /NA*UMG
gnomonic . . . . /NAUNK, /MAUNK, /GAUNK
gnomy (*see also* nomy) . . . . /GO*IM
gnosia . . . . /GOENS
gnosis . . . . /GOENSZ
gnosist . . . . /GOENT
gnostic . . . . /NA*US, /NAUFK, /GA*US
gnostics . . . . /NAUFKS, /NA*USZ, /GA*USZ
gnosy . . . . /NO*IZ
go . . . . /GO
gogic . . . . /GAUJ
gogue (*see also* agogue) . . . . /GO*EG
goitrogenic . . . . /GOIRNG
gold . . . . /GOLD
gonad . . . . /GOEND
gonadal . . . . /GOENL
gonadism . . . . /GOIFM
gonadotropic . . . . /GROFK
gonadotropin . . . . /GROFN
gone . . . . /GON
gonesis . . . . /GAOENSZ
gonia . . . . /GO*EN
gonial . . . . /GO*ENL
gonic . . . . /GO*ENG
gonimiasis . . . . /GAOISZ
gonioma . . . . /GO*EM
goniometer . . . . /GOIRMT
gonioscope . . . . /GO*EP
gonium . . . . /GOUM
gonorrhea . . . . /GRAOE
gonorrheic . . . . /GRAEK

gonous . . . . /GOUNS
gony. . . . . /GO*N
gorge . . . . /GORJ
gorged . . . . /GORJD
gout . . . . /GO*UT
gradation . . . . /GAEGS, /GAIDZ
grade. . . . /GRAID
graft . . . . /GRAFT
grafting. . . . /GRAFGT
gram . . . . /GRAM
grammatism . . . . /GRAFMT
grammic. . . . /GRAMG
grams . . . . /GRAMS
granular . . . . /GRURL, /GRARL
granulocyte . . . . /GRANLT
granulocytic. . . . /GRAKT
granulocytosis. . . . /GRANS, /GROELT
granuloma . . . . /GRAUM
granulomatosis . . . . /GROEMTS
granuloplastic. . . . /GLAF
granulosis . . . . /GROELS
graph . . . . /GRAF
grapher . . . . /GRAFR
graphia . . . . /GRIF
graphic . . . . /GRAFK
graphical . . . . /GRAKL
graphics . . . . /GRAFKS
graphies. . . . /GRAEFS
graphism. . . . /GRA*FM
graphs. . . . /GRAFS
graphy. . . . /GRAEF
gravics . . . . /GRAVKS
gravid . . . . /GRIVD
gravida . . . . /GRAVD
gravidic . . . . /GRAVK, /GRIVK
gravimeter . . . . /GRIVMT, /GRAVMT
gravity . . . . /GRAVT
gression. . . . /GRIGS
gressive . . . . /GRIV
grondation . . . . /GRONGS
group . . . . /GROUP, /GRAOUP
growing . . . . /GROEG
grown . . . . /GROUN
growth . . . . /GRO*ET
grundation . . . . /GRUNGS

gryphosis . . . . . . /GROEPZ
gryposis . . . . . . /GROEPSZ
guanidine . . . . . . /GAOEND
guanidinemia . . . . . . /GAOEM
guanine . . . . . . /GA
gummatous . . . . . . /GOUMT, /GOUMTS, /GUMTS
gustation . . . . . . /GUGS
gustometry . . . . . . /GROMT
gut . . . . . . /GUT
gymnasium . . . . . . /GIMZ
gymnastic . . . . . . /GIMT
gymnastics . . . . . . /GIMTS
gynecomastia . . . . . . /GAOIMT
gynic . . . . . . /JINK
gynogram . . . . . . /GAOING
gyny . . . . . . /GE
gyral . . . . . . /JAOIRL, /GAOIRL
gyrate . . . . . . /JAOIRT, /GAOIRT
gyration . . . . . . /JAOIRGS, /GAOIRGS
gyria . . . . . . /JAO*R, /JAO*IR
gyric . . . . . . /JAOIRK, /GAOIRK
gyrus . . . . . . /GRUS

H

habilitate . . . . . . /HIBLT, /HAEBLT
habilitation . . . . . . /HABLGS, /HIBLGS, /HAEBLGS
halation . . . . . . /HAILGS
halisteresis . . . . . . /HAOELTS
hallucination . . . . . . /HAOULGS
hallucinatory . . . . . . /HAOURLT
hallux . . . . . . /HUX
hang . . . . . . /HANG
hazard . . . . . . /HAFRD
hazardous . . . . . . /HAOFRD, /HAOFRDZ
hearing . . . . . . /HAERG
hebotomy . . . . . . /HAOEBT
hedonia . . . . . . /HAOEND
hedonism . . . . . . /HAOEFM, /HOFM
hedral . . . . . . /HAOERLD
helcosis (*see also* elcosis) . . . . . . /HELS, /HOEKLS
heliosis . . . . . . /HAOELSZ
helix . . . . . . /HAOELX
hemagglutination . . . . . . /HUNGS

hemagglutinin . . . . /HAEG
hemal . . . . /HA*EM
hemalbumin . . . . /HAO*UM
hemangioma . . . . /HAOM
hemarthrosis . . . . /HO*ET
hematin . . . . /HAENT, /H*ENT
hematocele . . . . /HAOELT
hematocrit . . . . /HAERKT
hematogenous . . . . /HOJ, /HOJT
hematology . . . . /HAOLG
hematoma . . . . /HAOEMT
hematometra . . . . /HOIRMT
hematonephrosis . . . . /HOEFSZ
hematopenia . . . . /HAOPT
hematopoiesis . . . . /HOIPTS
hematopoietic . . . . /HOIPT
hematoporphyrin . . . . /HOEFR
hematous . . . . /HEMTS
hematuria . . . . /HAOUR
hematuric . . . . /HAO*URK
heme . . . . /HAOEM
hemeral . . . . /HA*ERM
hemia . . . . /HAIM, /HAO*EM
hemic . . . . /HEMG
hemin . . . . /HAOEN
heminephrectomy . . . . /HEFKT
hemiplegic . . . . /H-J
hemispheric . . . . /HAOEFRK
hemoblast . . . . /HA*S
hemochromogen . . . . /HO*EJ
hemoglobin . . . . /HOB, /HEG
hemoglobinemia . . . . /HAOEBL
hemoglobinometer . . . . /HAOERMG
hemoglobinuria. . . . . /HAOURG, /HAOELG
hemolysin . . . . /HONLS
hemolysis . . . . /HOLS, /HOLSZ
hemolytic . . . . /HOLG
hemometer . . . . /HAOERMT
hemopericardium . . . . /HAURMD
hemophilia . . . . /HAOEF
hemophiliac . . . . /HAOEFG
hemopoiesis . . . . /HOISZ
hemopoietic . . . . /HO*IK
hemoptysis . . . . /HAUP
hemorrhagic . . . . /HIRJ

hemorrhagica . . . . /HAIG
hemorrhea . . . . /H*ERM
hemostasis . . . . /HAOEFMT, /HAIFSZ
hemotachometer . . . . /HAERMT
hemotherapy . . . . /HAIRP
hemothorax . . . . /HORX
hemotoxin . . . . /HOEFN
hemotoxism . . . . /HO*EFM
hemotransfusion . . . . /HAOUFGS
heparinemia . . . . /HAO*ERN
hepatectomy . . . . /HAEPGT
hepatia . . . . /HAEP, /HA*EPT
hepatic . . . . /HAEPG
hepaticus . . . . /HAEPGZ
hepatitic . . . . /HIPGT
hepatitis . . . . /HAEPT
hepatocele . . . . /HAOEPT
hepatogenic . . . . /HENK
hepatoma . . . . /HOEMT
hepatomegalia . . . . /HAOPG
hepatomegaly . . . . /HAOMG
hepatopexy . . . . /HEX
hepatorenal . . . . /HAOENL
hepatostomy . . . . /HO*S
hepatotomy . . . . /HAUT
hereditary . . . . /HA*IRD
hermaphrodite . . . . /HEFMT
hermaphroditism . . . . /HEFM
hernia . . . . /HAERN
hernial . . . . /HAERNL
herniorrhaphy . . . . /HAORP
hertz . . . . /HERZ
hesion . . . . /HAO*EGS
heteroagglutinin . . . . /HAOUNT
heterogeneity . . . . /HENGT
heterolysin . . . . /HOFN, /HOFRN
heteroplasty . . . . /HARPT
heterotopia . . . . /HAIPT
heterotroph . . . . /HOEFT
heterotrophic . . . . /HOEFK
hiatal . . . . /HOILT
hidria (*see also* idria) . . . . /*IRD, /YOIRD
hidrosis (*see also* idrosis *and* drosis) . . . . /DROESZ
hidrotic (*see also* idrotic *and* ydrotic) . . . . /DROK
hieric . . . . /HAO*ERK

hilar . . . /HIRL, /HAO*IRL
histaminic . . . /HIFMG
histioblast . . . /HAOBL, /HAOBT
histiocytary . . . /HOIFR
histiocytic . . . /HOIFKT
histiocytoma . . . /HOEFM
histiocytosis . . . /HAOEFT
histiodieresis . . . /HAOEFD
histioplasmacytic . . . /HAOKT
histochemical . . . /HAOFL
histochemistry . . . /HERMZ
histofluorescence . . . /HIFNS, /HIFRNS
histogenesis . . . /HENSZ
histologic . . . /HIFRK
histological . . . /HIFRL
histology . . . /HOELG
histon . . . /HAUFN
histone . . . /HIFN
history . . . /HIFT
homogeneity . . . /HAOEJT
hormonal . . . /HOERL, /HOERNL
hormone . . . /HOERM
horn . . . /HORN
humeral . . . /H*URL, /H-RL
humeralis . . . /H-RLS, /HURLZ
humerals . . . /H*URLS, /H-RLZ
humidifier . . . /HAOUFR
humor . . . /HAOURM
humoral. . . . /HAORL
hyal . . . /HYAL, /HYAOIL
hyalin. . . . /HIN
hyaline . . . /HAOIN
hyalinosis . . . /HAOILSZ
hyaloid . . . /HAOILD
hybrid . . . /HAOIBD
hydatidosis . . . /HOETSZ, /HOETSDZ
hydramnios . . . /HAOIRMS
hydranencephaly . . . /HAOIFLG
hydrate . . . /HAOIRT
hydrated . . . /HAOIRTD
hydration . . . /HAOIRGS
hydraulic . . . /DRAUK
hydremia . . . /HAOIRMD
hydria . . . /H*IRD, /HAO*IRD
hydric. . . . /H*IK

hydrocele . . . . . /HOIL, /HOIRL
hydrocephalus . . . . . /HAOIFLS
hydrocephaly . . . . . /HAOIFL, /HAOEFL
hydrochloria . . . . . /HOERKL
hydrochloric . . . . . /HORKL
hydrochloride . . . . . /HAOIRLD, /KHOIRD
hydrochloridia . . . . . /HORKLD
hydrogenate . . . . . /HORJ
hydrolysis . . . . . /DROLZ
hydrometer . . . . . /DROMT
hydrometra . . . . . /HAORMT
hydromyelia . . . . . /HAO*ERL
hydronephrosis . . . . . /HOEFS
hydropericardium . . . . . /HERPD
hydroperitoneum . . . . . /HOIRPT
hydropexis . . . . . /HIRPXZ
hydropexy . . . . . /HIRPX
hydropic . . . . . /HOIRK
hydrorrhea . . . . . /DRAE
hydrosis (*see also* ydrosis) . . . . . /DROES
hydrotherapy . . . . . /HAIRPT, /HO*IRP
hydrothorax . . . . . /HAORX
hydrotic . . . . . /HAOIRKT
hydroxide . . . . . /HOIX
hydroxy . . . . . /HOIRX
hydruria . . . . . /HAO*UR, /HAOR
hygroma . . . . . /GROIM
hygrometer . . . . . /HAOIRMG
hyloma . . . . . /HOIM
hymen . . . . . /HAO*IM
hymenal . . . . . /HAOINL
hymeneal . . . . . /HAO*ENL
hymenia . . . . . /HAO*EN
hymenic . . . . . /HAO*ENG
hymenitis . . . . . /HIMTS
hyoid . . . . . /HOD
hyoidean . . . . . /HO*IND
hypalgesia . . . . . /HAOELZ, /PAOELZ
hypercholesterolemic . . . . . /HOERMG
hypercytosis . . . . . /HAOIRPTS, /HAOIRPSZ
hyperemia . . . . . /HAOIRM
hyperesthesia . . . . . /HAOEPTS
hyperglycemia . . . . . /HAOIRPG
hyperhidrosis . . . . . /HOERPS
hyperidrosis . . . . . /HAOERPS

hyperkalemia . . . /HOIRM
hypermenorrhea . . . /HYEM
hypermetria . . . /HAOERPT
hyperparathyroidism . . . /HAOIFMD
hyperplasia . . . /HAIPS
hyperreflexia . . . /HAOIFX
hypersarcosis . . . /HOEPSZ
hypertension . . . /HAOIPGS
hypertensive . . . /HAOIFRB
hypertonia . . . /HAOIPT
hypertonic . . . /HAUNG
hypertrichosis . . . /HOEKSZ
hypertrophia . . . /HAOFK
hypertrophic . . . /HAOIFK
hypertrophy . . . /HAOIRPT
hypesthesia . . . /HAO*ETS
hypnia . . . /H*IP
hypnosis . . . /SNOP
hypnotic . . . /SNOPG, /SNOPK
hypnotism . . . /SNOFM
hypoblast . . . /HOIBT
hypocytosis . . . /HOIPSZ
hypoderma . . . /HAORM
hypoesthesia . . . /HO*ETS
hypogammaglobulinemia . . . /HAOEB
hypogastric . . . /HOIRKT, /HAORK
hypogonadism . . . /HOIFM
hypomenorrhea . . . /HYOM
hypometria . . . /HOERMT
hypoparathyroidism . . . /HOIFMD
hypophosphatasia . . . /HAEPTS
hypophyseal (*see also* hypophysial) . . . /HAUFL
hypophysectomy . . . /HAUFK, /PAUFK
hypophyses . . . /HEFSZ, /PEFSZ
hypophysial (*see also* hypophyseal) . . . /HOIFL
hypophysis . . . /HAUFSZ, /PAUFSZ
hypophysitis . . . /HOIFT, /HOIFTS
hypopituitarism . . . /HAOFM
hypoplasia . . . /HAIPZ
hypotensive . . . /HOIFRB
hypothermy . . . /HIRT
hypothyroidism . . . /HAOIFM
hypotonia . . . /HONT
hypotonic . . . /HOENG
hypoxia . . . /HAOIPX

hysterectomy .... /HIFRT
hysterocolpectomy .... /HYEKT
hysterogram .... /HIFRG
hysterograph .... /HAEFG
hysterography .... /HAEFR
hystero-oophorectomy .... /HAOFR
hysteropexy .... /HIFRX
hysterosalpingectomy .... /HIJT
hysterosalpingo-oophorectomy .... /HIMP, /HAOMP
hysterotomy .... /HOFRT

I

ia .... /A*I
iac .... /YAIK
ial .... /YAL
ials .... /YALS
ian .... /YA*N
iasis .... /AOISZ
iation .... /YAIGS
iatria .... /YART
iatric .... /YAOERT
iatrician .... /YIRGS
iatricians .... /YIRGSZ
iatrics .... /YAOERTS
iatrist .... /AOIFT, /YAOIFT
iatrists .... /AOIFTS, /YAOIFTS
iatrogenic .... /YAOENG
iatry .... /YAOET
ic .... /*IK
icidal (*see also* cidal) .... /YAOILD
icide (*see also* cide) .... /YAOID
icism .... /SIFM
icity (*see also* city) .... /ST*I
ics .... /*IX
ictal .... /YAKL, /IKLT
icteric .... /IRKT, /YIKT
-icteric .... /*IRKT, /YIRKT
icterus .... /YUX, /YIX
id (*see also* oid) .... /O*ID
idal (*see also* oidal) .... /O*ILD
idea .... /Y–D
ides .... /AOIDZ
idism (*see also* oidism) .... /O*IFMD

idria (*see also* hidria) . . . . /Y*IRD
idrosis (*see also* hidrosis *and* drosis) . . . . /DRO*ESZ, /DROIZ
idrotic (*see also* hidrotic *and* ydrotic) . . . . /DRO*KT
ids (*see also* oids) . . . . /O*IDZ
ifacient (*see also* facient) . . . . /FAERBT
ifaction (*see also* faction) . . . . /FWAIX
ifactive (*see also* factive) . . . . /FIVK, /FIFK
iferous (*see also* ferous) . . . . /FOIRS
ifiable . . . . /IFBL
ific . . . . /IFK
ification (*see also* fication) . . . . /IFX, /–FX
ifier . . . . /AOIFR
iform (*see also* form) . . . . /FOIRM
iforms (*see also* forms) . . . . /FOIRMS
ileac . . . . /YAEK
ileal . . . . /YAEL
ileitis . . . . /YAOITS
ilemmoma . . . . /YAO*EL
ileocutaneous . . . . /YAOUNTS
ileoneocystostomy . . . . /YO*NS
ileostomy . . . . /YOIFT
ileotomy . . . . /YOFT
ileum . . . . /YAEM
ileus . . . . /YILS
iliac . . . . /YAK
iliacs . . . . /YAKZ
iliitis . . . . /YOITS, /LOITS
imeter (*see also* meter) . . . . /MIRMT, /IRMT
imetry (*see also* metry) . . . . /ERMT
immune . . . . /MAOUN
-immune . . . . /MAO*UN
immune globulin . . . . /MAOUBL
immunity . . . . /MAOUNT, /MUNT
immunization . . . . /KBAOUNGS
immunoassay . . . . /SMAESZ
immunodetection . . . . /M–NX
immunodiffusion . . . . /SMAOUFGS, /DMAOUFGS
immunoelectrophoresis . . . . /MAOEFSZ
immunoglobulinemia . . . . /KBLAOEM
immunoimaging . . . . /MAOUJ
immunologic . . . . /KB–J
immunology . . . . /KBOLG
immunoprecipitation . . . . /MAOUPGS
immunoscintigraphy . . . . /MAOUFN, /MAOUFRN
immunosorbent . . . . /MOERBT

implant . . . . /KBLANT
implantation . . . . /KBLANGS
impregnation . . . . /KBRAEGS
impression . . . . /KBREGS
in . . . . /*IN
inactivation . . . . /NAEVGS, /NAEFGS
incineration . . . . /SIRNGS
incisal . . . . /SNAOILZ
incision . . . . /SNIGS
incisor . . . . /SNAOIRZ
incompatibility . . . . /KPIBLT
incompatible . . . . /KPIBL
incompetent . . . . /IP
indicanemia . . . . /DAOENK
indicant . . . . /DINKT, /DANKT
induce . . . . /SPWAOUS
induction . . . . /SPWUX
inert . . . . /NERT
infarct . . . . /FAURK, /N–FRKT
infarction . . . . /FAURX, /N–FRX
infection . . . . /NEFX, /NEFGS
-infection . . . . /N*EFX
infectious . . . . /NERB
-infectious . . . . /N*ERB
infective . . . . /NEVK
-infective . . . . /NIVK
inferior . . . . /FAOR
inferiorly . . . . /FAORL
infestation . . . . /FAIFGS
inflammatory . . . . /FLAMT
-inflammatory . . . . /FLA*MT, /FLAORMT
inflation . . . . /FLAIGS
influenza . . . . /FLAONS
influenzal . . . . /FLAONL
infraction . . . . /NAFX
infraorbital . . . . /FRORBL
infusion . . . . /NAOUFGS
ingestion . . . . /N*EGS
inguinal . . . . /GINL
inhibition . . . . /BIX
inhibitor . . . . /NORBT
inhibitory . . . . /NOERBT
inic . . . . /N–NG
injection . . . . /JOIX
injector . . . . /JOIRK

innervation . . . . . /NAEFRBGS
inoculation . . . . . /NOGS
inoma (*see also* noma) . . . . . /N*IM
inosemia . . . . . /SNAOEM
inosis . . . . . /NOSZ
inositol . . . . . /SNOL
insected . . . . . /SNEKTD
insertion . . . . . /SNERGS
instrument . . . . . /STRUMT
insular . . . . . /SNAOURL
-insular . . . . . /SNAO*URL
insulinar . . . . . /SLIRN
insulinemia . . . . . /SLAEM
insulinism . . . . . /SLIFM
integration . . . . . /GRAIGS
integrator . . . . . /GRAIRT, /GRORT
integumental . . . . . /SPWAEMT
intelligible . . . . . /JIBL
intense . . . . . /SPWENS
intercostal . . . . . /SPWOFL
interference . . . . . /SPWR–FRNS, /SPW–FRNS
internal . . . . . /SPWERNL
interstitial . . . . . /SPWIRBL
intestinal . . . . . /SPWEL, /SPWELS
intimal . . . . . /SPWA*M
intoxicant . . . . . /SPWANT
intoxication . . . . . /SPWOX
intraligamentous . . . . . /SPWLIG
intubation . . . . . /SPWAEGS
invasion . . . . . /VA*EGS
invasive . . . . . /VAEV
invertase . . . . . /NAEVS
investment . . . . . /VEFMT
involution . . . . . /NOULGS
iodide . . . . . /DAOD
iodidism . . . . . /DAOFM
iodinated . . . . . /YAINTD
iodine . . . . . /AOIND
ion . . . . . /AOIN
ionic . . . . . /AOING
ionics . . . . . /AOINGZ
iosis . . . . . /YAOESZ
ipara . . . . . /PIRP
iparous (*see also* parous) . . . . . /PA*IRZ
iprivous (*see also* privous) . . . . . /PROIVS

iridian . . . . /IRND
iridocyclitis . . . . /YAOIKL, /YAOIKLS
iritis . . . . /AOIRTS, /TRAOITS
iritomy . . . . /TROIMT
iron . . . . /AOIRN
irritability . . . . /IRBLT
irritable . . . . /IRBL
irritant . . . . /IRNT
irritation . . . . /IRGS
irritative . . . . /IVRT
is . . . . /S–
ischemia . . . . /SHAOEM, /IRK
-ischemia . . . . /SKHAOEM
ischemic . . . . /SHAOEMG
-ischemic . . . . /SHAO*EMG
ischia . . . . /SKAE, /SHAOE
ischiac . . . . /SHAOEK, /SKHAK
ischiadic . . . . /SHAOEKD
ischial . . . . /SHAOEKL, /SHIKL, /SKHAL
-ischial . . . . /SHAOERBL, /SHOIRBL
ism . . . . /IFM
ismal . . . . /SM–L
ismic . . . . /SMIZ
ismus . . . . /SMUS
isomer . . . . /AOIRM
isomeric . . . . /AOIRMG, /AOIRMK
isomerism . . . . /AOIFM
isotonia . . . . /SAONT
isotonic . . . . /SONT
isotropy . . . . /STROEP
ist . . . . /*IS
isthmian . . . . /SM*INT
istic . . . . /IFKT
ists . . . . /*ISZ
ite . . . . /AOIT
ites . . . . /AOITSZ
itic . . . . /*IKT
itide . . . . /TO*ID
itides (*see also* tides) . . . . /TOIDZ
itis . . . . /AOITS
itogen . . . . /TO*EJ
itogenic (*see also* togenic) . . . . /TOIJ
itogenous (*see also* togenous) . . . . /TO*J
ive . . . . /IV
ively . . . . /IVL

iveness . . . . /IVNS
ization . . . . /SAIGS
ize . . . . /AO*IS
ized . . . . /AOIFD
izema . . . . /ZIM
izer . . . . /AOIRS
izes . . . . /AOIFS
izing . . . . /AOIFG

J

jacent . . . . /JAINT
jaundice . . . . /JAUN
jection . . . . /J*EX, /J–X
jejunitis . . . . /JITS, /GITS
jejunocolic . . . . /JOKL
jejunoesophagostomy . . . . /JUFT
jejunogastrostomy . . . . /JAO*S
jejunoplasty . . . . /JAOP, /JAOPT
jejunostomy . . . . /JOS, /JO*S, /JOJ
jejunum . . . . /JEJ, /GEJ
jet . . . . /JET
joule . . . . /JAO*UL, /JAOL
jugal . . . . /JAOULG
jugular . . . . /JARL, /JAUR
junction . . . . /JUNGS
jut . . . . /JUT

K

kalemia . . . . /KLA*EM
kalemic . . . . /KLA*EMG, /KLAOEMG
kaliemia . . . . /KLAO*EM
kaluresis . . . . /KLURS
kamnosis (*see also* camnosis) . . . . /KOEMZ
karyoblast (*see also* caryoblast) . . . . /KBAOFT
karyocyte (*see also* caryocyte) . . . . /KRAOT
karyocytopoiesis . . . . /KROIPS
karyocytosis . . . . /KRAOTS
karyon (*see also* caryon) . . . . /KRAUN
karyosis . . . . /KARSZ
karyote (*see also* caryote) . . . . /KO*ET

karyotic (*see also* caryotic) . . . . /KRAOKT
katal . . . . /KALT
kelidosis (*see also* celidosis) . . . . /KLOEDZ
kentric . . . . /K*ENT
keratic . . . . /KERKT
keratin . . . . /KERNT
keratinization . . . . /KERX, /KERNGS
keratinize . . . . /KAOIFD
keratinized . . . . /KAOIS
keratitis (*see also* ceratitis) . . . . /KERTS
keratoconjunctivitis . . . . /KRIVTS
keratodermia . . . . /KRAERM
keratoiritis . . . . /KAOIRTS
keratology . . . . /KAERLG
keratoma . . . . /KRAUM
keratomycosis . . . . /KOESZ
keratophakia . . . . /KRAIFK
keratoplasty . . . . /KERPT
keratoprosthesis . . . . /KRAOEPT, /KRAOEPTS
keratoscope . . . . /KRO*EP
keratosis (*see also* ceratosis) . . . . /KROETS
keratotic . . . . /KAIRKT
kerosis . . . . /KAOERSZ
kesis . . . . /KESZ
ketal . . . . /KAOELT
ketogenesis . . . . /KAOEJS
ketonemia . . . . /KWAOEM
ketonuria . . . . /KWAOUR
ketosis . . . . /KWOESZ
kidney . . . . /KAOEND
kinase . . . . /KAIZ
kine . . . . /KO*IN
kinemia . . . . /KMAE
kinemic . . . . /KMAEG
kinesia . . . . /KAOEZ, /KAOENS
kinesimeter . . . . /KIRMT
kinesis . . . . /KAOESZ, /KAOENSZ
kinesograph . . . . /KAOEFG
kinesthesia (*see also* cinesthesia) . . . . /KAO*ETS, /KAO*ENT
kinesthetic . . . . /K*INT
kinetic . . . . /KENGT, /KINGT
kinetics . . . . /KENGTS, /KINGTS
kinin (*see also* cinin) . . . . /KAOIN
klasis (*see also* clasis) . . . . /KLAESZ
klastic (*see also* clastic) . . . . /KLAFZ

kleisis . . . . /KLAO*ISZ, /KLOIZ
klony . . . . /KLO*IN
koimesis (*see also* coimesis) . . . . /KOIMZ, /KOIMSZ
kolpos (*see also* colpos). . . . . /KOLZ
konia . . . . /KAUN
koniosis . . . . /KAUNS
kophosis . . . . /KOEFZ
koria (*see also* coria). . . . . /KAO*R
kousis . . . . /KOUSZ
kraurosis . . . . /KRAURS
kurtic . . . . /K*URK
kyme . . . . /KAO*IM, /KIM
kymia . . . . /KOIM
kymogram . . . . /KMAM
kymograph . . . . /KMAF
kymographic . . . . /KMAFK, /KAOIMG
kymography . . . . /KMAEF
kyphectomy . . . . /KEFK, /KAOIFK
kyphoses . . . . /KAOEFS, /KAOEFZ
kyphosis. . . . . /KOEFSZ, /KAOIFSZ

L

la . . . . /LA*
labe. . . . . /LA*EB
labeled . . . . /LAIBLD
labia . . . . /LA*IB
labial . . . . /LABL
labialis . . . . /LABLS
labile. . . . . /LOIBL
lability. . . . . /LOIBLT
labiopulpal . . . . /LAUP
labyrinthine . . . . /RAO*ENT
labyrinthitis. . . . . /RO*INT, /RO*INTS
labyrinthopexy . . . . /RAOPX
laceration . . . . /LARGS
lacrimal . . . . /LARKL
lactacidemia . . . . /LAOEMD
lactation . . . . /LAIX
lacteal . . . . /LAKL, /LAEKL
lactic. . . . . /TLAKT
lactose. . . . . /TLOEK
lactovegetarian . . . . /LAERJ, /LAIRJ
lactovegetarianism . . . . /LAIFM

lacunae . . . . . . /LAENK
lacunia . . . . . . /LUNK
lagnia . . . . . . /LA*G
lagnist . . . . . . /LAGT
lagny . . . . . . /LOIG
lalia . . . . . . /LAIL
lalism . . . . . . /LAFM
lambert . . . . . . /LERBT
lamella . . . . . . /L*EL
lamellar . . . . . . /L*ERL
laminar . . . . . . /LAIRM
laminate . . . . . . /LAIMT
lamination . . . . . . /LAMGS
laminectomy . . . . . . /LEMT, /LAEMT
lamp . . . . . . /LAMP
laparotomy . . . . . . /LARPT
lapaxy . . . . . . /LAPXZ
lapse . . . . . . /LAPS
lapsus . . . . . . /LAUPS
lar . . . . . . /LAR
large . . . . . . /LARJ
larged . . . . . . /LARJD
laryngeal . . . . . . /LAIRNL, /LAERNL
laryngectomy . . . . . . /LAIRNG
laryngitis . . . . . . /LAIRNTS
laryngologist . . . . . . /LARGT
laryngology . . . . . . /LARG
laryngoscopy . . . . . . /LAORNG
laryngotomy . . . . . . /LARNGT, /LAERNGT
larynx . . . . . . /LAIRNX
lase . . . . . . /LAES
late . . . . . . /LAIT
lated . . . . . . /LAITD
lateral . . . . . . /LARL
lateralism . . . . . . /LAEFM
laterally . . . . . . /LAERL
lateral sclerosis . . . . . . /LARLS, /LOELS
lation . . . . . . /LAIGS
lavage . . . . . . /LAVJ
lay . . . . . . /LAI
layer . . . . . . /LAER
lead . . . . . . /L*ED, /LAOED
leakage . . . . . . /LA*EJ
learning . . . . . . /LERNG
lecithal . . . . . . /SL*ET

lecithin . . . /SL*INT
legal . . . /LEL
leiomyofibroma . . . /LOIFM
leiomyoma . . . /LOIM
lemma . . . /LA*EM
lemmal . . . /L*EM
lemmic . . . /LEMG
lemmitis . . . /LEMTS
lemmoma (*see also* ilemmoma) . . . /LAUM
lemmosarcoma . . . /LOEM
lemmous . . . /LEMZ
lent . . . /LENT
lental . . . /LENLT
lentia . . . /LAERB
lenticular . . . /LERNL
lepidoma . . . /LOEMD
leprosy . . . /LERPZ
lepsia . . . /LOIPZ
lepsis . . . /LEPSZ
lepsy . . . /LEPZ
lept . . . /L*EPT
leptanalgesia . . . /LA*NL
leptanalgesic . . . /LA*NG
leptanesthesia . . . /LA*EN
leptanesthetic . . . /LA*ENG
leptic . . . /LEPGT
leptiform . . . /LEFPT
leptoid . . . /LOIPTD
leptomeningitis . . . /LAOIPT, /LAOIPTS
leptynsis . . . /LENTS
lesion . . . /LAOEGS
lesional . . . /LAOELGS
let . . . /LET
lethal . . . /LAO*ET
leucitis (*see also* leukitis) . . . /LAOUTS
leukemia . . . /LOUM
leukemic . . . /LOUMG
leukin . . . /LOUNK
leukitis (*see also* leucitis) . . . /LAOUKTS
leukoagglutinin . . . /LAOUGT
leukoblast . . . /LAOBT
leukoblastosis . . . /LOEBSZ
leukocyte . . . /LOUK
leukocythemia . . . /LAOMT
leukocytic . . . /LOIKT

leukocytosis . . . . /LOUKT, /LOUKTS
leukoderma . . . . /LAERMD
leukodystrophy . . . . /LAOFD
leukoma . . . . /LOEMG
leukopenia . . . . /LAOUN
leukorrhea . . . . /LAOURK
leukoscope . . . . /LAOUP
leukosis . . . . /LAOUKSZ
leukotoxin . . . . /LAOUNX
lever . . . . /LEVR
levosity . . . . /LOVT
levous . . . . /LOUVS
lexia . . . . /L–X
lexic . . . . /L*K
li . . . . /L*I
liasis . . . . /LAOISZ
lienal . . . . /LOINL
lienography . . . . /LAEFG
lienomegaly . . . . /LELG
ligamentary . . . . /LIRMT
ligamentous . . . . /LOUGTS
ligation . . . . /LAOIGS
liminal . . . . /L*IL
limit . . . . /LIMT
limitation . . . . /LIMGTS, /LIJTS
lin . . . . /LIN
line . . . . /LAOIN
linear . . . . /LIRN
lines . . . . /LAOINS
lingual . . . . /LINL
linguistic . . . . /LINGT
linguistics . . . . /LINGS, /LINGTS
linguitis . . . . /LUGT
linguoaxial . . . . /LIXL
linguo-occlusal . . . . /LAOULZ
linguopulpal . . . . /LOUP
lipase . . . . /LAEPZ
lipectomy . . . . /LEPKT
lipemia . . . . /PAEM
lipemic . . . . /PAEMG
lipid . . . . /PID
lipidemia . . . . /LAO*EM
lipidemic . . . . /LAOEMG
lipidoses . . . . /LAOEPDZ
lipidosis . . . . /LIPDZ

lipids . . . . /PIDZ
lipochondroma . . . . /PLOEMD
lipodystrophic . . . . /PLOFK, /PLOEFK
lipodystrophy . . . . /PLOEF
lipofibroma . . . . /LAOIRP
lipoid . . . . /POID
lipoidemia . . . . /LOIMD
lipoidosis . . . . /POEDZ
lipoleiomyoma . . . . /LO*IM
lipoma . . . . /LOEMP
lipomatosis . . . . /LAMS
lipomatous . . . . /LOEMPT
lipoprotein . . . . /LOIRN
lipoproteinemia . . . . /LAOEPT
liposis . . . . /LOEPSZ, /POSZ
lipsis . . . . /LIPSZ
lism . . . . /LIFM
listhesis . . . . /LAOEFS
listhetic . . . . /L*EKT
lite . . . . /LAO*IT
liter . . . . /LAOERT
literal . . . . /LIRL
lites . . . . /LO*ITS
lith . . . . /L*IT
lithalopaxy . . . . /LAOPT
lithectomy . . . . /L*ET
lithemia . . . . /LAO*EMT
lithiasis . . . . /LAO*ITS
lithic . . . . /LIFK
lithics . . . . /LIFKZ
lithology . . . . /LILG, /LOLG
lithotomy . . . . /LO*T, /LA*UT
lithotripsy . . . . /LIPT
lithotrity . . . . /L*IRT
lithotroph . . . . /LOEPT
lithotrophic . . . . /LOEPGT
lithotrophy . . . . /LOEPG
liths . . . . /L*ITS
lithuria . . . . /L*URT
load . . . . /LOED
lobar . . . . /LORB
lobate . . . . /LOEBT
lobed . . . . /LOEBD
lobitis . . . . /LOEBTS
lobular . . . . /LORBL

lobulate . . . . /LAIBT
lobulated . . . . /LAIBTD
lobulitis . . . . /LOBLT, /LOBLTS, /LAOUBLT, /LAOUBLTS
localization . . . . /LOLGS, /LOEFLGS
locate . . . . /LOEK
locatio . . . . /LOERBT
location . . . . /LOEX
locator . . . . /LOERKT
locomotion . . . . /LOEMGS
locular . . . . /LORKL
loculate . . . . /LAEKT
loculated . . . . /LAEKTD
log . . . . /LOG
logia . . . . /LAUJ, /LAOJ
logic . . . . /L–J
logical . . . . /LAJ
logically . . . . /LOIJ
logies (*see also* ologies *and* tologies) . . . . /–LGS, /O*LGS
logism . . . . /LOEFM
logist (*see also* ologist *and* tologist) . . . . /–LT, /O*LT
logists (*see also* ologists *and* tologists) . . . . /–LTS, /O*LTS
logous . . . . /LOUGS
logue . . . . /LO*G, /LO*UG
logy (*see also* ology *and* tology) . . . . /–LG, /O*LG
loid . . . . /LOID
loquence . . . . /KWUNS, /KW*ENS
loquism . . . . /KWIFM, /KWOFM
loquist . . . . /KWOEFT, /KWUFT
loquy . . . . /LO*EK, /KWAO*E
lordosis . . . . /LOERDZ
losis . . . . /LOESZ
louse . . . . /LOUS
loxia . . . . /LO*IX
loxy . . . . /LOIX
lucency . . . . /LAOUSZ
lucent . . . . /LAOUS
luetic . . . . /LAOUKT, /LAO*KT
lumbalis . . . . /LUBLS
lumbar . . . . /L*UB, /L*UM, /KBAR
lumbocostoabdominal . . . . /LUBL
luminal . . . . /LAONL, /LAO*UL
luminescence . . . . /LUMS
luminescent . . . . /LUMT
lunar . . . . /LAOURN
lunare . . . . /LAIRN

lunate . . . . . /LAINT
lupoid . . . . . /LOIPD
lus . . . . . /LUS
lutein . . . . . /LAOUT
luvium . . . . . /LUVM
luxation . . . . . /LUGS
ly . . . . . /LI
lygmus . . . . . /L*IG
lymph . . . . . /YIMP
lympha . . . . . /YAMP
lymphadenitis . . . . . /YINTS
lymphangeal . . . . . /YAENL
lymphangial . . . . . /YOINL
lymphangioma . . . . . /YOEJ
lymphangitis . . . . . /YAOINTS
lymphatic . . . . . /YIMPT
lymphemia . . . . . /YAOEMP
lymphia . . . . . /YAIMP
lymphic . . . . . /YIMPG
lymphitis . . . . . /YIFTS
lymphocele . . . . . /YAOEL
lymphocyte . . . . . /YAOIT, /YOIT
lymphocytic . . . . . /YAOIK, /YAOIKT
lymphocytosis . . . . . /YOEMP, /YOEMPS
lymphoidocyte . . . . . /LOIFT
lymphoma . . . . . /YOEM
lymphomatosis . . . . . /YOEFS, /YOEFSZ
lymphoplasia . . . . . /YAEMP, /YAEMPZ
lymphoscintigraphy . . . . . /YIFG
lysate . . . . . /LAIFT
lyse . . . . . /LAO*IS
lyses (*see also* olyses) . . . . . /LEZ, /LAOEZ
lysin (*see also* olysin) . . . . . /LIFN
lysine . . . . . /LOIFN
lysinemia . . . . . /LAOEFMS
lysinogen . . . . . /LAOIJ
lysinuria . . . . . /LAOURNS
lysis (*see also* olysis) . . . . . /LISZ, /O*LS
lysosome . . . . . /LOEMS, /LAOIMS
lyte . . . . . /YAOILT
lytic (*see also* olytic) . . . . . /LIKT
lytics (*see also* olytics) . . . . . /LIKTS
lytopoietic (*see also* olytopoietic) . . . . . /LAOIPGT
lyzable . . . . . /LAOIFBL
lyzation . . . . . /LAOIFGS

lyze . . . . /LAO*IZ
lyzer . . . . /LAO*IRZ

M

macria . . . . /MA*K
macroglossia . . . . /MOFL
macromolecule . . . . /KMAOKL
macular . . . . /MOURL, /MARKL
madesis . . . . /MAEDZ
magnesemia . . . . /MAGZ
magnet . . . . /MAEGT
magnetic . . . . /MAEKT
magnetism . . . . /MAEFMG
malacia . . . . /MAERB
malacic . . . . /MAERK, /MAEKL
malacosis . . . . /MALSZ
malar . . . . /MAERL
malarial . . . . /MLAIRL, /LAIRL
maleficence . . . . /MIFRB
malignancy . . . . /MALG
malignant . . . . /MALGT
malleal . . . . /MLAUL
malleolar . . . . /MLAURL
malleolus . . . . /MLAOELS
mamillary . . . . /MA*ERL
mammary . . . . /MAERM
mammography . . . . /MARMG
mammotropin . . . . /MAOFN, /MAOFRN
mancy . . . . /MA*NS
mandible . . . . /MABL
mandibular . . . . /MIRBL
mandibularitis . . . . /MIRBLT
mandibulectomy . . . . /MAKT
mandibulodyscephaly . . . . /MAOFBL
mania . . . . /MA*IN, /YAIN
maniac . . . . /MAINK, /YAINK
maniacal . . . . /MAO*ING
manipulation . . . . /MIPGS
manipulator . . . . /M*IRP
manometer . . . . /MAURMT
manometric . . . . /MARNT
manual . . . . /MANL
marasmus . . . . /MARMZ

margarine	/MOIRJ
marginal	/MAURJ
marital	/MAERLT
marriage	/MAIRJ, /MAERJ
mass	/MASZ
massage	/MAUJ
masseur	/MAORS
mast	/MA*S
mastectomy	/MEKT
mastia	/MA*FT
mastic	/MAIFK
mastigote	/MOGT
mastitis	/MIFTS
mastography	/MAOFG
mastoid	/MOITD
mastoiditis	/MOIDZ
mastoidostomy	/MOIMT
mastopathy	/MAO*PT, /MAEPT
masturbation	/MAURBGS, /MURBGS
masty	/MA*ES
mata	/MA*UT
material	/TERL
mathematical	/MA*LT
mathematics	/MAFKT, /MAFKTS
matism	/MAFMT
matoid	/MAOTD
matoma	/MAOMT
matosis (*see also* omatosis)	/MAMS, /O*EMZ
matous	/MOUTS
matrix	/MRAIXT
matrixoma	/MAIFM
mature	/MAUR
maturity	/MAURT
maxilla	/MIXL
maxillare	/MAEXL
maxillaritis	/MARXL
maxillary	/MAXL
maxillectomy	/MAXT
maximal	/M–XL
mazia	/MAZ, /MAIZ
meatal	/MAILT
meatotomy	/MAEMT
mechanical	/M–KL
mechanics	/M–KS
mechanism	/MEFM

mechanotherapy	/MAERPT
medial	/MAELD, /MAO*ELD
medialysis	/MAOELDZ
median	/MAOEND
mediastinal	/MAEFLT
mediastinogram	/MAFGT
mediastinography	/MAEFGT
mediastinum	/MAOEMT
medic	/MEKD
medical	/MEL
medicant	/MENGT
medication	/MEGS
medicine	/M–N
medullary	/MAERLD, /MEJD
medullated	/MAELTD
medullitis	/MULTS
medullotropic	/MAOUPG
megacolon	/MAIKL
megalia	/MAEG
megalic	/MEKL
megalogigantism	/MOEGT
megalopsia	/MAOPS
megalovirus	/MAOIV, /MAOV
megaly	/MELG
meganephronia	/MOIFN
meganephronic	/MAEFK
megasoma	/MAO*M
meiotic	/MAOIKT
melalgia	/M*ELG
melancholia	/MAOKL
melanin	/MLA*N
melanoma	/MLAEM
melanoses	/MAOELSZ
melanosis	/MELSZ, /MELS
melia	/MA*EL
melias	/MA*ELS
melic	/MAOEKL
melics	/MAOEKLS
melus	/MULZ
member	/MEB
membrane	/BRAEM
membrane disease	/BRAEMD
membranosus	/BROEMSZ
membranous	/BRAEMZ, /BRANZ
menarchal	/MA*URKL

menarche . . . /MA*URK
menia . . . /MAO*EN
menial . . . /MAO*ENL
menic . . . /MAO*ENG
meningeal . . . /JAO*EL
meninges . . . /MOIJS
meningioma . . . /JOEM
meningitis . . . /JAOIT
meningocele . . . /JOIL
meningomyelitis . . . /MENGTS
meningopathy . . . /GOP, /JOP
meninx . . . /MAOENKS
meniscitis . . . /MENTS, /MAOIFT, /MAOIFTS
meniscus . . . /MEFKS
menopausal . . . /MAUFL
menopause . . . /MAUZ
menorrhagia . . . /MRAEJ
menorrhea . . . /MRAOEN
menstrual . . . /MRENL
menstruation . . . /MRENGS
menstruum . . . /MAOURM
mensual . . . /MENLS
ment . . . /–MT
mental . . . /MENL
menthol . . . /M*ENT
mer . . . /M*ER
meral . . . /MERL
merase . . . /MAERZ
mercurial . . . /MOIRKL
mere . . . /MER, /MAOER
merge . . . /MERJ
meric . . . /M*ERK
merism . . . /MEFRM
merization . . . /MERGS
merocele . . . /MAOERLS
merorachischisis . . . /MAOERXZ
merotomy . . . /MAIRMT
merous . . . /MOURS
mesad . . . /MAOEFD
mesal . . . /MAEFL, /SMELZ, /MOIFL
mesenchyme . . . /MAOIFM
mesenteric . . . /MERKS
mesial . . . /MELZ
mesoblast . . . /MEBZ
mesoderm . . . /MERMS, /MERMD

mesodialysis . . . . . . /MALDZ
meson. . . . . . /SMEZ
mesophalangia . . . . . . /MLAING
metabolic . . . . . . /BLAUK, /BL*IK
metabolism . . . . . . /BLIFM
metabolite. . . . . . /BLOIT
metacarpal . . . . . . /MARP
metacarpalia . . . . . . /MA*URP
metacarpalism . . . . . . /MA*URM
metacarpia . . . . . . /MAURP
metachoresis. . . . . . /MAOETSZ
metagenesis. . . . . . /MEJS
metal . . . . . . /MAELT
metallic. . . . . . /MAELGT
metameric. . . . . . /M-RKT
metamorphosis . . . . . . /MORP
metaplasia . . . . . . /MAISZ
metaplastic . . . . . . /MEPT
metapody . . . . . . /MOETD
metastasis. . . . . . /MAEFT
metastatic . . . . . . /MAEFKT
metatarsal. . . . . . /MAURLS
metatarsalia. . . . . . /MAURLZ
metatarsalism . . . . . . /MAUFRM
metatarsia . . . . . . /MAURTS
metatarsus . . . . . . /MAURZ
meter (*see also* ometer) . . . . . . /MAOERT
meters (*see also* ometers). . . . . . /MAOERTS
methane . . . . . . /MA*INT
methemoglobin. . . . . . /MAOEMG
methioninemia . . . . . . /MAO*EMT
methyl . . . . . . /MY-L
metra (*see also* ometra) . . . . . . /MAOE
metrectomy. . . . . . /MOEKT
metria . . . . . . /MIRT
metrial . . . . . . /MAOERLT
metric. . . . . . /MERKT
metrics . . . . . . /MERKTS
metrioid. . . . . . /MOIRTD
metrioma . . . . . . /MO*EM
metriosis. . . . . . /MROESZ
metriotic. . . . . . /MAOERKT
metrist . . . . . . /MAO*ETS
metritic . . . . . . /MIRKT
metritis . . . . . . /MRAOITS

metrium . . . . /MAO*ERM
metrocolpos . . . . /MOPZ
metrogram . . . . /MOERG
metrograph . . . . /MAOEFG
metrography . . . . /MAERGT, /MAEFG
metrometer . . . . /MAOERMT
metropathism . . . . /MRO*EFM
metrope . . . . /MAOEP
metropia . . . . /MAOEPT
metropic . . . . /MAOEPG
metropsia . . . . /MOPTS
metrorrhagia . . . . /MRA*IJ
metrosalpingitis . . . . /MAOEPTS
metroscope . . . . /MAOERP
metry (*see also* ometry *and* imetry) . . . . /MRE
micra . . . . /MAO*IRK
micria . . . . /M*IRK
microbe . . . . /MROEB
microbial . . . . /MROEBL
microbic . . . . /MROEK
microcephaly . . . . /MAOEF
microcurie . . . . /MAOURK
microgram . . . . /MAOIRG
micrograph . . . . /MRAOF
micrography . . . . /MRAOFG
micrometer . . . . /MAOIRKT
micron . . . . /MIRN, /MAOIRNG
microns . . . . /MIRNS, /MAOIRNGS
microscope . . . . /MAOIRK
microscopic . . . . /MAOIRP
-microscopic . . . . /MAO*IRP
microscopical . . . . /MAOIRKL
microscopy . . . . /MOIRP
microsome . . . . /MAOIRM
microsomia . . . . /MAORM
mictio . . . . /MAO*ERB
miction . . . . /MO*IX
micturation . . . . /MAERGS
micturition . . . . /MAOURGS
migration . . . . /MAOIGS
millimeter . . . . /M–M
mimesis . . . . /MAOEMZ
mimetic . . . . /MIMT
mimetry . . . . /M–MT, /M*IRMT
mimia . . . . /M*IM

mimic . . . . . /MIMG
mimicry . . . . . /MAOERK
mine . . . . . /MAOIN
mineral. . . . . /MIRNL
mineralization . . . . . /MIRLGS
minerals . . . . . /MIRNLS
minimus . . . . . /MIMZ
miosis. . . . . /MOEZ
miotic . . . . . /M–KT
missible . . . . . /M–FBL
mission . . . . . /MIGS
mitochondria . . . . . /MAUND
mitochondrial . . . . . /MAUNLD
mitochondrion. . . . . /MAURND
mitosis . . . . . /MAOTS
mitotic . . . . . /MAUKT
mixis . . . . . /M*IXZ
mnemonic . . . . . /NONK
mnemonike . . . . . /N–MG
mnesia . . . . . /N–Z, /NAES
mnesic . . . . . /NAEFK
mnesis . . . . . /N–SZ, /NA*ESZ
mobility. . . . . /MOEBLT
modal. . . . . /MALD
model . . . . . /MOELD
modeling. . . . . /MOELGD
modulation . . . . . /MAEGS
modulator . . . . . /MAERJT
modulatory . . . . . /MORJ
moid . . . . . /MO*ID
molar . . . . . /MOEL, /MAO*RL
mole . . . . . /MO*EL
molecular . . . . . /KMERK, /KMARK
molecule. . . . . /KMAOUL
mongoloid . . . . . /MAUNG
monocyte . . . . . /MAO*INT
monomolecular . . . . . /MAORKL
morbid . . . . . /MOERBD
moron . . . . . /MAURN
morph . . . . . /MOEFR, /MOEF
morphia . . . . . /MAOFR
morphic. . . . . /MOEFRK, /MOERK
morphine . . . . . /MOFRB, /MOEFRN, /MOEFN
morphinism . . . . . /MOFRM
morphinisms . . . . . /MOFRMS

morphism	/MOIFM, /MOEFRM
morphogenesis	/MOFRJ
morphologist	/MOEFRLT
morphology	/MOEFRLG
morphophobia	/MOEFRB
morphopsia	/MOFPS
morphosis	/MOEFSZ, /MOEFRS
morphotic	/MOFRT
morphous	/MOUFS
morphy	/MOIFR
mortal	/MAORLT
motility	/MOILT
motion	/MOEGS
motivate	/MOEVT
motivation	/MOEVGS
motive	/MOEV
motonometer	/MAURNT
motor	/MOERT
motorius	/MOURTS
motory	/MO*ERT
mphalic (*see also* omphalic)	/O*EFK
mphalis (*see also* omphalis)	/O*EFZ
mphalocele (*see also* omphalocele)	/FLAO*EL
mphalos (*see also* omphalos)	/OEFMS
mphalus (*see also* omphalus)	/OUFMZ
mphraxis (*see also* emphraxis)	/KBRA*X
mucin	/MAOUNZ
mucinous	/MOUNS
mucoid	/MOIKD
mucoprotein	/MOIPT
mucormycosis	/MOERX
mucosa	/MOEKS
mucosal	/MOUKL, /MO*EKLS
mucotropic	/MAORPG
mucous	/MAOUK
mucus	/MAOUKS
munition	/MAO*UNGS
munitive	/MAOUV, /MAOUVT
mural	/MAOURL
mus	/M*UZ
muscular	/MUFRL
musculoskeletal	/MUKS, /MUFLZ
mutation	/MAIGS, /TAOUMGS
myal	/MYAL
myalgia	/MAOILG

myasthenia . . . /MENZ
myasthenic . . . /MENK
myatrophy . . . /MAOIF
myces . . . /MAOESZ
mycete . . . /MYAOET
mycetes . . . /MYAOETS
mycetic . . . /MYEKT
mycetolysis . . . /MAOIFLT, /MAOIFLTS
mycin . . . /SMIN, /MAOIFN
mycodermitis . . . /MIRMTS
mycosis . . . /MOESZ, /MAOIKS
mycotic . . . /MOKT
mycteria . . . /MOIRKT
myelencephalitis (*see also* myeloencephalitis) . . . /MEFLT
myelia . . . /MAO*EL, /MYAOEL
myelin . . . /MAOINL
myelinated . . . /MAOINLTD
myelination . . . /MAINGS
myelinic . . . /MOINK
myelinogenesis . . . /MOINSZ
myelinosis . . . /MAOINZ, /MAOINLSZ
myelins . . . /MAOINLZ
myelis . . . /MAOILZ
myelitic . . . /MIKT
myelitides . . . /MAOILTD, /MAOILTDZ
myelitis . . . /MAOILT, /MAOILTS
myeloblast . . . /YAFT
myeloblastosis . . . /YOEFT
myelocele . . . /YAOELS
myelocyte . . . /YLOIT
myelodysplasia . . . /YAIS
myeloencephalitis (*see also* myelencephalitis) . . . /MEFLTS, /YEFTS
myelogenous . . . /YOJS
myelography . . . /MAEF
myeloid . . . /MOILD
myelolymphocyte . . . /YOILT, /MIMPT
myeloma . . . /YOL
myelomalacia . . . /YAERB
myelomeningocele . . . /MOILS
myeloneuropathy . . . /MO*PT
myelopathy . . . /YO*PT
myelophthisis . . . /MAOIFSZ
myelopore . . . /MOERP
myeloradiculitis . . . /MOILTS
myeloradiculopathy . . . /MAOPT

myelosis . . . . . . /YOES
myelus . . . . . . /MAO*ILS
myesthesia . . . . . . /MAOES
myiasis . . . . . . /MAOIZ
myic . . . . . . /MO*IK
myitis . . . . . . /MAO*ITS
myloid . . . . . . /MO*ILD
myoblastoma . . . . . . /MAOIBL
myocardiac . . . . . . /MAURK
myocardial . . . . . . /MARL, /MA*URL
myocarditis . . . . . . /MAOITD
myoclonic . . . . . . /MAOINK
myoclonus . . . . . . /MAUKZ
myoclonus multiplex . . . . . . /MAUXZ
myodynia . . . . . . /MIND
myoendocarditis . . . . . . /MAOIDZ
myofibroma . . . . . . /MYOEM
myogenic . . . . . . /MOENK
myogram . . . . . . /MOIRM
myograph . . . . . . /MRAF
myography . . . . . . /MRAFG
myoid . . . . . . /MOID
myolipoma . . . . . . /MOEMP
myoliposis . . . . . . /MOEPSZ
myolysis . . . . . . /MOLSZ
myoma . . . . . . /MOIM
myomatosis . . . . . . /MOEMZ
myomatous . . . . . . /MYOEMT
myomectomy . . . . . . /MOIKT
myometer . . . . . . /MAOIRMT
myometrial . . . . . . /MAOIMT
myometritis . . . . . . /MAOIMTS
myomotomy . . . . . . /MOUT
myoneuroma . . . . . . /MOERM
myopathic . . . . . . /MAOIFK
myopathy . . . . . . /MA*ET
myopexy . . . . . . /MAOIPX
myopia . . . . . . /MAOP
myoplasty . . . . . . /MAS
myoplegia . . . . . . /MAO*EJ
myosarcoma . . . . . . /MO*ERM, /SKMOEM
myosin . . . . . . /MAOINS
myosinogen . . . . . . /MYENG
myosis . . . . . . /MOISZ
myositis . . . . . . /MAOITS

myotomy . . . . /MOT
myotonia . . . . /MOINT
myotonus . . . . /MOENTS
myotrophy . . . . /MOIF
myringitis . . . . /MAOIRNTS
mysia . . . . /MY–S
mysial . . . . /MAOEFLS, /MY–LS
mysiitis . . . . /MOITS
mysium . . . . /MAOIMZ, /MYUM
myxedema . . . . /MAOEMD
myxia . . . . /MAOEKS, /MAOEKZ
myxoadenoma . . . . /MOIMD
myxochondroma . . . . /MYOEMD
myxoma . . . . /MAUM
myxorrhea . . . . /MAOERX
myxosarcoma . . . . /MAURM
myxovirus . . . . /MAOIVR
myxoviruses . . . . /MAOIVRS

N

nanosoma . . . . /NAONS
narcoanalysis . . . . /NAURLS
narcolepsy . . . . /NARP
narcosis . . . . /NARKSZ
narcotic . . . . /NARKT
narcotism . . . . /NAOFM
nares . . . . /NAERZ
narial . . . . /NA*IRL
nasal . . . . /NAILZ
nasale . . . . /NAELZ
nasality . . . . /NAILTS
nasion . . . . /NONZ
natal . . . . /NAILT
natalogist . . . . /NAOLT
natant . . . . /NAINT
nate . . . . /NAIT
nated . . . . /NAITD
nation . . . . /NAIGS
natology . . . . /NAOLG
natremia . . . . /NAOERMT
natremic . . . . /NAOERMG
natriuresis . . . . /NAOERTS
natruria . . . . /TRAOUR

natured /NAIFPD

nauseant /NAUNT

navicular /NAFRBL, /NAFRL

ncus (*see also* oncus) /O*NG

nebulous /NEB

necrectomy /NERKT

necronectomy /NONGT

necrosis /NEXZ

necrospermia /NAERMS

necrotic /NROKT

ncus (*see also* oncus) /O*NG

nebulous /NEB

necrectomy /NERKT

necronectomy /NONGT

necrosis /NEXZ

necrospermia /NAERMS

necrotic /NROKT

necteur /N*URKT

nectin /NENK

nectins /NENKS

nectomy /N*EKT

nector /NAORKT

needle /NAOELD

negative /NEG

negativity /NAIGT, /NAEGT

nema /NA*EM

neme /N*EM

nemia /NAO*EM

neocystostomy /NAOEFT

neocytosis /SNOETS

neogenesis /NOJSZ, /NEJSZ

neogenetic /NOJT

neoplasia /NLAIS

neoplasm /NAZ

neoplastic /NLAS

neopyelostomy /NAOEPT

neostomy /NAO*EZ

neovaginorectal /NAOEVJ, /NAOEVRJ

neovulvar /NUVL

nephrectomy /FREKT

nephria /FRAIF

nephrial /FREFL

nephric /FROIK

nephrine /NEFRN

nephritic /FRIKT

nephritis . . . . /FRAOITS
nephrium . . . . /FRUFM, /FR*UM
nephrogenesis . . . . /FREJSZ
nephrogenic . . . . /FROEG
nephroi . . . . /FROI
nephroid. . . . /NOIPD
nephrolithiasis. . . . /NAO*ITS
nephroma . . . . /FROEM
nephromegaly . . . . /NEFMG
nephron. . . . /FRON
nephronia . . . . /FRAON
nephronic . . . . /FRAONG
nephropathy. . . . /FROP
nephropexy . . . . /NAOFX
nephroptosis. . . . /FROPT
nephros. . . . /NEFZ, /FROS
nephrosclerosis . . . . /FROESZ
nephrosis . . . . /FROES
nephrostomy . . . . /FROMT
nephrotic . . . . /FROKT
nephrotoxin . . . . /FROX
nephroureterectomy . . . . /NEFRKT
nephrous . . . . /FROUZ
nerval. . . . /NEFRBL
ness . . . . /*NS
neural . . . . /NURL
neuralgia . . . . /NAULG, /NAJ
neuralgic . . . . /NAUKL
neurasthenia . . . . /NAOENT
neure . . . . /NAO*R
neurectomy . . . . /NURKT
neuria. . . . /N*IR
neurial . . . . /NOIRL, /N*IRL
neuric . . . . /N*URK
neurine. . . . /NIRN
neurite . . . . /NAORT
neuritic. . . . /N*IRKT
neuritis . . . . /NAOIRTS
neurium . . . . /NIRM
neuroanastomosis. . . . /NO*ES
neuroblastoma . . . . /NOURM
neurocytoma . . . . /NOIRMT
neurofibroma. . . . /NOEFM
neurography. . . . /NAEF
neuroimmunology. . . . /NOURLG

neurologic . . . . . /NURK
neurology . . . . . /NURLG
neurolysis . . . . . /NOURLS
neuroma . . . . . /NOERM
neuromatosis . . . . . /NOEMS
neuromere . . . . . /NAO*ERM
neuromyelitis . . . . . /NAOILT, /NAOILTS
neuromyography . . . . . /NAEFG
neuromyoma . . . . . /NAOIRM
neuromyositis . . . . . /NOURMTS
neuron . . . . . /NAOURN
neuronal . . . . . /NAOURNL
neuronophagia . . . . . /NAIRJ, /NA*IJ
neurons . . . . . /NAOURNS
neuropathic . . . . . /NURPG
neuropathy . . . . . /NURPT
neuroradiculitis . . . . . /NAURLT
neurorrhaphy . . . . . /NAFP, /NAEFP
neuroses . . . . . /NAOURSZ
neurosis . . . . . /NAOURS
neurositis . . . . . /NAORTS
neurosurgeon . . . . . /NAORN
neurosurgeons . . . . . /NAORNS
neurosurgery . . . . . /NAORNG
neurotic . . . . . /NAOURKT
neurotization . . . . . /NURGS
neurotome . . . . . /NOEMT
neurotomy . . . . . /NAUT
neurotoxin . . . . . /NOURX
neutron . . . . . /NAORNT
neutrophil . . . . . /NAOUFLT
neutrophile . . . . . /NAOIFL
neurotropic . . . . . /NOPG
nevus . . . . . /NAOEVS
nidal . . . . . /NOILD
nigral . . . . . /NAOILG
nin . . . . . /N*IN
nine . . . . . /NAOIN
nitrate . . . . . /NAOIRT
nitremia . . . . . /NAOEMT
nitrogen . . . . . /NAOIJ
nitroglycerin . . . . . /NAOIRNG
nitroglycerol . . . . . /NAOIRL
nocardiosis . . . . . /NOEKD, /NAURKD
nodal . . . . . /NAOLD

node . . . . /NOED
nodi . . . . /N*ID
noditis . . . . /NO*ITS
nodular . . . . /NAOURLD
nodulate . . . . /NAORLT
noduli . . . . /NOUD
nodus . . . . /NOUDZ
noia . . . . /NO*I
noid . . . . /NO*D
noma (*see also* inoma) . . . . /NAO*M
nome . . . . /NOM
nomia . . . . /NA*M
nomic . . . . /NAUMG
nomics . . . . /NAUMGS
nominate . . . . /NOMT
nomous . . . . /NOMS
nomy (*see also* gnomy) . . . . /NO*IM
normal . . . . /NOL
normalcy . . . . /NOLZ
normality . . . . /NOILT
normally . . . . /NOIL
normity . . . . /NO*RMT
normoblast . . . . /NORBL
normocytosis . . . . /NORMSZ
nosic . . . . /NOFK
nosis (*see also* osis) . . . . /NO*ESZ
nosology . . . . /SNOLG
nosus . . . . /NUSZ
ntogenic (*see also* ontogenic) . . . . /O*NGT
nuclear . . . . /NAOUKL
nuclease . . . . /NLAIZ
nucleate . . . . /NAOUKLT
nucleated . . . . /NAOUKLTD, /NAOUKTD
nucleation . . . . /NAOUKLGS
nucleolar . . . . /KLAOURL
nucleolus . . . . /KLULS, /NOEKLS
nucleoprotein . . . . /NAOUPG
nucleoside . . . . /NAOUKLD
nucleosis . . . . /NOELZ
nucleotide . . . . /NAOULGD
nucleus . . . . /NAOUX
nuclide . . . . /NUK, /NUKD
nuclides . . . . /NUKZ, /NUKDZ
numerary . . . . /NA*ERM
nutrient . . . . /TRAOENT

nutrients . . . . /TRAOENTS
nutrition . . . . /TRURB, /NUGS
nychia (*see also* onychia) . . . . /AO*NK
nychial (*see also* onychial) . . . . /AOFP
nychium (*see also* onychium) . . . . /O*UM
nychon (*see also* onychon) . . . . /O*FP
nychosis (*see also* onychosis) . . . . /O*EFPS
nym . . . . /NY*M
nymous . . . . /NOUMS
nymy (*see also* onymy) . . . . /NY–M
nystagmograph . . . . /NIFG
nystagmography . . . . /NAOEFG
nystagmus . . . . /N*IS
nystaxis . . . . /NAXZ
nyx (*see also* onyx) . . . . /O*NX, /ONGZ
nyxis (*see also* onyxis) . . . . /O*NXZ

O

obesity . . . . /OEBT
obstruction . . . . /BRUX
-obstruction . . . . /BR*UX
occipital (*see also* ccipital) . . . . /SIPT
-occipital . . . . /S*IPT
occiput . . . . /SPUT
occlude . . . . /KLAOD
occlusal (*see also* cclusal *and* clusal) . . . . /KLAOL
-occlusal . . . . /KLAOLS, /KLAO*L
occlusion (*see also* clusion) . . . . /KLAOGS
-occlusion . . . . /KLAO*GS
occlusive . . . . /KLAOV
-occlusive . . . . /KLAOF
oclasis (*see also* clasis) . . . . /KLAOZ
oclastic (*see also* clastic) . . . . /KLAFKT
oclusion (*see also* occlusion) . . . . /KLOUGS
ocular (*see also* cular) . . . . /AUK
-ocular . . . . /A*UK
ocularity (*see also* cularity) . . . . /AUKLT
-oculogram . . . . /AUKL
-oculography . . . . /AUFK
ocyte (*see also* cyte) . . . . /SO*IT
ode . . . . /O*ED
odinia (*see also* dinia) . . . . /DO*IN
odmia . . . . /OMD

odontalgia . . . . /DAONL
-odontalgia . . . . /DAONLG
odontalgic. . . . . /DAONK
odontia (*see also* dontia) . . . . /DORBT
odontiasis (*see also* dontiasis). . . . . /DAOIRB
odontitis (*see also* dontitis) . . . . /DAOINTS, /DAO*ITS
odontium (*see also* dontium) . . . . /DAO*ERB
odontodynia . . . . /DAOND
-odontodynia. . . . . /DAO*ND
odontoid . . . . /OIND
-odontoid . . . . /OINTD
odontoma (*see also* dontoma) . . . . /DWOM
-odontoma. . . . . /DWAUM
odynia (*see also* dynia). . . . . /DOIND, /DO*EN
official. . . . . /FIRBL
ogen (*see also* gen) . . . . /OIG
ogenesis (*see also* genesis) . . . . /G*ENSZ, /J*ENSZ
ogenetic (*see also* genetic) . . . . /G*ENT
ogenetics (*see also* genetics) . . . . /G*ENTS
ogenic (*see also* genic) . . . . /G*ENG
ogenicity (*see also* genicity) . . . . /G*INT
ogenics (*see also* genics). . . . . /G*ENGS
ogenous (*see also* genous). . . . . /O*J
ogens (*see also* gens) . . . . /OIGS
ogeny (*see also* geny) . . . . /GO*IN
ohm . . . . /O*EM
-ohm . . . . /O*IM
oid . . . . /OID
oidal (*see also* idal) . . . . /OILD
oidism (*see also* idism) . . . . /OIFMD
oids (*see also* ids) . . . . /OIDZ
oliguric . . . . /GLURK
olivary . . . . /LAIV, /LOIVL
-olivary . . . . /LAIVR
ologies (*see also* logies *and* tologies) . . . . /OLGS
ologist (*see also* logist *and* tologist) . . . . /OLT
ologists (*see also* logists *and* tologists). . . . . /OLTS
ology (*see also* logy *and* tology) . . . . /OLG
olyses (*see also* lyses). . . . . /OLZ
olysin (*see also* lysin) . . . . /LOFN
olysis (*see also* lysis *and* tolysis) . . . . /OLS
olytic (*see also* lytic *and* tolytic). . . . . /L*IKT, /LOKT
olytics (*see also* lytics) . . . . /LOKTS, /L*IKTS
olytopoietic (*see also* lytopoietic) . . . . /LOIPGT
oma . . . . /OEM

omas . . . /OEMS
omatosis (*see also* matosis) . . . /OEMZ
omentopexy . . . /MAOPX
-omentopexy . . . /MOEPX
ometer (*see also* meter) . . . /MAO*ERT
ometers (*see also* meters) . . . /MAO*ERTS
ometra (*see also* metra) . . . /MA*ERT
ometry (*see also* metry) . . . /MR*E
omohyoid . . . /O*IMD
omphalic (*see also* mphalic) . . . /OEFK
omphalis (*see also* mphalis) . . . /OEFS
omphalocele (*see also* mphalocele) . . . /FLAOEL
omphalos (*see also* mphalos) . . . /OEFM
omphalus (*see also* mphalus) . . . /OUFMS, /OUMZ
on . . . /ON
-oncogene . . . /O*UNG
oncogenic . . . /OEJ
oncology . . . /AUNL
-oncology . . . /A*UNL
oncotic . . . /AUNGT
-oncotic . . . /A*UNGT
oncus (*see also* ncus) . . . /ONG
one . . . /O*EN, /WUN
ontogenesis . . . /OENTS
ontogenetic . . . /OENGT
ontogenic (*see also* ntogenic) . . . /ONGT
onychia (*see also* nychia) . . . /AONK
onychial (*see also* nychial) . . . /AOFPL
onychium (*see also* nychium) . . . /OUM
onychomycosis . . . /OEMSZ
onychon (*see also* nychon) . . . /OFP
onychosis (*see also* nychosis) . . . /OEFPS
onymy (*see also* nymy) . . . /NA*UM
onyx (*see also* nyx) . . . /ONX
onyxis (*see also* nyxis) . . . /ONXZ
oophorectomy . . . /FAOFK
-oophorectomy . . . /FAOFR, /FAO*FK
oophoritis . . . /FROETS
-oophoritis . . . /FRO*ETS
-oophorocele . . . /FRAOFL
oophorosalpingitis . . . /FRAOIPT, /FRAOIPTS
oothecitis . . . /AO*TS
-oothecitis . . . /A*UTS
-oothecocele . . . /THOEK, /THOEKL
oothecosalpingitis . . . /THAOIJ, /THAOIJS

opacity (*see also* pacity) . . . . . /PAOFT
–opacity . . . . . /PAO*FT
opalgia. . . . . /PAOLG, /AOLG
opaque . . . . . /PAEG
opathic (*see also* pathic) . . . . . /PAOFK, /OPG
opathies (*see also* pathies). . . . . /O*PTS
opathy (*see also* pathy). . . . . /O*PT
ope . . . . . /O*EP
openia (*see also* penia) . . . . . /PO*EN
opening. . . . . /OEPG
operable . . . . . /PRAIBL
operative . . . . . /PRAIV
operculum . . . . . /PERKL
ophage (*see also* phage). . . . . /FA*EJ
ophagia (*see also* phagia) . . . . . /FA*IJ
ophagous (*see also* phagous). . . . . /FO*UG
ophagy (*see also* phagy) . . . . . /FO*IJ
ophobia (*see also* phobia) . . . . . /FOB
ophrys . . . . . /FROIS
ophthalmia (*see also* phthalmia). . . . . /FAUM
ophthalmic (*see also* phthalmic) . . . . . /FAUK, /FAUMG
ophthalmitis (*see also* phthalmitis) . . . . . /FAUMT, /FAUMTS
-ophthalmitis. . . . . /FOIMTS
ophthalmodonesis (*see also* phthalmodonesis) . . . . . /MAOEFS
ophthalmologist . . . . . /MOLT
-ophthalmologist . . . . . /MO*LT
ophthalmologists . . . . . /MOLTS
ophthalmology. . . . . /MOLG
-ophthalmology . . . . . /MO*LG
ophthalmometer (*see also* phthalmometer) . . . . . /FAORMT
ophthalmoncus . . . . . /FONGS
ophthalmopathy . . . . . /FAEPT
-ophthalmopathy . . . . . /FA*EPT
ophthalmos (*see also* phthalmos) . . . . . /FOS
ophthalmoscope (*see also* phthalmoscope). . . . . /FOEPT
-ophthalmoscope . . . . . /FOPT
ophthalmotomy (*see also* phthalmotomy) . . . . . /MAUPT
ophthalmous (*see also* phthalmous) . . . . . /FOUMS
ophthalmus (*see also* phthalmus) . . . . . /FAUS
ophthisis (*see also* phthisis) . . . . . /THAO*ISZ
ophthongia (*see also* phthongia). . . . . /PONG
opia (*see also* pia) . . . . . /AOP, /YOP
opic (*see also* pic) . . . . . /AOPG, /YOPG
oplasty (*see also* plasty) . . . . . /PLAOS
ops . . . . . /OPZ

opsia (*see also* psia) . . . . /AUPZ
opsin. . . . /A*UPS
opsis (*see also* psis) . . . . /AUPSZ
opsonic . . . . /PO*PG
opsonin (*see also* psonin). . . . /POPZ
-opsonin . . . . /PO*PS
opsy (*see also* psy) . . . . /OIPS
opter . . . . /OIPT
opterygium (*see also* pterygium) . . . . /TROEJ
optic (*see also* ptic) . . . . /AUPT, /TAUPT
-optic . . . . /TA*UPT
optics (*see also* ptics) . . . . /AUPTS, /TAUPTS
optimal. . . . /AUM
optometer (*see also* ptometer). . . . /AURMT
-optometer . . . . /A*URMT
optometry (*see also* ptometry). . . . /TROMT
optosia (*see also* ptosia) . . . . /O*EPT, /TO*EZ
optosis (*see also* ptosis) . . . . /O*EPTS, /TO*ESZ
optotic (*see also* ptotic). . . . /TOPGT
optysis (*see also* ptysis) . . . . /TAO*ISZ
orad . . . . /OERD
oral . . . . /ORL
-oral . . . . /O*RL
orbicular . . . . /BARKL, /BIRKL
-orbicular . . . . /BAORKL, /BA*RKL
orbit . . . . /ORBT
orbita . . . . /AORBT
orbital (*see also* rbital) . . . . /ORBL
-orbital. . . . /OERBL
orbitale . . . . /ORBLT
orbititis . . . . /AOIBTS
orbitography . . . . /OIFRG
-orbitography. . . . /O*IFRG
orchial. . . . /ORKL
orchid (*see also* rchid) . . . . /AORKD
orchidectomy (*see also* rchidectomy) . . . . /OERKT
orchidia (*see also* rchidia). . . . /OIKD
-orchidia. . . . /O*IKD
orchidic (*see also* rchidic) . . . . /OERKTD
orchidism . . . . /OERKD
-orchidism . . . . /O*ERKD
orchidium . . . . /KHORK
orchidopexy (*see also* rchidopexy) . . . . /OEPX
orchidostomy . . . . /OFPD
-orchidostomy . . . . /OEFPD

orchis . . . . /ORKZ
orchism . . . . /OFRM
orchitis . . . . /KHAOIRTS
-orchitis . . . . /KHAO*IRTS
orchium (*see also* rchium) . . . . /OURM
order . . . . /OD
orexia . . . . /OERX
organic . . . . /GANK
organism . . . . /GOFM, /GIFM
organization . . . . /ORGS
orient . . . . /OERNT
orientation . . . . /OERNGS
orificial . . . . /AOFRL, /OIFRL
orrhagia (*see also* rrhagia) . . . . /RO*ERJ
orrhea (*see also* rrhea) . . . . /RAO*E
orthic . . . . /OIRK, /O*IRT
orthics . . . . /OIRX, /O*IRTS
orthist . . . . /OIRT
orthists . . . . /OIRTS
orthocytosis . . . . /STO*RT
-orthocytosis . . . . /STO*RTS
orthography . . . . /THOEF
orthopnea . . . . /THOPT
-orthopter . . . . /THRORPT
orthosis . . . . /THOESZ
ory . . . . /OIR
oscheocele (*see also* scheocele) . . . . /SKAEL
oscheos . . . . /SKHES
oscheotomy (*see also* scheotomy) . . . . /SKROT
oscillometer . . . . /SKLAOERMT
-oscillometer . . . . /SKLAO*ERMT
oscopies (*see also* scopies) . . . . /SKOIPZ, /SKO*IPS
oscopy (*see also* scopy) . . . . /SKO*IP
osculate . . . . /SKLAT, /SKLAOT
osculating . . . . /SKLAGT, /SKLAOGT
osculation . . . . /SKLAGS
ose (*see also* se) . . . . /O*ES
osed . . . . /OEFD
oses (*see also* ses) . . . . /SESZ
osis (*see also* tosis *and* sis) . . . . /OESZ
ositol (*see also* sitol) . . . . /SO*ILT
osmatic (*see also* smatic) . . . . /SMAUK
osmia (*see also* smia) . . . . /OMS, /OZ
osmic (*see also* smic) . . . . /SMAUS
osmolality . . . . /SMALT

osmolarity (*see also* smolarity) . . . . . . /SMAIRLT
-osmolarity . . . . . . /SMAERLT
osmole . . . . . . /SMOELS, /SMOLS
osmometer (*see also* smometer) . . . . . . /SMORMT
osmosis (*see also* smosis) . . . . . . /SMOES
-osmosis . . . . . . /SMOESZ
osmotic (*see also* smotic) . . . . . . /SMIKT, /SMOEKT
-osmotic . . . . . . /SMOT
osmous (*see also* smous) . . . . . . /OUMS
osphrasia (*see also* sphrasia) . . . . . . /SFRAIS
osphresia (*see also* sphresia) . . . . . . /SFRAOEZ
osphresis . . . . . . /SFRAOESZ
osseal . . . . . . /SA*EL
osseous . . . . . . /SUSZ
-osseous . . . . . . /S*USZ
ossification . . . . . . /SOFGS
ost . . . . . . /A*UZ
ostasis (*see also* stasis) . . . . . . /OSZ
osteal (*see also* steal) . . . . . . /STEL
ostealgia (*see also* stealgia) . . . . . . /STELG
ostectomy . . . . . . /STAOKT
osteitis (*see also* steitis) . . . . . . /STOIT, /STOITS
ostenosis (*see also* stenosis) . . . . . . /SNO*ESZ
osteoarthropathy . . . . . . /TWARPT, /TWORPT
osteochondrodysplasia . . . . . . /STAIDZ, /TWAIDZ
-osteochondrodysplasia . . . . . . /STA*IDZ, /TWA*IDZ
-osteodysplasia . . . . . . /TWLAIS
osteodystrophy . . . . . . /TWROF
-osteodystrophy . . . . . . /TWRO*F
osteogenesis . . . . . . /TWEJS
osteogeny . . . . . . /TWOJ
osteoid . . . . . . /TWO*ID
osteology . . . . . . /TWOLG
osteolysis . . . . . . /TWOLS
-osteolysis . . . . . . /TWOLSZ
osteoma (*see also* steoma) . . . . . . /TWOEM
-osteoma . . . . . . /TWOM
osteomalacia . . . . . . /TWAERB
-osteomalacia . . . . . . /TWA*ERB
-osteomalacic . . . . . . /TWA*ERK
osteomalacic . . . . . . /TWAERK
osteomyelitis . . . . . . /TWAOILTS
osteon (*see also* steon) . . . . . . /STAOEN
osteopathy . . . . . . /TWAEPT
osteophlebitis . . . . . . /TWEP

-osteophlebitis . . . . . . TW*EP
osteophyte (*see also* steophyte) . . . . . . /TWHAOIT
osteoplasia . . . . . . /TWAEZ
osteoplasty . . . . . . /TWAS
-osteoplasty . . . . . . /TWA*S
osteorrhaphy . . . . . . /TWRAEF
osteosis (*see also* steosis) . . . . . . /TWOEFS
osteotomy . . . . . . /TWOT
osteum (*see also* steum) . . . . . . /STEMT, /TWEMT
ostitis (*see also* stitis) . . . . . . /TWOIT, /TWOITS
ostium (*see also* stium) . . . . . . /TWUMT, /STUMT
ostogavage (*see also* stogavage) . . . . . . /STAOVJ
ostolavage (*see also* stolavage) . . . . . . /TLAOVJ
ostoma (*see also* stoma) . . . . . . /STO*EM
ostomies (*see also* stomy) . . . . . . /O*SZ
ostomy (*see also* stomy) . . . . . . /O*S
ostoses . . . . . . /STAOEZ
ostosis (*see also* stosis) . . . . . . /STAUSZ, /TWOSZ
ostotic (*see also* stotic) . . . . . . /STO*EKT
otia (*see also* tia) . . . . . . /TWOIK, /SHAE
otic (*see also* tic) . . . . . . /OKT
otics (*see also* tics) . . . . . . /OKTS
otitis (*see also* titis) . . . . . . /TWAOTS
-otitis . . . . . . /TWAO*TS
otology (*see also* tology) . . . . . . /TAULG, /TOELG
-otology . . . . . . /TA*ULG, /TO*ELG
otome (*see also* tome) . . . . . . /TO*EM
otomes (*see also* tomes) . . . . . . /TO*EMS
otomies (*see also* tomies) . . . . . . /OTS
otomy (*see also* tomy) . . . . . . /OT
otoscope (*see also* toscope) . . . . . . /TOEPS
otus (*see also* tus) . . . . . . /YOETS
ous (*see also* tous) . . . . . . /OUS
oval . . . . . . /OVL
ovaria (*see also* varia) . . . . . . /VA*IR
ovarial . . . . . . /OIVL, /OIVRL
ovarian . . . . . . /AOVN, /VARN, /OIVN
-ovarian . . . . . . /VA*RN, /VA*IRN
ovarianism (*see also* varianism) . . . . . . /AOVNS
-ovarianism . . . . . . /AOVNZ
-ovariectomy . . . . . . /AO*K
ovariotomy . . . . . . /OIVT
-ovariotomy . . . . . . /OEVT
ovarism . . . . . . /AOVM
ovaritis . . . . . . /AOFT, /AOFTS

-ovaritis . . . . . /OEVRTS
ovarium (*see also* varium) . . . . . /VAIRM
-ovarium . . . . . /VAORM
oviparous . . . . . /VIPS
ovovegetarian . . . . . /VAORJ
-ovovegetarian . . . . . /VORJ
ovular . . . . . /OEVRL, /AOVRL
-ovular . . . . . /VOURL
ovulation . . . . . /OVLGS, /OEVLGS
-ovulation . . . . . /AOVLGS
ovulatory . . . . . /OEVRLT, /AOVRLT
ovum (*see also* vum) . . . . . /OEVM
oxaluria . . . . . /KPLAOUR
oxanthine (*see also* xanthine) . . . . . /ZAONT
oxemia (*see also* xemia) . . . . . /KPIM
oxenous (*see also* xenous) . . . . . /KPOUS
oxia . . . . . /O*X
oxic (*see also* xic) . . . . . /KPOK
oxidant . . . . . /KPOKD
oxidants . . . . . /KPOKDZ
oxidase . . . . . /SDAIS
-oxidase . . . . . /SDAIZ
oxidation (*see also* xidation) . . . . . /SHAEGS
oxide . . . . . /KPAOID
oxides . . . . . /KPAOIDZ
oxidosis (*see also* xidosis) . . . . . /OEXZ
oxiduria . . . . . /KPAOUR
oxygen . . . . . /SHEN
oxygenase . . . . . /SHAIS, /SHAIZ
-oxygenase . . . . . /SHAES, /SHAEZ
oxygenases . . . . . /SHAISZ
-oxygenases . . . . . /SHAESZ
oxygenation . . . . . /SHAIGS

P

pacer . . . . . /PAIFR
pachia . . . . . /POIFP
pachy . . . . . /PAUFP
pachyderma . . . . . /PA*ERM, /PAERKD
pachymeningitis . . . . . /PAOIMT, /PAOIMTS
pachynsis . . . . . /PAXZ
pacing . . . . . /PAIFG
pacity (*see also* opacity) . . . . . /PO*IFT

pagus . . . . /PUGS
paic . . . . /PA*IK
pain . . . . /PAIN
pains . . . . /PAINS
palatal . . . . /PLA*L
palatine . . . . /PLAOIN
palatinus . . . . /PLUNS
palatodigital . . . . /PLIJ, /PLIJT
palatopharyngoplasty . . . . /PLAOPS
palinal . . . . /PLAUNL
pallesthesia . . . . /PLAO*ETS, /PLAOEZ
pallial . . . . /PLAIL
pallidal . . . . /PLALD
pallidectomy . . . . /PLIKD
pallidothalamectomy . . . . /PAOKT
pallidotomy . . . . /PAOLTD
pallium . . . . /PLUL
palmar . . . . /PRAUM
palmus . . . . /PUMZ
palpation . . . . /PALGS
palpebral . . . . /PREBL
palpitation . . . . /PAIPGS
paludal . . . . /PLULD
paludism . . . . /PLUFM, /PLIFMZ
pancreas . . . . /PAENK
pancreatectomy . . . . /PRAENGT
pancreatic . . . . /PRAENK
pancreatism . . . . /PRAEFM
pancreatitis . . . . /PAOITS
pancreatography . . . . /PRAEF, /PRAEFT
pancreorrhea . . . . /PRAOENK
panendoscopy . . . . /PRO*IP
papillary . . . . /PLAER
papilledema . . . . /PLAOEMD
papillitis . . . . /PLOITS
papilloma . . . . /PLAUM
papular . . . . /PLAURP
papule . . . . /PLAOUL
paque . . . . /PAUK
para (*see also* ipara) . . . . /PA*UR
paracentesis . . . . /PRAOENTS
parallaxis . . . . /PLAURXZ
parallel . . . . /PAERL
paralysis . . . . /PRALS
paralytic . . . . /PAIRLT, /PRALT

paraplegia . . . . /PLAOEJ
parasalpinx . . . . /PRINX
parasite . . . . /PROIT
parasitic . . . . /PROIK
parasiticide . . . . /PROITD
parasitism . . . . /PROIFM
parasitus . . . . /PRARTS
parathyreosis . . . . /PO*ETS
parathyroidectomy . . . . /PR*EKT
parathyroidism . . . . /PAOIFM
parathyroprival . . . . /PAUVL
parathyroprivic . . . . /PRAIVK
parathyrosis . . . . /PRAOIRSZ
parectasis . . . . /PRAIKTS
parelkysis . . . . /PREKLS
parenchyma . . . . /PRAN
parenchymal . . . . /PRANL
parenchymatous . . . . /PROUNTS
parency . . . . /PARNSZ
parent . . . . /PARNT
parental . . . . /PARNLT
paresis . . . . /PRAOES
paresthesia . . . . /PRAOEZ
paretic . . . . /PARKT, /PAERKT
pareunia . . . . /PRAO*UN
paric . . . . /PA*URK
parietal . . . . /PRAOILT
parietopexy . . . . /PRAOIPX
parity . . . . /PAIRT
parkinsonism . . . . /PRAFM
parotidism . . . . /PROFMD
parotitis . . . . /PAORTS
parous (*see also* iparous) . . . . /PAIRZ
paroxysmal . . . . /PROXL
partal . . . . /PAURLT
partial . . . . /PARB
particle . . . . /PARL
partite . . . . /PA*URT
partum . . . . /PAURMT
parturient . . . . /PRAOURNT
patch . . . . /PAFP
patellar . . . . /PLART
patent . . . . /PAENT
path . . . . /PA*T
pathetic . . . . /TH*EKT

pathia . . . . /PA*IT
pathic (*see also* opathic) . . . . /PAFK
pathical . . . . /PAFBL, /PAFKL
pathies (*see also* opathies) . . . . /PA*ETS
pathism . . . . /PAFMT, /PA*FM
pathist . . . . /PAFT, /PAIFT
pathists . . . . /PAFTS, /PAIFTS
pathogen . . . . /PENG, /PA*GT
pathogenesis . . . . /PENSZ
pathogenetic . . . . /PENGT
pathogenic . . . . /PENK
pathogenicity . . . . /PEJ, /PEJT
pathologic . . . . /THOJ
pathological . . . . /THALT
pathologies . . . . /THOLGS, /THAOLGS
pathologist . . . . /THOLT, /THAOLT
pathology . . . . /THAOLG, /THOLG
pathophobia . . . . /POEB
paths . . . . /PA*TS
pathy (*see also* opathy) . . . . /PA*ET
patient . . . . /PAIRB, /PAIRBT
pause . . . . /PAUS
pax . . . . /PA*X
peak . . . . /PAEK
pectic . . . . /POIKT
pectin . . . . /P*EKT
pectineal . . . . /PAENGT
pectoral . . . . /PEKL
pectoralis . . . . /PEKLS, /PRILS
pedal . . . . /PELD
pedesis . . . . /PAOEDZ
pedia . . . . /PAED
pedic . . . . /P–KD
pedics . . . . /PAEDZ, /PAOEKS
pedicular . . . . /PARKL, /PAOERKL
pediculate . . . . /PAOEKL
pedion . . . . /PYOND
pedist . . . . /PAEFT
pedium . . . . /PAO*EMD
peduncular . . . . /PURKL
peia . . . . /PA*E
peic . . . . /PAO*EK
pelade . . . . /PLA*D
peliopexy . . . . /PLAOEX
pellic . . . . /P*EKL

pellous . . . . . /PLELS
pelvectomy . . . . . /PEFKT, /PEVKT
pelvic . . . . . /PEFK, /PEVK
pelvimetry . . . . . /PEVMT, /PEFMT
pelvioneostomy . . . . . /PAOEVT
pelvioplasty . . . . . /PAVLT
pelviperitoneal . . . . . /PEVRNL, /PEVNL
pelviperitonitis . . . . . /PEVLT, /PEVLTS
pelyx . . . . . /PEKLZ
penetrance . . . . . /PRANZ
penetration . . . . . /PRAINGS
penia (*see also* openia) . . . . . /PAOEN
penial . . . . . /PAONL
penic . . . . . /PAOENG
penile . . . . . /PAOINL
penis. . . . . . /PAOENS
penniform . . . . . /POFM
pepsia . . . . . /PEPS
pepsin . . . . . /PEFN, /PEPZ
pepsinemia . . . . . /PAOEFMS
pepsinia . . . . . /PENZ
pepsinogen . . . . . /PEPGS
pepsinuria . . . . . /PAOURN
pepsis . . . . . /PEPSZ
peptic . . . . . /PEPT
peptid . . . . . /PEPTD
peptidase . . . . . /PAIDZ
peptide . . . . . /PAOIPTD
peptidorrhachia . . . . . /PREPTD
peptin . . . . . /P*EPT
peptone . . . . . /POEPT
peptonuria . . . . . /PAORP
perception . . . . . /SPEPGS
perceptive . . . . . /SPIV
percolation . . . . . /PERX
percussion . . . . . /PRURB, /PRURBGS
perforate . . . . . /FRAET
perfusion . . . . . /PUFGS
periarteritis . . . . . /PRAERTS
pericardiac . . . . . /PRAURK
pericardial . . . . . /PRARL
pericardiopexy . . . . . /PRAOX
pericarditis . . . . . /PRARD
pericardium . . . . . /PAURMD, /PARMD
pericyte . . . . . /POIRT

pericytoma. . . . . . /POEM, /POEMT
perimyocarditis . . . . . . /PRARMD
perineal . . . . . . /PRAOENL
perineoplasty. . . . . . /PIRNS
perineorrhaphy . . . . . . /PAEFG
perineoscrotal . . . . . . /PROELT
perineostomy . . . . . . /PRO*ES
perineotomy. . . . . . /PAOERNT
perinephrosis . . . . . . /PROEFSZ
perineuritis . . . . . . /PERTS
period . . . . . . /PERD
periodic . . . . . . /PERGD
periodicity. . . . . . /PEFRT
periodism . . . . . . /PEFRM
periodontitis. . . . . . /PRONTS
periodynia . . . . . . /PROED
periosteal . . . . . . /PRAOEL
periosteals . . . . . . /PRAOELZ
periosteum . . . . . . /PRUMT, /PRAOM
periostitis. . . . . . /PRIT, /PRITS
periphacitis . . . . . . /PAOIFTS
periphakitis . . . . . . /PAOIKS
periphery . . . . . . /PRAOEF
peristalsis . . . . . . /PRELZ, /PRELSZ
peristaltic . . . . . . /PERLT
peristole . . . . . . /PRIFLT
perithelium . . . . . . /PRAOELT
peritoneal . . . . . . /PIRNL
peritoneoabdominal. . . . . . /PRAONL
peritoneography . . . . . . /PRIFG
peritoneopelvic . . . . . . /PRAOVK
peritoneum . . . . . . /PIRM
peritonia . . . . . . /PRAONT
peritonitis . . . . . . /PRAOITS
permeability . . . . . . /P–BLT
permeable . . . . . . /P–BL
peroneal . . . . . . /PRONL
peroxidase . . . . . . /PRAIKD, /PRAIKDZ
peroxide . . . . . . /PROKD, /PRAOIX
personal . . . . . . /PERNL
personalization . . . . . . /PERNLGS
personification . . . . . . /PERNGS
perspirant. . . . . . /SPRIRNT, /SPARNT
pertussis . . . . . . /PRUSZ
pestis. . . . . . /PETSZ

petal . . . . . /PAELT
petrosal . . . . . /PROELZ
petrosis . . . . . /PROETS
petrotic . . . . . /P*ERKT
pexia . . . . . /PA*EX
pexic . . . . . /PEKZ
pexies . . . . . /PAOEXZ
pexin . . . . . /P*EX
pexis . . . . . /PEXZ
pexostomy . . . . . /PO*X
pexotomy . . . . . /PAUKT
pexy . . . . . /PEX
phacitis . . . . . /FAOIFTS
phacomatosis (*see also* phakomatosis) . . . . . /FOEMZ
phage (*see also* ophage) . . . . . /FAEJ
phagia (*see also* ophagia) . . . . . /FAIJ
phagic . . . . . /FAIG
phagies . . . . . /FAEJS
phagism . . . . . /FAIFM
phagocyte . . . . . /FAOGT
phagocytes . . . . . /FAOGTS
phagocytic . . . . . /FAGT
phagocytosis . . . . . /FOEGT, /FOEGTS
phagology . . . . . /FALG
phagous (*see also* ophagous) . . . . . /FOUG
phagus . . . . . /FAUG
phagy (*see also* ophagy) . . . . . /FOIJ
phakia . . . . . /FA*IK
phakitis . . . . . /FAOIKS
phakomatosis (*see also* phacomatosis) . . . . . /FOEKSZ
phakus . . . . . /FUKS
phalangeal . . . . . /FLAENL
phalangectomy . . . . . /FLENGT
phalangia . . . . . /FLAING
phalangism . . . . . /FLAFM
phalangy . . . . . /FLOIJ
phalanx . . . . . /FLANKZ
phallic . . . . . /FAKL
phallus . . . . . /FLAUS
phane . . . . . /FA*IN
phanerosis . . . . . /FAERNZ
phanes . . . . . /FA*INS
phania . . . . . /FA*EN
phanic . . . . . /FANK
phanic acid . . . . . /FANKD

phantom . . . . . /FAOMT
phany . . . . . /FA*N
pharmaceutical . . . . . /FARL, /FAURL
pharmaceuticals . . . . . /FARLS, /FAURLS
pharmaceutics . . . . . /FAOUKS
pharmacologic . . . . . /FAURMG
pharmacological . . . . . /FAUJ
pharmacologist . . . . . /FARKT
pharmacologists . . . . . /FARKTS
pharmacology . . . . . /FAURM
pharmacy . . . . . /FARMZ
pharyngeal . . . . . /FAIRNL, /FAIRJ
pharyngeum . . . . . /FREJ
pharyngeus . . . . . /FRAJS
pharyngioma . . . . . /FRAUJ
pharyngitis . . . . . /FAIRNTS
pharyngocele . . . . . /FRAOELG, /FAOERJ
pharyngography . . . . . /FRAOFG
pharyngolaryngoscope . . . . . /FLARP
pharyngolith . . . . . /FLA*RT
pharyngorrhaphy . . . . . /FROERG
pharyngoscope . . . . . /FAORP
pharyngoscopy . . . . . /FAORPG
pharynx . . . . . /FAIRNX
phase . . . . . /FAIZ
phasia . . . . . /FA*IZ
phasic . . . . . /FAIFK
phasis . . . . . /FAESZ
phemesthesia . . . . . /FEMS
phemia . . . . . /F*EM
phemic . . . . . /FEMG, /F*EMG
phemy . . . . . /FO*IM
phenic . . . . . /FAOENG
phenics . . . . . /FAOENGS
phenomenon . . . . . /FON
phenotype . . . . . /FOIP
phenylalaninemia . . . . . /FAO*EM
pheresis (*see also* apheresis) . . . . . /PRAOESZ
pherous . . . . . /FERZ
phil . . . . . /F*IL
phile . . . . . /FAO*IL
philia . . . . . /FAO*EL
philiac . . . . . /FAO*ELG
philic . . . . . /F*ILG
philin . . . . . /FLIN

philioid . . . /FLO*ID
philism . . . /FLIFM
philosis . . . /FLOESZ
philous . . . /FLOUZ, /FOUZ
phils . . . /F*ILS
philuria . . . /FLIRL
phily . . . /FO*IL
phimosis . . . /FAOIMZ, /FAOIMS
phlebectasia . . . /FLAIBS
phlebectasis . . . /FLAIBSZ
phlebitic . . . /FLIBT
phlebitis . . . /FLEBT, /FLEBTS
phlebography . . . /FLAEFG
phlebostomy . . . /FLOFT
phlebotomy . . . /FLOB
phlegma . . . /FLEG, /FLEMG
phlegmasia . . . /FLAIGZ
phlegmatic . . . /FLEGT
phlegmon . . . /FLOM
phlogistic . . . /FLOEJ
phlysis . . . /FLISZ
phobe . . . /FO*EB
phobia (*see also* ophobia) . . . /FOEB
phobiac . . . /FO*IB, /FO*IK
phobic . . . /FOIB
phobophobia . . . /FAOB
phone . . . /FOEN
phonesis . . . /FOENSZ
phonia . . . /FAON
phonic . . . /FAUNG
phonocardiography . . . /FAOFG
phonoscope . . . /FOEP
phony . . . /FO*IN
phora . . . /FAO*R
phoral . . . /FO*RL
phoralgia . . . /FRALG
phore . . . /FO*R
phoregram . . . /FRA*M
phoresis . . . /FOERS, /FOERSZ
phoretic . . . /FOERKT
phoretogram . . . /FRAOEGT
phoria . . . /FOIR
phoriant . . . /FOIRNT
phoric . . . /FO*RK
phorin . . . /FAORN

phorins . . . . . /FAORNZ
phoritis . . . . . /FOIRT, /FOIRTS
phorometer . . . . . /FRORMT
phoroscope . . . . . /FROEP
phorotropic . . . . . /FROPK
phorous . . . . . /FOURZ
phorus . . . . . /FROUS
phose . . . . . /FOEZ
phosis . . . . . /FO*ES
phosphatasemia . . . . . /SFAEMT
phosphatase . . . . . /SFAIZ
phosphatases . . . . . /SFAISZ
phosphatasia . . . . . /SFAEZ
phosphate . . . . . /SFAIT
phosphatemia . . . . . /SFEM, /FAOEMT
phosphatemic . . . . . /SFEMG, /SFOFG
phosphates . . . . . /SFAITS
phosphaturia . . . . . /SFAOURT
phospheremia . . . . . /SFERM
phospholipid . . . . . /SFLIPD
phosphometer . . . . . /SFOTS
phosphoremia . . . . . /SFRAOEM
phosphoric . . . . . /SFOERK
phosphoric acid . . . . . /SFOERKD
phosphorous . . . . . /SFOURS
phosphorous acid . . . . . /FOD
phosphorus . . . . . /FOSZ, /SFOS
phosphorylase . . . . . /FLAEZ
phosphorylation . . . . . /SFAELGS, /SFAILGS
photesthesia . . . . . /FAO*ETS
photochromogen . . . . . /FROEJ
photochromogenic . . . . . /FROEK
photodermatitis . . . . . /FOERMTS
photofluorimetry . . . . . /FLAOERMT
photofluorometer . . . . . /FLOERMT
photograph . . . . . /FRAF
photography . . . . . /FRAEF
photometer . . . . . /FAOERMT
photometric . . . . . /FROEKT
photometry . . . . . /FRAOEMT
photomicrograph . . . . . /FAOIRMG
photomicrography . . . . . /FAERG
phototherapy . . . . . /FAORPT
phragma . . . . . /FRA*G
phrasia . . . . . /FRAZ, /FRAIZ

phraxis . . . . . /FRA*X
phrenal. . . . . /FR*ENL
phrenia . . . . . /FREN
phrenic . . . . . /FRENG
phrenitis . . . . . /FRAOENTS, /FRENTS
phryon . . . . . /FROIN
phthalmia (*see also* ophthalmia). . . . . /FA*UM
phthalmic (*see also* ophthalmic) . . . . . /FA*UK, /FA*UMG
phthalmitis (*see also* ophthalmitis) . . . . . /FA*UMT, /FA*UMTS
phthalmodonesis (*see also* ophthalmodonesis) . . . . . /MAOEFZ
phthalmometer (*see also* ophthalmometer) . . . . . /FAO*RMT
phthalmos (*see also* ophthalmos) . . . . . /FO*S
phthalmoscope (*see also* ophthalmoscope) . . . . . /FO*EPT
phthalmotomy (*see also* ophthalmotomy) . . . . . /MA*UPT
phthalmous (*see also* ophthalmous) . . . . . /FOUMZ
phthalmus (*see also* ophthalmus) . . . . . /FA*US
phthisic . . . . . /THAOIKS, /TIKZ
phthisis (*see also* ophthisis) . . . . . /THAOISZ
phthongia (*see also* ophthongia) . . . . . /PAONG
phycomycosis. . . . . /FOESZ
phygous . . . . . /FOUGS
phylactia . . . . . /FLAOERB
phylactic . . . . . /FLIKT, /FLA*KT
phylactics . . . . . /FLIKTS, /FLA*KTS
phylaxes . . . . . /FLAOEX
phylaxia . . . . . /FLAOIX
phylaxis . . . . . /FLAXZ
phyletic. . . . . /FLAOIKT
phyletism . . . . . /FLOIFM
phylic . . . . . /FAOIKL
phylum . . . . . /FLAOIM, /FLOIM
phyma . . . . . /FAOIM, /FOIM
phymas . . . . . /FOIMS
phyogenetic . . . . . /FENT
physeal . . . . . /SFAEL, /FILZ
physectomy . . . . . /SFEKT
physeoportal (*see also* physioportal) . . . . . /SFOPT
physeoprivic (*see also* physioprivic) . . . . . /SPRIVK, /SFRIVK
physeotropic (*see also* physiotropic) . . . . . /SFROPG
physes. . . . . /FAO*EZ
physial . . . . . /SFILS
physic . . . . . /FWIK
physical . . . . . /F–L
physicist . . . . . /FW*IS, /FWIFT
physics . . . . . /FWIX

physin . . . . /SFAOIN
physiologic . . . . /FLIJ
physiological . . . . /FLOJ
physiologies . . . . /FOJS
physiologist . . . . /FOLZ
physiology . . . . /FOJ
physioportal (*see also* physeoportal) . . . . /SFOEPT
physioprivic (*see also* physeoprivic) . . . . /SPRIV
physiotropic (*see also* physeotropic) . . . . /SFROEPG
physis . . . . /FOISZ
physitis . . . . /FOITS
physometra . . . . /FAOIRMT
phyte . . . . /FAO*IT
phytic . . . . /F*IKT
phytid . . . . /FAOITD
phytin . . . . /FOINT, /FO*IT
phytoma . . . . /FAO*IMT
phytosis . . . . /FAOIPTS
phytum . . . . /FOIMT
pia (*see also* opia) . . . . /AO*P, /YO*P
pial . . . . /PYAOEL
pic (*see also* opic) . . . . /AO*PG, /YO*PG
piesia . . . . /PAEZ, /PAOIRB
piesis . . . . /PAESZ
piesotherapy . . . . /PAERPS
pietic . . . . /PAEKT, /PAOIKT
piezometer . . . . /PAOIZ
piezometry . . . . /PAOIRZ
pigment . . . . /PIMT
pigmentation . . . . /PIMGS
pil . . . . /PAO*IL
pile . . . . /PAOIL
pine . . . . /PAO*EN, /PAOIN
pineal . . . . /PAENL
pinealism . . . . /PAEFM
pinemia . . . . /PAO*EM
pinuria . . . . /PAO*IRN
pionia . . . . /PO*IN
pipet . . . . /PIPT
pipette . . . . /PAOIPT
pituicyte . . . . /PAO*IT
pituitarism . . . . /PIFM
place . . . . /PLAIS
placement . . . . /PLAIFMT
placenta . . . . /PLAENT, /PLAEFNT

placental . . . . . /PLAENL, /PLAEFNL
placentography . . . . . /PLAEFG
plakia . . . . . /PLA*IK
plane . . . . . /PLAEN
planesia . . . . . /PLAENZ
planesis . . . . . /PLAENSZ
plania . . . . . /PLA*IN
plankton . . . . . /PLAONK
plant . . . . . /PLANT
plantar . . . . . /PLAUR, /PLA*RNT
plantation . . . . . /PLANGS
planting . . . . . /PLANGT
plany . . . . . /PLOIN
plaque . . . . . /PLAK
plasia . . . . . /PLAEZ
plasis . . . . . /PLAESZ
plasm . . . . . /PLAFM
plasma . . . . . /PLAFMS, /PLAZ
plasmal . . . . . /PLALZ
plasmapheresis . . . . . /PLAOEFSZ
plasmatic . . . . . /PLAFMT
plasmia . . . . . /PLAOFM
plasmic . . . . . /PLAMG, /PLAFMG
plasmin . . . . . /PLAFMZ
plasmolysis . . . . . /PLOLS
plasmoma . . . . . /PLOMS
plasmosis . . . . . /PLOEMS
plasmotherapy . . . . . /PLAIRP
plast . . . . . /PLAFT
plasts . . . . . /PLAFTS
plastic . . . . . /PLAS, /PLAFK
plastica . . . . . /PLOIF
plastics . . . . . /PLASZ, /PLAFX
plastid . . . . . /PLAFD
plastigenic . . . . . /PLENG
plastin . . . . . /PLAFN
plastinogen . . . . . /PLAOFN
plasty (*see also* oplasty) . . . . . /PLA*S
plata . . . . . /PLA*T
plate . . . . . /PLAET
platelet . . . . . /PLAILT
plating . . . . . /PLAEGT
plax . . . . . /PLAX
plaxoma . . . . . /PLOEMX
plectic . . . . . /PL*EKT, /PLAOEKT

plegia . . . . . /PLAOEG
plegic . . . . . /PLEK
plethysmograph . . . . . /PL*EGT
plethysmography . . . . . /PLA*EGT
pleura . . . . . /PLER
pleural . . . . . /PLERL
pleure . . . . . /PL*ER
pleuric . . . . . /PLURK, /PL*ERK
pleuritis . . . . . /PLERTS
pleuroparietopexy . . . . . /PLERP
pleuropneumonia . . . . . /PLAOURM
plex . . . . . /PLEX
plexia . . . . . /PLOIXZ
plexis . . . . . /PLIX, /PLIXZ
plexus . . . . . /PLEKZ, /PLEXZ
plexy . . . . . /PLOIX
plication . . . . . /PLAOIGS
ploid . . . . . /PLO*ID
ploidy . . . . . /PLO*D
pnea . . . . . /NAE
pneic . . . . . /NAO*EK
pneumatic . . . . . /NAOUMT
pneumatosis . . . . . /NOEMTS
pneumocholecystitis . . . . . /NOEFPT
pneumococcal . . . . . /NAOKL
pneumococcic . . . . . /NAOXZ
pneumoconiosis . . . . . /NAOMSZ
pneumocyst . . . . . /NAOFT
pneumogony . . . . . /NOIMG
pneumograph . . . . . /NAOMG
pneumography . . . . . /NAOG
pneumohepatitis . . . . . /NAEPTS
pneumon . . . . . /NAOUN
pneumonia . . . . . /NAOUM
pneumonic . . . . . /NAOUMG
pneumonitis . . . . . /NAOIMTS
pneumonium . . . . . /NOUM
pneumonolysis . . . . . /NAOULS
pneumopathy . . . . . /NOIPT
pneumopericardium . . . . . /NAURMD
pneumoperitoneum . . . . . /NAORMT
pneumoperitonitis . . . . . /NOIMTS
pneumopexy . . . . . /NAOUPX
pneumoplasty . . . . . /NAPZ
pneumoplethysmography . . . . . /NA*EGT

pneumoradiography . . . . /NOIFP
pneumoroentgenography . . . . /NAOFG
pneumothorax . . . . /NAOURX
pocket . . . . /POKT
pod . . . . /PO*D
podal . . . . /POLD
podalgia . . . . /PAOJ
podia . . . . /PAOD
podiasis . . . . /PAOIDZ
podic . . . . /POEGD
podium . . . . /POEMD
podous . . . . /POUDZ
pods . . . . /PODZ, /PO*DZ
pody . . . . /PO*ED
poiesic . . . . /PO*IK
poiesis . . . . /POISZ
poietic . . . . /POIK
poietin . . . . /POIT
poikilocytosis . . . . /POIKLSZ
poikilosis . . . . /POIX, /POIKLS
poikilotic . . . . /POIKLT
poison . . . . /POI
poisonous . . . . /POUS
polar . . . . /POERL
polarimeter . . . . /PLOMT
polariscope . . . . /PLAORP
polarization . . . . /POELGS
polarize . . . . /POELT
polarized . . . . /POELTD
polarizing . . . . /POELGT
pole . . . . /POEL
polesis . . . . /POELS
poliodystrophy . . . . /PLAOEF
poliomyelitis . . . . /PLAOILT, /PLAOILTS
poliosis . . . . /PLOELS
polycyte . . . . /POLGT
polycythemic . . . . /PLAOIMG
polydystrophy . . . . /PLOEFD
polygyria . . . . /PLAOIRG
polymer . . . . /PLERM
polymeric . . . . /PLERK
polymerization . . . . /PLERMGS
polyneuritis . . . . /PAOIRTS
polyp . . . . /PLIP
polypeptidemia . . . . /PLEPTD

polyploid . . . . /POILD
polyploidy . . . . /PLOILD, /PLOLD
polypnea . . . . /PLAOEP
polypneic . . . . /PLAOEPG
polyposis . . . . /PLIPSZ
polypus . . . . /PLUPS, /PLUPZ
polysaccharide . . . . /PLAKD, /PLAFP
polysaccharidosis . . . . /PLOEKD, /PLOEKDZ
polyuria . . . . /PLAOUR
pompholyx . . . . /PLIFX
pompic . . . . /POMPG, /POMP
ponderal . . . . /PONLD
ponesis . . . . /PONSZ
ponetic . . . . /PONGT
ponia . . . . /PAON
ponic . . . . /PAONK
pontia . . . . /PORB
pontile . . . . /PONL, /PAUNLT
pontine . . . . /PAUNT
popliteal . . . . /PLILT, /PLOPT, /PLAOEPT
poration . . . . /POERGS
pore . . . . /POER
poria (*see also* aporia) . . . . /PO*R
poritis . . . . /POERTS
porosis . . . . /PROESZ
porotic . . . . /PROIKT
porous . . . . /POERZ
porphyria . . . . /POIFR, /PAOFR
porphyrin . . . . /POEFR, /POFRN
porphyrinemia . . . . /POEFRM
porphyrinism . . . . /PIFRM
porphyrinogen . . . . /POEFRG
porphyrinuria . . . . /PAOUFR
port . . . . /PORT
portal . . . . /PORLT
porter . . . . /PRORT
portion . . . . /PORGS
portogram . . . . /PO*RM
portography . . . . /POERGT
pose . . . . /POES
posed . . . . /POEFD
posia . . . . /PAOS
position . . . . /POGS
positive . . . . /POZ, /POS, /POV
posterior . . . . /PAO*R, /PYAOR

posthitis . . . . /PAO*ITS
posy. . . . . . . /PO*IS
potassemia . . . . /PAUTS
potassemic . . . . /PAUGT
potassium . . . . /PAUT
potency . . . . /PO*ENTS
potent . . . . /PO*ENT
potentia . . . . /POERB
potential. . . . . . . /POERBL
potentiality . . . . /POERBLT
potentiation . . . . /POERBGS
potentiator . . . . /PROERBT
potomy. . . . . . . /POMT
pragia . . . . /PRAIJ
pragic . . . . /PRAJ
prandial . . . . /PRANLD
prasin. . . . . . . /PRAINZ
praxia . . . . /PRA*X
praxic . . . . /PRA*K
praxis . . . . /PRAXZ
praxy . . . . /PROIX
precipitate . . . . /PRIP
precipitation. . . . . . . /PRAIPGS, /PR*IPGS
precipitin . . . . /PRIPT
predator. . . . . . . /PRED
pregnancy . . . . /PRAEG
preputial. . . . . . . /PRAOUL, /PRAOURB
presbyopia . . . . /PRAUP, /PRAOP
preservation . . . . /PREFRX
press . . . . /PRESZ
pressed . . . . /PREFD
pressor. . . . . . . /PRERSZ
pressure . . . . /PRERB
prevention . . . . /PREFNGS, /PREVNGS
prisis . . . . /PROISZ
prism . . . . /PRIFM
prival . . . . /PRIVL, /PRAVL
privia . . . . /PROIV
privic . . . . /PRIVK
privous (*see also* iprivous) . . . . /PROUVS
proaccelerinemia . . . . /PRAERM
probasia . . . . /PRAIBZ
probe . . . . /PROEB
proconvertinemia . . . . /PRAOEVM
proctectomy. . . . . . . /PROEKT

proctia . . . . /PRORB
proctic . . . . /PRO*KT
proctitis . . . . /PROKTS, /PROKZ
proctium . . . . /PR*UM
proctocolectomy . . . . /PROKL
proctostomies . . . . /PROFKTS
proctostomy . . . . /PROFKT
product . . . . /PRUT
production . . . . /PRUGS, /PRUX
professional . . . . /PR–FL
prognosis . . . . /PROEG
proinsulin . . . . /PLINZ
proinsulinemia . . . . /PRUN, /PLA*EM
projection . . . . /PROEJ
projector . . . . /PRORJ
prolactinemia . . . . /PLAOEMT
prolactinemic . . . . /PLAOEMG
proliferative . . . . /PLOIFT, /PLIVT
prolinemia . . . . /PLOIM
promontory . . . . /PROERM
pronation . . . . /PROENGS
prone . . . . /PROEN
prophylactic . . . . /FLAKT
prophylaxis . . . . /FLAKZ
proportion . . . . /PRORGS
prosexia . . . . /PR*EX
prosody . . . . /PROEDZ
prosopalgia . . . . /PROELG
prosope . . . . /PRO*EP
prosopia . . . . /PROIPS
prosopic . . . . /PROIPG
prosopous . . . . /PROUPS
prosopus . . . . /PRUPS
prostaglandin . . . . /PRAONG, /PRAONGD
prostate . . . . /PRAET
prostatectomy . . . . /PRAEKT
prostatic . . . . /PROFK
prostatitis . . . . /PRAOIFT, /PRAOIFTS
prosthesis . . . . /PRAOET, /PRAO*ET
prosthetic . . . . /PRO*T
prosthetics . . . . /PRO*TS
protease . . . . /PROIS
protectant . . . . /PRANT
protectants . . . . /PRANTS
protection . . . . /PREX

protective . . . . /PREVK
proteic. . . . /PRAO*EK
protein . . . . /PROIN
proteinemia . . . . /PRAOEMT
proteinemic. . . . /PRAOEMG
proteinia . . . . /PRO*I, /PRAOENT
proteinic. . . . /PROING
proteinosis . . . . /PROINSZ, /PROENSZ
proteinuria . . . . /PRAOURT
proteosis . . . . /PROETSZ
prothrombin. . . . /THRAUB
prothrombinemia . . . . /THRAOEB
protoplasmic . . . . /PRAPG
proximal . . . . /PRO*X
pruritic . . . . /PRAOURK
psammus . . . . /SAMZ
psathyrosis . . . . /SO*ETS, /SA*T
pselaphesia . . . . /SFAOES
-pseudohypoparathyroidism . . . . /SO*IFMD
pseudohypoparathyroidism . . . . /SOIFMD
psia (*see also* opsia) . . . . /A*UPZ
psis (*see also* opsis) . . . . /A*UPSZ
psoas . . . . /SWAS, /SWAOS, /SWOES
psonin (*see also* opsonin). . . . /PO*PZ
psoriasis . . . . /SOERSZ
psoriatic . . . . /SOERKT
psy (*see also* opsy) . . . . /O*IPS
psychiatric . . . . /SKAOIK
psychiatrically . . . . /SKAOIKL
psychiatrist. . . . /SKAOIT
psychiatrists . . . . /SKAOITS
psychiatry . . . . /SKRAOE
psychic. . . . /SKOIK, /SK*IK
psychical . . . . /SKOIKL, /SKIKL
psychologic . . . . /SK–J
psychological . . . . /SKOJ
psychologically . . . . /SKOEJ
psychologist. . . . /SKOLT
psychologists . . . . /SKOLTS
psychology . . . . /SKOLG
psychomotor . . . . /SMOERT, /SKMOERT
psychopathic . . . . /SKPAFK
psychopathy . . . . /SKOP
psychopharmacology . . . . /SKAURM
psychosis . . . . /SKOES, /SKOEZ

psychosocial . . . . . . /SKOERBL
psychotic . . . . . . /SKOK
pteric . . . . . . /TAERK
pterin . . . . . . /T*IRN
pterins . . . . . . /T*IRNS, /TIRNZ
pterygium (*see also* opterygium) . . . . . . /TREJ
pterygoid . . . . . . /TOIGD
ptic (*see also* optic) . . . . . . /A*UPT
ptics (*see also* optics) . . . . . . /A*UPTS, /TA*UPTS
ptilosis . . . . . . /TILSZ
ptometer (*see also* optometer) . . . . . . /AURPT
ptometry (*see also* optometry) . . . . . . /TRO*MT
ptosia (*see also* optosia) . . . . . . /TOEZ
ptosis (*see also* optosis) . . . . . . /TOESZ, /OEPTS
ptotic (*see also* optotic) . . . . . . /TAUPGT
ptyalism . . . . . . /TYAOIFM, /TLAOIFM
ptychial . . . . . . /TAOIKL
ptysis (*see also* optysis) . . . . . . /TAOISZ
puberal . . . . . . /PAOURBL
pubertal . . . . . . /PAOURBLT
puberty . . . . . . /PAOUBT
pubescence . . . . . . /PAOUBSZ
pubescent . . . . . . /PAOUBTS
pubic . . . . . . /PAOUB
pubiotomy . . . . . . /POBT
pulmonary . . . . . . /PLOM
pulmonism . . . . . . /PAOFM
pulmonography . . . . . . /PLAEF
pulmonum . . . . . . /PLAO*M
pulpal . . . . . . /POUPL
pulsation . . . . . . /PULGS
pulsion . . . . . . /PAOLGS, /P*ULGS
pulvinectomy . . . . . . /PUVLT
puncture . . . . . . /PUNG
pupillary . . . . . . /PLAOURP
purgia . . . . . . /PAORJ
purine . . . . . . /PRAO*EN
purpurin . . . . . . /PRURN
purulent . . . . . . /PAOURLT
purulents . . . . . . /PAOURLTS
pus . . . . . . /PUS
pustular . . . . . . /PAOUFL
pustule . . . . . . /PAOUL
putrefactive . . . . . . /PAOUVKT
pyelectasia . . . . . . /PLAIKT

pyelectasis . . . . /PLEKTS
pyelia . . . . /PYAEL
pyelitis . . . . /PAOILT
pyelography . . . . /PLOLG
pyelolithotomy . . . . /PLO*T
pyeloneostomy . . . . /PLO*S
pyelonephritis . . . . /PLENTS
pyelonephrostomy . . . . /PLOFT
pyeloplasty . . . . /PLAOIP
pyelostomy . . . . /PLOS
pyemia . . . . /POIM
pyemic . . . . /POIMG, /PAOEMG
pyesis . . . . /PAO*ESZ
pyetic . . . . /PYEKT
pyga . . . . /PY–J
pygia . . . . /PYIJ
pygous . . . . /PYOUS
pyic . . . . /PAO*IK
pyknic . . . . /PYINK
pyknosis . . . . /POEKSZ
pyknotic . . . . /POEKT
pyle . . . . /PYAO*IL
pylephlebitis . . . . /FLAOEB, /FLAOEBS
pylic . . . . /PLAO*IK, /PYIK
pylorectomy . . . . /PLEKT
pyloric . . . . /PLOERK
pyoculture . . . . /PYOULT
pyogenic . . . . /PYENG
pyogenous . . . . /PYOJ, /PYOJS
pyon . . . . /PA*UN
pyonephrosis . . . . /POEFSZ
pyopericardium . . . . /PAOIRM
pyorrhea . . . . /PRAOE
pyosalpinx . . . . /PINX, /PAOINX
pyosis . . . . /PAOISZ
pyotherapy . . . . /PYAERP, /PYAIRP
pyothorax . . . . /PORX
pyoureter . . . . /PYAOURT
pyra . . . . /PYAR, /P*IR
pyramid . . . . /PIRMD
pyramidal . . . . /PAIRMD
pyramidial . . . . /PA*IRMD
pyranose . . . . /PAOIRNZ
pyremia . . . . /PAOERM, /PYAOIRM
pyresis . . . . /PYAOESZ

pyretic . . . /PAOIRK, /PYEK
pyrexia . . . /PAOIRX
pyrexial . . . /PAOIRL
pyrism . . . /PRAOIFM
pyrogenic . . . /PYERNG
pyrosis . . . /PAOIRSZ
pyrotic . . . /PYOK, /PYOKT
pyrous . . . /PROUZ
pyuria . . . /PYAOUR

Q

quantimeter . . . /KWIRMT
quantitative . . . /KWAIV
quest . . . /KW*ES
quetral . . . /KWAOET
quetrous . . . /KWAOETS
quetrum . . . /KWAOERT
quinol . . . /KWONL
quinone . . . /KWIN

R

rabies . . . /RAIBS
racemose . . . /RAMZ
rachia . . . /WRAIFP
rachicentesis . . . /RAENTS
rachidian (*see also* rhachidian *and* rrhachidian) . . . /RAFP
rachis . . . /RAIFPS
rachischisis (*see also* rhachischisis *and* rrhachischisis) . . . /RISZ
rachitic . . . /RIFPT
rachitis . . . /RAOIFPT, /RAOIKT, /RAOIKTS
rad . . . /RAD
radial . . . /RAOLD
radialis . . . /RAILDZ, /RULZ
radiation . . . /YAEGS, /RA*EGS
radical . . . /RALD
radicular . . . /RA*R, /RARKL
radiculitis . . . /RAOILTS
radiculodysplasia . . . /RAIPZ
radiculoneuritis . . . /ROISZ
radiculoneuropathy . . . /ROIPT, /RURPT

radiculopathy . . . . /RAOP, /RAOPT
radiculopolyneuronitis . . . . /RAONTS
radiogram . . . . /RAORM, /RAORG
radiograph . . . . /RAOFP
radiographic . . . . /RAOFPG
radiography . . . . /ROIFP
radiologist . . . . /RAOLT, /ROLT
radiology . . . . /RAOLG
radiometer . . . . /RAOERMT
radiometric . . . . /RAORKT
radiometry . . . . /ROMT
radionecrosis . . . . /ROENSZ
radiotherapy . . . . /RAERPG
radius . . . . /RUS
ramous . . . . /ROUMS
ranging . . . . /RA*ING
rational . . . . /RAL
rbital (*see also* orbital) . . . . /O*RBL
rchid (*see also* orchid) . . . . /AO*RKD
rchidectomy (*see also* orchidectomy) . . . . /O*ERKT
rchidia (*see also* orchidia) . . . . /OIRKD
rchidic (*see also* orchidic) . . . . /OIFPD
rchidopexy (*see also* orchidopexy) . . . . /O*EPX
rchium (*see also* orchium) . . . . /O*URM
reaching . . . . /RAOEFPG
reactant . . . . /RANGT, /RANKT
reaction . . . . /RAX
reactivation . . . . /RAEVX
reactive . . . . /RAVK
reactivity . . . . /RAVKT
realization . . . . /ROIFGS
reception . . . . /SEPGS
receptive . . . . /SEVP
receptor . . . . /SOERPT
receptors . . . . /SOERPTS
recidive . . . . /RIVD
rectal . . . . /REKL
rectitis . . . . /REKTS
rectoneostomy . . . . /RONGT
rectopexy . . . . /R*EPX
rector . . . . /RERKT
rectostomy . . . . /ROFK, /ROFKT
rectum . . . . /RUM, /RUMT
rectus . . . . /RUKTS
recumbent . . . . /RUBT

recurrence . . . . . /RURNZ
reduction . . . . . /RAOUGS
reductive . . . . . /RUVK, /RAOUVK
reflex . . . . . /R–FX
reflexes . . . . . /R–FXZ
reflexia . . . . . /REFX
refractive . . . . . /FRAEVK
refractometer . . . . . /REFRKT
refringence . . . . . /REFRJS
refringent . . . . . /REFRJT
regeneration . . . . . /GRENGS
regulation . . . . . /REGS
regulator . . . . . /R–GT
regulators . . . . . /R–GTS
regulatory . . . . . /R–RGT
rehabilitation . . . . . /RABLGS
reinfusion . . . . . /RAOUFGS
relapse . . . . . /RAPZ
relate . . . . . /RELT
relaxation . . . . . /RAEX
renal . . . . . /RAENL
-renal . . . . . /RA*ENL
renalectomy . . . . . /RAENGT
renalopathy . . . . . /RAEPT
renin . . . . . /R*IN
reninemia . . . . . /RAO*EM
reninemic . . . . . /RAOEMG
renogenic . . . . . /RAOENG, /RENK
renogram . . . . . /RAOERM
renopathy . . . . . /R*EPT
renoscope . . . . . /ROP
renoscopy . . . . . /ROIPG
renotropic . . . . . /ROPG
replica . . . . . /KPAE
repressor . . . . . /WRERP
resection . . . . . /RAOEX
resistance . . . . . /R*INS, /RA*NS
resistant . . . . . /RINT, /RA*NT
resonance . . . . . /RANS
respiration . . . . . /SPAOIRX
respiratory . . . . . /SPAOIRT
respirometer . . . . . /SPAOIRMT
responder . . . . . /SPROND
response . . . . . /SPONS
responsive . . . . . /SPOIV

responsiveness . . . . /SPOIVNS
rest . . . . /R*ES
retention . . . . /RENGTS
reticular . . . . /RURKT
reticulate . . . . /RIKLT
reticulated . . . . /RIKLTD
reticuloendothelioma . . . . /RO*ET
reticuloma . . . . /RAUM
reticulosis . . . . /ROEKSZ
reticulum . . . . /R*ET
retina . . . . /RAENT
retinal . . . . /RAENLT
retinitis . . . . /RAOINTS, /RAOINT
retinitis pigmentosa . . . . /RAOIPTS
retinogram . . . . /WRAM
retinograph . . . . /RAFG
retinography . . . . /RAEFG
retinopathia . . . . /RA*IT
retinopathy . . . . /ROPT, /RO*PT
retroperitoneum . . . . /ROERM
retroviral . . . . /TRAOIVL
reversal . . . . /RERL
reversible . . . . /RERBL
reversion . . . . /RERGS
rhachia . . . . /WRAIK
rhachidia . . . . /WHAOEK
rhachidian (*see also* rachidian *and* rrhachidian) . . . . /RA*K, /WRA*K
rhachischisis (*see also* rachischisis *and* rrhachischisis) . . . . /WRIXZ
rheography . . . . /WRAEFG
rheology (*see also* rrheology) . . . . /WRAOELG, /RAO*ELG
rheostat . . . . /WRAET
rheostosis . . . . /WRAOETS
rheumatic . . . . /RAOUMT, /WRAOUMT
rheumatism . . . . /RAOUFM, /WRAOUFM
rhexis . . . . /R*EX, /WRIX
rhinal . . . . /WRAOINL
rhine . . . . /WRAO*IN
rhinia . . . . /WRAIN
rhinic . . . . /WRAOINK
rhinitis . . . . /ROINT, /ROINTS
rhinocystotomy . . . . /WROT
rhinolaryngology . . . . /RAOINL
rhinology . . . . /RAOILG
rhinoplasty . . . . /WRAPT
rhinorrhea . . . . /WRAE

rhinoscopy . . . . . /WROIP
rhizoclasia . . . . . /WRAIZ
rhodopsin . . . . . /WROPD
rhombic . . . . . /ROMG
rhythm . . . . . /THIM
rhythmia (*see also* rrhythmia) . . . . . /R*IMT, /WR*IT
rhythmic . . . . . /WRIMG, /THIMG
rhythms . . . . . /THIMS
riboflavin . . . . . /RAIVN
riboflavinosis . . . . . /RAIVNS
ribonuclease . . . . . /RAEBS, /RAEBZ
ribosome . . . . . /RAOIBS
rickets . . . . . /ROIKT, /ROIKTS
riding. . . . . . /RAOIGD
roentgen . . . . . /ROENGT
roentgenography . . . . . /ROEFG
roentgentherapy . . . . . /RAIRPG
rooted . . . . . /RAOTD
rose . . . . . /ROEZ
rosein . . . . . /ROENZ
rostral . . . . . /RAOFL
rotary . . . . . /TRORT
rotate . . . . . /TROET
rotation . . . . . /TROEGS
rotatory . . . . . /RAO*RT, /TRO*RT
rrhachia . . . . . /RAEFP
rrhachic . . . . . /WRAEK
rrhachidian (*see also* rachidian *and* rhachidian) . . . . . /WR*IK
rrhachis . . . . . /RAIKS, /RAIKZ
rrhachischisis (*see also* rachischisis *and* rhachischisis) . . . . . /WRISZ, /R*ISZ
rrhachitis . . . . . /WRAOITS
rrhage . . . . . /RAJ
rrhagenic . . . . . /RAENG, /GAENG
rrhagia (*see also* orrhagia) . . . . . /ROERJ, /RA*IJ
rrhagic . . . . . /RAEG
rrhagin . . . . . /WRAEJ
rrhagins . . . . . /WRAEJS
rrhagiparous . . . . . /ROUPS, /JIPS
rrhaphe . . . . . /RAIF
rrhaphy . . . . . /RAEF
rrhea (*see also* orrhea) . . . . . /RAOE
rrheal. . . . . . /RAO*EL, /WRAOEL
rrheals . . . . . /RAO*ELS, /WRAOELS
rrhectic . . . . . /WR*EKT
rrheic . . . . . /RAO*EK

rrheics . . . . /RAO*EKS
rrheid . . . . /WRAOED, /RAO*ED
rrheology (*see also* rheology) . . . . /WROELG
rrhesis . . . . /WRAOESZ
rrhexis . . . . /WREX
rrhiasis . . . . /WRAOISZ
rrhine . . . . /RAO*IN
rrhinia . . . . /RAO*N
rrhodin . . . . /WROEND
rrhodinogen . . . . /WROEGD
rrhoic . . . . /WROEK
rrhoid . . . . /WROID, /ROID
rrhoidal . . . . /WROILD, /ROILD
rrhoidectomy . . . . /WREKT
rrhoids . . . . /WROIDZ, /ROIDZ
rrhoncus . . . . /RONK
rrhythmia (*see also* rhythmia) . . . . /WR*IMT
rubella . . . . /ROUB
rubin . . . . /RAOUB
rubinemia . . . . /RAOEB
rubral . . . . /RAORBL
rubricyte . . . . /ROIBT
rum . . . . /R*UM
rupture . . . . /RUPT

S

s . . . . /–S, /–Z
sa . . . . /SA
sac . . . . /SKA, /SKRA
saccades . . . . /SKAIDZ
saccharide . . . . /SKRAOID
saccharides . . . . /SKRAOIDZ
saccharose . . . . /SKROEZ
saccharum . . . . /SKHUM
saccular . . . . /SKAOURL
sacculotomy . . . . /SAKLT, /SOKLT
sacral . . . . /SKRAL
sacralization . . . . /SKRALGS
sacrum . . . . /SKRUM
sadism . . . . /SDIFM
safety . . . . /SAIFT
sagittal . . . . /SAJT
sal . . . . /SAL

salemia . . . . /SLAOEM
salination . . . . /SLAINGS
saline . . . . /SLAOEN
salivary . . . . /SAVL
salivation . . . . /SLAOIVGS
salivogram . . . . /SAVLG
salpingeal . . . . /SPLAEL
salpingectomy . . . . /SPINK
salpingiosis . . . . /SPOEJS
salpingitis . . . . /SPAOITS, /SPAOINTS
salpingography . . . . /SPOG
salpingoma . . . . /SPOEM
salpingo-oophoritis . . . . /SPRAOITS
salpingoovaritis . . . . /SPAOIVT, /SPAOIVTS
salpingo-ovaritis . . . . /SPAOIFT, /SPAOIFTS
salpingostaphylinus . . . . /SPLAOINS
salpingostomy . . . . /SPO*S
salpingotomy . . . . /SPAUT
salpinx . . . . /SPINX
salt . . . . /SALT
salubrious . . . . /SLAOB
san . . . . /SAN
sane . . . . /SAIN
sanguinate . . . . /SWAENGT
sanguination . . . . /SWANGS
sanguine . . . . /SWANG
sanguineous . . . . /SWUS
sanitary . . . . /SNAIRT
sanity . . . . /SANT
sans . . . . /SANS
sapremia . . . . /SPRA*EM
sarc . . . . /SA*URK
sarca . . . . /SAURK
sarcia . . . . /SARS
sarcocele . . . . /SARKL
sarcocleisis (*see also* sarcokleisis) . . . . /SA*RKS, /SLARKS
sarcoidosis . . . . /SKOIDZ
sarcokleisis (*see also* sarcocleisis) . . . . /SARKS
sarcoma . . . . /SKOEM
sarcomatosis . . . . /SKOEMT
sarcomatous . . . . /SKOEMTS
sarcomphalocele . . . . /SFLAOEL
sarcosinemia . . . . /SAURM
sarcosis . . . . /SKOESZ
sarcotoxin . . . . /SAURX

sarcotoxism . . . . . . /SAUFM
sarcous . . . . . . /SARKZ
satiable . . . . . . /SAIRBL
sation . . . . . . /SAEGS
saturate . . . . . . /SAFP
saturation . . . . . . /SAFPGS
scabietic . . . . . . /SKAOEB, /SKAOEBT
scan . . . . . . /SKAN
scanner . . . . . . /SKARN
scaphocephaly . . . . . . /SKAOFL
scaphoid . . . . . . /SKAFD, /SKOIFD, /SKAOFD
scapilium . . . . . . /SKLIM, /SKLIP
scapula . . . . . . /SKLAP
scapular . . . . . . /SKLAURP
scapularis . . . . . . /SKLAURPS
scapulohumeral . . . . . . /SKHURL, /SKHAOURL, /SKHAOURM
scapulum . . . . . . /SKLAOUP
scarlatina . . . . . . /SKARLT
scarlatinal . . . . . . /SKLARLT
scarlet . . . . . . /SKLET
scelia . . . . . . /SKLE
scelous . . . . . . /SKLES
scelus . . . . . . /SKLEZ
scheocele (*see also* oscheocele) . . . . . . /SKA*EL
scheotomy (*see also* oscheotomy) . . . . . . /SKRO*T
schesis . . . . . . /SKESZ
schisis . . . . . . /SKISZ
schism . . . . . . /SKIFM
schizia . . . . . . /SKHIZ
schlerema . . . . . . /SKLAOEM
schwannoma . . . . . . /SWOEM
sciatic . . . . . . /SKAK
science . . . . . . /SAOINS
scientist . . . . . . /SAOINT
scientists . . . . . . /SAOINTS
scintigram . . . . . . /STRAMG, /STRIMG
scintigraphy . . . . . . /STRAF
scintogram . . . . . . /STRAOMG
scirrhus . . . . . . /SKHIRS, /SKHUS, /SKIRS
scission . . . . . . /SKIGS
sclera . . . . . . /SKLAER, /SKLA
scleral . . . . . . /SKLERL, /SKLAERL
scleria . . . . . . /SKLAOR
scleritis . . . . . . /SKLAOIT, /SKLAOITS
sclerium . . . . . . /SKLUM

scleroderma . . . . . /SKLERD
scleroma . . . . . /SKLOERM
scleronectomy . . . . . /SKLENT
sclerosis . . . . . /SKLOEZ
sclerotic . . . . . /SKLOK
sclerotitis . . . . . /SKLOITS
scoliosis . . . . . /SKOELZ, /SKLOL
scope . . . . . /SKOEP
scopes . . . . . /SKOEPS
scopic . . . . . /SKOPG
scopical . . . . . /SKPAL
scopics . . . . . /SKOPGS
scopies (*see also* oscopies) . . . . . /SKOIPS
scopist . . . . . /SKOEFT
scopy (*see also* oscopy) . . . . . /SKOIP
scorbutic . . . . . /SKBAOUK
scotoma . . . . . /SKAUMT
scotometry . . . . . /SMRE
scotosis . . . . . /SKOETS
scribe . . . . . /SKRAOIB
scription . . . . . /SKR–PGS
scrotal . . . . . /SKROELT
scrotum . . . . . /SKROET
se (*see also* ose) . . . . . /SE
sebacea . . . . . /SBAOERB
sebacia . . . . . /SBAERB
seborrheic . . . . . /SBRAOEK
second . . . . . /SEK
secretin . . . . . /SKRAOENT
secretion . . . . . /SKRAOEGS
secretor . . . . . /SKRERT
secretory . . . . . /SKROIRT
sect . . . . . /SEKT
sectio . . . . . /SHEX, /SHAOX
section . . . . . /S–X
sectomy . . . . . /S–KT
sector . . . . . /SERKT
security . . . . . /SKURT
sedation . . . . . /SDAEGS
sedative . . . . . /SDAEV
segment . . . . . /SAEMT
segmental . . . . . /SMAENLT
segmentation . . . . . /SGEGS
seisis . . . . . /SOISZ
seism . . . . . /SOIFM

seismography . . . . . . /SMAEFG
seizure . . . . . . /SHAOEZ, /SHAOES
selection . . . . . . /SLEX
selective . . . . . . /SLEV, /SLEVK
selectivity . . . . . . /SLEVT
selenium . . . . . . /SLOIM
self . . . . . . /S*EFL
sellar . . . . . . /SLAER, /SLA*R
semeiology . . . . . . /SMAULG
semia . . . . . . /SMAOEN
seminalvesiculectomies . . . . . . /SMAVKS, /SMEVKS
seminalvesiculectomy . . . . . . /SMAVK, /SMEVK
semiology . . . . . . /SMAOELG
senile . . . . . . /SNAOIL
senility . . . . . . /SNILT
senium . . . . . . /SNOIM
sensation . . . . . . /SENGS
sense . . . . . . /SENS
sensibility . . . . . . /SNIBLT
sensible . . . . . . /SNIBL
sensitive . . . . . . /SNIV
sensitiveness . . . . . . /SNIVNS
sensitivity . . . . . . /SNIVT
sensitization . . . . . . /STAOIFGS
sensitize . . . . . . /STAOIS
sensitized . . . . . . /STAOIFD
sensitizer . . . . . . /STAOIFR, /STAOIRS
sensor . . . . . . /SOERN, /SORNS
sensorial . . . . . . /SORNL, /SOERNL
sensory . . . . . . /SROERN, /SRORNS
sepsis . . . . . . /SEPSZ
septal . . . . . . /SPALT
septate . . . . . . /STAIPT
septic . . . . . . /SPEP, /SPEPG
septicemia . . . . . . /SPAOEM
septitis . . . . . . /STEPTS
septopexy . . . . . . /SPAOPT, /SPAOX
septoplasty . . . . . . /SPLAOS, /SPLAO*S
septum . . . . . . /STEPT
sepulture . . . . . . /SPURLT
serodiagnosis . . . . . . /SAOERDZ
serosa . . . . . . /SAO*ERS
serosal . . . . . . /SAO*ERLS
serosis . . . . . . /SERSZ
serositis . . . . . . /SAOERTS

serotherapy . . . . . /SAERP, /SAIRP
serothorax . . . . . /STHORX, /STHOERX
serotonemia . . . . . /STOERM
serous . . . . . /SOUS
serrate . . . . . /SAIRT
serum. . . . . /SAOERM
ses (*see also* oses) . . . . . /SES
sex . . . . . /SEX
sexual . . . . . /SEXL, /SWAL
sexuality. . . . . /SEXLT, /SWAELT
sexualization. . . . . /SELGS, /SWAELGS
sexualize. . . . . /SWALS
shaping . . . . . /SHAIPG
sheathed . . . . . /SHAO*ETD
shock . . . . . /SHOK
shoot . . . . . /SHAOT
sialadenitis . . . . . /SLAOINTS
sialagogue . . . . . /SLOG, /SGAUG
sialemesis . . . . . /SLEMS
sialia . . . . . /SLAL
sialic . . . . . /SLOIK
sialidosis . . . . . /SAOLD, /SAOLDZ
sialography . . . . . /SGRAOF
sialorrhea . . . . . /SLAOIR
sialosis. . . . . /SLOESZ
sibilant . . . . . /SIBLT
siccant . . . . . /SK-NT
siccate . . . . . /SKAIK
siccation . . . . . /SKAEGS
siccative. . . . . /SKIV
side . . . . . /SAOID
sideratio . . . . . /SDRAERB
sideration . . . . . /SDRAEGS
sideric . . . . . /SDRERK
siderin . . . . . /SDRIN
siderinuria . . . . . /SDRAOUR
siderosis . . . . . /SDROESZ, /SIRDZ
sides . . . . . /SAOIDZ
sidosis. . . . . /SDOEZ
sight . . . . . /SAOIT
sigmoid . . . . . /SMOID
sigmoidal . . . . . /SMOILD
sigmoidectomy . . . . . /SMOIKT
sigmoiditis. . . . . /SMOIT, /SMOITS
sigmoidopexy. . . . . /SMOIX

sigmoidoscope . . . . /SMOIP
sigmoidoscopy . . . . /SMOIPG
sigmoidostomy . . . . /SMOFT
silicosis . . . . /SILZ
sin . . . . /SIN
sinal. . . . . /SAOINL
sinase . . . . /SNAES
sine . . . . /SAO*IN, /SAO*EN
sinemia . . . . /SNEM
sinister . . . . /SN*IRS
sinistral . . . . /SNAURL
sinistrous . . . . /SNIRTS
sinogen. . . . . /SNOG
sinoidal . . . . /SNOILD
sinose . . . . /SNOEZ
sinous. . . . . /SNOUS
sins . . . . /SINZ
sinuitis . . . . /SNAOUT, /SNAOUTS
sinuous . . . . /SNOUZ, /SNAOS
sinuria . . . . /SNIR
sinusectomy . . . . /SNAOUKT
sinusitis . . . . /SNUT, /SNUTS
sinusoidal . . . . /SNOILDZ, /SNO*ILD
sis (*see also* osis) . . . . /SIS
site . . . . /SAO*IT
sites . . . . /SAO*ITS
sitic . . . . /ST–K
sitis . . . . /SO*ITS
sitol (*see also* ositol) . . . . /SOILT
sity . . . . /STO*I
skeletal . . . . /SKAELT
skeleton . . . . /SKELT
skelic. . . . . /SKEKL
skellic. . . . . /SKLEKL
skeocytosis . . . . /SKAOETS
sleep . . . . /SLAOEP
slide. . . . . /SLAOID
smallpox . . . . /SMAUX
smatic (*see also* osmatic) . . . . /SMA*UK
smear. . . . . /SMAOER
smia (*see also* osmia) . . . . /O*MS, /O*Z
smic (*see also* osmic). . . . . /SMAUZ
smolarity (*see also* osmolarity) . . . . /SMA*IRLT
smometer (*see also* osmometer) . . . . /SMO*RMT
smosis (*see also* osmosis). . . . . /SMO*ES

smotic (*see also* osmotic) . . . . /SM*IKT, /SMO*EKT
smous (*see also* osmous) . . . . /O*UMS
social . . . . /SORBL
sodic . . . . /SDOIK
sodium . . . . /SDUM
soft . . . . /SOFT
sol . . . . /SOL
solenitis . . . . /SLOINTS
solization . . . . /SOILGS
soluble . . . . /SOBL
solution. . . . . /SLAOUGS
solve. . . . . /SOVL
solvent . . . . /SOFLT, /SOVLT
solving . . . . /SOVLG
soma . . . . /SAOM
somal . . . . /SMAOL
somatia. . . . . /SMAERB
somatic . . . . /SOMT
somatize . . . . /SMOIS
somatogenesis . . . . /SEJS
somatognosis . . . . /SGOENS, /SGOENSZ
somatotropism . . . . /STROFM
somatous . . . . /SMOUTS
some . . . . /SOM
somes . . . . /SOMS
somia. . . . . /SO*M
somiasis . . . . /SMAOIZ
somic. . . . . /SOMG
somite. . . . . /SMAO*IT
somnia . . . . /SM–N
somniac . . . . /SM–NG
somnias . . . . /SM–NS
somnolence . . . . /SLENZ
somus . . . . /SOEMS
somy . . . . /SMAOE
sonic . . . . /SAUNG
sonics . . . . /SAUNGS
sonogram . . . . /SOENG
sonograph . . . . /SNAUF
sonographer . . . . /SOEFR, /SNOEFR
sonographic . . . . /SAFK
sonography . . . . /SOEFG, /SNOEFG
sonoscopy . . . . /SNOIPS
sophy . . . . /SHOF
sopor. . . . . /SPO*ER

sorbate . . . . . /SAEBT
sorbates . . . . . /SAEBTS
sorbent . . . . . /SOERNT
sorption. . . . . /SORPGS
sound . . . . . /SOUN
source. . . . . /SORS
space . . . . . /SPAIS
spacial . . . . . /SPAIF
spadia . . . . . /SPAED
spadiac . . . . . /SPAEGD
spadial. . . . . /SPAELD
spadias . . . . . /SPAEDZ
spasia . . . . . /SPAEZ
spasis . . . . . /SPAESZ
spasm. . . . . /SPAFM
spasmia . . . . . /SPAOFM
spasmodic . . . . . /SMOD
spasmolytic. . . . . /SMOKL
spasmus . . . . . /SPAMS
spastic . . . . . /SPAS, /SPAFKT
spatial . . . . . /SPAIL, /SPAL
specialty. . . . . /SPAERBLT
species . . . . . /SPAOES
specific . . . . . /SPEF
spection . . . . . /SP*X, /SP*EGS
spective. . . . . /SPEVK
spectrin . . . . . /SPREN
spectrogram . . . . . /SPRAM
spectrography. . . . . /SPRAEF
spectrometry . . . . . /SPRET
spectrophotometer . . . . . /SPROEMT
spectrophotometry. . . . . /SPRAOEMT
spectroscope . . . . . /SPOEPT
spectroscopy . . . . . /SPOS
sperm . . . . . /SPERM
spermasia . . . . . /SPAERMS
spermatic . . . . . /SPAERMT
spermatism. . . . . /SPAEFM, /SPEFRM
spermatitis . . . . . /SPAOIMT, /SPAOIMTS
spermatocele . . . . . /SPAOELT
spermatogenesis . . . . . /SPERJS, /SPEJS
spermia. . . . . /SPAERM
spermic. . . . . /SPERMG
spermid . . . . . /SPIRMD
spermism . . . . . /SPIFM

spermitis . . . . /SPOIRMT, /SPOIRMTS
spermotoxin . . . . /SPOERX
spermous . . . . /SPOUZ
spermy . . . . /SPAOERM
sphacelus . . . . /SFAFLS
sphenoid . . . . /SFOID
sphenoiditis . . . . /SFOIDZ
sphenosyndactylia . . . . /SFAOENL
sphere . . . . /SFAOER
spherectomy . . . . /SFREK
spheres . . . . /SFAOERS
spheric . . . . /SFAOERK
spherinemia . . . . /SFAOERM
spherium . . . . /SFRUM
spherocyte . . . . /SFOIT
spherocytosis . . . . /SFOESZ
spherolith . . . . /SFLIT, /SFL*IT
spherulosis . . . . /SFAOURLZ, /SFAOURLSZ
sphincterectomy . . . . /SFERKT
sphincterotomy . . . . /SFOKT
sphrasia (*see also* osphrasia) . . . . /SFRAIZ
sphresia (*see also* osphresia) . . . . /SFRAOES, /SFRAO*EZ
sphygmia . . . . /SFOIG
sphygmic . . . . /SMIK
sphygmograph . . . . /SMAF
sphygmy . . . . /SFOIM
sphyxia . . . . /SF*IX, /SYIX
spike . . . . /SPAOIK
spinal . . . . /SPAOINL
spinale . . . . /SPLAOE
spinalis . . . . /SPAOINLS
spinatus . . . . /SPAINT, /SPAINTS
spindle . . . . /SPINL
spinogram . . . . /SPAOIM
spinography . . . . /SPAEF
spinous . . . . /SPUS
spiral . . . . /SPAOIRL
spirator . . . . /SPRAERT
spire . . . . /SPAO*IR
spirillary . . . . /SPLAIRL, /SPLIRL
spirillosis . . . . /SPROEL, /SPROELS, /SPIRLS
spirochetal . . . . /SPOIRKL
spirochetosis . . . . /SPROETS
spirography . . . . /SPRAEFG, /SPRIFG
spiroma . . . . /SPRAUM

spirometer . . . . . . /SPROMT
spirometry . . . . . . /SPRAOERMT
spirosis . . . . . . /SPROEZ
spissate . . . . . . /SPAIFT
splanchnia . . . . . . /SPLAENG
splanchnic . . . . . . /SPLANK
splanchnitis . . . . . . /SPLANGS, /SPLAOINTS
splanchnopleuric . . . . . . /SPLERK, /SPLURK
splenectomy . . . . . . /SPLEK, /SPLEKT
splenia . . . . . . /SPLAEN
splenial . . . . . . /SPLINL, /SPLAOENL
splenic . . . . . . /SPLENG
splenin . . . . . . /SPL–N
splenism . . . . . . /SPLEFM
splenitis . . . . . . /SPLAOITS, /SPLENTS
splenograph . . . . . . /SPLAF
splenography . . . . . . /SPLAEF
splenomegaly . . . . . . /SPLELG
splenometry . . . . . . /SPLEM
splenopathy . . . . . . /SPLA*ET
splenopexy . . . . . . /SPLOEX
splenotomy . . . . . . /SPLOMT
spondylia . . . . . . /SPLIL
spondylic . . . . . . /SPLIK
spondylisis . . . . . . /SPAUNLS
spondylism . . . . . . /SPLIFM
spondylitis . . . . . . /SPLONT, /SPLONTS
spondylolisthesis . . . . . . /SPLAOESZ
spongia . . . . . . /SPAOG
spongioblastosis . . . . . . /SBLOESZ
spongioma . . . . . . /SPO*EM, /SPOM
spongiosis . . . . . . /SPAOJZ, /SPOEJ
spongiosus . . . . . . /SPUJS
spongium . . . . . . /SPUMG
spora . . . . . . /SPAOR
sporangia . . . . . . /SPOERNG
sporangium . . . . . . /SPRAJ
sporanic . . . . . . /SPRANK
spore . . . . . . /SPOER
sporiasis . . . . . . /SPOIRS
sporid . . . . . . /SPRID
sporidia . . . . . . /SPOIRD
sporidiasis . . . . . . /SPAOIRDZ
sporidiosis . . . . . . /SPOERDZ
sporin . . . . . . /SPORN, /SPO*RN

sporium . . . . /SPURM
sporoblast . . . . /SPRAFT
sporogenic . . . . /SPROEG
sporosis . . . . /SPOERSZ
sporous . . . . /SPOURS
spray . . . . /SPRAI
squamosal . . . . /SKWAIL
squamous . . . . /SKWAM
stabile . . . . /STAOIBL, /STA*IBL
stability . . . . /STABLT, /STAIBLT
stable . . . . /STAIBL
stage . . . . /STAIJ
stain . . . . /STAIN
stalsis . . . . /STAULSZ
staltic . . . . /STAULT
stance . . . . /STANS
standard . . . . /ST–D
stapedial . . . . /STAIPD
stapediopexy . . . . /STAIPX
staphylia . . . . /STOIFL
staphyline . . . . /STLAOIN
staphylinus . . . . /STLAOINS
staphylococcic . . . . /STAOFX, /STAOLX
staphylolysin . . . . /STLAOFN
staphyloplasty . . . . /STAOFT
staphylorrhaphy . . . . /STAEF
staphyloschisis . . . . /STAOSZ
stases . . . . /STAESZ
stasia . . . . /STAIZ
stasic . . . . /STAIFK
stasis (*see also* ostasis) . . . . /STAISZ, /STAZ
stasy . . . . /STAEZ
stat . . . . /STAT
state . . . . /STAIT
static . . . . /STAKT
statics . . . . /STAKTS
statism . . . . /STAFMT
statistics . . . . /STATS
statometer . . . . /STOERMT
status . . . . /STAUS
staxis . . . . /STAXZ
steal (*see also* osteal) . . . . /STAEL
stealgia (*see also* ostealgia) . . . . /ST*ELG
stealith . . . . /STLIT, /STAELT
stearate . . . . /STAOERT

steatolysis . . . . /STAOELS, /STAELS
steatoma . . . . /STAOEMT
steatomatous . . . . /STOEMTS
steatosis . . . . /STOETS
stegnosia . . . . /STEGZ
stegnosis . . . . /STEGS
steitis (*see also* osteitis) . . . . /STO*IT, /STO*ITS
stenium . . . . /STWUM
stenocephalic . . . . /STEFK
stenochoria . . . . /STOERK
stenol . . . . /STONL
stenolysis . . . . /STLISZ
stenoma . . . . /STAUM
stenomelia . . . . /SNAEL
stenosis (*see also* ostenosis) . . . . /SNOESZ
stenotic . . . . /STOKT
stenotomy . . . . /SNOMT
steoma (*see also* osteoma) . . . . /TWO*EM
steon (*see also* osteon) . . . . /STAO*EN
steophyte (*see also* osteophyte) . . . . /TWHOIT
steosis (*see also* osteosis) . . . . /TWOEFZ
step . . . . /STEP
stereognosis . . . . /STOEGS
stereoradiography . . . . /STROG, /STROIFP
stereoscope . . . . /STOERP
stereoscopy . . . . /STOIP, /STAOERP
steresis . . . . /STRAOESZ
steric . . . . /ST*ERK
sterility . . . . /STERLT
sterilization . . . . /STERLGS
sterin . . . . /ST*IRN, /ST–RN
sterism . . . . /STAOEFM
sternal . . . . /STURNL, /ST*ERNL
sternia . . . . /STARN
sternomastoid . . . . /SMAOTD
sternoplasty . . . . /SPLAZ
sternum . . . . /STURM
steroid . . . . /STERD, /STOIRD
sterol . . . . /STROL, /STRAOL
sterolemia . . . . /STLAOEM
sterols . . . . /STROLS, /STRAOLS
stethograph . . . . /STHRAF
stethophone . . . . /STOEFN
stethoscope . . . . /STHOEP, /THOEP
steum (*see also* osteum) . . . . /ST*EMT, /TW*EMT

sthenia (*see also* asthenia) . . . . . /STHAOEN
stheniant . . . . . /STHAOENT
sthenic (*see also* asthenic) . . . . . /STHENG, /STHENK
sthenin . . . . . /STHIN
sthenometer . . . . . /STHOMT
sthenuria . . . . . /STHAOUR
sthesia (*see also* esthesia) . . . . . /STHAO*ES
stigmatic . . . . . /SGIKT, /SMAIKT
stigmatism . . . . . /SMIFM
stillation . . . . . /STILGS
stimulant . . . . . /STLANT
stimulation . . . . . /STLAIGS
stimulism . . . . . /STLIM, /STLUFM
stimulus . . . . . /STLUS
stitis (*see also* ostitis) . . . . . /TWO*IT, /TWO*ITS
stium (*see also* ostium) . . . . . /TW*UMT, /ST*UMT
stixis . . . . . /STIXZ
stogavage (*see also* ostogavage) . . . . . /STAVJ
stolavage (*see also* ostolavage) . . . . . /TLAVJ
stole . . . . . /STOEL
stolic . . . . . /STOKL
stolithotomy . . . . . /STLO*T
stoma (*see also* ostoma) . . . . . /STOEM
stomal . . . . . /SMOL
stomatitis . . . . . /STOMTS
stomatocleisis . . . . . /SKLAOIS
stomatomy . . . . . /SMAUMT
stomatoplasty . . . . . /STAOPT
stomatous . . . . . /STOUMS
stome . . . . . /STO*M
stomia . . . . . /STO*IM
stomiasis . . . . . /STOEMZ, /STAOIMSZ
stomies (*see also* ostomy) . . . . . /STOIMZ
stomize . . . . . /SMOIZ
stomized . . . . . /SMOIFD
stomizes . . . . . /SMOISZ, /SMOIFS
stomizing . . . . . /SMOIFG
stomy (*see also* ostomy) . . . . . /STOIM
stosis (*see also* ostosis) . . . . . /STOSZ
stotic (*see also* ostotic) . . . . . /STOEKT
strabismus . . . . . /STRABS
strain . . . . . /STRAIN
stratal . . . . . /STRALT
stratified . . . . . /STRAFD, /STRAFTD
stratum . . . . . /STRAIMT, /STRAMT

stream . . . . . /STRAOEM
strepsis . . . . . /STREPSZ
streptococcic . . . . . /STROK
streptolysin . . . . . /STROFN
stress . . . . . /STRESZ
striate . . . . . /STRAOIT, /STROIT
striated . . . . . /STRAOITD, /STROITD
striatum . . . . . /STRAOIM
stroboscope . . . . . /STRO*EP, /STRAUP
stroma . . . . . /STROEM
stromal . . . . . /STRAUL
stromatic . . . . . /STRAULT
stromin . . . . . /STRO*M
stromuhr . . . . . /STROERM
strontium . . . . . /STRONT
strophe . . . . . /STROEF
strophy . . . . . /STROIF
structural . . . . . /STRURL
structure . . . . . /STRUR
struma . . . . . /STRAOUM
strumectomy . . . . . /SMEKT
strumitis . . . . . /STRAOMTS, /SMAOITS
strumous . . . . . /STRAOUMS
style . . . . . /STAOIL
stypsis . . . . . /STIPSZ
styptic . . . . . /STIPT
styrene . . . . . /STAOIRN
subarachnoid . . . . . /SRAFPD, /SWRAFPD
subclavian . . . . . /SKLAIVN, /SKLAIFN
substantiation . . . . . /STAENGS
substituted . . . . . /STUTD
succorrhea . . . . . /SKHAOE
succus . . . . . /SKUZ
suction . . . . . /SUX
sudate . . . . . /SWAOT
sudation . . . . . /SWAOGS
sudopathy . . . . . /SDOPT
sudoral . . . . . /SAORLD
sudotherapy . . . . . /SDAERP, /SDAIRP
sufficiency . . . . . /SUFS
sufficient . . . . . /SUF
sufflation . . . . . /SFLAEGS
sugar . . . . . /SHUG
suggestibility . . . . . /SGUBLT
suggestion . . . . . /SUGS

suicide . . . /SWAOID
sulcus . . . /SKLUK
sulfate . . . /SUFLT
sulfide . . . /SUFLD
sulfite . . . /SFAOILT
sulfur . . . /SUFRL
sulfuric . . . /SUFK
sulfuric acid . . . /SUFKD
sum . . . /SUM
superior . . . /SYOR, /SAOR
supination . . . /SAOUPGS, /SUPGS
supine . . . /SWAOUP
suppressant . . . /SPRENT
suppression . . . /SPREGS
suppressive . . . /SPREF
suppurative . . . /SPRAOUV, /SPRUFRB
suprarenal . . . /SPRAENL
suprarenalism . . . /SPRAEFM
suprarenoma . . . /SPROEM
sure . . . /SHAOUR
surgery . . . /SURG
surgical . . . /SURL
suria . . . /SOIR
surveillance . . . /SWAINS
survey . . . /SWAE
sus . . . /SUS
susceptibility . . . /STIBLT
susceptible . . . /STIBL
susception . . . /SWEPGS
susceptive . . . /STIVP
susceptum . . . /SWUMT
suscipiens . . . /SPUNS
suspension . . . /SWENGS
suture . . . /SAOUFP
sylvian . . . /SIVN
symbiont . . . /SBONT
symbiosis . . . /SBOES
symmetry . . . /SMAOET
sympathectomy . . . /SMAEKT
sympathetic . . . /STHIK
sympathicotonia . . . /SPAONT
sympathicotonus . . . /SPAONTS, /SPO*ENTS
sympatholytic . . . /SPLOKT
sympathomimetic . . . /SMIMT
symphysial . . . /SFIFL

symphysis . . . /SIMPS
symptomatic . . . /STOMT
synapsis . . . /SNAPZ
synaptic . . . /SNAPT
synchronism . . . /SKROIFM
synchysis . . . /SINKSZ
synclitism . . . /SKLIFM
syndactylia . . . /SDAOEKL
syndactyly . . . /SDAK
syndesis . . . /SDAOESZ
syndrome . . . /SDROEM
synechia . . . /SNAEK, /SNEFP
synergia . . . /SNAORJ, /SN*ERJ
synergy . . . /SNERJ
synitis . . . /SNOITS
synizesis . . . /SNESZ
synostosis . . . /SNAUSZ
synovectomy . . . /SEVK, /SEVKT
synovia . . . /SNOV, /SNOEV
synovial . . . /SNOVL, /SNOEVL
synovitis . . . /SNITS
synthesis . . . /STHES
synthetic . . . /STHEK
syphilide . . . /SFLAOID
syphilis . . . /SIFLS
syphilitic . . . /SFLIK
syphilology . . . /SFLOLG
syphilopathy . . . /SFLAPT
syringitis . . . /SIRJ
syringomyelia . . . /SMAOEL
syringosis . . . /SRINGSZ
syrinx . . . /SYAOINX
systaltic . . . /STLAUK
systaltism . . . /STLIFM
system . . . /S–M
systematic . . . /S–MT
systemic . . . /S–MG
systole . . . /STLAOE
systolic . . . /STLOK
systrophy . . . /STROFG, /STRIFG

T

tabes . . . . /TAIBS
tabetic. . . . /TBEK, /TBEKT
tachogram . . . . /TAOFPG
tachograph . . . . /TRAFG
tachometer . . . . /TAORMT
tachometry . . . . /TRAOMT
tachygraph. . . . /TRAFPG
tachygraphy . . . . TRAEFG
tactic . . . . /TWAK
tactics . . . . /TWAKZ
tactor . . . . /TAORK
tad . . . . /TAD
take. . . . /TAIK
talar . . . . /TLAURL, /TA*RL, /TLA*RL
tarachia. . . . /TRAIFP
tarsal. . . . /TARL
tarsalgia . . . . /TARLG
tarsectomy . . . . /TARKT
tarsi . . . . /TAURZ
tarsium . . . . /TARMZ
tarsophalangeal . . . . /TARNL
tarsus. . . . /TARSZ, /TAURSZ
tasia . . . . /TAESZ
tasis . . . . /TASZ
tast . . . . /TAFT
taste . . . . /TA*IS
tatic. . . . /TWAKT
taxia . . . . /TAEKZ
taxic . . . . /TIXZ
taxine . . . . /TAOENX
taxis . . . . /TAEXZ
taxy. . . . /TWAEX
technic . . . . /T–N
technics . . . . /T–NS
technique . . . . /NAOEK
techniques. . . . /NAOEKZ
technology . . . . /T–J
tecta . . . . /TAEKT
tectal. . . . /TAEKL
tegmental. . . . /TELGT
tegumental . . . . /TELT
tegumentary . . . . /TAIRT

telangiectasia . . . /TLAIS
-telangiectasia . . . /TLA*IS
telectasia . . . /TLAEKZ
telectasis . . . /TLAKZ
telemetry . . . /TLEMT
teleosis . . . /TLOS
teleotic . . . /TLOK
telephalangia . . . /TLAING
telephalangy . . . /TLAOENG
telia . . . /TYAOEL
telic . . . /T*ELG
telism . . . /TEFM
tellurium . . . /TLURM
telorism . . . /TLOFM
temesis . . . /TEMSZ
temper . . . /TREMP
temporal . . . /TAORL
temporale . . . /TOIRL
tend . . . /TEND
tendency . . . /TENTSDZ
tender . . . /TERND
tendineum . . . /TWIM
tendinitis . . . /TOINTS
tendinobursitis . . . /TBURTS
tendinosus . . . /TOENTS
tendinous . . . /TOINZ
tendon . . . /TOIN
tendonitis . . . /TONTS
tenic . . . /TENK
tenon . . . /TA*UN
tenonitis . . . /TAONTS
tenontoplasty . . . /TWEPT
tenositis . . . /TWOTS
tenosynovitis . . . /TAOIVT, /TAOIVTS
tenotomy . . . /TWOMT
tensinogen . . . /TENG
tension . . . /TENGS
tensive . . . /TEFRB, /TEV
tensor . . . /TORNS
tentorial . . . /TWOERL
teric . . . /TERK
term . . . /TERM
terma . . . /T-RM
terminal . . . /TAERL
tertian . . . /TERB

test . . . . . /T*ES
testis . . . . . /T*ETS
testoidism . . . . . /TWOIFM
testosterone . . . . . /TO*S, /TAO*S, /STROEN
tetanic . . . . . /TAENK
tetanus . . . . . /TETS
tetany . . . . . /TAOENT
texis . . . . . /TEXZ
thalamectomy . . . . . /THOIMT, /TH*EMT
thalamic . . . . . /THAMG, /THAULG
thalamohypophysial . . . . . /THOIFL
thalamotomy . . . . . /THOMT
thalamus . . . . . /THALS
thalaxia . . . . . /THAX
thanasia . . . . . /THAINS
thanatology . . . . . /THAONG
theca . . . . . /THAOEK
thecal . . . . . /THAOEKL
thecitis . . . . . /THAOETS
thecohysterectomy . . . . . /THIFRT
thecosis . . . . . /THAOEKS
thele . . . . . /THA*EL
thelia . . . . . /TLA
thelial . . . . . /TLAL, /TLAEL
thelialization . . . . . /THAOELGS
theliitis . . . . . /THILT, /THILTS
thelioblastoma . . . . . /THAOEBL
theliochorial . . . . . /THOKL
theliocyte . . . . . /THROIT
theliocytes . . . . . /THROITS
theliocytosis . . . . . /THOITS
thelioid . . . . . /THAOELD
theliolysin . . . . . /THONLS
theliolytic . . . . . /THIFK
thelioma . . . . . /TLOEM
theliomatosis . . . . . /THOEMT, /THOEMTS
theliomyoma . . . . . /TLAOM
theliosarcoma . . . . . /THOERKL
theliosis . . . . . /THAOELZ, /THAOELSZ
theliotoxin . . . . . /THOX
thelitis . . . . . /THAOELT, /THAOELTS
thelium . . . . . /TLUM, /TLIM, /THAO*EL
thelization . . . . . /THELGS
thenar . . . . . /THAOERN
thenic . . . . . /THAOENK, /TH*ENK

thenics . . . . . /THENKS
therapeutic . . . . . /THAOUP, /THAOUPT
therapeutics . . . . . /THAOUPS, /THAOUPTS
therapies . . . . . /THAERPS, /THAIRPS
therapist . . . . . /THAERPT, /THAIRPT
therapy . . . . . /THAERP, /THAIRP
therm . . . . . /THURM
thermal . . . . . /TH*ERM, /TH*ERL
thermalgesia . . . . . /THAOELS
thermanous . . . . . /THOURMS
thermesthesia . . . . . /THERMS
thermesthesiometer . . . . . /THAOERMT
thermia . . . . . /THAORM, /THO*IRM
thermic . . . . . /THIRM, /THIRMG
thermism . . . . . /THEFRM
thermoanesthesia . . . . . /THAOEMZ
thermoesthesia . . . . . /STHAOELS
thermognosis . . . . . /THOGS
thermomassage . . . . . /THAUJS
thermometer . . . . . /THERMT
thermometry . . . . . /THORMT
thermosystaltic . . . . . /THAUKL
thermotherapy . . . . . /THURP
thermous . . . . . /THOUMS
therms . . . . . /THURMS
thermy . . . . . /THOIRM
thesis . . . . . /THAOEZ
thetic . . . . . /THAOEKT
thetics . . . . . /THEKTS, /THAOEKTS
thioglycerol . . . . . /THOEL
thion . . . . . /THO*IN
thionammonemia . . . . . /THAO*IN
thionemia . . . . . /THAOIN
thionuria . . . . . /THAOUR
thlasia . . . . . /TLAIZ
thlipsia . . . . . /THLIPZ
thlipsis . . . . . /TLIPSZ
thoracia . . . . . /THAORK
thoracic . . . . . /THORK
thoracotomy . . . . . /THAORKT
thorax . . . . . /THORX, /THOERX
thorium . . . . . /THOERM
threpsia . . . . . /THREPS
threpsy . . . . . /THREPSZ
thricosis . . . . . /THRAOIX

thrix. . . . . /THRIX
thrombia . . . . /THROMP
thrombin. . . . . /THRIB
thrombinemia . . . . /THROIM
thromboagglutinin. . . . . /TLAOUT
thrombocyte . . . . /THRAOIT
thrombophlebitis. . . . . /THROBT
thromboplastin. . . . . /THON
thromboplastinemia . . . . /THOEN
thrombosis. . . . . /THROMS, /THROEBS
thrombotic. . . . . /THRAUBT
thrombus. . . . . /THRUB
thrypsis . . . . /THRIPS
thymia. . . . . /THOIM
thymiac . . . . /THAOK
thymic . . . . /THAOIMG, /THOIMG
thymism . . . . /THAOIFM
thymization . . . . /THAOIMGS
thymopexy . . . . /THOIX
thymus . . . . /THAOIMS
thyrea . . . . /THAER
thyreoiditis . . . . /THAOIRTS, /THAOERTS
thyreosis . . . . /THAOERSZ
thyreotomy. . . . . /THAOIRT
thyrin . . . . /THAOIRN
thyroid . . . . /THROID, /THAOIRD
thyroidal. . . . . /THAOIRLD
thyroideal . . . . /THOIRLD
thyroidean . . . . /THOIRND
thyroidectomize. . . . . /THRAOIZ
thyroidectomy . . . . /THREKT
thyroideus . . . . /THOIRDZ
thyroidism . . . . /THIFM, /THROIFM
thyroiditis. . . . . /THAOITS
thyroidoma . . . . /THROEMD
thyroidotomy . . . . /THROIMTD
thyropathy . . . . /THAOIRP, /THAOIRPT
thyropexy . . . . /THREX
thyroprival . . . . /THRIFL, /THRAVL
thyroprivia. . . . . /THRIF
thyrosis . . . . /THAOIRSZ
thyrotomy. . . . . /THAOIRMT, /THROIMT
thyrotoxic . . . . /THAOIRK, /THROIK
thyrotoxicosis . . . . /THROEXZ
thyrotrophic . . . . /THROEFG

thyrotropic . . . . . /THROIPG
thyroxin . . . . . /THROIX
thyroxine . . . . . /THROX
thyroxinemia . . . . . /THRONX
tia (*see also* otia) . . . . . /TWO*IK, /SHA
tiatrics . . . . . /TAOERTS
tibial . . . . . /TIBL
tibial band . . . . . /TIBLD
tic (*see also* otic) . . . . . /TIK
tics (*see also* otics) . . . . . /TIKS
tid . . . . . /TID
tide . . . . . /TAOID
tides (*see also* itides) . . . . . /TAOIDZ
tility . . . . . /TLIT
timbria . . . . . /TBRIM
timer . . . . . /TAOIRM
tin . . . . . /TIN
tinic . . . . . /TINK
tism . . . . . /TIFM
tissular . . . . . /TIRBL
tist . . . . . /T*IS
titis (*see also* otitis) . . . . . /TAOITS
tize . . . . . /TOIZ
tized . . . . . /TOIFD
tizes . . . . . /TOIFS
tizing . . . . . /TOIFG
tmesis . . . . . /TAOEMSZ
tocia . . . . . /TOERB
tocic . . . . . /TWOK
tocograph . . . . . /TOEFK
tocography . . . . . /TAOEFK
tocous . . . . . /TOUKS
toe . . . . . /TOE
togenic (*see also* itogenic) . . . . . /TO*IJ
togenous (*see also* itogenous) . . . . . /TOJ
toid . . . . . /TOID
tolerance . . . . . /TLANS
tolerant . . . . . /TLANT
tologies (*see also* ologies *and* logies) . . . . . /TOLGS
tologist (*see also* ologist *and* logist) . . . . . /TOLT
tology (*see also* ology *and* otology) . . . . . /TOLG
tolysis (*see also* olysis *and* lysis) . . . . . /TOLS, /TLISZ
tolytic (*see also* olytic *and* lytic) . . . . . /TLOKT
toma . . . . . /TAOM
tome (*see also* otome) . . . . . /TOEM

tomias . . . . . /TOEMZ
tomic . . . . . /TOMG
tomies (*see also* otomies) . . . . . /TOMS, /O*TS
tomist . . . . . /T*IMS
tomists. . . . . /T*IMSZ
tomize . . . . . /TOIMS
tomized . . . . . /TOIMD
tomizes . . . . . /TOIMZ
tomizing . . . . . /TOIMG
tomoclasis. . . . . /TAUXZ
tomogram . . . . . /TOEMG
tomographic . . . . . /TOIFK
tomography . . . . . /TOEFG
tomous. . . . . /TOUMS
tomy (*see also* otomy) . . . . . /TOM, /O*T
tone . . . . . /TOEN
tones . . . . . /TOENZ
tonia. . . . . /TO*N
tonic . . . . . /TAUNK, /TONG
tonicity . . . . . /TOFT
tonin . . . . . /TO*IN
tonograph . . . . . /TO*ENG
tonoid . . . . . /TOIND
tonometer. . . . . /TAUMT
tonometry . . . . . /TOERMT
tonos . . . . . /TONS
tonoscopy. . . . . /TOIPS
tonsillar . . . . . /TAURNL, /TORNL
tonsillectomy . . . . . /TAUNG, /TAUNLG
tonsillitis . . . . . /TAUNLT
tonus . . . . . /TOENS
tony . . . . . /TO*EN
topagnosia. . . . . /TAOPZ
topagnosis. . . . . /TAOPSZ
tope . . . . . /TOEP
tophagous . . . . . /TOFS
topia . . . . . /TA*UP
topic . . . . . /TAUP
topicity . . . . . /TAUFT
topography . . . . . /TOEPG
topokinesia . . . . . /TAOENSZ
topy . . . . . /TO*IP
toreusis. . . . . /TRAOSZ
torsion . . . . . /TORGS, /TOERGS
toscope (*see also* otoscope) . . . . . /TO*EPS

tosis (*see also* osis) . . . . . /TOISZ, /O*ESZ
tosus . . . . . /TOUSZ
total . . . . . /TOELT
totic . . . . . /TOIKT
tous (*see also* ous) . . . . . /TOUS
toxemia . . . . . /TAOEMZ, /KPAOEM
toxia . . . . . /T–X
toxic . . . . . /TOK
toxication . . . . . /TOGS
toxicity . . . . . /TOFX, /TOFK
toxicologist . . . . . /TOEKT
toxicology . . . . . /TOEKL
toxicosis . . . . . /TOEXZ, /TWOX
toxigen . . . . . /TOENK
toxigenic . . . . . /TONK
toxin . . . . . /TOX
toxinemia . . . . . /TAOENZ
toxinization . . . . . /TAINX
toxinogen . . . . . /TOENG
toxins . . . . . /TOXZ
toxis . . . . . /TAUKZ
toxism . . . . . /TOFM
toxoid . . . . . /TOIKD
toxon . . . . . /TONX, /TAONX
toxy . . . . . /TYOX
tracer . . . . . /TRAIRS
tracheal . . . . . /TRAIKL, /TRAEKL
tracheitis . . . . . /TRAOIKS
trachelectasia . . . . . /TRAIKLS
trachelectomy . . . . . /TRAEKT
trachelitis . . . . . /TRAOIKLS
tracheloplasty . . . . . /TRAIPT
trachelorrhaphy . . . . . /TRAEF
trachelos . . . . . /TRAEKLS
trachelotomy . . . . . /TROKT
trachelus . . . . . /TRAOEKLS
tracheobronchitis . . . . . /TRONTS
tracheobronchoscopy . . . . . /TROPS
tracheoscopy . . . . . /TRAEPS
tracheotomy . . . . . /TRAIKT
trachoma . . . . . /TRO*EM
tract . . . . . /TRAKT
tracted . . . . . /TRAKTD
traction . . . . . /TRAX
tractor . . . . . /TRAOK

tragicus . . . /TRUS
tragus . . . /TRAIG
train. . . . /TRAIN
transducer . . . /TRAORS
transduction . . . /TRUGS
transference . . . /TR–FRNS
transformation . . . /TR–GS, /TR–FMGS
transfusion . . . /TR–FGS, /TRAOUFGS
transmission . . . /TR–MGS
transmitter . . . /TR–RMT
transmitters . . . /TR–RMTS
transparency. . . . /TR–PZ
transparent. . . . /TR–P
transplant . . . /TRAPT
transplantation . . . /TRAPGS
transport . . . /TR–PT
transversalis . . . /TRAEFL, /TRAEVL
transversarius . . . /TRAURS
transverse . . . /TRAFRB
transversectomy . . . /TREKT
transversostomy . . . /TRO*S, /TRAFRT
trap . . . /TRAP
trapezial. . . . /TRAOEPZ
trauma . . . /TRAUM
traumas . . . /TRAUMS
traumatic . . . /TRAUMT
treatment. . . . /TREMT, /TRAOEMT
tremor. . . . /TRERM
trepanation . . . /TRAEPGS
tresia. . . . /TRAEZ
tresis. . . . /TRAOESZ
tribe. . . . /TRAOIB
trichate . . . /TRIFPD
trichia . . . /TRAFP
trichial. . . . /TRAIFPL
trichiasis . . . /TRAOIXZ
trichic . . . /TRIFPG
trichiniasis. . . . /TRAOIFPS
trichinosis . . . /TRIFPS
trichium . . . /TROIFM
trichomonal . . . /TROENL
trichophobia . . . /TROEB
trichophrydia . . . /TRID
trichosis . . . /TROEXZ
trichotic. . . . /TRIFPT

trichous . . . . . /TRIFPZ
triginous . . . . . /TRIJS
triglyceridemia . . . . . /TLAOED
trigo . . . . . /TRAO*IG
trigonitis . . . . . /TROING
trigonoenterostomy . . . . . /TRONT, /TRONGT
trigonosigmoidostomy . . . . . /TROIND
tripsis . . . . . /TRIPSZ
tripsy . . . . . /TRIPS
triptic . . . . . /TRIPGT
triptor . . . . . /TRIRPT
triptoscope . . . . . /TROEPT
triptoscopy . . . . . /TROIPT
trismus . . . . . /TRIMZ
trist . . . . . /TR*IS
trists . . . . . /TR*ISZ
trite . . . . . /TRAOIT
trochanterian . . . . . /TROENK
trochanteric . . . . . /TROERK
trochlea . . . . . /TROKL
trochlear . . . . . /TRORKL
tron . . . . . /TRO*N
trope . . . . . /TROEP
tropes . . . . . /TROEPS
troph . . . . . /TROIF
trophasthenia . . . . . /TREN
trophe . . . . . /TRAUF
trophia . . . . . /TRAOEF
trophic . . . . . /TROEFG, /TROIFG, /TROFG
trophin . . . . . /TROEFN
trophoblast . . . . . /TROEFB
trophodynia . . . . . /TROEFD
trophoneurosis . . . . . /TROERZ, /TRAOURS
trophy . . . . . /TROEF
tropia . . . . . /TROIP
tropic . . . . . /TROPG, /TROIPG
tropin . . . . . /TROFN
tropins . . . . . /TROFNS
tropion . . . . . /TRAUN
tropism . . . . . /TROFM
tropometer . . . . . /TROPT, /TRAOERMT
tropous . . . . . /TROUPZ
tropy . . . . . /TRAOEP, /TRO*EP
trosis . . . . . /TROESZ
truncus . . . . . /TRUNKZ

trusion . . . . . /TRAOGS
trypesis . . . . . /TRAOEPS
trypsia . . . . . /TROIPS
trypsin . . . . . /TRINS, /TR*IPS
tryptic . . . . . /TR–PK, /TR*IPG
tubal . . . . . /TUBL
tubate . . . . . /TAEBT
tubation . . . . . /TAOUBGS
tube . . . . . /TAOUB
tuberal . . . . . /TAOBL
tubercle. . . . . /TAOURKL
tubercular. . . . . /BERL
tuberculate . . . . . /BERLT
tuberculin . . . . . /BERKL, /TBLIN
tuberculoma. . . . . /TAOUKL
tuberculoses . . . . . /BERKZ
tuberculosis . . . . . /BERK
tuberculotic. . . . . /BERKT, /BLOKT, /TBLOK
tuberculous . . . . . /BERKS
tuberous . . . . . /TAOUBZ
tubography . . . . . /TAOUFB
tubular . . . . . /TAOURBL
tubule . . . . . /TAOUBL
tumesce . . . . . /TAOUMZ
tumescence . . . . . /TAOUMS
tumor . . . . . /TAOURM
tumorigenic . . . . . /TAOURMG
turbinal . . . . . /TURNL
turbinate . . . . . /TBAET
turia . . . . . /TAOUR
tus (*see also* otus) . . . . . /YO*ETS
tussive . . . . . /TUV
ty . . . . . /TI
tylosis . . . . . /TAOILSZ, /TLOSZ
tylus. . . . . /TAOILZ
tympanal. . . . . /TAMPL
tympanic . . . . . /TIMPG, /TWANK
tympanites . . . . . /TIMPT
tympanitis . . . . . /TIMPTS
tympanotomy . . . . . /TWAUT
tympanum . . . . . /TWUM, /TUMP
tympany. . . . . /TWEMP
type. . . . . /TAOIP
types . . . . . /TAOIPS
typhlic . . . . . /TIFK

typhlitis . . . . . /TAOIFLT, /TAOIFLTS
typhlon . . . . . /TIFN
typhlosis . . . . . /TOEFLS
typhlotomy . . . . . /TOFLT
typhoid . . . . . /TWOID
typhoid fever . . . . . /TWAOEVR
typhosis . . . . . /TOEFSZ
typic . . . . . /TWIPG, /TOIPK
typical . . . . . /TOIP
typing . . . . . /TAOIPG
typology . . . . . /TOIPG
typy . . . . . /TAO*IP
tyrosinemia . . . . . /TRAO*EM

U

ulcerative . . . . . /UVLT
ulis . . . . . /YOULS
ulnar . . . . . /ARNL
um . . . . . /UM
umbilical . . . . . /BIKL
umbilication . . . . . /BAILGS
umbilicus . . . . . /BIKLS
uncle . . . . . /UNK
uncles . . . . . /UNKS
ungual . . . . . /GAUNL
unguia . . . . . /*UNG
unguial . . . . . /UNL
unit . . . . . /UNT
unsaturated . . . . . /NAFPD
urachal . . . . . /YURKL
urachus . . . . . /YAOFP
uranic . . . . . /URNG
uratic . . . . . /YAORKT
urea . . . . . /YAOR, /YAO*UR
uremia . . . . . /YAOURM
uresia . . . . . /YAOERZ
uresis . . . . . /YAOES
ureter . . . . . /AOURT
ureteral . . . . . /YERLT, /AOURLT
ureterectasis . . . . . /YAOURTS
ureterectomy . . . . . /AOURKT
ureteria . . . . . /YAERKT
ureteric . . . . . /YERKT

ureteritis . . . . . /AOURTS
ureterocystectomy . . . . . /YAOERKT
ureterocystotomy . . . . . /YAURS
ureterogram . . . . . /AOURGT
ureterography . . . . . /YOERG
ureterolysis . . . . . /YOERLS
ureteronephrosis . . . . . /YOEFZ
ureteroplasty . . . . . /YA*RS
ureteropyelitis . . . . . /YAOILTS
ureteropyelonephritis . . . . . /YAOIFLT
ureteroradiography . . . . . /YAOEFG
ureteroscopy . . . . . /YAOURP
ureterosis . . . . . /YAOETS
ureterostomy . . . . . /AOUFT
-ureterostomy . . . . . /AO*UFT
ureterotomy. . . . . /YAURT
ureteroureterostomy . . . . . /YUFT
urethra . . . . . /AO*URT
urethral . . . . . /YARLT, /YA*LT
urethralis . . . . . /YARLTS, /YA*LTS
urethria . . . . . /YAO*ERT
urethritis . . . . . /AO*URTS
urethrocele. . . . . /AOELT
urethrogram . . . . . /AOURG
urethrography . . . . . /AO*URGT
urethropexy . . . . . /AOURX
urethroscope . . . . . /AOURP
urethroscopy . . . . . /AOURPG
urethrotome . . . . . /YO*EMT
uretic . . . . . /YERK
uria . . . . . /YAOUR
uriasis . . . . . /YAOIRS
uric . . . . . /YAOURK
uricacidemia . . . . . /YAOEKD
uricaciduria. . . . . /YAOIRKS
uricemia . . . . . /YAOURMS, /YAOERM
uricemic . . . . . /YAOERMG
uricide . . . . . /YAOIRD
uricuria . . . . . /YAOERK, /YAO*URK
uricuric . . . . . /YOURK
urid . . . . . /YURD
urobilin . . . . . /AOURBL
urocrinia . . . . . /YAOUNK
urography . . . . . /YAOURG, /YAOUFRG
urolithic . . . . . /YIFK, /YAOFK

urology . . . /YAOURLG
uterine . . . /YAOURT
ureteroscopy . . . /YAOURP
uterotomy . . . /YAOUMT
uterotropic . . . /YURPG
uterovaginal . . . /YAVL
uvular . . . /YAOUVL

V

vaccinal . . . /VAUNL
vaccination . . . /VAGS, /VAIX
vaccine . . . /VAX, /VAO*EN
vaccinial . . . /VOINL
vacuolar . . . /VAORKL
vacuole . . . /VAOKL
vagal . . . /VA*LG
vaginal . . . /VLAJ
vaginalitis . . . /VLAJT, /VLAJTS, /VLOIJ
vaginitis . . . /VAOIJS
vagino-enterocele . . . /VAOL
vaginorectal . . . /VARKT
vagogram . . . /VA*M
vagotomy . . . /VAOT
vagotony . . . /VONT
valence . . . /VAINLS
valency . . . /VAINLZ
valent . . . /VAINT, /VAINLT
valeric . . . /VAERK
valgus . . . /VALGZ
valinemia . . . /VAEM
valvar . . . /VAVRL, /VAUVRL
valve . . . /VAFL, /VAVL
valvotomy . . . /VAOMT
valvular . . . /VAURL
valvulitis . . . /VAOIVLT, /VAOIFLT
valvulotome . . . /VOEMT
valvulotomy . . . /VAVLT
vaporization . . . /VAIRPGS
var . . . /VA*R
varia (*see also* ovaria) . . . /VAOR
variance . . . /VAIRNS
varianism (*see also* ovarianism) . . . /OIVNS
variant . . . /VAIRNT

variate . . . . . /VART
varication . . . . . /VARGS
varicosis . . . . . /VARSZ
varicosity . . . . . /VAIFT
variola . . . . . /VOERL
varium (*see also* ovarium) . . . . . /VA*IRM
varus . . . . . /VARS
vasation . . . . . /VAZ
vascular . . . . . /VAFR, /VAUFR
vascularization . . . . . /VAFRGS, /VAUFRGS
vascularly . . . . . /VAFRL, /VAUFRL
vasculature . . . . . /VAOUT
vasculitis . . . . . /VOIT, /VOITS
vasectomy . . . . . /VEKT
vasology . . . . . /VAOFLG
vasomotor . . . . . /VOERMT
vasostomy . . . . . /VAO*S
vection . . . . . /V*EX
vector . . . . . /VERKT
vegetarian. . . . . . /VAIRJ
vegetarianism . . . . . /VAIFM
vegetative. . . . . . /VAIJ
venation . . . . . /VAINGS
venereal . . . . . /VAIRL
venitis . . . . . /VAOENTS
venogram . . . . . /VAOENG
venography . . . . . /VAOEFG
venom . . . . . /VEM
venomous . . . . . /VEMS
venosity . . . . . /VAONT, /VOFT
venostomy . . . . . /VEFT
venous . . . . . /VENZ
venter . . . . . /V–RNT, /V*ERNT
ventilation . . . . . /VAENGS
vention . . . . . /V*ENGS
ventrad . . . . . /VARTD
ventral . . . . . /VARL
ventricle . . . . . /VENK
ventricular. . . . . . /VANK
ventricularis. . . . . . /VANKS
ventriculi . . . . . /VIRK, /VL*I, /VLAO*I
ventriculography . . . . . /VAEFG
ventriculus . . . . . /VEKLZ
venular . . . . . /VAORNL
verbal . . . . . /VERBL

verdin . . . . /VIRND
vergence . . . . /VERJS
verse . . . . /VERS
versioflexion . . . . /VEFN, /VEFRN
version . . . . /VERGS
versus . . . . /VERZ
vert . . . . /VERT, /VOIRT
vertebra . . . . /VA
vertebral . . . . /BRAL, /VAUL
verted . . . . /VERTD, /VOIRTD
verter . . . . /V*ERT
vertical . . . . /VERL
vertiginous . . . . /VIJZ
vertigo . . . . /VERG, /VERGT
vesical . . . . /VAEFL
vesicle . . . . /VEKL, /VELS
vesicofixation . . . . /VEFX
vesicopexy . . . . /VOEPX
vesicoplasty . . . . /VAEFK
vesicostomy . . . . /VAUFT
vesicular . . . . /VEFRL
vesiculectomies . . . . /VLEKTS
vesiculectomy . . . . /VLEKT
vesiculitis . . . . /VIKL, /VIKLS
vesiculography . . . . /VOG
vesiculosis . . . . /VOKLS
vest . . . . /V*ES
vestibular . . . . /VEBL
vestibulitis . . . . /VAOIBTS
viable . . . . /VAOIBL
villi . . . . /VLI
villous . . . . /VILS
villus . . . . /VL*US
vinyl . . . . /VAOINL
violet . . . . /VO*ILT
viral . . . . /VAOIRL
virotic . . . . /VAOIRK
virulence . . . . /VERLS
virulent . . . . /VURLT, /VAOULT
virus . . . . /VAOIR
visceral . . . . /VIFRL
visceration . . . . /VIFRGS
visceritis . . . . /VAOIFT, /VAOIFTS
viscidosis . . . . /V–FDZ
viscosimetry . . . . /VAOERMT, /SKAOERMT

viscosity . . . . /VIFT
vision . . . . /VIGS
visor . . . . /VAOIRZ
visual . . . . /VIRBL
vital . . . . /VALT
vitamin . . . . /VAOIM, /VAOIMT
vitaminosis . . . . /VOIMT, /VOIMTS
vitaminotic . . . . /VOIK
vitellin . . . . /VAOINLT
vitelline . . . . /VINLT
vitreous . . . . /VIT
vitrinal . . . . /VIRNLT
vivescence . . . . /VAOIVNS
vivification . . . . /VAIFGS, /VAIVGS
vivisection . . . . /VIVGS
vocational . . . . /VORBL, /VOEXL
voice . . . . /VOIS
volemia . . . . /VAO*EM, /VAOEM
volemic . . . . /VAOEMG
volia . . . . /VAO*L
volitional . . . . /VOILGS
volt . . . . /VOLT, /VOELT
voltage . . . . /VOJ
voltmeter . . . . /VOERLT
voltometer . . . . /VORLT
volution . . . . /V–LGS
volvulus . . . . /VAOUFL, /VAOUFLS
vomerine . . . . /VOIRM
vomiting . . . . /VOMG, /VOMGT
vorous . . . . /VOURS
vulvar . . . . /VUFRL, /VUVRL
vum (*see also* ovum) . . . . /OVM

W

waking . . . . /WAIG
watt . . . . /WAT
wave . . . . /WAEV
waves . . . . /WAEVS
weight . . . . /WAET
welding . . . . /WELGD
well . . . . /WEL

X

xanthene . . . . /ZENT
xanthin . . . . /ZINT, /KP*INT
xanthine (*see also* oxanthine) . . . . /ZAENT, /KPA*NT
xanthoendothelioma . . . . /KPOEMT
xanthoma . . . . /ZOEMT
xanthopsia . . . . /SAUPS, /ZAUPZ
xanthosarcoma . . . . /ZKOEM
xanthose . . . . /ZANTS
xemia (*see also* oxemia) . . . . /KP*IM
xenia . . . . /SA*EN
xenic . . . . /ZAOENG, /ZAENG
xenitis . . . . /ZAOENTS
xenosis . . . . /KPOENS
xenous (*see also* oxenous) . . . . /KPO*US
xeny . . . . /ZNAOE
xerasia . . . . /ZAOERZ
xerosis . . . . /KPROESZ
xerotic . . . . /KPROKT
xic (*see also* oxic) . . . . /KPIK
xidation (*see also* oxidation) . . . . /SHA*EGS
xidosis (*see also* oxidosis) . . . . /O*EXZ
xiphoid . . . . /ZIFD
xyster . . . . /ZIFR, /ZIFRT

Y

ydrosis (*see also* hydrosis) . . . . /DRO*ES
ydrotic (*see also* hidrotic *and* idrotic) . . . . /DRO*K
ysterocyesis . . . . /JAOIFSZ

Z

zemia . . . . /ZAEM
zoa . . . . /ZOE
zoal . . . . /ZOEL
zoan . . . . /ZAON
zoiasis . . . . /ZAOIS
zoic . . . . /ZOIK
zoicide . . . . /ZOID
zoin . . . . /ZOIN

zoite . . . . /SWAOIT, /ZWAOIT
zonal . . . . /ZAUNL
zone . . . . /ZOEN
zonular . . . . /ZOERNL
zoological . . . . /ZAOL
zoology . . . . /ZAOLG
zoon . . . . /ZON
zoonosis . . . . /ZONSZ
zoosis . . . . /ZOEZ, /SWOESZ
zoospermatism . . . . /ZOIRMT
zoospermia . . . . /ZOIRM
zootic . . . . /ZAOKT
zygomatic . . . . /ZAOIGT
zygosis . . . . /ZOESZ
zygosity . . . . /ZOGT, /ZOFT
zygote . . . . /ZAOIG, /ZOEGT
zygotic . . . . /ZOKT
zygous . . . . /ZUS
zyme . . . . /ZYAOIM
zymin . . . . /ZMIN
zymogen . . . . /ZGEN
zymogenic . . . . /ZGENG
zymosis . . . . /SMOEZ, /ZMOEZ
zymotic . . . . /ZMOK, /ZMOKT

SUFFIXES (BY STENO)

A

/ABL . . . . . abdominal
/ABZ . . . . . abscess
/A*D . . . . . ad
/AE . . . . . ae
/AEBD . . . . . antibody
/AEFB . . . . . ankyloblepharon
/AEFG . . . . . arteriography
/AEFLG . . . . . alveolography
/AEFPT . . . . . -aperture (*hyphenated*)
/AEFRNT . . . . . afferent
/AEGT . . . . . aggregate
/AEJ . . . . . antigen
/AEJS . . . . . antigens
/AEK . . . . . acme
/A*EL . . . . . ale
/AELZ . . . . . alis
/A*EM . . . . . amine
/AEMDZ . . . . . amidase
/AEMP . . . . . ampere
/AEMSZ . . . . . emesia
/AEN . . . . . anesthesia
/AENG . . . . . antigenic
/AENL . . . . . angle
/A*ENL . . . . . -angle (*hyphenated*)
/A*EP . . . . . apnea
/A*EPG . . . . . apneic

Steno	Suffix
/AEPX	apex
/AERK	architecture
/AERKL	architectural
/AERL	arterial
/AERZ	aerosol
/AET	ate
/AETD	ated
/AEVL	alveolar
/AFK	aphic
/AFP	arche
/AFPT	aperture
/A*I	ia
/AIBL	able
/AIF	aphia
/AIFM	erethism
/AIFNT	affinity
/AIGS	ation
/AIMDZ	amidase
/AINKSZ	ankyloses
/AINKZ	ankylosis
/AINL	anal
/AIPZ	aplasia
/A*IR	are
/AIRGS	aeration
/AIRJ	aerophagy
/AIRLG	aerophilic
/A*IRP	aerophil
/A*IRS	ares
/AISZ	ases
/AIVL	auriculovertebral
/AIZ	ase
/AK	act
/AKL	algic
/AKT	act
/A*KT	atic
/A*KTS	atics
/AL	al
/ALG	algia
/AN	an
/ANG	antigenic
/ANGT	actinic
/ANLS	ankyloses
/ANT	ant
/ANTS	ants
/AOB	antibody

/AOBD . . . . . antibody
/AOEJD . . . . . electrocardiogram
/AOEKS . . . . . auxesis
/AOEKT . . . . . emetic
/AOELT . . . . . urethrocele
/AOEM . . . . . emia
/AOEMG . . . . . emic
/AOEMS . . . . . aminos
/AO*EMS . . . . . aminos
/AOERJ . . . . . ergy
/AOERLS . . . . . aerocele
/AO*ERM . . . . . eremia
/AOERMTS . . . . . erythematous
/AOERSZ . . . . . erysis
/AO*ERT . . . . . erythema
/AOERX . . . . . erection
/AOERZ . . . . . eresis
/AO*ET . . . . . ether
/AOFP . . . . . nychial
/AOFPL . . . . . onychial
/AOFRL . . . . . orificial
/AOFT . . . . . ovaritis
/AOFTS . . . . . ovaritis
/AOIBTS . . . . . orbititis
/AOIDZ . . . . . ides
/AO*IDZ . . . . . eidosis
/AOIFD . . . . . ized
/AOIFG . . . . . izing
/AOIFM . . . . . isomerism
/AOIFP . . . . . archy
/AOIFR . . . . . ifier
/AOIFS . . . . . izes
/AOIFT . . . . . iatrist
/AOIFTS . . . . . iatrists
/AOIMD . . . . . amide
/AOIMT . . . . . amnionitis
/AOIMTS . . . . . amnionitis
/AOIN . . . . . ion
/AOIND . . . . . iodine
/AOING . . . . . ionic
/AOINGZ . . . . . ionics
/AOINK . . . . . enchyme
/AOIRL. . . . . . aerophile
/AOIRM . . . . . isomer
/AOIRMG . . . . . isomeric

/AOIRMK . . . . . isomeric
/AOIRN . . . . . iron
/AOIRS . . . . . izer
/AOIRSZ . . . . . ereisis
/AOIRTS . . . . . iritis
/AO*IS . . . . . ize
/AOISZ . . . . . iasis
/AOIT . . . . . ite
/AOITS . . . . . itis
/AOITSZ . . . . . ites
/AOIVLT . . . . . alveolitis
/AOIVLTS . . . . . alveolitis
/AOIVMT . . . . . avitaminosis
/AOIVMTS . . . . . avitaminosis
/AO*K . . . . . -ovariectomy (*hyphenated*)
/AOLG . . . . . opalgia
/AOMG . . . . . ammoniac
/AON . . . . . anomaly
/AONK . . . . . onychia
/AO*NK . . . . . nychia
/AONKS . . . . . -antitoxin (*hyphenated*)
/AONLS . . . . . anomalous
/AONX . . . . . antitoxin
/AONZ . . . . . ansotomy
/AOP . . . . . opia
/AO*P . . . . . pia
/AOPG . . . . . opic
/AO*PG . . . . . pic
/AOR . . . . . anterior
/AORBS . . . . . aortic bodies
/AORBT . . . . . orbita
/AORD . . . . . auditory
/AORG . . . . . aortography
/AORKD . . . . . orchid
/AO*RKD . . . . . rchid
/AORKT . . . . . aortic
/AORTS . . . . . aortitis
/AO*S . . . . . atriostomy
/AO*TS . . . . . oothecitis
/AOUFM . . . . . eurysm
/AOUFT . . . . . ureterostomy
/AO*UFT . . . . . -ureterostomy (*hyphenated*)
/AOUGT . . . . . autogram
/AOUK . . . . . autonomic
/AO*UM . . . . . autoimmune

/AOUNL . . . annular
/AOURBL . . . urobilin
/AOURG . . . urethrogram
/AOURGT . . . ureterogram
/AO*URGT . . . urethrography
/AOURKT . . . ureterectomy
/AOURLT . . . ureteral
/AOURNT . . . eurynter
/AOURP . . . urethroscope
/AOURPG . . . urethroscopy
/AOURT . . . ureter
/AO*URT . . . urethra
/AOURTS . . . ureteritis
/AO*URTS . . . urethritis
/AOURX . . . urethropexy
/AOVLGS . . . -ovulation (*hyphenated*)
/AOVM . . . ovarism
/AOVN . . . ovarian
/AOVNS . . . ovarianism
/AOVNZ . . . -ovarianism (*hyphenated*)
/AOVRL . . . ovular
/AOVRLT . . . ovulatory
/AOX . . . antitoxin
/APG . . . apical
/APGS . . . aptation
/APLS . . . aplasia
/APT . . . apt
/A*R . . . ar
/A*RKT . . . arctia
/ARLT . . . arteriole
/A*RMT . . . ammeter
/ARNL . . . ulnar
/A*RS . . . aster
/A*RTS . . . arthros
/ARXL . . . axillary
/ARZ . . . ars
/AUBL . . . audible
/AUFK . . . -oculography (*hyphenated*)
/AUFPT . . . auchenotomy
/AUFPTS . . . auchenitis
/A*UGS . . . augmentation
/AUK . . . ocular
/A*UK . . . -ocular (*hyphenated*)
/AUKL . . . -oculogram (*hyphenated*)
/AUKLT . . . ocularity

/AUKZ . . . . auxis
/AUM. . . . . optimal
/AUNGT . . . . oncotic
/A*UNGT . . . . -oncotic (*hyphenated*)
/AUNL . . . . oncology
/A*UNL . . . . -oncology (*hyphenated*)
/A*UPS. . . . . opsin
/AUPSZ. . . . . opsis
/A*UPSZ. . . . . psis
/AUPT . . . . optic
/A*UPT. . . . . ptic
/AUPTS . . . . optics
/A*UPTS . . . . ptics
/AUPZ. . . . . opsia
/A*UPZ . . . . psia
/AURKL . . . . auricular
/AURKLS . . . . auricularis
/AURKT . . . . arcuate
/AURL . . . . aural
/A*URL . . . . aurale
/AURMT. . . . . optometer
/A*URMT . . . . -optometer (*hyphenated*)
/AURPT . . . . ptometer
/A*URT. . . . . arthria
/A*UTS . . . . -oothecitis (*hyphenated*)
/AUVGT . . . . augmentive
/A*UX. . . . . auxe
/A*UZ . . . . ost
/AX . . . . action
/AXL . . . . axial

B

/BAEKT . . . . bacteria
/BAELZ. . . . . basial
/BAERP. . . . . bacteriotherapy
/BAFRM . . . . barism
/BAIFK . . . . basic
/BAIFRL . . . . behavioral
/BAILGS . . . . umbilication
/BAILZ . . . . basal
/BAINT . . . . butane
/BAIS. . . . . base
/BAIVRL . . . . behavioral

/BAIZ . . . . . basia
/BAKT . . . . . bacteria
/BAL . . . . . balance
/BALG . . . . . balancing
/BALZ . . . . . basilar
/BAND . . . . . band
/BANG . . . . . bang
/BANK . . . . . bank
/BAOERL . . . . . bacterial
/BAOERM . . . . . bacterium
/BAOES . . . . . bacteriaceae
/BAOEZ . . . . . bezoar
/BAOFRL . . . . . bifemoral
/BAOIFM . . . . . albinism
/BAOILG . . . . . bilinogen
/BAOIN . . . . . bion
/BAOINL . . . . . bulbospinal
/BAOINT . . . . . biont
/BAOINTS . . . . . bionts
/BAOIRTS . . . . . bursitis
/BAOISZ . . . . . biasis
/BAOIT . . . . . bite
/BAOKL . . . . . buccal
/BAOKTS . . . . . biotaxis
/BAOL . . . . . boulia
/BAO*L . . . . . bolia
/BAOMGS . . . . . biodynamics
/BAOR . . . . . baria
/BAORKL . . . . . -orbicular (*hyphenated*)
/BAORLS . . . . . borreliosis
/BAORLT . . . . . abortal
/BAORT . . . . . borate
/BAOUBS . . . . . bubonocele
/BAOUK . . . . . ambulic
/BAOUL . . . . . bulia
/BAOULG . . . . . bulic
/BAOUM . . . . . albumin
/BAOUMS . . . . . albuminous
/BAOUMT . . . . . albuminimeter
/BAOUN . . . . . albuminemia
/BAOUR . . . . . albumosuria
/BAOURK . . . . . barbituric
/BAOURKD . . . . . barbituric acid
/BAOURM . . . . . albuminuria
/BAOURMT . . . . . albuminmetry

/BAOXL	buccoaxial
/BAR	bar
/BARBL	barbital
/BARBT	barbital
/BA*RK	baric
/BARKL	orbicular
/BA*RKL	-orbicular (*hyphenated*)
/BARKT	bacteri
/BARL	bacterial
/BARP	bicarbonate
/BARPT	baropathy
/BAUKL	binocular
/BAZ	basis
/BEFRL	bifemoral
/BEKTS	biotaxes
/BENSZ	biogenesis
/BERK	tuberculosis
/BERKL	tuberculin
/BERKS	tuberculous
/BERKT	tuberculotic
/BERKZ	tuberculoses
/BERL	tubercular
/BERLT	tuberculate
/BEVL	bevel
/BIFLG	basophilic
/BIFRL	bifemoral
/BIKL	umbilical
/BIKLS	umbilicus
/BIKTS	biotaxis
/BIPT	bicipital
/BIRKL	orbicular
/BIRMT	amebimeter
/BIRNL	abdominoperitoneal
/B*IRT	birth
/BIX	inhibition
/BLA	bilia
/–BL	able
/BLADZ	bladders
/BLAEF	blepharia
/BLAEFK	blepharic
/BLAFK	blastic
/BLAFM	ambulism
/BLAFMG	ambulic
/BLAFT	blast
/BLAFTS	blasts

/BLAGS	ablation
/BLAIGS	ambulation
/BLAIS	basioglossus
/BLAL	biological
/BLAMT	blastomata
/BLAOB	bilirubin
/BLAOEB	bilirubinemia
/BLAOEFP	bleach
/BLAO*EM	bilinemia
/BLAOEMT	blastema
/BLAOEPT	blastopenia
/BLAOER	blennorrhea
/BLAOIKS	blastomycosis
/BLAOJ	bilirubinogen
/BLAOL	bucco-occlusal
/BLAOUL	blastula
/BLAOUN	bilirubin
/BLAOURN	bilinuria
/BLARD	bladder
/BLARDZ	bladders
/BLA*S	blast
/BLA*SZ	blasts
/BLAUK	metabolic
/BLAURB	bulbar
/BLAV	ablative
/BL*E	boly
/BLEFM	blepharism
/BLEFN	blepharon
/BLEFRN	blepharon
/BLEFT	blastemia
/BLEJ	blepharopterygium
/BLEK	blastemic
/BL*EN	blennia
/BLEPS	blepsia
/BLEPSZ	blepsis
/BL*ES	blood test
/BL*IB	bulbia
/BLIFM	metabolism
/BL*IK	metabolic
/BLIKT	bilinicterus
/BLIM	ballism
/BLIMS	ballismus
/BL*IN	bilin
/BLIR	biliary
/BL–J	biologic

/BLOEFM . . . . . bolism
/BLOEM . . . . . blastoma
/BLOEMS . . . . . blastomas
/BLOEMT . . . . . blastomatosis
/BLOEP . . . . . amblyopia
/BLOESZ . . . . . blastosis
/BLOFKT . . . . . blastotic
/BLOGT . . . . . blotting
/BLOID . . . . . blastoid
/BLOIF . . . . . blephary
/BLOIM . . . . . blastomyoma
/BLOIP . . . . . amblyopia
/BLOIT . . . . . metabolite
/BLOK . . . . . block
/BLOKT . . . . . tuberculotic
/BLOT . . . . . blot
/BLOUBS . . . . . bulbous
/BLOULS . . . . . bullous
/-BLT . . . . . ability
/BLUBS . . . . . bulbus
/BLURK . . . . . albuminuric
/BLUS . . . . . bilious
/BLUT . . . . . blood test
/BOD . . . . . body
/BODZ . . . . . bodies
/BOEB . . . . . biophobia
/BO*EL . . . . . bole
/BO*EM . . . . . boma
/BOEP . . . . . bioscope
/BOEPG . . . . . bioscopy
/BOERKD . . . . . boric acid
/BOERLS . . . . . borreliosis
/BOERLT . . . . . bolometer
/BOES . . . . . albumose
/BOESZ . . . . . albuminosis
/BOIFM . . . . . biotism
/BOIM . . . . . bium
/BOIMD . . . . . albumoid
/BOINK . . . . . bionic
/BOINT . . . . . biotin
/BOISZ . . . . . biosis
/BOIT . . . . . biotic
/BOITS . . . . . biotics
/BOKL . . . . . binocular
/BOLG . . . . . biology

/BOLGT . . . . . biologist
/BOLGTS . . . . . biologists
/BOLTS . . . . . biologists
/BONT . . . . . biont
/BONTS . . . . . bionts
/BORN . . . . . born
/BOUK . . . . . bulbic
/BOUN . . . . . bound
/BOUP . . . . . buccopulpal
/BOX . . . . . box
/BRAEGS . . . . . abrasion
/BRAELS . . . . . borreliosis
/BRAEM . . . . . membrane
/BRAEMD . . . . . membrane disease
/BRAEMZ . . . . . membranous
/BRAERD . . . . . abrader
/BRAESZ . . . . . bronchiectasis
/BRAFL . . . . . brachiocephalia
/BRAFPZ . . . . . brachius
/BRAID . . . . . bradia
/BRAIFP . . . . . brachia
/BRAIFPL . . . . . brachial
/BRAIKL . . . . . brachial
/BRAIN . . . . . brain
/BRAKD . . . . . brachydactyly
/BRAL . . . . . vertebral
/BRANG . . . . . branchial
/BRANZ . . . . . membranous
/BRAOE . . . . . albumorrhea
/BRAOIMD . . . . . bromide
/BRAOITS . . . . . bronchitis
/BRAORL . . . . . bronchiolar
/BRAOTS . . . . . bronchiolitis
/BREFK . . . . . brachycephalic
/BREFL . . . . . brachycephaly
/BREGT . . . . . bregmatic
/BRELG . . . . . bronchomegaly
/BREM . . . . . bicarbonatemia
/BRERN . . . . . brenner
/BRIFM . . . . . barism
/BRIFP . . . . . barbiturate
/BRIFPS . . . . . barbiturates
/BR*IK . . . . . baric
/BRIKL . . . . . brachydactylia
/BROEMD . . . . . bromidrosis

/BROEMSZ . . . . membranosus
/BROEMT . . . . bromate
/BROEMTD . . . . bromated
/BROENSZ . . . . anabrosis
/BROERNL . . . . bronchiolar
/BROES . . . . bacteriosis
/BROIM . . . . brachium
/BROIN . . . . bothrion
/BROIP . . . . bronchoscopy
/BRO*IT . . . . bothritis
/BROM . . . . bromic
/BRONGT . . . . bronchotomy
/BRONLG . . . . bronchial
/BRONTS . . . . bronchitis
/BROUMD . . . . bromous acid
/BROUMS . . . . bromous
/BRUX . . . . obstruction
/BR*UX . . . . -obstruction (*hyphenated*)
/BULG. . . . . bulge
/BURLS . . . . bursal
/BURTS . . . . bursitis
/BYAUN. . . . . byon
/BYOIT . . . . biote
/BYO*N. . . . . byon

D

/–D. . . . . ed
/DAEFGS. . . . . differentiation
/DAEFTD . . . . differentiate
/DA*EM . . . . dema
/DAENL . . . . dentale
/DAENT . . . . dependent
/DAERL . . . . dermal
/DAERLGS . . . . dermalization
/DAERLS . . . . dermals
/DAERM. . . . . derma
/DA*ERM . . . . dermia
/DAERMS . . . . dermas
/DAERNT . . . . determinant
/DAES . . . . diastase
/DAEZ . . . . dermectasia
/DAFM . . . . dactylism
/DAFN . . . . diaphany

/DAIJS . . . . digitation
/DAJT . . . . digita
/DAKLS . . . . dactylus
/DAL . . . . dialysis
/DA*L . . . . dal
/DALT . . . . dalton
/DAMT . . . . dominant
/DANKT. . . . . indicant
/DAOD . . . . iodide
/DAOE . . . . dia
/DAOELT . . . . dermatocele
/DAO*EM . . . . edema
/DAOENK . . . . indicanemia
/DAOENZ . . . . dentes
/DAOEPS . . . . diapedesis
/DAOERB . . . . dontium
/DAO*ERB. . . . . odontium
/DAOEX. . . . . decussation
/DAOFM . . . . iodidism
/DAOI . . . . die
/DAOIB. . . . . diabetes
/DAOIBT . . . . diabetic
/DAOIDZ . . . . dermides
/DAOIFK . . . . diaphragmatic
/DAOIFN . . . . diaphane
/DAOIFRM . . . . diaphragm
/DAOIFT. . . . . diastasis
/DAOIFTS. . . . . diastasis
/DAOIKL . . . . ductile
/DAOIL . . . . dial
/DAO*IN . . . . dyne
/DAOINT . . . . dynamometer
/DAOINTS . . . . odontitis
/DAOIRB. . . . . odontiasis
/DAOIRBS . . . . dontiasis
/DAOIRKT . . . . diametric
/DAOIRM . . . . diaphragm
/DAOIRS . . . . dieresis
/DAOIRT . . . . dieretic
/DAOIRTS . . . . epidermitis
/DAOISZ. . . . . diosis
/DAO*IT . . . . diathesis
/DAOITS . . . . dontitis
/DAO*ITS. . . . . odontitis
/DAOKT . . . . endarterectomy

/DAOND . . . . odontodynia
/DAO*ND . . . . -odontodynia (*hyphenated*)
/DAONK. . . . . odontalgic
/DAONL. . . . . odontalgia
/DAONLG . . . . -odontalgia (*hyphenated*)
/DAO*P. . . . . dopa
/DAOPS . . . . dipsomania
/DAORD . . . . dorsad
/DAORMT . . . . dormital
/DAOUFG . . . . durography
/DAOUR . . . . aldosteronuria
/DAOURGS . . . . duration
/DAO*URM . . . . durogram
/DAOURN . . . . dysneuria
/DAOURT. . . . . denture
/DAPGS. . . . . adaptation
/DARJ. . . . . discharge
/DAUKT . . . . ductal
/DAULG. . . . . dontalgia
/DAULS . . . . diastalsis
/DAUNL . . . . dontology
/DAUNLT . . . . dontologist
/DA*UNT . . . . dont
/DAUP. . . . . dopa
/D–BL . . . . digestible
/DBUX . . . . abduction
/DEFLS . . . . adelphus
/DEFRNL . . . . deferential
/DEFRNTS. . . . . deferentitis
/DEGS . . . . degradation
/D*EGS. . . . . detection
/DEKL . . . . delic
/D*EKT . . . . dectomy
/DELTD. . . . . deltoid
/D*EM . . . . demia
/D*EMG. . . . . demic
/DENK. . . . . adenic
/DENL . . . . dental
/DENS . . . . dense
/D*ENS . . . . density
/DENSZ . . . . dentosis
/DENT . . . . dent
/DENZ . . . . dens
/DERB. . . . . dentium
/DERBS . . . . dentia

/DERGS . . . . determination
/DERJ . . . . dysergia
/DERKL . . . . dermoclysis
/DERKT. . . . . diphtheritic
/DERM . . . . derm
/DERMDZ . . . . dermidosis
/DERMG . . . . dermic
/DERMGS . . . . dermization
/DERMS . . . . dermis
/DERMSZ. . . . . dermiasis
/DERMT . . . . dermatitis
/DERNTS . . . . densitometer
/DERP . . . . dermoplasty
/DERPT. . . . . dermoperiostosis
/DERSZ . . . . dermosis
/DESZ . . . . desis
/D–FK. . . . . disc
/D–FRNT . . . . deferentectomy
/D–GS. . . . . diagnosis
/D–GT . . . . diagnostic
/D–GTS . . . . diagnostics
/DIFGS . . . . differentiation
/DIFK . . . . disk
/D*IFK . . . . disc
/DIFT . . . . different
/DIJ . . . . digit
/DIJT . . . . digital
/D*IK . . . . dic
/DIKL . . . . dicliditis
/D*IKT. . . . . dectic
/DILGS . . . . dilution
/D*IN . . . . dynia
/DINKT . . . . indicant
/D*INS . . . . dynias
/DINTS. . . . . dentitis
/DIPGS . . . . dipsic
/D*IPT . . . . diphtheria
/DIPZ . . . . dipsia
/DIRKT . . . . diametric
/DIRMG. . . . . dermic
/DIRMGS . . . . dermics
/DIRMT . . . . densimeter
/DIRMTS . . . . dermitis
/DIRS . . . . adenoscirrhus
/DIRX . . . . dermics

/DISZ . . . . discus
/DIVRM . . . . diverticulum
/DJAIGS . . . . degeneration
/DJAIV . . . . degenerative
/D–JS . . . . digestion
/DLAEGS . . . . delineation
/DLAFM . . . . dactylism
/DLAFT . . . . dermatoplasty
/DLAIGS . . . . dilation
/DLAIGT . . . . dilating
/DLAIRT . . . . dilator
/DLAIV . . . . dilative
/DLAK . . . . dactylic
/DLAOEJ . . . . diplegia
/DLAOEK . . . . dactyly
/DLAOEL . . . . dactylia
/DLAOIKS . . . . dermatoclysis
/DLAOIKT . . . . dialytic
/DLAOIRS . . . . dialyzer
/DLAOIRT . . . . dilator
/DLAO*ITS . . . . dermolithiasis
/DLAOIVT . . . . diverticulitis
/DLAOIVTS . . . . diverticulitis
/DLAOULS . . . . distocclusal
/DLA*S . . . . dermatoplasty
/DLAUM . . . . dendroglioma
/DLAVR . . . . diverticular
/DLENS . . . . adolescence
/DLENT . . . . adolescent
/DLEPGT . . . . dysleptic
/DLEPT . . . . dysleptic
/DLIGS . . . . dilatation
/DLIRM . . . . delirium
/DLIT . . . . dacryolith
/DL*IT . . . . dacryolith
/DLOEP . . . . diplopia
/DLOID . . . . deltoid
/DLOIP . . . . diploid
/DLOIPD . . . . diploidy
/DLOIPS . . . . adenoleukopoiesis
/DLOM . . . . dendroglioma
/DLON . . . . dolichocolon
/DLOUKS . . . . dactylous
/DLUKZ . . . . dactylus
/DLUM . . . . delirium

/DLUVM . . . . diverticulum
/DLUVR. . . . . diverticular
/DMA . . . . desma
/DMAEL . . . . dolichomelia
/DMAL . . . . didymal
/DMAOEL . . . . dermatocele
/DMAOITS . . . . didymitis
/DMAOS. . . . . desmia
/DMAOUFGS . . . . immunodiffusion
/DMAT . . . . dermatomy
/DMAUM . . . . dermoma
/DMAUT . . . . desmata
/DMEJ . . . . dynamogenic
/DMEK . . . . desmic
/DMERB. . . . . dementia
/DMIFM . . . . desmism
/DMIGS . . . . admission
/DMIK . . . . demic
/DMIS . . . . didymis
/DMOEM. . . . . dermatome
/DMOES. . . . . endosmosis
/DMOESZ . . . . dermatosis
/DMOEZ. . . . . dermosis
/DMOF . . . . dynamograph
/DMOFL . . . . desmodial
/DMOFM . . . . dermotropism
/DMOID. . . . . dermoid
/DMOILD. . . . . dermoidal
/DMOMT . . . . dynamometer
/DMORMT . . . . dynamometry
/DMOUS . . . . dermatous
/DMUM . . . . desmium
/DMUS . . . . didymus
/D*N . . . . dinia
/DNOURS . . . . dermatoneurosis
/DOEFM . . . . aldosteronism
/DOEJ . . . . dosage
/DOELGS. . . . . depolarization
/DOEMT. . . . . dentinoma
/DOEMZ. . . . . desmos
/DO*EN. . . . . odynia
/DOENS . . . . donesis
/DOEPT . . . . dochoplasty
/DOERBGS . . . . adsorption
/DOERBT . . . . adsorbent

/DOERKL . . . . endotheliosarcoma
/DOERL . . . . endocardial
/DOERLT . . . . depolarizer
/DOERPGS . . . . adsorption
/DOES . . . . dose
/DOET . . . . dote
/DOETS. . . . . dermatosis
/DOETSZ . . . . dermatoses
/DOFG . . . . endography
/DOFM . . . . dontism
/DOFPT. . . . . dochotomy
/DOFT . . . . dontist
/DOID . . . . edematoid
/DOIFM . . . . dyniotropism
/DOIFPT . . . . dochitis
/DOIFPTS. . . . . dochitis
/DOIK. . . . . dectoma
/DOIKLS . . . . dermatopoikilosis
/DOIKT. . . . . ductitis
/DOIKTS. . . . . ductitis
/DOIMS . . . . didymus
/DOIMTS . . . . didymitis
/DOIN . . . . dynia
/DO*IN . . . . odinia
/DOIND . . . . odynia
/DOINK . . . . dynic
/DOINKS . . . . dynics
/DOINS . . . . dynias
/DOIRM . . . . diathermy
/DO*IRM . . . . diathermy
/DOIRMT. . . . . dermatosis
/DOIRMTS . . . . dermatoses
/DOITD . . . . edematoid
/DOLG . . . . dermatology
/DOLS . . . . dontolysis
/DOMS . . . . dominance
/DO*MT . . . . dominant
/DONGT. . . . . dontic
/DONL. . . . . dontal
/DONS. . . . . dontia
/DONT . . . . dont
/DO*NT . . . . dontist
/DONTS . . . . dontics
/DO*NTS . . . . dontitis
/DONX . . . . dontics

/DOP . . . . endopathy
/DORB . . . . dontia
/DORBT . . . . odontia
/DORLS . . . . dorsal
/DORMGS . . . . dormition
/DORNZ. . . . . dornase
/DORX . . . . decortication
/DOS . . . . duodenostomy
/DO*S . . . . duodenostomy
/DOUMS . . . . edematous
/DOUMT . . . . edematous
/DOUNTS . . . . dontous
/DOURMTS . . . . dermatoneurosis
/DPLAOEG . . . . diplegia
/DRAE. . . . . hydrorrhea
/DRAEM . . . . aldosteronemia
/DRAFM . . . . andrism
/DRAIBL . . . . degradable
/DRAIGS . . . . duration
/DRAIJ . . . . drainage
/DRAIS . . . . dyscrasia
/DRAKT . . . . dermatic
/DRAL . . . . dural
/DRAMGT . . . . diagrammatic
/DRANT . . . . depressant
/DRAOEFM . . . . adrenalism
/DRAO*EK . . . . diarrheic
/DRAOEL . . . . diarrheal
/DRAOENL . . . . adrenal
/DRAOF . . . . dermatrophia
/DRAOIT . . . . dendrite
/DRAO*M . . . . dromia
/DRAOND. . . . . android
/DRAOSZ . . . . diaphoresis
/DRAOTS . . . . endometritis
/DRAOUGS . . . . distribution
/DRAOUX . . . . distribution
/DRAPG . . . . drepanocytic
/DRAUK . . . . hydraulic
/DRAUM . . . . drama
/DRAUMT . . . . drometer
/DRERJ . . . . adrenergic
/DREXL . . . . directional
/DREXT . . . . dexterity
/DREZ . . . . diuresis

/DRI . . . . drive
/DRIFM . . . . adrenocorticism
/DRIPT . . . . dontrypy
/DR*IT . . . . dysrhythmia
/D-RK . . . . detector
/DR-K. . . . . epidermic
/DR-L . . . . epidermal
/DROEFM . . . . dontotropism
/DROEG. . . . . androgen
/DROEKD . . . . dextrocardia
/DRO*EL. . . . . dromal
/DROEM . . . . drome
/DRO*EM . . . . dromia
/DROENT . . . . androsterone
/DROEP . . . . dontropy
/DROEPS . . . . drepanocytosis
/DROEPSZ . . . . ephidrosis
/DROES . . . . hydrosis
/DRO*ES . . . . ydrosis
/DROESZ . . . . hidrosis
/DRO*ESZ . . . . idrosis
/DRO*ETS . . . . diarthrosis
/DROFM. . . . . adrenocorticalism
/DROFMT . . . . dicrotism
/DROIKT. . . . . dendritic
/DRO*IM . . . . dromy
/DROIMD. . . . . dermoid
/DROITS . . . . endocarditis
/DROIZ . . . . idrosis
/DROK . . . . hidrotic
/DRO*K . . . . ydrotic
/DRO*KT . . . . idrotic
/DROLZ . . . . hydrolysis
/DROMG . . . . dromic
/DROMS. . . . . dromus
/DROMT . . . . hydrometer
/DRON . . . . dendron
/DRO*N . . . . deron
/DROPGT . . . . dioptric
/DROSZ . . . . drosis
/DROT . . . . dicrotic
/DROUFM . . . . andromorphism
/DROUFS . . . . andromorphous
/DROUMS. . . . . dromous
/DROUX . . . . dextrous

/DR-P	depressor
/DRUG	drug
/DRUK	adductor
/DRUPGS	disruption
/DUKL	ductal
/DUKLS	dactylous
/DUKT	duct
/DUP	duplicate
/DUPGS	duplication
/D*URK	duric
/DURKT	ductor
/DURKTS	ductors
/DURMTS	dermatous
/D*UX	duction
/D-VP	depressive
/DWAEF	adenography
/DWAIGS	deviation
/DWAIRX	adenovarix
/DWAISZ	adenectasis
/DWALG	adenalgia
/DWAM	dynamic
/DWAMG	adynamic
/DWAMS	dynamics
/DWAOE	adenia
/DWAOED	diadochokinesia
/DWAOEL	adenocele
/DWAOEMS	desmoses
/DWAOEN	adenia
/DWAOERB	deficiency
/DWAOERBD	deficiency syndrome
/DWAOIP	diopter
/DWAOUGS	diffusion
/DWAUM	-odontoma (*hyphenated*)
/DWAUMT	adenocystoma
/DWEKT	adenectomy
/DWEMG	endemic
/DW*EN	aden
/DWENK	adenic
/DWENTS	adenitis
/DWIM	dynamia
/DWIMT	adenolymphitis
/DWIMTS	adenolymphitis
/DWINT	dentin
/DWIRBT	deficient
/DW*IS	adenocyst

/DWOD . . . . duodenum
/DWOEM . . . . adenoma
/DWOEMTS . . . . adenomatosis
/DWOEMZ . . . . desmosis
/DWOENTS . . . . dontosis
/DWOEP . . . . diascope
/DWOEPK . . . . adenotropic
/DWOEPSZ . . . . adiposis
/DWOES . . . . adipose
/DWOESZ . . . . adenosis
/DWOI . . . . adenoid
/DWOIKT . . . . adenoidectomy
/DWOIL . . . . adenoidal
/DWOIP . . . . duodenoscopy
/DWO*IP . . . . diascopy
/DWOIPS . . . . adipsia
/DWOIT . . . . duodenitis
/DWOITS . . . . duodenitis
/DWOKT . . . . duodenectomy
/DWOLD . . . . duodenal
/DWOM . . . . odontoma
/DWO*M . . . . dontoma
/DWONG . . . . adenoncus
/DWONL . . . . duodenal
/DWO*P . . . . adenopathy
/DWOPT . . . . adiposity
/DWO*PT . . . . adenopathy
/DWOS . . . . duodenostomy
/DWO*S . . . . duodenostomy
/DWOT . . . . adenotomy
/DWOUS . . . . adenous
/DWRAM . . . . adenogram
/DWROEM . . . . adenocarcinoma
/DWUNGS . . . . disjunction
/DWUS . . . . adenosus
/DYAF . . . . diagraph
/DYAOIN . . . . dyne
/DYA*S . . . . diaclast
/DYENS . . . . dysgenesia
/DYENSZ . . . . dysgenesis
/DYENT . . . . audient
/DYENZ . . . . dysgenesia
/DYIN . . . . dyscrinia
/DYOT . . . . dictiotomy
/D–Z . . . . disease

E

/EFLTS . . . . elephantiasis
/EFPSZ . . . . ecchysis
/EFRMS . . . . estrum
/EFRNT . . . . efferent
/EFRS . . . . estrus
/EFRZ. . . . . estrous
/EKD . . . . ectoderm
/EKLS . . . . elcus
/EKT . . . . ectomy
/*EKT . . . . ectome
/EKTS . . . . ectomies
/ELZ . . . . elasma
/EMGS . . . . emization
/EMS . . . . emesis
/EMSZ . . . . emesis
/ENK . . . . enchyma
/ENKL . . . . enchymal
/ENL. . . . . enamel
/EPLD . . . . epidemiology
/ERJ . . . . ergia
/ERK . . . . ergic
/ERMT . . . . imetry
/ERPD . . . . epidermoid
/ERZ . . . . erism
/ESZ . . . . esis

F

/FAEFK . . . . aphasic
/FAEFM . . . . ferrism
/FAEJ . . . . phage
/FA*EJ. . . . . ophage
/FAEJS . . . . phagies
/FAEL . . . . female
/FAEM . . . . family
/FA*EN . . . . phania
/FA*EPT . . . . -ophthalmopathy (*hyphenated*)
/FAEPT . . . . ophthalmopathy
/FAERBT . . . . ifacient
/FAERG . . . . photomicrography
/FAERK . . . . ferric

/FAERNZ . . . . phanerosis
/FAERT . . . . ferritin
/FAES . . . . aphasia
/FAESZ . . . . phasis
/FA*ESZ . . . . aphasis
/FA*ET . . . . amphetamine
/FAEVK . . . . affective
/FAEVT . . . . affectivity
/FAFLS . . . . fascialis
/FAGT. . . . . phagocytic
/FAIFGS. . . . . infestation
/FAIFK. . . . . phasic
/FAIFM . . . . phagism
/FAIG . . . . phagic
/FAIJ . . . . phagia
/FA*IJ. . . . . ophagia
/FA*IK . . . . phakia
/FA*IN. . . . . phane
/FA*INS . . . . phanes
/FAIRBL . . . . facial
/FAIRBLS . . . . facialis
/FAIRBT . . . . facient
/FAIRJ . . . . pharyngeal
/FAIRN . . . . ferrin
/FAIRNL . . . . pharyngeal
/FAIRNTS . . . . pharyngitis
/FAIRNX . . . . pharynx
/FAIRS . . . . ferious
/FAIS . . . . face
/FAIX. . . . . fixation
/FAIZ . . . . phase
/FA*IZ. . . . . phasia
/FAKL . . . . phallic
/FAKT . . . . factor
/FALG . . . . phagology
/FA*N . . . . phany
/FANK. . . . . phanic
/FANKD . . . . phanic acid
/FAOB . . . . phobophobia
/FAOEB . . . . feedback
/FAOEGTS . . . . fetation
/FAO*EL . . . . philia
/FAO*ELG . . . . philiac
/FAOELT . . . . fetal
/FAOEM . . . . ferremia

/FAO*EM . . . . phenylalaninemia
/FAOEMG . . . . ferremic
/FAOEMS . . . . ferricemia
/FAOEMT . . . . phosphatemia
/FAOENG. . . . . phenic
/FAOENGS . . . . phenics
/FAOERJ . . . . pharyngocele
/FAOERMT . . . . photometer
/FAOETS . . . . fetus
/FAO*ETS. . . . . photesthesia
/FAOEZ . . . . fecia
/FAO*EZ. . . . . physes
/FAOFG . . . . phonocardiography
/FAOFK . . . . oophorectomy
/FAO*FK . . . . -oophorectomy (*hyphenated*)
/FAOFR . . . . oophorectomy
/FAOGT . . . . phagocyte
/FAOGTS . . . . phagocytes
/FAOIB. . . . . fiber
/FAOIBS . . . . fibrous
/FAOIFTS. . . . . phacitis
/FAO*IG . . . . fying
/FAOIKL. . . . . phylic
/FAOIKS . . . . phakitis
/FAO*IL. . . . . phile
/FAOIM. . . . . phyma
/FAOIMS . . . . phimosis
/FAO*IMT . . . . phytoma
/FAOIMZ . . . . phimosis
/FAOIP. . . . . fiberscope
/FAOIPTS . . . . phytosis
/FAOIRB. . . . . fibra
/FAOIRMG . . . . photomicrograph
/FAOIRMT . . . . physometra
/FAO*IT . . . . phyte
/FAOITD . . . . phytid
/FAOK . . . . factor
/FAOKL. . . . . factorial
/FAOMT. . . . . phantom
/FAON . . . . phonia
/FAOR . . . . inferior
/FAO*R . . . . phora
/FAORL . . . . inferiorly
/FAORM. . . . . foramina
/FAORMT. . . . . ophthalmometer

/FAO*RMT . . . . phthalmometer
/FAORN . . . . phorin
/FAORNZ . . . . phorins
/FAORP . . . . pharyngoscope
/FAORPG . . . . pharyngoscopy
/FAORPT . . . . phototherapy
/FAOT . . . . foot
/FAOUFBL . . . . fusible
/FAOUFL . . . . fusal
/FAOUG . . . . fugal
/FAOUGS . . . . fusion
/FAOUGZ . . . . fugous
/FAOUJ . . . . fuge
/FAOUK . . . . fugic
/FAOUKS . . . . pharmaceutics
/FAOURBS . . . . fuscinosis
/FAOUZ . . . . fuse
/FARBL . . . . fascial
/FARBLZ . . . . fascialis
/FARBTS . . . . fascitis
/FARGS . . . . faradization
/FARKT . . . . pharmacologist
/FARKTS . . . . pharmacologists
/FARL . . . . pharmaceutical
/FARLS . . . . pharmaceuticals
/FARMZ . . . . pharmacy
/FA*S . . . . fast
/FASZ . . . . aphasis
/FAT . . . . fat
/FAUG . . . . phagus
/FAUJ . . . . pharmacological
/FAUK . . . . ophthalmic
/FA*UK . . . . phthalmic
/FAUM . . . . ophthalmia
/FA*UM . . . . phthalmia
/FAUMG . . . . ophthalmic
/FA*UMG . . . . phthalmic
/FAUMT . . . . ophthalmitis
/FA*UMT . . . . phthalmitis
/FAUMTS . . . . ophthalmitis
/FA*UMTS . . . . phthalmitis
/FA*UN . . . . fauna
/FAUNG . . . . phonic
/FAURD . . . . farad
/FAURDZ . . . . faradism

/FAURK . . . . infarct
/FAURKL . . . . fascicular
/FAURL . . . . pharmaceutical
/FAURLS . . . . pharmaceuticals
/FAURM . . . . pharmacology
/FAURMG. . . . . pharmacologic
/FAUS . . . . ophthalmus
/FA*US . . . . phthalmus
/FAVK . . . . factive
/FA*X . . . . faction
/FBLAFT . . . . fibroblast
/FBROID . . . . fibroid
/FEFRN . . . . ferrin
/FEK . . . . effect
/F*EM . . . . phemia
/FEMG . . . . phemic
/F*EMG . . . . phemic
/FEMS. . . . . phemesthesia
/FENT . . . . phyogenetic
/FERD . . . . ephedrine
/FERJ . . . . fermentation
/FERK . . . . effector
/FERL. . . . . fertile
/FERLT . . . . fertility
/FERMGS . . . . fermentation
/FERMT . . . . ferment
/FERNT . . . . ferient
/FERS . . . . ferous
/FERZ . . . . pherous
/FET . . . . amphetamine
/FEVK. . . . . fective
/F*EX. . . . . fection
/F*I. . . . . fy
/F*ID . . . . fid
/FIFK . . . . ifactive
/FIFN . . . . fibrinolysin
/FIFP . . . . fiche
/FIFRN. . . . . fibrinolysin
/FIG . . . . figure
/FIGD . . . . figured
/F*IK . . . . fic
/F*IKT . . . . phytic
/F*IL . . . . phil
/FILG . . . . filling
/F*ILG . . . . philic

/F*ILS . . . . phils
/FILZ . . . . physeal
/FIM . . . . film
/FIRB . . . . efficient
/FIRBL . . . . official
/FIRLGS . . . . filtration
/FIRLT . . . . filter
/FIRLZ . . . . fissural
/FIRZ . . . . fissure
/FIVK . . . . ifactive
/FIX . . . . fix
/F–L . . . . physical
/FLAEFG . . . . phlebography
/FLAEGS . . . . flagellation
/FLAEM . . . . filaremia
/FLAENL . . . . phalangeal
/FLA*ER . . . . filaria
/FLAEX . . . . flexia
/FLAEZ . . . . phosphorylase
/FLAF . . . . electrophysiolograph
/FLAFM . . . . phalangism
/FLAFPT . . . . flatulent
/FLAIBS . . . . phlebectasia
/FLAIBSZ . . . . phlebectasis
/FLAIFN . . . . flavin
/FLAIGS . . . . inflation
/FLA*IGS . . . . flation
/FLAIGZ . . . . phlegmasia
/FLAIJ . . . . flagellate
/FLAIJS . . . . flagellation
/FLAING . . . . phalangia
/FLAIRL . . . . filarial
/FLAIVN . . . . flavin
/FLAIVS . . . . flavous
/FLAJ . . . . flagellate
/FLAKT . . . . prophylactic
/FLA*KT . . . . phylactic
/FLA*KTS . . . . phylactics
/FLAKZ . . . . prophylaxis
/FLAMT . . . . inflammatory
/FLA*MT . . . . -inflammatory (*hyphenated*)
/FLANKZ . . . . phalanx
/FLANXZ . . . . anaphylaxis
/FLAOEB . . . . pylephlebitis
/FLAOEBS . . . . pylephlebitis

/FLAOEL . . . . omphalocele
/FLAO*EL . . . . mphalocele
/FLAOERB . . . . phylactia
/FLAOERMT . . . . photofluorimetry
/FLAOEX . . . . phylaxes
/FLAOGS . . . . fistulization
/FLAOID . . . . formaldehyde
/FLAOIKT . . . . phyletic
/FLAOIM . . . . phylum
/FLAOIX . . . . phylaxia
/FLAOM . . . . electrophysiologram
/FLAONL . . . . influenzal
/FLAONS . . . . influenza
/FLAORMT . . . . -inflammatory (*hyphenated*)
/FLAOUD . . . . fluid
/FLAOURD . . . . fluoride
/FLAOUVM . . . . fluvium
/FLAOVM . . . . fluvium
/FLAOZ . . . . fluorescein
/FLAR . . . . fistular
/FLARK . . . . follicular
/FLARP . . . . pharyngolaryngoscope
/FLA*RT . . . . pharyngolith
/FLARX . . . . folliculitis
/FLAUM . . . . folliculoma
/FLAUS . . . . phallus
/FLAXZ . . . . phylaxis
/FLEBT . . . . phlebitis
/FLEFN . . . . flexion
/FLEG . . . . phlegma
/FL*EGS . . . . flection
/FLEGT . . . . phlegmatic
/FLEKD . . . . flexed
/FLEMG . . . . phlegma
/FLENGT . . . . phalangectomy
/FLENS . . . . fluorescence
/FLENT . . . . fluorescent
/FLER . . . . filar
/FLERL . . . . filarial
/FLES . . . . fluorescent
/FLEVN . . . . flavine
/FL*EX . . . . flexion
/FLIBL . . . . fibular
/FLIBT . . . . phlebitic
/FLIFM . . . . philism

/FLIJ . . . . physiologic
/FLIKT . . . . phylactic
/FLIKTS . . . . phylactics
/FLIL . . . . familial
/FLIMT . . . . filament
/FLIMTS. . . . . filaments
/FLIN . . . . philin
/FLINGT . . . . anaphylactic
/FLINL . . . . faciolingual
/FLINS . . . . fluorescin
/FLIR . . . . fleur
/FLIRB . . . . fibrilla
/FLIRL . . . . philuria
/FLIRMT . . . . flowmeter
/FLISZ . . . . phlysis
/FL–KT. . . . . flect
/FLOB . . . . phlebotomy
/FLOE . . . . flow
/FLOEB . . . . fibroblastoma
/FLOEJ . . . . phlogistic
/FLOEMP. . . . . fibrolipoma
/FLOERMT . . . . photofluorometer
/FLOERP. . . . . fluoroscope
/FLOESZ. . . . . philosis
/FLOFT . . . . phlebostomy
/FLO*ID . . . . philioid
/FLOIF . . . . electrophysiolography
/FLOIFM . . . . phyletism
/FLOIJ . . . . phalangy
/FLOIM. . . . . phylum
/FLOIMT. . . . . flowmeter
/FLOIRD . . . . fluoride
/FLOIVD . . . . flavonoid
/FLOIVDZ . . . . flavonoids
/FLOJ. . . . . physiological
/FLOKLGS . . . . flocculation
/FLOKLZ . . . . flocculus
/FLOM . . . . phlegmon
/FLONGT . . . . flocculent
/FLOR. . . . . fluorescent
/FLO*R . . . . flora
/FLORK . . . . fluoric
/FLORMT . . . . fluorometer
/FLORNS . . . . florescence
/FLORS. . . . . fluorescence

/FLOUMT . . . . filamentous
/FLOUMTS . . . . filamentous
/FLOUZ. . . . . philous
/FL*UG . . . . fluctuating
/FLUGS . . . . fluctuation
/FLUKL . . . . flocculus
/FL*UM . . . . folium
/FLUNZ . . . . fluence
/FLURG. . . . . fluorography
/FLURM. . . . . fluorogram
/FLURP . . . . fluoroscopy
/FLURSZ. . . . . fluorosis
/FLURT . . . . flutter
/FLUX . . . . flux
/FOB . . . . ophobia
/FOD . . . . phosphorous acid
/FOEB . . . . phobia
/FO*EB . . . . phobe
/FOEFG. . . . . focusing
/FOEFL . . . . focal
/FOEGT . . . . phagocytosis
/FOEGTS . . . . phagocytosis
/FOEKL . . . . focal
/FOEKSZ . . . . phakomatosis
/FOEMZ. . . . . phacomatosis
/FOEN . . . . phone
/FOENSZ . . . . phonesis
/FOEP . . . . phonoscope
/FOEPD . . . . fundoscope
/FOEPT . . . . ophthalmoscope
/FO*EPT . . . . phthalmoscope
/FOERKT . . . . phoretic
/FOERMG. . . . . formic
/FOERMTS . . . . photodermatitis
/FOERS. . . . . phoresis
/FOERSZ. . . . . phoresis
/FO*ES . . . . phosis
/FOESZ. . . . . phycomycosis
/FOEZ . . . . phose
/FOFRB . . . . formative
/FOIB . . . . phobic
/FO*IB. . . . . phobiac
/FOIJ . . . . phagy
/FO*IJ . . . . ophagy
/FO*IK . . . . phobiac

/FO*IL . . . . phily
/FOIM . . . . phyma
/FO*IM . . . . phemy
/FOIMS . . . . phymas
/FOIMT . . . . phytum
/FOIMTS . . . . -ophthalmitis (*hyphenated*)
/FO*IN . . . . phony
/FOINSZ . . . . anaphysis
/FOINT . . . . phytin
/FOIP . . . . phenotype
/FOIR . . . . phoria
/FOIRM . . . . iform
/FOIRMS . . . . iforms
/FOIRNT . . . . phoriant
/FOIRS . . . . iferous
/FOIRT . . . . phoritis
/FOIRTS . . . . phoritis
/FOISZ . . . . physis
/FO*IT . . . . phytin
/FOITS . . . . physitis
/FOJ . . . . physiology
/FOJS . . . . physiologies
/FOLGD . . . . folding
/FOLZ . . . . physiologist
/FON . . . . phenomenon
/FONGS . . . . ophthalmoncus
/FOPT . . . . -ophthalmoscope (*hyphenated*)
/FO*R . . . . phore
/FO*RGS . . . . foration
/FO*RK . . . . phoric
/FO*RL . . . . phoral
/FORM . . . . form
/FO*RM . . . . form
/FORMGS . . . . formation
/FORMS . . . . forms
/FO*RMS . . . . forms
/FORNS . . . . fensor
/FOS . . . . ophthalmos
/FO*S . . . . phthalmos
/FOSZ . . . . phosphorus
/FOUG . . . . phagous
/FO*UG . . . . ophagous
/FOUGS . . . . phygous
/FOUMS . . . . ophthalmous
/FOUMZ . . . . phthalmous

/FOURZ . . . . phorous
/FOUZ . . . . philous
/FOVT . . . . formative
/FRAEF . . . . photography
/FRAEJ . . . . frigeration
/FRAEM . . . . foramen
/FRAET . . . . perforate
/FRAEVK . . . . refractive
/FRAF . . . . photograph
/FRA*G . . . . phragma
/FRAIF . . . . nephria
/FRAIFT . . . . fenestria
/FRAIRBL . . . . fibrillary
/FRAIRL . . . . fibrillary
/FRAIZ . . . . phrasia
/FRAJS . . . . pharyngeus
/FRAK . . . . fracture
/FRAKT . . . . fracture
/FRALG . . . . phoralgia
/FRA*M . . . . phoregram
/FRAMG . . . . fasciogram
/FRAMT . . . . fragment
/FRAOEBL . . . . febrile
/FRAOEDZ . . . . aphrodisiac
/FRAOEGT . . . . phoretogram
/FRAOEJ . . . . fibrinogenemia
/FRAOELG . . . . pharyngocele
/FRAOEMT . . . . photometry
/FRAOEMZ . . . . fructosemia
/FRAOENTS . . . . phrenitis
/FRAOEP . . . . femoropopliteal
/FRAOES . . . . aphrodisia
/FRAOFG . . . . pharyngography
/FRAOFL . . . . -oophorocele (*hyphenated*)
/FRAOIBL . . . . febrile
/FRAOIBS . . . . fibrositis
/FRAOINGS . . . . fructokinase
/FRAOIP . . . . fiberscopy
/FRAOIPT . . . . oophorosalpingitis
/FRAOIPTS . . . . oophorosalpingitis
/FRAOITD . . . . aphrodite
/FRAOITS . . . . nephritis
/FRAOL . . . . femoral
/FRAON . . . . nephronia
/FRAONG . . . . nephronic

/FRAONS . . . . furanose
/FRAOUK . . . . fructose
/FRAOUKT . . . . fructose
/FRAOUN . . . . furan
/FRAPS . . . . femoroplasty
/FRASZ . . . . apheresis
/FRAUJ . . . . pharyngioma
/FRAUM . . . . fibrosarcoma
/FRAUR . . . . fracture
/FRA*X . . . . phraxis
/FRAZ . . . . phrasia
/FREFL . . . . nephrial
/FREJ . . . . pharyngeum
/FREJSZ . . . . nephrogenesis
/FREKT . . . . nephrectomy
/FREKZ . . . . frequency
/FREMSZ . . . . fibromatoses
/FREN . . . . phrenia
/FRENG . . . . phrenic
/FR*ENL . . . . phrenal
/FRERK . . . . ferric
/FRIBL . . . . fibril
/FRIFM . . . . aphrodism
/FRIFMT . . . . aphroditism
/FRIGS . . . . friction
/FRIKT . . . . nephritic
/FR*IKT . . . . fibrinolytic
/FRILT . . . . filtrate
/FRIND . . . . ephedrine
/FRING . . . . fibrinogen
/FRIRBL . . . . fibrillar
/FRIRBLT . . . . fibrillatory
/FROBT . . . . fibrotic
/FROEB . . . . fibroma
/FROEBS . . . . fibromas
/FROEBSZ . . . . fibrosis
/FROEG . . . . nephrogenic
/FROEJ . . . . photochromogen
/FROEK . . . . photochromogenic
/FROEKT . . . . photometric
/FROEM . . . . nephroma
/FRO*EM . . . . fibrosarcoma
/FROEMS . . . . fibromatosis
/FROEMSZ . . . . fibromatosis
/FROEP . . . . phoroscope

/FROEPT . . . . femoroplasty
/FROERG. . . . . pharyngorrhaphy
/FROES . . . . nephrosis
/FROESZ . . . . nephrosclerosis
/FROET . . . . forate
/FROETS. . . . . oophoritis
/FRO*ETS . . . . -oophoritis (*hyphenated*)
/FROI . . . . nephroi
/FROIBD . . . . fibroid
/FROIK . . . . nephric
/FROIM . . . . fibromyoma
/FROIN . . . . phryon
/FROIP. . . . . fibroscopy
/FROIS . . . . ophrys
/FROKT . . . . nephrotic
/FROLS . . . . fibrinolysis
/FROMT . . . . nephrostomy
/FRON. . . . . nephron
/FRONL . . . . frontal
/FRONLS . . . . frontalis
/FROP. . . . . nephropathy
/FROPK . . . . phorotropic
/FROPT. . . . . nephroptosis
/FRORBL . . . . infraorbital
/FRORMT . . . . phorometer
/FROS . . . . nephros
/FROUBS . . . . fibrinous
/FROUS . . . . phorus
/FROUZ . . . . nephrous
/FROX . . . . nephrotoxin
/FRUFM. . . . . nephrium
/FRUGS . . . . fragous
/FRUKTS . . . . fructokinase
/FR*UM. . . . . nephrium
/FUFS . . . . fuscin
/FUKS . . . . phakus
/FUNGS . . . . function
/FUNLGS . . . . functional
/FURGS . . . . furcation
/F*URK . . . . furca
/FURKT . . . . furcate
/FURKTD. . . . . furcated
/FURZ . . . . fissura
/FUVN . . . . fulvin
/FWAIX . . . . ifaction

/FWAT . . . . . fatty
/FWAX . . . . . faction
/FWIFT . . . . . physicist
/FWIK . . . . . physic
/FW*IS . . . . . physicist
/FWIX . . . . . physics
/FWUND . . . . . fecundity
/FWUNGS . . . . . fecundation
/FWUNL . . . . . fungal
/F–X . . . . . fication
/–FX . . . . . ification

G

/GAEFM . . . . . genitalism
/GAEGS . . . . . gradation
/GAEJ . . . . . engage
/GAEMT . . . . . engagement
/GAENG . . . . . rrhagenic
/GAENGS . . . . . genization
/GAENL . . . . . genital
/GAER . . . . . geria
/GAERN . . . . . gasserian
/GAFMT . . . . . gamist
/GAFR . . . . . gaster
/GAFRM . . . . . gastrogram
/GAIDZ . . . . . gradation
/GAIG . . . . . gage
/GAILTS . . . . . genitalis
/GAIM . . . . . game
/GAIMT . . . . . gametocyte
/GAIRK . . . . . ergastic
/GAIRN . . . . . gainer
/GAIRZ . . . . . ergasia
/GAISZ . . . . . gasis
/GAIZ . . . . . gasia
/GAKT . . . . . aganactesis
/GAKTS . . . . . aganactesis
/GAM . . . . . gamma
/GA*M . . . . . gamy
/GANGTS . . . . . ganglitis
/GANK . . . . . organic
/GANLT . . . . . genetical
/GANTS . . . . . gangliitis

/GAOE . . . . gee
/GAOEK . . . . geneic
/GAOEL . . . . gastrocele
/GAOEM . . . . guanidinemia
/GAOEMT . . . . gamete
/GAOEN . . . . gene
/GAOEND . . . . guanidine
/GAOENGS . . . . geneization
/GAO*ENL . . . . genal
/GAOENS . . . . genes
/GAOENSZ . . . . gonesis
/GAOENT . . . . geneity
/GAOENZ . . . . genus
/GAOERM . . . . gastrinemia
/GAOESZ . . . . geusis
/GAOET . . . . gametophyte
/GAOEZ . . . . geusesthesia
/GAOIFT . . . . antagonist
/GAOIM . . . . gastromyotomy
/GAOIMT . . . . gynecomastia
/GAOING . . . . gynogram
/GAOIRGS . . . . gyration
/GAOIRK . . . . gyric
/GAOIRL . . . . gyral
/GAOIRT . . . . gyrate
/GAOISZ . . . . gonimiasis
/GAONSZ . . . . agnosis
/GAOTS . . . . geustia
/GAOUL . . . . genual
/GAOUS . . . . ageusia
/GAOUZ . . . . ageusia
/GAOX . . . . geusic
/GAOZ . . . . geusia
/GA*UG . . . . agogue
/GAUJ . . . . gogic
/GAUN . . . . guanine
/GAUNK . . . . gnomonic
/GAUNL . . . . ungual
/GA*US . . . . gnostic
/GA*USZ . . . . gnostics
/GAUT . . . . gastrotomy
/GAVGS . . . . galvanization
/GAVJ . . . . gavage
/GAVM . . . . galvanism
/GE . . . . gyny

/GEJ . . . . . jejunum
/GEKL . . . . . genetical
/GEKT . . . . . gastrectomy
/GEL . . . . . gel
/GELT . . . . . gelatin
/G*EM . . . . . gemina
/GEMT . . . . . gametic
/GEMTS . . . . . gamentous
/GEMZ . . . . . geochemistry
/G*EN . . . . . gen
/GENG . . . . . genic
/G*ENG . . . . . ogenic
/GENGS . . . . . genics
/G*ENGS . . . . . ogenics
/G*ENS . . . . . gens
/GENSZ . . . . . genesis
/G*ENSZ . . . . . ogenesis
/GENT . . . . . genetic
/G*ENT . . . . . ogenetic
/GENTS . . . . . genetics
/G*ENTS . . . . . ogenetics
/GENZ . . . . . geneous
/GERK . . . . . generic
/GERTS . . . . . geriatrics
/GERZ . . . . . gerus
/GEV . . . . . congestive
/GIFM . . . . . organism
/GIKT . . . . . genolytic
/GIMT . . . . . gymnastic
/GIMTS . . . . . gymnastics
/GIMZ . . . . . gymnasium
/GINL . . . . . inguinal
/GINT . . . . . genicity
/G*INT . . . . . ogenicity
/GISZ . . . . . gastroschisis
/GITS . . . . . jejunitis
/GL– . . . . . gala
/GLA . . . . . glia
/GLAEK . . . . . glycolate
/GLAEL . . . . . gluteal
/GLAEM . . . . . glycemia
/GLAEMG . . . . . glycemic
/GLAEMT . . . . . glutamate
/GLAERMT . . . . . glomerator
/GLAF . . . . . granuloplastic

/GLAIBD . . . . globinated
/GLAIK . . . . glycorrhachia
/GLAIRMT . . . . glomerator
/GLAKD . . . . galactoside
/GLAKDZ. . . . . galactosides
/GLAKT . . . . galactic
/GLAL. . . . . glial
/GLANTS . . . . glandulitis
/GLAOBL . . . . gammaglobulin
/GLAOEB . . . . gammaglobulinemia
/GLAOEK. . . . . galactorrhea
/GLAOEL. . . . . galactocele
/GLAOEMS. . . . . glyoxylemia
/GLAOEMX. . . . . glyoxylemia
/GLAOEP . . . . glycopenia
/GLAOERK . . . . glyceric
/GLAOES . . . . glycosemia
/GLAOIGD . . . . gliding
/GLAOIJ . . . . glycoconjugate
/GLAOIK . . . . glycogen
/GLAOIMS . . . . glycoplasmia
/GLAOINT . . . . ganglionitis
/GLAOINTS . . . . ganglionitis
/GLAOIP . . . . glycoprotein
/GLAOIS . . . . glycinemia
/GLAOISZ . . . . glycemosis
/GLAOIT . . . . gliocyte
/GLAOITS . . . . glossitis
/GLAOIZ. . . . . glycin
/GLAOKD . . . . glucoside
/GLAOMD . . . . glutamic acid
/GLAOS . . . . glossia
/GLAOSZ . . . . glossis
/GLAOTD . . . . agglutinoid
/GLAOUB. . . . . globulin
/GLAOUBS . . . . globulins
/GLAOUJ . . . . agglutinogen
/GLAOUK. . . . . glucose
/GLAOUKD . . . . glucosidase
/GLAOUNGS . . . . agglutination
/GLAO*UNGS . . . . gglutination
/GLAOUR . . . . globinuria
/GLAOURB . . . . globulinuria
/GLAOURK . . . . globininuric
/GLAOURN . . . . globulinuria

/GLAOURNS . . . . glycinuria
/GLAOUT . . . . agglutinin
/GLAO*UT . . . . gglutinin
/GLAOUV . . . . agglutinative
/GLAR . . . . glandular
/GLARB . . . . galactia
/GLARND . . . . glanders
/GLAT . . . . gliacyte
/GLA*UB . . . . gammaglobulin
/GLAUBL . . . . globular
/GLAUK . . . . glaucoma
/GLAUL . . . . ganglial
/GLAUM . . . . glioma
/GLAUMS . . . . gliomas
/GLAUN . . . . ganglion
/GLAUNG . . . . ganglionic
/GLAUNSZ. . . . . ganglionosis
/GLAUR . . . . angular
/GLAUS . . . . glaucin
/GLAUTD . . . . glottid
/GLAVN . . . . galvanic
/GLAVNG . . . . galvanic
/GLEFRB . . . . glossal nerve
/GLEKT . . . . glossectomy
/GLEM . . . . glycerolemia
/GLEND . . . . glenoid
/GLEPS . . . . globinopepsia
/GLERL . . . . glomerular
/GLERT . . . . glucosometer
/GLEVRB . . . . glossal nerve
/GLIBL . . . . agglutinable
/GLID . . . . glyceridemia
/GLIFG . . . . globinophilic
/GLIFRT . . . . glycerate
/GLIFT . . . . glycerate
/GLIGD . . . . glyceridemic
/GLIK . . . . glyphic
/GLIKT . . . . genolytic
/GLIM . . . . ganglioma
/GLIR . . . . gliar
/GLIRD . . . . glyceride
/GLIRDZ . . . . glycerides
/GLITS . . . . ganglitis
/GLIX . . . . glyphics
/GLOBL . . . . globulin

/GLOBLS . . . . globulins
/GLOBS. . . . . globinous
/GLOBT . . . . globinopathy
/GLOBTS . . . . globinopathies
/GLOBZ . . . . globose
/GLODZ . . . . epiglottideus
/GLOEB . . . . globin
/GLO*EBS . . . . globose
/GLOEBSZ. . . . . globulosis
/GLOEBZ . . . . globus
/GLOEKS . . . . galactosis
/GLOEL . . . . globinocholia
/GLOEM . . . . globinemia
/GLO*EM . . . . glioma
/GLO*EMS. . . . . gliomas
/GLOEMT . . . . gliomatosis
/GLOEMTS . . . . gliomatosis
/GLOEN . . . . globin
/GLOEND . . . . globinated
/GLOERM . . . . glioneuroma
/GLOERMT . . . . globinometry
/GLOESZ . . . . gliosis
/GLOEZ. . . . . globulose
/GLOFL. . . . . glossal
/GLOIB . . . . glioblastoma
/GLOIM . . . . gliocytoma
/GLOIN . . . . glucoprotein
/GLOIND . . . . agglutinoid
/GLOISZ . . . . glioses
/GLOKL . . . . glycolic
/GLOKLD. . . . . glycolic acid
/GLOKT . . . . glottic
/GLOL . . . . glycerol
/GLOLS . . . . globinolysis
/GLOLSZ . . . . glycogenolysis
/GLONL. . . . . globulinemia
/GLONT. . . . . conglutinin
/GLOPG . . . . epiglottic
/GLO*PT . . . . globulinopathy
/GLORB . . . . globar
/GLORMT . . . . globinometer
/GLOS . . . . glossa
/GLOTD . . . . epiglottidean
/GLO*TD . . . . glottid
/GLOTS . . . . glottis

/GLOUKT . . . . galactous
/GLOUP . . . . glucopenia
/GLOURD . . . . glutamic aciduria
/GLOURK . . . . glycosuric
/GL–TS . . . . gangliitis
/GLU . . . . glandula
/GLUB . . . . globin
/GLUBD . . . . globinated
/GLUKS . . . . glucokinase
/GLUNGS . . . . agglutination
/GL*UNGS . . . . gglutination
/GLURK . . . . oliguric
/GL*URK . . . . glycosuric
/GLURS . . . . glycosuria
/GLUS . . . . glomerulus
/GLUSZ . . . . glossus
/GLUTS . . . . gluteus
/GMA . . . . gamma
/GO . . . . go
/GOE . . . . ego
/GOEG . . . . agogue
/GO*EG . . . . gogue
/GOEJ . . . . agogy
/GO*EM . . . . gonioma
/GOEMS . . . . gastroanastomosis
/GOEMZ . . . . gastrostomosis
/GO*EN . . . . gonia
/GOEND . . . . gonad
/GO*ENG . . . . gonic
/GOENL . . . . gonadal
/GO*ENL . . . . gonial
/GOENS . . . . gnosia
/GOENSZ . . . . gnosis
/GOENT . . . . gnosist
/GOENZ . . . . agnosia
/GOEP . . . . gastroscope
/GO*EP . . . . gonioscope
/GOERM . . . . germinoma
/GOFM . . . . organism
/GO*G . . . . agogue
/GOIFM . . . . gonadism
/GOIK . . . . gastroscopy
/GOIM . . . . gamy
/GO*IM . . . . gnomy
/GOIMT . . . . gamety

/GOIN . . . . geny
/GO*IN . . . . ogeny
/GOIP . . . . gastroduodenoscopy
/GOIRMT . . . . goniometer
/GOIRNG . . . . goitrogenic
/GOJ . . . . agogic
/GOLD . . . . gold
/GOLS . . . . genolysis
/GOMT . . . . galvanometer
/GON . . . . gone
/GO*N . . . . gony
/GONL . . . . agonal
/GONSZ . . . . genosis
/GOP . . . . meningopathy
/GORJ . . . . gorge
/GORJD . . . . gorged
/GOS . . . . gastrostomy
/GO*S . . . . gastrostomy
/GOUM . . . . gonium
/GOUMS . . . . gamous
/GOUMT . . . . gummatous
/GOUMTS . . . . gummatous
/GOUNS . . . . gonous
/GO*UT . . . . gout
/GRAEF . . . . graphy
/GRAEFP . . . . gastrorrhaphy
/GRAEFS . . . . graphies
/GRAEK . . . . gonorrheic
/GRAENZ . . . . gangrenous
/GRAF . . . . graph
/GRAFGT . . . . grafting
/GRAFK . . . . graphic
/GRAFKS . . . . graphics
/GRA*FM . . . . graphism
/GRAFMT . . . . grammatism
/GRAFR . . . . grapher
/GRAFS . . . . graphs
/GRAFT . . . . graft
/GRAG . . . . agra
/GRAID . . . . grade
/GRAIGS . . . . integration
/GRAIRT . . . . integrator
/GRAKL . . . . graphical
/GRAKT . . . . granulocytic
/GRA*L . . . . agral

/GRALG	gastralgia
/GRAM	gram
/GRAMG	grammic
/GRAMS	grams
/GRANLT	granulocyte
/GRANS	granulocytosis
/GRAOE	gonorrhea
/GRAOEM	gastrium
/GRAOEZ	agogatresia
/GRAOF	autograph
/GRAOIF	agraphia
/GRAOIT	gastritis
/GRAOITS	gastritis
/GRAON	gastrone
/GRAOULGS	gastrulation
/GRAOULT	gastrula
/GRAOUP	group
/GRARL	granular
/GRA*S	gastria
/GRAUM	granuloma
/GRAVD	gravida
/GRAVK	gravidic
/GRAVKS	gravics
/GRAVMT	gravimeter
/GRAVT	gravity
/GREM	epigastrium
/GRENGS	regeneration
/GRIF	graphia
/GRIGS	gression
/GRIK	gastric
/GR*IK	agric
/GRINS	gastrin
/GRISZ	gastroschisis
/GRIV	gressive
/GRIVD	gravid
/GRIVK	gravidic
/GRIVMT	gravimeter
/GROEG	growing
/GROELS	granulosis
/GROELT	granulocytosis
/GROEMTS	granulomatosis
/GROEPSZ	gryposis
/GROEPZ	gryphosis
/GRO*ET	growth
/GROF	gastrograph

/GROFG . . . . gastrography
/GROFK . . . . gonadotropic
/GROFN . . . . gonadotropin
/GROFT . . . . gastrostomy
/GROIF . . . . autography
/GROIM . . . . hygroma
/GROMT . . . . gustometry
/GRONGS . . . . grondation
/GRORT . . . . integrator
/GROUN . . . . grown
/GROUP . . . . group
/GROUS . . . . agrous
/GRUM . . . . gastrium
/GRUNGS . . . . grundation
/GRURL . . . . granular
/GRUS . . . . gyrus
/GR*US . . . . gastrius
/GUGS . . . . gustation
/GUMTS . . . . gummatous
/GUMZ . . . . gamus
/GUT . . . . gut

H

/HABLGS . . . . habilitation
/HAEBLGS . . . . habilitation
/HAEBLT . . . . habilitate
/HAEFG . . . . hysterograph
/HAEFR . . . . hysterography
/HAEG . . . . hemagglutinin
/HA*EM . . . . hemal
/HAENT . . . . hematin
/HAEP . . . . hepatia
/HAEPG . . . . hepatic
/HAEPGT . . . . hepatectomy
/HAEPGZ . . . . hepaticus
/HAEPT . . . . hepatitis
/HA*EPT . . . . hepatia
/HAEPTS . . . . hypophosphatasia
/HAERG . . . . hearing
/HAERKT . . . . hematocrit
/HA*ERM . . . . hemeral
/HAERMT . . . . hemotachometer
/HAERN . . . . hernia

/HAERNL . . . . . hernial
/HAFRD . . . . . hazard
/HAIFSZ . . . . . hemostasis
/HAIG . . . . . hemorrhagica
/HAILGS . . . . . halation
/HAIM . . . . . hemia
/HAIPS . . . . . hyperplasia
/HAIPT . . . . . heterotopia
/HAIPZ . . . . . hypoplasia
/HA*IRD . . . . . hereditary
/HAIRP . . . . . hemotherapy
/HAIRPT . . . . . hydrotherapy
/HALD . . . . . aldehyde
/HAMT . . . . . enhancement
/HANG . . . . . hang
/HAOBL . . . . . histioblast
/HAOBT . . . . . histioblast
/HAOEB . . . . . hypogammaglobulinemia
/HAOEBL . . . . . hemoglobinemia
/HAOEBT . . . . . hebotomy
/HAOEF . . . . . hemophilia
/HAOEFD . . . . . histiodieresis
/HAOEFG . . . . . hemophiliac
/HAOEFL . . . . . hydrocephaly
/HAOEFM . . . . . hedonism
/HAOEFMT . . . . . hemostasis
/HAOEFRK . . . . . hemispheric
/HAOEFT . . . . . histiocytosis
/HAO*EGS . . . . . hesion
/HAOEJT . . . . . homogeneity
/HAOELG . . . . . hemoglobinuria
/HAOELSZ . . . . . heliosis
/HAOELT . . . . . hematocele
/HAOELTS . . . . . halisteresis
/HAOELX . . . . . helix
/HAOELZ . . . . . hypalgesia
/HAOEM . . . . . heme
/HAO*EM . . . . . hemia
/HAOEMT . . . . . hematoma
/HAOEN . . . . . hemin
/HAO*EN . . . . . hymenia
/HAOEND . . . . . hedonia
/HAO*ENG . . . . . hymenic
/HAOENL . . . . . hepatorenal
/HAO*ENL . . . . . hymeneal

/HAOEPT . . . hepatocele
/HAOEPTS . . . hyperesthesia
/HAO*ERK . . . hieric
/HAO*ERL . . . hydromyelia
/HAOERLD . . . hedral
/HAOERMG . . . hemoglobinometer
/HAOERMT . . . hemometer
/HAO*ERN . . . heparinemia
/HAOERPS . . . hyperidrosis
/HAOERPT . . . hypermetria
/HAO*ETS . . . hypesthesia
/HAOFK . . . hypertrophia
/HAOFL . . . histochemical
/HAOFM . . . hypopituitarism
/HAOFR . . . hystero-oophorectomy
/HAOFRD . . . hazardous
/HAOFRDZ . . . hazardous
/HAOIBD . . . hybrid
/HAOIFK . . . hypertrophic
/HAOIFL . . . hydrocephaly
/HAOIFLG . . . hydranencephaly
/HAOIFLS . . . hydrocephalus
/HAOIFM . . . hypothyroidism
/HAOIFMD . . . hyperparathyroidism
/HAOIFRB . . . hypertensive
/HAOIFX . . . hyperreflexia
/HAOILD . . . hyaloid
/HAOILSZ . . . hyalinosis
/HAO*IM . . . hymen
/HAOIN . . . hyaline
/HAOINL . . . hymenal
/HAOIPGS . . . hypertension
/HAOIPT . . . hypertonia
/HAOIPX . . . hypoxia
/HAO*IRD . . . hydria
/HAOIRGS . . . hydration
/HAOIRKT . . . hydrotic
/HAO*IRL . . . hilar
/HAOIRLD . . . hydrochloride
/HAOIRM . . . hyperemia
/HAOIRMD . . . hydremia
/HAOIRMG . . . hygrometer
/HAOIRMS . . . hydramnios
/HAOIRPG . . . hyperglycemia
/HAOIRPSZ . . . hypercytosis

/HAOIRPT . . . . hypertrophy
/HAOIRPTS . . . . hypercytosis
/HAOIRT . . . . hydrate
/HAOIRTD . . . . hydrated
/HAOKT . . . . histioplasmacytic
/HAOLG . . . . hematology
/HAOM . . . . hemangioma
/HAOMG . . . . hepatomegaly
/HAOMP . . . . hysterosalpingo-oophorectomy
/HAOPG . . . . hepatomegalia
/HAOPT . . . . hematopenia
/HAOR . . . . hydruria
/HAORK . . . . hypogastric
/HAORL. . . . . humoral
/HAORM . . . . hypoderma
/HAORMT. . . . . hydrometra
/HAORP . . . . herniorrhaphy
/HAORX . . . . hydrothorax
/HAOUFGS . . . . hemotransfusion
/HAOUFR . . . . humidifier
/HAOULGS . . . . hallucination
/HAO*UM . . . . hemalbumin
/HAOUNT. . . . . heteroagglutinin
/HAOUR . . . . hematuria
/HAO*UR . . . . hydruria
/HAOURG . . . . hemoglobinuria
/HAO*URK . . . . hematuric
/HAOURLT . . . . hallucinatory
/HAOURM . . . . humor
/HA*RNS . . . . enhancer
/HARPT . . . . heteroplasty
/HA*S . . . . hemoblast
/HAUFK . . . . hypophysectomy
/HAUFL. . . . . hypophyseal
/HAUFN . . . . histon
/HAUFSZ . . . . hypophysis
/HAUNG . . . . hypertonic
/HAUP . . . . hemoptysis
/HAURMD. . . . . hemopericardium
/HAUT . . . . hepatotomy
/HEFKT . . . . heminephrectomy
/HEFM . . . . hermaphroditism
/HEFMT . . . . hermaphrodite
/HEFSZ . . . . hypophyses
/HEG . . . . hemoglobin

/HELS . . . . . helcosis
/HEMG . . . . . hemic
/HEMTS . . . . . hematous
/HENGT . . . . . heterogeneity
/HENK . . . . . hepatogenic
/HENSZ . . . . . histogenesis
/H*ENT . . . . . hematin
/H*ERM . . . . . hemorrhea
/HERMZ . . . . . histochemistry
/HERPD . . . . . hydropericardium
/HERZ . . . . . hertz
/HEX . . . . . hepatopexy
/HIBLGS . . . . . habilitation
/HIBLT . . . . . habilitate
/HIFMG . . . . . histaminic
/HIFN . . . . . histone
/HIFNS . . . . . histofluorescence
/HIFRG . . . . . hysterogram
/HIFRK . . . . . histologic
/HIFRL . . . . . histological
/HIFRNS . . . . . histofluorescence
/HIFRT . . . . . hysterectomy
/HIFRX . . . . . hysteropexy
/HIFT . . . . . history
/HIJT . . . . . hysterosalpingectomy
/H*IK . . . . . hydric
/HIMP . . . . . hysterosalpingo-oophorectomy
/HIMTS . . . . . hymenitis
/HIN . . . . . hyalin
/H*IP . . . . . hypnia
/HIPGT . . . . . hepatitic
/H*IRD . . . . . hydria
/HIRJ . . . . . hemorrhagic
/HIRL . . . . . hilar
/HIRPX . . . . . hydropexy
/HIRPXZ . . . . . hydropexis
/HIRT . . . . . hypothermy
/H–J . . . . . hemiplegic
/HOB . . . . . hemoglobin
/HOD . . . . . hyoid
/HOEFK . . . . . heterotrophic
/HOEFM . . . . . histiocytoma
/HO*EFM . . . . . hemotoxism
/HOEFN . . . . . hemotoxin
/HOEFR . . . . . hematoporphyrin

/HOEFS . . . . hydronephrosis
/HOEFSZ . . . . hematonephrosis
/HOEFT . . . . heterotroph
/HO*EJ . . . . hemochromogen
/HOEKLS . . . . helcosis
/HOEKSZ . . . . hypertrichosis
/HOELG . . . . histology
/HOEMT . . . . hepatoma
/HOENG . . . . hypotonic
/HOEPSZ . . . . hypersarcosis
/HOERKL . . . . hydrochloria
/HOERL . . . . hormonal
/HOERM . . . . hormone
/HOERMG . . . . hypercholesterolemic
/HOERMT . . . . hypometria
/HOERNL . . . . hormonal
/HOERPS . . . . hyperhidrosis
/HO*ET . . . . hemarthrosis
/HO*ETS . . . . hypoesthesia
/HOETSDZ . . . . hydatidosis
/HOETSZ . . . . hydatidosis
/HOFM . . . . hedonism
/HOFN . . . . heterolysin
/HOFRN . . . . heterolysin
/HOFRT . . . . hysterotomy
/HOIBT . . . . hypoblast
/HOIFKT . . . . histiocytic
/HOIFL . . . . hypophysial
/HOIFM . . . . hypogonadism
/HOIFMD . . . . hypoparathyroidism
/HOIFR . . . . histiocytary
/HOIFRB . . . . hypotensive
/HOIFT . . . . hypophysitis
/HOIFTS . . . . hypophysitis
/HO*IK . . . . hemopoietic
/HOIL . . . . hydrocele
/HOILT . . . . hiatal
/HOIM . . . . hyloma
/HO*IND . . . . hyoidean
/HOIPSZ . . . . hypocytosis
/HOIPT . . . . hematopoietic
/HOIPTS . . . . hematopoiesis
/HOIRK . . . . hydropic
/HOIRKT . . . . hypogastric
/HOIRL . . . . hydrocele

/HOIRM . . . . hyperkalemia
/HOIRMT . . . . hematometra
/HO*IRP . . . . hydrotherapy
/HOIRPT . . . . hydroperitoneum
/HOIRX . . . . hydroxy
/HOISZ . . . . hemopoiesis
/HOIX . . . . hydroxide
/HOJ . . . . hematogenous
/HOJT . . . . hematogenous
/HOLG . . . . hemolytic
/HOLS . . . . hemolysis
/HOLSZ . . . . hemolysis
/HONLS . . . . hemolysin
/HONT . . . . hypotonia
/HORJ . . . . hydrogenate
/HORKL . . . . hydrochloric
/HORKLD . . . . hydrochloridia
/HORN . . . . horn
/HORX . . . . hemothorax
/HO*S . . . . hepatostomy
/H-RL . . . . humeral
/H-RLS . . . . humeralis
/H-RLZ . . . . humerals
/HUNGS . . . . hemagglutination
/H*URL . . . . humeral
/H*URLS . . . . humerals
/HURLZ . . . . humeralis
/HUX . . . . hallux
/HYAOIL . . . . hyal
/HYEKT . . . . hysterocolpectomy
/HYEM . . . . hypermenorrhea
/HYOM . . . . hypomenorrhea

I

/IFBL . . . . ifiable
/IFK . . . . ific
/IFKT . . . . istic
/IFM . . . . ism
/IFX . . . . ification
/*IK ic
/IKLT . . . . ictal
/*IKT . . . . itic
/*IN . . . . in

/IP . . . . incompetent
/IRBL . . . . irritable
/IRBLT . . . . irritability
/*IRD . . . . hidria
/IRGS . . . . irritation
/IRK . . . . ischemia
/IRKT . . . . icteric
/*IRKT . . . . -icteric (*hyphenated*)
/IRND . . . . iridian
/IRNT . . . . irritant
/*IS . . . . ist
/*ISZ . . . . ists
/IV . . . . ive
/IVL . . . . ively
/IVNS . . . . iveness
/IVRT . . . . irritative
/*IX . . . . ics

J

/J– . . . . agent
/JAEF . . . . angiography
/JAEFG . . . . cineangiography
/JAEGS . . . . education
/JAEKT . . . . angiectatic
/JAEM . . . . geminal
/JA*EM . . . . gemmal
/JAENT . . . . genate
/JAENZ . . . . genesia
/JAEPZ . . . . angioplasia
/JAES . . . . genase
/JA*ES . . . . gesta
/JAESZ . . . . angiectases
/JAEV . . . . gingivae
/JAEZ . . . . genases
/JAFT . . . . angioblast
/JAIGS . . . . generation
/JAINT . . . . jacent
/JAIRGS . . . . degeneration
/JAIRN . . . . genarian
/JAISZ . . . . angiectasis
/JAIT . . . . generate
/JAITD . . . . generated
/JAIV . . . . degenerative

/JAIZ . . . . angiectasia
/JALGS . . . . ejaculation
/JAOB . . . . augiaphobia
/JAOEFK . . . . analgesic
/JAOEKT . . . . algetic
/JAO*EL . . . . meningeal
/JAOELG . . . . algesic
/JAOELS . . . . algesia
/JAOEN . . . . genia
/JAOERJ . . . . argyria
/JAOETS . . . . angiitis
/JAOEZ . . . . analgesia
/JAOFK . . . . angiopathic
/JAOFT . . . . angioenterostomy
/JAOIF . . . . genize
/JAOIFM . . . . gigantism
/JAOIFSZ . . . . ysterocyesis
/JAOIL . . . . angial
/JAOILTS . . . . angiocholitis
/JAOIMT . . . . angiopericytoma
/JAOIN . . . . angina
/JAOINL . . . . anginal
/JAO*IR . . . . gyria
/JAOIRGS . . . . gyration
/JAOIRK . . . . gyric
/JAOIRL. . . . . gyral
/JAOIRT . . . . gyrate
/JAOIT . . . . meningitis
/JAOITS . . . . angitis
/JAOL . . . . joule
/JAOLG. . . . . angiology
/JAOM . . . . angioma
/JAOMT . . . . angiomatosis
/JAON . . . . angion
/JAOP . . . . jejunoplasty
/JAOPT . . . . jejunoplasty
/JAO*R . . . . gyria
/JAO*S . . . . jejunogastrostomy
/JAOUG . . . . conjugate
/JAO*UL . . . . joule
/JAOULG . . . . jugal
/JAOUNG . . . . conjugant
/JAOUVT . . . . adjuvant
/JAPT. . . . . angioplasty
/JARK. . . . . angiosarcoma

/JARL . . . . . jugular
/JARM . . . . . angiogram
/JA*S . . . . . angioblast
/JAUFT . . . . . angiostomy
/JAULG . . . . . algiform
/JA*UN . . . . . angion
/JAUR . . . . . jugular
/JAURJ . . . . . argyrosis
/JAUT . . . . . angiotomy
/JAVL . . . . . gingival
/JEB . . . . . angiophlebitis
/JEBT . . . . . angiophlebitis
/JEFM . . . . . genism
/JEGS . . . . . gestation
/JEGT . . . . . gestate
/JEJ . . . . . jejunum
/JEKL . . . . . genically
/J*EKT . . . . . angiectomy
/JELGS . . . . . gestational
/JEMS . . . . . geminus
/JENSZ . . . . . genesis
/J*ENSZ . . . . . ogenesis
/JERG . . . . . engineering
/JERL . . . . . germinal
/JERND . . . . . gender
/JET . . . . . jet
/J*EX . . . . . jection
/J–F . . . . . geography
/J–GS . . . . . ejection
/JIBL . . . . . intelligible
/JIFM . . . . . argyrism
/JIFT . . . . . geneticist
/JIGT . . . . . angitic
/JIKT . . . . . angiectomy
/JINK . . . . . gynic
/JIPS . . . . . rrhagiparous
/JIRM . . . . . argyrum
/JITS . . . . . jejunitis
/JIVL . . . . . conjunctival
/JIVT . . . . . conjunctivitis
/JLAIR . . . . . angiocapillary
/JLOEZ . . . . . angiosclerosis
/J–NL . . . . . genal
/J–NS . . . . . genous
/JOEBL . . . . . angioendothelioblastoma

/JOEBSZ . . . . angiofibrosis
/JOEDZ . . . . angiectodes
/JOEFM . . . . angiofibroma
/JOELSZ . . . . gelosis
/JOEM. . . . . meningioma
/JOENL . . . . angioendothelioma
/JOERM . . . . angiocarcinoma
/JOESZ . . . . angiosis
/JOET. . . . . genote
/JOIL . . . . meningocele
/JO*IM . . . . geminum
/JOIMTS . . . . angiomyomatosis
/JOIP . . . . angioscopy
/JOIRK. . . . . injector
/JOITS. . . . . angeitis
/JOIX . . . . injection
/JOJ . . . . jejunostomy
/JOKL . . . . jejunocolic
/JOKT . . . . angiotic
/JOM . . . . angioblastoma
/JONSZ . . . . genosis
/JOP. . . . . meningopathy
/JOPT . . . . angiopathy
/JO*RM . . . . algiform
/JOS . . . . jejunostomy
/JO*S . . . . jejunostomy
/JOUMT . . . . angiomatous
/JOUMTS . . . . angiomatous
/JOURS. . . . . gerous
/J–S . . . . agents
/JUFT . . . . jejunoesophagostomy
/J*UM . . . . angium
/JUNGS. . . . . junction
/J*UR . . . . angiuria
/JUT. . . . . jut
/J–X. . . . . jection

K

/KAEFP . . . . cachexia
/KAEFPT . . . . cachectic
/KAEGS . . . . cation
/KAEKT . . . . canthectomy
/KAEM . . . . chromate

/KAENLS . . . . canales
/KAENS . . . . anacinesia
/KA*ENS . . . . anakinesia
/KAENSZ . . . . anakinesis
/KAENT . . . . cuneate
/KAENZ . . . . anacinesis
/KAERL . . . . cameral
/KAERLG . . . . keratology
/KAERN . . . . cancer
/KAERNL . . . . costosternal
/KAERNZ . . . . cancerous
/KAET . . . . cate
/KAFLG . . . . costalgia
/KAFLGS . . . . calcification
/KAFRNS . . . . cavernous
/KAID . . . . caudate
/KAILGS . . . . calyx
/KAILT . . . . calent
/KAILX . . . . calix
/KAINDZ . . . . cadence
/KAINLS . . . . canalis
/KAINT . . . . cadent
/KAIR . . . . care
/KAIRKT . . . . keratotic
/KA*IS . . . . cace
/KAIZ . . . . kinase
/KAKT . . . . cataract
/KAL . . . . cal
/KALG . . . . calcic
/KALS . . . . calcium
/KALSZ . . . . calcinosis
/KALT . . . . katal
/KALZ . . . . calcia
/KAMPZ . . . . campsia
/KAMS . . . . campsia
/KAMSZ . . . . campsis
/KAMZ . . . . campsis
/KANL . . . . canal
/KANLGS . . . . canalization
/KA*NTS . . . . acanthocytosis
/KAOBL . . . . connubial
/KAOEFG . . . . kinesograph
/KAOEFS . . . . kyphoses
/KAOEFZ . . . . kyphoses
/KAOEJS . . . . ketogenesis

/KAOEKS . . . . coccoses
/KAOELT . . . . ketal
/KAOEM . . . . chemotherapy
/KAO*EMS. . . . . calcinemia
/KAOEND . . . . kidney
/KAOENS . . . . kinesia
/KAOENSZ . . . . kinesis
/KAO*ENT . . . . kinesthesia
/KAOERBS . . . . canities
/KAOERN . . . . criterion
/KAOERSZ . . . . kerosis
/KAOESZ. . . . . kinesis
/KAO*ETS. . . . . kinesthesia
/KAOEZ . . . . kinesia
/KAOFLG . . . . costalgia
/KAOGS. . . . . constitution
/KAOIFD . . . . keratinized
/KAOIFK . . . . kyphectomy
/KAOIFMG . . . . chiasmic
/KAOIFMT . . . . chiasmatic
/KAOIFSZ. . . . . kyphosis
/KAOIL . . . . chyle
/KAO*IL. . . . . chylia
/KAOILS . . . . chylous
/KAOIM. . . . . chyme
/KAO*IM . . . . kyme
/KAOIMG . . . . kymographic
/KAOIN . . . . kinin
/KAOINLD. . . . . condyli
/KAOINT . . . . chitin
/KAOIP . . . . cheiloplasty
/KAOIRD . . . . cardii
/KAOIRL . . . . chyluria
/KAOIRMT . . . . eikonometer
/KAOIRTS . . . . keratoiritis
/KAOIS . . . . keratinize
/KAOITS. . . . . carditis
/KAOM . . . . coma
/KAON . . . . conia
/KAONGT. . . . . conchitis
/KAONL. . . . . conchal
/KAONTS . . . . conchitis
/KAO*R. . . . . koria
/KAORD. . . . . coordinate
/KAO*RD . . . . cordia

/KAORLD . . . . cordal
/KAO*RLD . . . . cordial
/KAORLGD . . . . cordialgia
/KAORM . . . . cormia
/KAORNGS . . . . coordination
/KAOSZ . . . . akusis
/KAO*TS . . . . acanthocytosis
/KAOUBLT . . . . cubital
/KAOUFM . . . . cuneiform
/KAOUFT . . . . acoustic
/KAOUFTS . . . . acoustics
/KAO*UGS . . . . cution
/KAOULT . . . . cuticle
/KAOUNL . . . . conule
/KAOUNLD . . . . conulid
/KAOUNTS . . . . cutaneostomy
/KAOURBL . . . . curable
/KAOURLT . . . . cuticular
/KAOURN . . . . cornu
/KAOURNT . . . . cornuate
/KAOURP . . . . cuprein
/KAOURPT . . . . curietherapy
/KAO*US . . . . acoustic
/KAO*USZ . . . . acoustics
/KAOUT . . . . acute
/KAOUTS . . . . cutaneous
/KAOUVR . . . . curative
/KAOUVRT . . . . curative
/KAO*UZ . . . . cusis
/KAPDZ . . . . capsid
/KARKL . . . . calcarine
/KARL . . . . cardial
/KARLS . . . . cardiolysis
/KARLT . . . . cartilage
/KARNLD . . . . cardinal
/KARP . . . . carp
/KARPL . . . . carpal
/KARPS . . . . carpus
/KARSZ . . . . karyosis
/KA*S . . . . cast
/KAUD . . . . caudal
/KA*UD . . . . caudad
/KAUFL . . . . causal
/KA*UGS . . . . cauterization
/KAUJS . . . . collagenous

/KAUKL . . . . coccal
/KAUL . . . . call
/KA*ULD . . . . caudal
/KAULTS . . . . catalysis
/KAUN . . . . konia
/KAUND . . . . chondral
/KAUNG . . . . condylic
/KAUNL . . . . condyle
/KAUNLS . . . . condylus
/KAUNS . . . . koniosis
/KAUPGS . . . . copulation
/KAUR . . . . cardia
/KAURD . . . . cardia
/KAURDZ . . . . cardosis
/KA*URGS . . . . cauterization
/KAURJ . . . . cardioplegia
/KAURK . . . . cardiac
/KA*URL . . . . cardial
/KAURMD . . . . cardium
/KAURMG . . . . cardiogram
/KAURND . . . . chondrial
/KAURP . . . . cardioplasty
/KAURPT . . . . cardiopathy
/KAURPX . . . . cardiopexy
/KA*URT . . . . cautery
/KAURTD . . . . cardotomy
/KAUX . . . . coccus
/KAUXZ . . . . coccosis
/KAV . . . . cava
/KAVG . . . . cavogram
/KAVL . . . . caval
/KAVRNS . . . . cavernous
/KAVRT . . . . cavitary
/KBAENT . . . . carbonate
/KBAIGS . . . . combination
/KBA*IGS . . . . amputation
/KBAISZ . . . . catabasis
/KBAIX . . . . amputation
/KBAOEM . . . . emphysema
/KBAOFT . . . . karyoblast
/KBAO*FT . . . . caryoblast
/KBAOIRTS . . . . calcaneobursitis
/KBAOL . . . . embolia
/KBAOUNGS . . . . immunization
/KBAR . . . . lumbar

/KBAULT . . . . cobalt
/KBEKT . . . . embolectomy
/KBINT . . . . ambient
/KB–J . . . . immunologic
/KBLANGS . . . . implantation
/KBLANT . . . . implant
/KBLAOEM . . . . immunoglobulinemia
/KBLAOISZ . . . . encleisis
/KBLAS . . . . ectoblast
/KBLIFM . . . . embolism
/KBL*IK . . . . embolic
/KBLOE . . . . ecbole
/KBLOFM . . . . catabolism
/KBLOISZ . . . . enclisis
/KBLOK . . . . catabolic
/KBLUS . . . . embolus
/KBOKLD . . . . carboxylic acid
/KBOLG . . . . immunology
/KBON . . . . carbon
/KBONT . . . . carbonate
/KBRAEGS . . . . impregnation
/KBRAEZ . . . . embryoplasia
/KBRAX . . . . emphraxis
/KBRA*X . . . . mphraxis
/KBREGS . . . . impression
/KBROEM . . . . embryoma
/KBROEN . . . . embryon
/KBROIN . . . . embryony
/KBRONG . . . . embryonic
/KBUBL . . . . combustible
/KBUMT . . . . cumbent
/KBURTS . . . . calcaneobursitis
/KEFK . . . . kyphectomy
/KEK . . . . connect
/K*EKT . . . . cardectomy
/KENGT . . . . kinetic
/KENGTS . . . . kinetics
/K*ENT . . . . kentric
/KENTS . . . . cardiocentesis
/KERKT . . . . keratic
/KERNGS . . . . keratinization
/KERNT . . . . keratin
/KERPT . . . . keratoplasty
/KERTS . . . . keratitis
/KERX . . . . keratinization

/KESZ . . . . kesis
/KEX. . . . . connection
/KHAEPT . . . . chondropathy
/KHA*EPZ . . . . achondroplasia
/KHAERB . . . . chetia
/KHAES . . . . chesia
/KHA*ET. . . . . chondropathy
/KHAEZ . . . . chezia
/KHAIDZ. . . . . chondrodysplasia
/KHAIJ . . . . change
/KHAING . . . . change
/KHA*IPS . . . . achondroplasia
/KHAIPZ . . . . achondroplasia
/KHAK . . . . chondriac
/KHALS. . . . . chalasia
/KHALSZ . . . . chalasis
/KHAMT . . . . chromat
/KHAO*EM . . . . chylema
/KHAOEVR . . . . achiever
/KHAOIL. . . . . chylia
/KHAO*IL . . . . cheilia
/KHAOILT . . . . cholitis
/KHAOILTS . . . . cholitis
/KHAO*IM . . . . chymia
/KHAOINS. . . . . cholecystokinin
/KHAO*INS . . . . -cholecystokinin (*hyphenated*)
/KHAOIP . . . . cheiloscope
/KHAOIR . . . . chiria
/KHAO*IR . . . . cheiria
/KHAOIRK. . . . . chirurgic
/KHAOIRL . . . . chiral
/KHAO*IRL . . . . cheiral
/KHAOIRLG . . . . chirurgical
/KHAOIRTS . . . . orchitis
/KHAO*IRTS. . . . . -orchitis (*hyphenated*)
/KHAOITS . . . . chondritis
/KHAOIZ. . . . . enchysis
/KHAOL . . . . cholia
/KHAOLT . . . . cholate
/KHAO*PT . . . . chondropathia
/KHAOR . . . . chorea
/KHAORLD . . . . chordal
/KHA*PT . . . . chondropathia
/KHARJ. . . . . charge
/KHAUG . . . . cholagogue

/KHAUKT . . . . chondrectomy
/KHAUR . . . . choria
/KHAURPS . . . . chondroscapularis
/KHEM . . . . chemical
/KHEMSZ . . . . chemistries
/KHEMZ . . . . chemistry
/KHERNT . . . . chorioretinitis
/KHEXZ . . . . ecchysis
/KHIFM . . . . chorism
/KHIFP . . . . chromotrichia
/KHIFT . . . . cholecyst
/KHIRLG . . . . chirurgical
/KHIRS . . . . chirus
/KHISZ . . . . chysis
/KHITS . . . . cholecystis
/KHIX . . . . ectothrix
/KHOEB . . . . chondrofibroma
/KHOEF . . . . chondrodystrophy
/KHOEFG . . . . cholecystography
/KHOEFM . . . . chondrofibrosarcoma
/KHOEFS . . . . chondrosteosis
/KHO*EK . . . . echoic
/KHOEKT . . . . cholecystocholedochectomy
/KHOELG . . . . cholic
/KHOELGD . . . . cholic acid
/KHOELT . . . . cholecystitis
/KHOELTS . . . . cholecystitis
/KHOEM . . . . chondroma
/KHOEMS . . . . chondrosarcoma
/KHOEMT . . . . cholesteatoma
/KHOEMTS . . . . chondromatosis
/KHOENDZ . . . . chondrogenesis
/KHOEP . . . . chronoscope
/KHOER . . . . chore
/KHOERM . . . . enchondroma
/KHOERN . . . . chorion
/KHOERNG . . . . chorionic
/KHOERSZ . . . . chondroses
/KHOESZ . . . . chondrosis
/KHOET . . . . chondrotomy
/KHOETS . . . . chondrostosis
/KHOF . . . . chondrodystrophia
/KHOFM . . . . alcoholism
/KHOFPS . . . . choledochostomy
/KHOFPT . . . . choledochotomy

/KHOID . . . . choroidea
/KHOIK . . . . chroic
/KHOIKT . . . . cholecystectomy
/KHO*IL . . . . chilia
/KHOIM. . . . . chemy
/KHOIN . . . . chronia
/KHOIPG . . . . echoscopy
/KHOIRD . . . . hydrochloride
/KHOIRL . . . . cheiral
/KHOITS . . . . chorditis
/KHOIX . . . . chondromyxoma
/KHOIZ . . . . chromhidrosis
/KHOL . . . . alcohol
/KHOLSZ. . . . . chondrolysis
/KHORD . . . . chord
/KHORK . . . . orchidium
/KHORL. . . . . chorial
/KHORM . . . . chondrium
/KHORN . . . . chordon
/KHORND . . . . chondria
/KHORNGD . . . . chondriac
/KHORNL . . . . chondriacal
/KHORNSZ . . . . chondriasis
/KHOS . . . . cholecystostomy
/KHO*S . . . . cholecystostomy
/KHOT . . . . cholecystotomy
/KHO*T . . . . cholecystotomy
/KHOTS . . . . chondroseotomy
/KHOUNS. . . . . chthonous
/KHOUR . . . . choluria
/KHOUS. . . . . chondrous
/KHOUZ . . . . chroous
/KHROIP. . . . . chromoprotein
/KIM. . . . . kyme
/KINGT . . . . kinetic
/KINGTS . . . . kinetics
/KINLD . . . . condylian
/KINS. . . . . anakinesia
/K*INT . . . . kinesthetic
/KIRMT. . . . . kinesimeter
/KIRNL . . . . cardioperitoneal
/K-KL . . . . collic
/KLAEF . . . . cochleograph
/KLAEFG . . . . cochleography
/KLAEFK . . . . cochleographic

/KLAEKT . . . . caliectasis
/KLA*EM . . . . kalemia
/KLA*EMG . . . . kalemic
/KLAEMP . . . . eclampsia
/KLAENL . . . . calcaneal
/KLAENSZ . . . . alkalescence
/KLAERB . . . . chalazia
/KLAERM . . . . cochleogram
/KLA*ERN . . . . calcanean
/KLA*ES . . . . cholinesterase
/KLAESZ . . . . klasis
/KLAFKT . . . . oclastic
/KLAFM . . . . cladism
/KLAFRL . . . . clavicular
/KLAFRLZ . . . . claviculars
/KLAFT . . . . clastic
/KLAFZ . . . . klastic
/KLAG . . . . cholangiogastrostomy
/KLAGT . . . . cartilago
/KLAIFN . . . . clavian
/KLA*IGS . . . . collation
/KLAIL . . . . echolalia
/KLAIMZ . . . . clysmia
/KLAIN . . . . alkaline
/KLAIR . . . . calary
/KLAISZ . . . . clasis
/KLAIT . . . . cholate
/KLAIV . . . . clave
/KLAIVN . . . . clavian
/KLAIVS . . . . clavius
/KLAIZ . . . . clasia
/KLAJS . . . . cartilaginous
/KLAKD . . . . cladic
/KLAKT . . . . catalytic
/KLALG . . . . condylalgia
/KLAMZ . . . . clamis
/KLANG . . . . cholangiostomy
/KLAOB . . . . coloboma
/KLAOD . . . . occlude
/KLAO*E . . . . coly
/KLAOEL . . . . caliceal
/KLAOEM . . . . chloremia
/KLAO*EM . . . . kaliemia
/KLAOEMD . . . . chloridemia
/KLAOEMG . . . . kalemic

/KLAO*EMG . . . . chloremic
/KLAOEMGS . . . . calcemic
/KLAOEMS . . . . calcemia
/KLAOERMG . . . . cholesteremic
/KLAOESZ. . . . . choleresis
/KLAOF . . . . -occlusive (*hyphenated*)
/KLAOFG . . . . cholangiography
/KLAOGS. . . . . occlusion
/KLAO*GS . . . . -occlusion (*hyphenated*)
/KLAOILD . . . . cleidal
/KLAOINL . . . . clinal
/KLAOIRD . . . . chlorhydria
/KLAOIRS. . . . . catalyzer
/KLAOIRTS . . . . corneascleritis
/KLAOIS . . . . clysis
/KLAOISZ. . . . . cleisis
/KLAO*ISZ . . . . kleisis
/KLAOIT. . . . . chlorite
/KLAOITS . . . . cholangitis
/KLAOJ . . . . cholangiojejunostomy
/KLAOL. . . . . occlusal
/KLAO*L . . . . -occlusal (*hyphenated*)
/KLAOLS . . . . -occlusal (*hyphenated*)
/KLAOMT. . . . . calicostomy
/KLAON . . . . clonia
/KLAOR. . . . . calorie
/KLAORK. . . . . caloric
/KLAORM. . . . . cholangiogram
/KLAORP . . . . chloropia
/KLAORT. . . . . chlorate
/KLAO*UGS . . . . collusion
/KLAOUM . . . . coulomb
/KLAOUR . . . . calciuria
/KLAOURGS. . . . . chloruration
/KLAOURL . . . . nucleolar
/KLAOURN . . . . calcinuria
/KLAOV. . . . . occlusive
/KLAOZ. . . . . oclasis
/KLARKL . . . . collicular
/KLARL . . . . collateral
/KLART . . . . cartilage
/KLAS . . . . clasty
/KLA*S . . . . clast
/KLASZ . . . . class
/KLAUL . . . . caulia

/KLAURM . . . . columnar
/KLAVRL . . . . clavicular
/KLAVRLZ . . . . claviculars
/KLAZ . . . . clasis
/KLED . . . . choledochus
/KLEF . . . . cancellous
/KLEKT . . . . colectomy
/KLEN . . . . choline
/KLENT . . . . cholangioenterostomy
/KLEP . . . . catalepsy
/KLEPGT . . . . calcipectic
/KLEPSZ . . . . clepsis
/KLEPX . . . . calcipexy
/KLEPZ . . . . clepsia
/KLER . . . . cholera
/KLERMT . . . . cholesteremia
/KLERN . . . . cholesterin
/KLES . . . . cholesterol
/KL*ES . . . . cholesterol
/KLESZ . . . . clesis
/KLET . . . . cholangeitis
/KLETS . . . . cholangeitis
/KL–GZ . . . . calation
/KLIB . . . . equilibrium
/KLIFD . . . . cholangiocystoduodenostomy
/KLIFMT . . . . climatologist
/KLIFN . . . . colysin
/KLIFR . . . . clyster
/KLIFRL . . . . clavicularis
/KLIJ . . . . cholinergic
/KLIKTS . . . . canaliculitis
/KLIL . . . . calyceal
/KLIMG . . . . climatology
/KLIN . . . . clinic
/KLINGS . . . . clination
/KLINL . . . . clinical
/KLINT . . . . alkalinity
/KLIP . . . . clip
/KLIR . . . . chloruria
/KLIRKL . . . . canalicular
/KLIS . . . . catalyst
/KLIT . . . . clitoris
/KLIVL . . . . clival
/KLIVRL . . . . clavicularis
/KLOEB . . . . coloboma

/KLOEDZ . . . . kelidosis
/KLOEFSZ . . . . cleidodysostosis
/KLOEG . . . . cologastrostomy
/KLOEKSZ . . . . calycosis
/KLOEL . . . . cholesterolia
/KLOEM . . . . clastoma
/KLOENL . . . . clonal
/KLOENLT . . . . clonality
/KLO*EP . . . . colonoscope
/KLOEPS . . . . colposcope
/KLOER . . . . cholera
/KLOERGS . . . . chloridation
/KLOERL . . . . chloral
/KLOERM . . . . cholesterolemia
/KLOERMG . . . . cholesterolemic
/KLOERZ. . . . . chlorization
/KLOF . . . . chlorophyll
/KLOFT. cholangioduodenostomy
/KLOGS . . . . clusion
/KLOGT . . . . clotting
/KLO*I . . . . clinoid
/KLOID . . . . colloid
/KLOIMTS . . . . climatics
/KLOIN . . . . colony
/KLO*IN . . . . klony
/KLOINTS . . . . condylitis
/KLOIPS . . . . colonoscopy
/KLOIPT . . . . colpitis
/KLOIPTS . . . . colpitis
/KLOIRD . . . . chloride
/KLOIRN . . . . chlorine
/KLOIRNGS. . . . . chlorination
/KLOISZ. . . . . clisis
/KLOIT. . . . . colitis
/KLOITD . . . . cleidomastoid
/KLOITDZ . . . . cleidomastoideus
/KLOITS . . . . colitis
/KLOITSDZ . . . . cleidomastoideus
/KLOIZ. . . . . kleisis
/KLOKL . . . . collic
/KLOMT. . . . . colotomy
/KLON . . . . colon
/KLONG . . . . colonic
/KLONK . . . . clonic
/KLONT . . . . colonitis

/KLONTS . . . . colonitis
/KLOPG . . . . colpectomy
/KLOPT . . . . coloptosis
/KLORGS . . . . coloration
/KLORK . . . . chloric
/KLORKT . . . . choleretic
/KLORMT . . . . colorimeter
/KLORN . . . . chlorin
/KLORNTD . . . . chlorinated
/KLOS . . . . colostomy
/KLO*S . . . . colostomy
/KLOUGS . . . . oclusion
/KLO*UR . . . . closure
/KLOURZ . . . . chlorous
/KLOUZ . . . . calculous
/K-LS . . . . collis
/KL-S . . . . calculus
/KL-T . . . . calate
/KL-TD . . . . calated
/KLUL . . . . clusal
/KLULS . . . . nucleolus
/KLULZ . . . . cclusal
/KLUNS . . . . clonus
/KLURK . . . . calcuria
/KLURS . . . . kaluresis
/KL-Z . . . . catalyze
/KMA . . . . comma
/KMAE . . . . kinemia
/KMAEF . . . . kymography
/KMAEG . . . . kinemic
/KMAERT . . . . colpometra
/KMAF . . . . kymograph
/KMAFK . . . . kymographic
/KMAIRT . . . . camerate
/KMAIS . . . . chromasia
/KMAIZ . . . . chromasia
/KMAKT . . . . climacteric
/KMAL . . . . comial
/KMAM . . . . kymogram
/KMAOE . . . . cardiotomy
/KMAOEFL . . . . chromophilia
/KMAOEM . . . . chromemia
/KMAOIF . . . . chromophile
/KMAOIKS . . . . coccidioidomycosis
/KMAOIZ . . . . ectomize

/KMAOKL . . . . macromolecule
/KMAOT . . . . commata
/KMAOUL. . . . . molecule
/KMAOURL . . . . commissural
/KMARK . . . . molecular
/KMAUM . . . . coccoma
/KMAUT . . . . cotomy
/KMAZ . . . . chromasy
/KM–D. . . . . compromised
/KMEFT . . . . chemist
/KMEFTS . . . . chemists
/KMENLS . . . . commensal
/KMERK . . . . molecular
/KM*ES. . . . . chemist
/KM*ESZ . . . . chemists
/KMIF . . . . chromophil
/KMIFM . . . . chromatism
/KMIK . . . . economic
/KMIKS . . . . economics
/KMIRMT . . . . corticomimetic
/KMOEFM . . . . chromism
/KMOEK . . . . chylomicronemia
/KMOEL. . . . . chromosomal
/KMO*EM . . . . enchymoma
/KMOEMS. . . . . chromosome
/KMOFG . . . . chromatography
/KMOK . . . . chromatotic
/KMO*S . . . . costomy
/KMUM . . . . conium
/KMUMD . . . . conidium
/KMUNGS . . . . communication
/K–ND . . . . conditioned
/K–NG. . . . . conditioning
/KOEFM. . . . . corticism
/KOEFMT. . . . . corticalism
/KOEFSZ . . . . kyphosis
/KOEFZ . . . . kophosis
/KOEKT . . . . ctony
/KOELG . . . . ecology
/KOELT . . . . ecologist
/KOEMSZ . . . . camnosis
/KOEMZ . . . . kamnosis
/KOEN . . . . cone
/KO*EN . . . . conia
/KOEN . . . . cone

/KOEND . . . conid
/KOENG . . . cogenic
/KO*ENG . . . conic
/KOENGS . . . conization
/KOENS . . . coniosis
/KO*ENT . . . acanthoma
/KOEP . . . cope
/KO*EP . . . copia
/KOEPT . . . colpotomy
/KOERG . . . corticogram
/KOERLT . . . cortical
/KOERM . . . cormus
/KOERNL . . . corneal
/KOERPT . . . corporectomy
/KOERSZ . . . coriasis
/KOERTS . . . cortisone
/KOERX . . . cortex
/KOESZ . . . keratomycosis
/KO*ET . . . karyote
/KO*ETS . . . acanthosis
/KOEVRNS . . . cavernosus
/KOFL . . . costal
/KOFLS . . . costalis
/KOFLZ . . . costals
/KOFM . . . cosm
/KOGS . . . cognition
/KOID . . . corticoid
/KO*ID . . . coccoid
/KOIFM . . . corticoidism
/KOIKD . . . coccoid
/KOIL . . . coil
/KOILT . . . coital
/KOIM . . . kymia
/KOIMS . . . calcinemia
/KOIMSZ . . . koimesis
/KOIMZ . . . koimesis
/KO*IN . . . kine
/KOINL . . . condyloid
/KOINLS . . . condylous
/KOINZ . . . anconeus
/KOIRNSZ . . . carynosis
/KOITS . . . coitus
/KOJ . . . accommodation
/KOKL . . . colic
/KOLG . . . ecology

/KOLS	colpos
/KOLT	colotomy
/KOLZ	kolpos
/KONLS	consciously
/KONS	conscious
/KONSZ	consciousness
/KOPG	copic
/KOPGS	copulation
/KORD	cord
/KORKT	cordectomy
/KORN	corn
/KORPGS	corporation
/KORPT	corporate
/KO*T	cotomy
/KOULT	culture
/KOUPX	cowpox
/KOURNS	cornous
/KOURS	course
/KOUS	continuous
/KOUSZ	kousis
/KOV	cognitive
/KOXZ	coccic
/KPABL	compatible
/KPABLT	compatibility
/KPAD	ectad
/KPAE	replica
/KPAENL	carpophalangeal
/KPAERL	ectodermal
/KPAERS	exairesis
/KPAES	competency
/KPAFLGS	capsulation
/KPAMGS	examination
/KPA*NT	xanthine
/KPAOEL	colpocele
/KPAOEM	toxemia
/KPAOERL	corporeal
/KPAOERMT	campimeter
/KPAOI	carpi
/KPAOID	oxide
/KPAOIDZ	oxides
/KPAOIGS	excitation
/KPAOILT	cystopyelitis
/KPAOILTS	cystopyelitis
/KPAOINL	corticospinal
/KPAOIRT	excitatory

/KPAON	axon
/KPAONG	axonography
/KPAONK	axonic
/KPAONL	axonal
/KPAOUL	capsule
/KPAOULGS	capsulization
/KPAOUR	oxiduria
/KPAOURL	capsular
/KPE	competent
/KPEK	carpectomy
/KPENGS	compensation
/KPERGS	exertion
/KPERK	exoteric
/KPERM	ectoderm
/KPERNL	external
/KPERS	exeresis
/KPES	competence
/KPEX	colopexy
/KP–FL	capsule
/KP–FLGS	capsulization
/KP–FRL	capsular
/KP–GS	examination
/KPIBL	incompatible
/KPIBLT	incompatibility
/KPIFG	existing
/KPIFGT	existing
/KPIFP	capitulate
/KPIFPGS	capitulation
/KPIGS	excision
/KPIK	xic
/KPIM	oxemia
/KP*IM	xemia
/KPIN	campsodynia
/KPINL	axiogingival
/KP*INT	xanthin
/KPIRT	excitory
/KPIZ	colpismus
/KP–K	capnic
/KPLAEZ	chondroplasia
/KPLAIR	capillary
/KPLAOEMG	complementemic
/KPLAOEMT	complementemia
/KPLAOIGS	coloplication
/KPLAOIT	capsulitis
/KPLAOS	coloplasty

/KPLAOUR . . . . oxaluria
/KPLA*S. . . . . colpoplasty
/KPLEMT . . . . complement
/KPLEMTD . . . . complemented
/KPLERL . . . . cardiopleural
/KPLERMT . . . . complementary
/KPLEX . . . . complex
/KPLIRS . . . . capillaris
/KPLOS . . . . coloplasty
/KP–N . . . . capnia
/KPOEFD . . . . composed
/KPOEGS . . . . composition
/KPOEMT . . . . xanthoendothelioma
/KPOEN . . . . axone
/KPOENS . . . . xenosis
/KPOENT. . . . . component
/KPOENTS . . . . components
/KPOEX . . . . ectomopexy
/KPOEZ . . . . exarthrosis
/KPOGS. . . . . composition
/KPOID . . . . axoid
/KPOIR. . . . . cataphoria
/KPOISZ . . . . ectyposis
/KPOIT . . . . capitate
/KPOITS. . . . . capitates
/KPOK . . . . oxic
/KPOKD . . . . oxidant
/KPOKDZ . . . . oxidants
/KPONK. . . . . axonic
/KPOR . . . . exophoria
/KPORL. . . . . corporal
/KPOUN . . . . compound
/KPOUS . . . . oxenous
/KPO*US . . . . xenous
/KPRAIGS . . . . expiration
/KPRAOERT . . . . excretory
/KPRAOUR . . . . cupriuria
/KPREFBL . . . . compressible
/KPREKT . . . . carpectomy
/KPREM . . . . cupremia
/KPROESZ. . . . . xerosis
/KPROFBL. . . . . compressible
/KPROFGS. . . . . compression
/KPROFR . . . . compressor
/KPROKT. . . . . xerotic

/KPROMD . . . . compromised
/KPROS. . . . . compress
/KPRUFL. . . . . corpuscular
/KPUM . . . . colpium
/KPURL. . . . . capsular
/KRAEF . . . . cardiorrhaphy
/KRAEFG . . . . corticography
/KRAELG . . . . acromegaly
/KRA*ENT . . . . creatine
/KRAEP . . . . cryotherapy
/KRAEPGS . . . . crepitation
/KRAEPT . . . . carpectomy
/KRA*EPT . . . . endocrinopathy
/KRAERM . . . . keratodermia
/KRAERP . . . . cryotherapy
/KRAEVG . . . . cavography
/KRAF . . . . cardiograph
/KRAFK . . . . cardiographic
/KRAFL . . . . cristal
/KRAFM . . . . cerastism
/KRAI . . . . acria
/KRA*I . . . . akria
/KRAIFGS . . . . castration
/KRAIFK . . . . keratophakia
/KRAIFT . . . . crotaphia
/KRAIK . . . . craniectomy
/KRA*IN. . . . . crania
/KRAINK . . . . cranic
/KRAINL . . . . cranial
/KRAINT . . . . craniotomy
/KRAINZ. . . . . cranius
/KRAIPS . . . . corticohyperplasia
/KRAIRB . . . . acratia
/KRAIRM . . . . cranium
/KRAISZ . . . . acrasia
/KRALT . . . . contractility
/KRAMT . . . . chromat
/KRAN . . . . crania
/KRAOE. . . . . curie
/KRAOEF . . . . cardiography
/KRAOEJ. . . . . celialgia
/KRAOEKL . . . . celic
/KRAOEKT . . . . celectomy
/KRAOEL. . . . . cele
/KRAO*EL. . . . . coel

/KRAOELS . . . . cryalgesia
/KRAOELT . . . . cystocele
/KRAOELTS . . . . celitis
/KRAO*EM . . . . creatinemia
/KRAOENS . . . . cenesthesia
/KRAO*ENT . . . . creatine
/KRAOEPT . . . . keratoprosthesis
/KRAOEPTS . . . . keratoprosthesis
/KRAOERMT . . . . craniometry
/KRAOERTS . . . . carteresis
/KRAO*ESZ . . . . catheresis
/KRAO*ET . . . . catheresis
/KRAOETS . . . . cardiocentesis
/KRAO*ETS . . . . cardicentesis
/KRAOEZ . . . . cryesthesia
/KRAOF . . . . cardiophonograph
/KRAOFL . . . . chromatophilia
/KRAOFT . . . . crotaphy
/KRAOIF . . . . cairograph
/KRAOIFL . . . . chromatophile
/KRAOIFM . . . . crinism
/KRAOIKT . . . . cricotomy
/KRAOIL . . . . cryalgesia
/KRAO*IL . . . . cryal
/KRAOIN . . . . crinin
/KRAOIND . . . . cyanide
/KRAOINTS . . . . cardiomediastinitis
/KRAOIP . . . . cryoscopy
/KRAOIRD . . . . cricothyroid
/KRAOIRMT . . . . cricothyrotomy
/KRAOIRP . . . . cryotherapy
/KRAOIRS . . . . cryptovirus
/KRAOISZ . . . . crisis
/KRAO*IT . . . . cryesthesia
/KRAO*ITS . . . . cytocatheresis
/KRAOKT . . . . karyotic
/KRAO*KT . . . . caryotic
/KRAOL . . . . crural
/KRAO*M . . . . chromia
/KRAOMT . . . . craniotomy
/KRAON . . . . corona
/KRAONL . . . . coronal
/KRAOP . . . . croup
/KRAO*R . . . . coria
/KRAOS . . . . crasia

/KRAOSZ . . . . . cariasis
/KRAOT . . . . . karyocyte
/KRAO*T . . . . . caryocyte
/KRAOTS . . . . . karyocytosis
/KRAR . . . . . catarrh
/KRARKT . . . . . catarctic
/KRARL . . . . . catarrhal
/KRARSZ. . . . . caryosis
/KRARX. . . . . catarxis
/KRA*S . . . . . crista
/KRAUB . . . . . carbia
/KRAUD . . . . . acardius
/KRAUFM. . . . . chronism
/KRAUKT. . . . . cauterectomy
/KRAUM . . . . . keratoma
/KRAUMT . . . . . chrometer
/KRAUN . . . . . karyon
/KRA*UN . . . . . caryon
/KRAUNL . . . . . condylar
/KRAURKD . . . . . cardic
/KRAURKT . . . . . carditic
/KRAURMT . . . . . cardiomyotomy
/KRAURN . . . . . cardian
/KRAURS . . . . . kraurosis
/KRAUT . . . . . cautery
/KRAX . . . . . contraction
/KREF . . . . . access
/KREFM . . . . . endocrinism
/KREFN . . . . . cardiophrenic
/KREFNS. . . . . crescence
/KREKT . . . . . cardiectomy
/KREL . . . . . cell
/KRELD . . . . . celled
/KREN. . . . . endocrine
/KRENGT . . . . . cardiokinetic
/KRENZ . . . . . endocrisia
/KREP . . . . . crepitant
/KRER . . . . . cere
/KRERKT. . . . . catheretic
/KRERN . . . . . chronorrhea
/KRERS . . . . . accessory
/KRERT . . . . . corneoscleretomy
/KRERTS . . . . . ceratitis
/KRES. . . . . access
/KR*ET. . . . . catheretic

/KRETS . . . . crotesis
/KREX . . . . correction
/KRI. . . . . create
/KRIFKT . . . . eccritic
/KRIFL. . . . . crystal
/KRIFNT . . . . chromogenicity
/KRIGS . . . . creation
/KRIKT . . . . eccritic
/KRIL . . . . critical
/KRIMPS . . . . cardiosymphysis
/KRIMZ . . . . crismus
/KRIN . . . . crine
/KR*IN . . . . crinia
/KRING . . . . carcinogen
/KRINGS . . . . chromatinization
/KRINK . . . . crinic
/KRINSZ. . . . . crinosis
/KRINTS . . . . crinitis
/KRIPGT . . . . cryptectomy
/KRIPKT . . . . cryptectomy
/KRIPSZ . . . . crypsis
/KRIPZ . . . . crypsis
/KRIRK . . . . citric
/KR*IS . . . . cyst
/KRISZ . . . . eccrisis
/KRIT. . . . . crit
/KRIVTS . . . . keratoconjunctivitis
/KRIZ. . . . . eccrisia
/KR-KT . . . . critic
/KR-M . . . . cardiogram
/KR-N. . . . . cornea
/KR-NL . . . . corneal
/KROEF. . . . . chronograph
/KROEFG. . . . . corticotrophic
/KROEFL . . . . chromophil
/KROEFM. . . . . chroism
/KROEFN. . . . . corticotropin
/KROEFRN. . . . . corticotropin
/KROEJ. . . . . chromogen
/KROEJS . . . . chromogens
/KROEKL . . . . coelic
/KROEL . . . . coele
/KROELS . . . . cellulose
/KROEM . . . . chrome
/KROEMG . . . . chromic

/KROEMGS . . . . chromatization
/KROEMS . . . . chromatosis
/KROEMSZ . . . . chromatosis
/KROEMT . . . . chromatin
/KROEMZ . . . . chromesthesia
/KRO*EN . . . . cardiophone
/KROENG . . . . endocrinology
/KROENGS . . . . endocrinologies
/KROENGT . . . . chromogenicity
/KROENK . . . . chromogenic
/KROENL . . . . endocrinology
/KROENLS . . . . endocrinologies
/KROEP . . . . cardioscope
/KRO*EP . . . . keratoscope
/KROEPG . . . . corticotropic
/KROEPT . . . . chromatopsia
/KROEPTS . . . . cryptosis
/KROERMT . . . . chromometer
/KROERNS . . . . cornis
/KROERNT . . . . cornate
/KROES . . . . chrosis
/KROESZ . . . . craniosis
/KRO*ET . . . . caryote
/KROETS . . . . keratosis
/KRO*ETS . . . . ceratosis
/KROEZ . . . . cirrhosis
/KROFRM . . . . cryptorchism
/KROG . . . . cardiography
/KRO*I . . . . chroia
/KROID . . . . choroid
/KRO*ID . . . . coracoid
/KROIDZ . . . . choroiditis
/KROIF . . . . chromatophil
/KROIFK . . . . chromatophilic
/KROIFM . . . . crotism
/KROIKT . . . . crotic
/KROIL . . . . acromial
/KROILD . . . . choroidal
/KRO*ILD . . . . chorioidal
/KRO*IM . . . . chromy
/KROIMSZ . . . . coimesis
/KROIMT . . . . cystorhinotomy
/KROIMZ . . . . coimesis
/KRO*IN . . . . chrony
/KROINL . . . . chronal

/KROINT . . . . coronitis
/KROINTS . . . . coronitis
/KROIPS . . . . karyocytopoiesis
/KROIPZ . . . . chromoscopy
/KROIS . . . . acariasis
/KRO*IS . . . . chrosy
/KROISZ . . . . chromidrosis
/KROITD . . . . cotyloid
/KROITDZ . . . . chorioiditis
/KROITS . . . . cranitis
/KRO*ITS . . . . corditis
/KROITSDZ . . . . chorioiditis
/KROKD . . . . carotic
/KROKT . . . . corticectomy
/KROL . . . . control
/KROM . . . . chromia
/KROMS . . . . chromous
/KROMT . . . . chromatic
/KRO*MT . . . . achromatic
/KRONK . . . . chronic
/KROPT . . . . achromatopsia
/KROPTS . . . . chromatopsy
/KRORMT . . . . cystometrography
/KRORZ . . . . cursor
/KRO*S . . . . cardiostomy
/KROSZ . . . . cross
/KRO*T . . . . cristopathy
/KROTD . . . . carotid
/KROUNZ . . . . chronous
/KROUP . . . . croup
/KROUR . . . . contracture
/KROUTS . . . . crotous
/KROUZ . . . . chrous
/KRUDZ . . . . cardius
/KRURL . . . . crural
/KRURNG . . . . caruncular
/KRURZ . . . . crureus
/KR–Z . . . . crisia
/KUFPS . . . . conchous
/KUFRB . . . . curve
/KUFRBGS . . . . curvation
/KUFRBT . . . . curvature
/KUNS . . . . conus
/KUPGS . . . . cuspation
/KUPGZ . . . . cusping

/KUPL . . . . . . couple
/K*URK . . . . . . kurtic
/KURKT . . . . . . conductor
/KURKTS . . . . . . conductors
/KURNT . . . . . . current
/KUS . . . . . . coccus
/KUSZ . . . . . . cuss
/K*UT . . . . . . cut
/KUVRS . . . . . . cursive
/KUVS . . . . . . cursive
/KWABL . . . . . . coagulable
/KWABLT . . . . . . coagulability
/KWAEF . . . . . . concave
/KWAEN . . . . . . akinesia
/KWAENZ . . . . . . akinesis
/KWAES . . . . . . aqueous
/KWAEV . . . . . . concave
/KWAFT . . . . . . coagulative
/KWAGS . . . . . . coagulation
/KWAIV . . . . . . quantitative
/KWANG . . . . . . coagulin
/KWANLT . . . . . . coagulant
/KWAO*E . . . . . . loquy
/KWAOEM . . . . . . ketonemia
/KWAOERT . . . . . . quetrum
/KWAOET . . . . . . quetral
/KWAOETS . . . . . . quetrous
/KWAOS . . . . . . acusia
/KWAOT . . . . . . acuity
/KWAOUM . . . . . . acousma
/KWAOUP . . . . . . acupuncture
/KWAOUR . . . . . . ketonuria
/KWAOUS . . . . . . acousia
/KWAOUSZ . . . . . . acusis
/KWAOUT . . . . . . acute
/KWAO*UT . . . . . . acuity
/KWAOUTS . . . . . . cutis
/KWAOUZ . . . . . . acousia
/KWARG . . . . . . coagulator
/KWARGS . . . . . . coarctation
/KWAT . . . . . . adequate
/KWATS . . . . . . adequacy
/KW*ENS . . . . . . loquence
/KWERGS . . . . . . conversion
/KW*ERNS . . . . . . coherence

/KWERNT . . . . coherent
/KWERNZ . . . . coherence
/KWERT . . . . convert
/KW*ES . . . . quest
/KWEX . . . . convex
/KWIFM . . . . loquism
/KWIN . . . . quinone
/KWIRMT . . . . quantimeter
/KWIRN . . . . convertin
/KWIV . . . . equivalent
/KWIVNS . . . . equivalence
/KWIVS . . . . equivalence
/KWOEFBL . . . . coercible
/KWOEFT . . . . loquist
/KWOEM. . . . . coma
/KWOEMT . . . . comatose
/KWOEND . . . . codone
/KWOES. . . . . cardiosis
/KWOESZ . . . . ketosis
/KWOEZ . . . . comatose
/KWOFM . . . . loquism
/KWONL. . . . . quinol
/KWOUS . . . . acousis
/KWOUSZ . . . . acousis
/KWOUZ . . . . comatous
/KWUFT . . . . loquist
/KWUNS . . . . loquence
/KWUNT . . . . convulsant
/KWUTS . . . . cutis
/KWUV . . . . convulsive
/KWUVNT . . . . convulsant

L

/LA* . . . . la
/LABL . . . . labial
/LABLS . . . . labialis
/LA*EB. . . . . labe
/LAEF. . . . . electrocardiograph
/LAEFG . . . . lienography
/LAEFM. . . . . lateralism
/LA*EJ . . . . leakage
/LAEKL . . . . lacteal
/LAEKT . . . . loculate

/LAEKTD . . . . loculated
/LA*EM. . . . . lemma
/LAEMS . . . . elasma
/LAEMT . . . . laminectomy
/LAEMZ . . . . elasmatosis
/LA*EN . . . . leptanesthesia
/LA*ENG. . . . . leptanesthetic
/LAENK . . . . lacunae
/LAEPZ. . . . . lipase
/LAER . . . . layer
/LAERB. . . . . lentia
/LAERJ . . . . lactovegetarian
/LAERL . . . . laterally
/LAERMD . . . . leukoderma
/LAERN . . . . allergen
/LAERNGT. . . . . laryngotomy
/LAERNL . . . . laryngeal
/LAES. . . . . lase
/LAFKT . . . . elastic
/LAFM . . . . lalism
/LAFN . . . . elastin
/LA*G . . . . lagnia
/LAGT. . . . . lagnist
/LAI . . . . lay
/LA*IB. . . . . labia
/LAIBLD . . . . labeled
/LAIBT. . . . . lobulate
/LAIBTD. . . . . lobulated
/LAIFM. . . . . lactovegetarianism
/LAIFT . . . . lysate
/LAIGS . . . . lation
/LAIL . . . . lalia
/LAIMT. . . . . laminate
/LAINT. . . . . lunate
/LAIPZ. . . . . alloplasia
/LAIRJ . . . . lactovegetarian
/LAIRL. . . . . malarial
/LAIRM. . . . . laminar
/LAIRN. . . . . lunare
/LAIRNG . . . . laryngectomy
/LAIRNL. . . . . laryngeal
/LAIRNTS. . . . . laryngitis
/LAIRNX. . . . . larynx
/LAIT . . . . late
/LAITD . . . . lated

/LAIV	olivary
/LAIVR	–olivary
/LAIX	lactation
/LAJ	logical
/LAKL	lacteal
/LAL	electrical
/LAMGS	lamination
/LAMP	lamp
/LAMS	lipomatosis
/LA*NG	leptanalgesic
/LA*NL	leptanalgesia
/LAOBT	leukoblast
/LAOED	lead
/LAOEFMS	lysinemia
/LAOEFS	listhesis
/LAOEGS	lesion
/LAOEKSZ	electrophoresis
/LAO*EL	allele
/LAOELG	allelic
/LAOELGS	lesional
/LAO*EM	lipidemia
/LAOEMD	lactacidemia
/LAOEMG	lipidemic
/LAOEMGS	alimentation
/LAO*EMT	lithemia
/LAOEPDZ	lipidoses
/LAOEPT	lipoproteinemia
/LAOERT	liter
/LAO*ET	lethal
/LAOEZ	lyses
/LAOFD	leukodystrophy
/LAOFLG	electroencephalography
/LAOIFBL	lyzable
/LAOIFGS	lyzation
/LAOIGS	ligation
/LAOIJ	lysinogen
/LAOIMS	lysosome
/LAOIN	line
/LAOINS	lines
/LAOIPGT	lytopoietic
/LAOIPT	leptomeningitis
/LAOIPTS	leptomeningitis
/LAOIRP	lipofibroma
/LAO*IRZ	lyzer
/LAO*IS	lyse

/LAOISZ . . . . liasis
/LAO*IT . . . . lite
/LAO*ITS . . . . lithiasis
/LAO*IZ . . . . lyze
/LAOJ . . . . logia
/LAO*KT . . . . luetic
/LAOMT . . . . leukocythemia
/LAONL . . . . luminal
/LAO*P . . . . alope
/LAOPT . . . . lithalopaxy
/LAORM . . . . electrocardiogram
/LAORNG . . . . laryngoscopy
/LAOUBLT . . . . lobulitis
/LAOUBLTS . . . . lobulitis
/LAOUGT . . . . leukoagglutinin
/LAOUKSZ . . . . leukosis
/LAOUKT . . . . luetic
/LAOUKTS . . . . leukitis
/LAO*UL . . . . luminal
/LAOULZ . . . . linguo-occlusal
/LAOUN . . . . leukopenia
/LAOUNX . . . . leukotoxin
/LAOUP . . . . leukoscope
/LAOURK . . . . leukorrhea
/LAOURN . . . . lunar
/LAOURNS . . . . lysinuria
/LAOURNT . . . . allantoinuria
/LAOUS . . . . lucent
/LAOUSZ . . . . lucency
/LAOUT . . . . lutein
/LAOUTS . . . . leucitis
/LAPS . . . . lapse
/LAPXZ . . . . lapaxy
/LAR . . . . lar
/LARG . . . . laryngology
/LARGS . . . . laceration
/LARGT . . . . laryngologist
/LARJ . . . . large
/LARJD . . . . larged
/LARKL . . . . lacrimal
/LARL . . . . lateral
/LARLS . . . . lateral sclerosis
/LARNGT . . . . laryngotomy
/LARPT . . . . laparotomy
/LAUJ . . . . logia

/LAUM . . . . lemmoma
/LA*UM. . . . . alum
/LAUP . . . . labiopulpal
/LAUPS . . . . lapsus
/LA*UT . . . . lithotomy
/LAVJ . . . . lavage
/L*ED. . . . . lead
/LEFK . . . . electricity
/LEFPT. . . . . leptiform
/LEKL. . . . . electrical
/LEKT. . . . . electric
/L*EKT . . . . listhetic
/LEL. . . . . legal
/L*EL . . . . lamella
/LELG . . . . lienomegaly
/L*EM . . . . lemmal
/LEMG . . . . lemmic
/LEMTS . . . . lemmitis
/LEMZ . . . . lemmous
/LENLT . . . . lental
/LENT . . . . lent
/LENTS . . . . leptynsis
/LEPG . . . . epileptic
/LEPGT . . . . leptic
/LEPKT . . . . lipectomy
/LEPS . . . . epilepsy
/LEPSZ . . . . lepsis
/L*EPT . . . . lept
/LEPZ . . . . lepsy
/LERBT . . . . lambert
/LERG . . . . allergenic
/LERJ . . . . allergic
/LERJS . . . . allergosis
/L*ERL . . . . lamellar
/LERNG . . . . learning
/LERNL . . . . lenticular
/LERPZ. . . . . leprosy
/LET . . . . let
/L*ET . . . . lithectomy
/LEVR . . . . lever
/LEZ . . . . lyses
/-LG . . . . logy
/LI . . . . ly
/L*I li
/LIFK . . . . lithic

/LIFKZ	lithics
/LIFM	lism
/LIFN	lysin
/L*IG	lygmus
/LIJTS	limitation
/LIKT	lytic
/L*IKT	olytic
/LIKTS	lytics
/L*IKTS	olytics
/L*IL	liminal
/LILG	lithology
/LIMGTS	limitation
/LIMT	limit
/LIN	lin
/LINGS	linguistics
/LINGT	linguistic
/LINGTS	linguistics
/LINL	lingual
/LIPDZ	lipidosis
/LIPSZ	lipsis
/LIPT	lithotripsy
/LIRL	literal
/LIRMT	ligamentary
/LIRN	linear
/L*IRT	lithotrity
/LISZ	lysis
/L*IT	lith
/L*ITS	liths
/LIXL	linguoaxial
/L–J	logic
/L*K	lexic
/L–MT	element
/L–MTS	elements
/LOBLT	lobulitis
/LOBLTS	lobulitis
/LOEBD	lobed
/LOEBSZ	leukoblastosis
/LOEBT	lobate
/LOEBTS	lobitis
/LOED	load
/LOEFLGS	localization
/LOEFM	logism
/LOEFTS	elastosis
/LOEK	locate
/LO*EK	loquy

/LOELS . . . . lateral sclerosis
/LOEM . . . . lemmosarcoma
/LOEMD . . . . lepidoma
/LOEMG . . . . leukoma
/LOEMGS . . . . locomotion
/LOEMP . . . . lipoma
/LOEMPT . . . . lipomatous
/LOEMS . . . . lysosome
/LOEMTS . . . . alimentosis
/LOEP . . . . alopia
/LOEPG . . . . lithotrophy
/LOEPGT . . . . lithotrophic
/LOEPSZ . . . . liposis
/LOEPT . . . . lithotroph
/LOERBT . . . . locatio
/LOERDZ . . . . lordosis
/LOERKT . . . . locator
/LOERNT . . . . allergosorbent
/LOERX . . . . allocortex
/LOESZ . . . . losis
/LOEX . . . . location
/LOFG . . . . electrocardiography
/LOFN . . . . olysin
/LOG . . . . log
/LO*G . . . . logue
/LOIBL . . . . labile
/LOIBLT . . . . lability
/LOID . . . . loid
/LOIFM . . . . leiomyofibroma
/LOIFN . . . . lysine
/LOIFT . . . . lymphoidocyte
/LOIG . . . . lagny
/LOIJ . . . . logically
/LOIKT . . . . leukocytic
/LOIM . . . . leiomyoma
/LO*IM . . . . lipoleiomyoma
/LOIMD . . . . lipoidemia
/LOIMDZ . . . . elasmoidea
/LOINK . . . . allantoic
/LOINL . . . . lienal
/LOINT . . . . allantois
/LOIPD . . . . lupoid
/LOIPGT . . . . olytopoietic
/LOIPTD . . . . leptoid
/LOIPZ . . . . lepsia

/LOIRN . . . . lipoprotein
/LOITS . . . . iliitis
/LO*ITS . . . . lites
/LOIVL . . . . olivary
/LOIX . . . . loxy
/LO*IX . . . . loxia
/LOKT . . . . olytic
/LOKTS . . . . olytics
/LOLG . . . . lithology
/LOLGS . . . . localization
/LORB . . . . lobar
/LORBL . . . . lobular
/LORKL . . . . locular
/LORKT . . . . electrophoretic
/LORNT . . . . allergosorbent
/LO*T . . . . lithotomy
/LO*UG . . . . logue
/LOUGS . . . . logous
/LOUGTS . . . . ligamentous
/LOUK . . . . leukocyte
/LOUKT . . . . leukocytosis
/LOUKTS . . . . leukocytosis
/LOUM . . . . leukemia
/LOUMG . . . . leukemic
/LOUNK . . . . leukin
/LOUP . . . . linguopulpal
/LOUS . . . . louse
/LOUVS . . . . levous
/LOVT . . . . levosity
/L–RGS . . . . allergization
/L–RJ . . . . allergy
/L–RJS . . . . allergies
/–LT . . . . logist
/–LTS . . . . logists
/L*UB . . . . lumbar
/LUBL . . . . lumbocostoabdominal
/LUBLS . . . . lumbalis
/LUGS . . . . luxation
/LUGT . . . . linguitis
/L*UM . . . . lumbar
/LUMS . . . . luminescence
/LUMT . . . . luminescent
/LUNK . . . . lacunia
/L*URT . . . . lithuria
/LUS . . . . lus

/LUVM . . . . luvium
/L–X . . . . lexia

M

/MABL . . . . mandible
/MAEDZ . . . . madesis
/MAEF . . . . myelography
/MAEFG . . . . metrography
/MAEFGT . . . . mediastinography
/MAEFK . . . . meganephronic
/MAEFKT . . . . metastatic
/MAEFL . . . . mesal
/MAEFLT . . . . mediastinal
/MAEFMG . . . . magnetism
/MAEFT . . . . metastasis
/MAEG . . . . megalia
/MAEGS . . . . modulation
/MAEGT . . . . magnet
/MAEKL . . . . malacic
/MAEKT . . . . magnetic
/MA*EL . . . . melia
/MAELD . . . . medial
/MAELGT . . . . metallic
/MA*ELS . . . . melia
/MAELT . . . . metal
/MAELTD . . . . medullated
/MAEMT . . . . meatotomy
/MAEPT . . . . mastopathy
/MAERB . . . . malacia
/MAERGS . . . . micturation
/MAERGT . . . . metrography
/MAERJ . . . . marriage
/MAERJT . . . . modulator
/MAERK . . . . malacic
/MAERL . . . . malar
/MA*ERL . . . . mamillary
/MAERLD . . . . medullary
/MAERLT . . . . marital
/MAERM . . . . mammary
/MAERPT . . . . mechanotherapy
/MA*ERT . . . . ometra
/MAERZ . . . . merase
/MA*ES . . . . masty

/MA*ET . . . . myopathy
/MAEXL . . . . maxillare
/MAFGT . . . . mediastinogram
/MAFKT . . . . mathematics
/MAFKTS . . . . mathematics
/MAFMT . . . . matism
/MA*FT . . . . mastia
/MA*G . . . . agmia
/MAGZ . . . . magnesemia
/MAIFK . . . . mastic
/MAIFM . . . . matrixoma
/MAIGS . . . . mutation
/MAIKL . . . . megacolon
/MAILT . . . . meatal
/MA*IN . . . . mania
/MAINGS . . . . myelination
/MAINK . . . . maniac
/MA*INT . . . . methane
/MAIRJ . . . . marriage
/MAIRMT . . . . merotomy
/MAISZ . . . . metaplasia
/MAIZ . . . . mazia
/MA*K . . . . macria
/MAKT . . . . mandibulectomy
/MALD . . . . modal
/MALDZ . . . . mesodialysis
/MALG . . . . malignancy
/MALGT . . . . malignant
/MALSZ . . . . malacosis
/MA*LT . . . . mathematical
/MAMS . . . . matosis
/MANL . . . . manual
/MA*NS . . . . mancy
/MAOE . . . . metra
/MAOEF . . . . microcephaly
/MAOEFD . . . . mesad
/MAOEFG . . . . metrograph
/MAOEFLS . . . . mysial
/MAOEFS . . . . ophthalmodonesis
/MAOEFSZ . . . . immunoelectrophoresis
/MAOEFZ . . . . phthalmodonesis
/MAO*EJ . . . . myoplegia
/MAOEKL . . . . melic
/MAOEKLS . . . . melics
/MAOEKS . . . . myxia

/MAOEKZ . . . . myxia
/MAO*EL. . . . . myelia
/MAO*ELD . . . . medial
/MAOELDZ. . . . . medialysis
/MAOELSZ. . . . . melanoses
/MAOEMD . . . . myxedema
/MAOEMG. . . . . methemoglobin
/MAOEMT. . . . . mediastinum
/MAO*EMT . . . . methioninemia
/MAOEMZ . . . . mimesis
/MAO*EN. . . . . menia
/MAOEND. . . . . median
/MAO*ENG . . . . menic
/MAOENKS. . . . . meninx
/MAO*ENL . . . . menial
/MAOEP . . . . metrope
/MAOEPG. . . . . metropic
/MAOEPT . . . . metropia
/MAOEPTS . . . . metrosalpingitis
/MAOER . . . . mere
/MAO*ERB. . . . . mictio
/MAOERK . . . . mimicry
/MAOERKT. . . . . metriotic
/MAOERLS. . . . . merocele
/MAOERLT . . . . metrial
/MAO*ERM. . . . . metrium
/MAOERMT . . . . metrometer
/MAOERP. . . . . metroscope
/MAOERT. . . . . meter
/MAO*ERT . . . . ometer
/MAOERTS . . . . meters
/MAO*ERTS . . . . ometers
/MAOERX . . . . myxorrhea
/MAOERXZ . . . . merorachischisis
/MAOES . . . . myesthesia
/MAOESZ . . . . myces
/MAO*ETS . . . . metrist
/MAOETSZ. . . . . metachoresis
/MAOFBL . . . . mandibulodyscephaly
/MAOFG. . . . . mastography
/MAOFN . . . . mammotropin
/MAOFR . . . . morphia
/MAOFRK . . . . amorphic
/MAOFRN . . . . mammotropin
/MAOIBL . . . . myoblastoma

/MAOIBZ. . . . . amebiasis
/MAOIDZ . . . . myoendocarditis
/MAOIF . . . . myatrophy
/MAOIFK . . . . myopathic
/MAOIFLT . . . . mycetolysis
/MAOIFLTS . . . . mycetolysis
/MAOIFM . . . . mesenchyme
/MAOIFN . . . . mycin
/MAOIFSZ . . . . myelophthisis
/MAOIFT . . . . meniscitis
/MAOIFTS. . . . . meniscitis
/MAOIGS. . . . . migration
/MAOIKS. . . . . mycosis
/MAOIKT . . . . meiotic
/MAOILG . . . . myalgia
/MAO*ILS. . . . . myelus
/MAOILT . . . . myelitis
/MAOILTD . . . . myelitides
/MAOILTDZ . . . . myelitides
/MAOILTS . . . . myelitis
/MAOILZ . . . . myelis
/MAOIMT . . . . myometrial
/MAOIMTS. . . . . myometritis
/MAOIMZ . . . . mysium
/MAOIN . . . . mine
/MAO*ING . . . . maniacal
/MAOINK . . . . myoclonic
/MAOINL. . . . . myelin
/MAOINLSZ . . . . myelinosis
/MAOINLTD . . . . myelinated
/MAOINLZ . . . . myelins
/MAOINS . . . . myosin
/MAO*INT . . . . monocyte
/MAOINZ . . . . myelinosis
/MAOIPX . . . . myopexy
/MAOIRG. . . . . microgram
/MAOIRK . . . . microscope
/MAO*IRK . . . . micra
/MAOIRKL. . . . . microscopical
/MAOIRKT . . . . micrometer
/MAOIRM . . . . microsome
/MAOIRMT . . . . myometer
/MAOIRNG . . . . micron
/MAOIRNGS. . . . . microns
/MAOIRNTS . . . . myringitis

/MAOIRP . . . . microscopic
/MAO*IRP . . . . -microscopic (*hyphenated*)
/MAOITD . . . . myocarditis
/MAOITS . . . . myositis
/MAO*ITS . . . . myitis
/MAOIV . . . . megalovirus
/MAOIVR . . . . myxovirus
/MAOIVRS . . . . myxoviruses
/MAOIZ . . . . myiasis
/MAOKL. . . . . melancholia
/MAO*M . . . . megasoma
/MAOMT. . . . . matoma
/MAOP. . . . . myopia
/MAOPS . . . . megalopsia
/MAOPT . . . . myeloradiculopathy
/MAO*PT. . . . . mastopathy
/MAOPX . . . . omentopexy
/MAORKL . . . . monomolecular
/MAO*RL . . . . molar
/MAORLT . . . . mortal
/MAORM . . . . microsomia
/MAORMT. . . . . anemometer
/MAORPG . . . . mucotropic
/MAORS . . . . masseur
/MAOTD . . . . matoid
/MAOTS. . . . . mitosis
/MAOUBL . . . . immune globulin
/MAOUFN. . . . . immunoscintigraphy
/MAOUFRN. . . . . immunoscintigraphy
/MAOUJ. . . . . immunoimaging
/MAOUK . . . . mucous
/MAOUKS . . . . mucus
/MAOUN . . . . immune
/MAO*UN . . . . -immune (*hyphenated*)
/MAO*UNGS . . . . munition
/MAOUNT . . . . immunity
/MAOUNZ . . . . mucin
/MAOUPG . . . . medullotropic
/MAOUPGS . . . . immunoprecipitation
/MAOURGS . . . . micturition
/MAOURK . . . . microcurie
/MAOURL. . . . . mural
/MAOURM . . . . menstruum
/MAOUV . . . . munitive
/MAOUVT. . . . . munitive

/MAOV . . . . megalovirus
/MARKL . . . . macular
/MARL . . . . myocardial
/MARMG . . . . mammography
/MARMZ . . . . marasmus
/MARNT . . . . manometric
/MARP . . . . metacarpal
/MARXL . . . . maxillaritis
/MAS . . . . myoplasty
/MA*S . . . . mast
/MASZ . . . . mass
/MAUFL . . . . menopausal
/MAUFRM . . . . metatarsalism
/MAUFS . . . . amorphous
/MAUJ . . . . massage
/MAUKT . . . . mitotic
/MAUKZ . . . . myoclonus
/MAUM . . . . myxoma
/MAUND . . . . mitochondria
/MAUNG . . . . mongoloid
/MAUNK . . . . gnomonic
/MAUNLD . . . . mitochondrial
/MAUPT . . . . ophthalmotomy
/MA*UPT . . . . phthalmotomy
/MAUR . . . . mature
/MAURBGS . . . . masturbation
/MAURJ . . . . marginal
/MAURK . . . . myocardiac
/MA*URK . . . . menarche
/MA*URKL . . . . menarchal
/MAURKT . . . . amaurotic
/MA*URL . . . . myocardial
/MAURLS . . . . metatarsal
/MAURLZ . . . . metatarsalia
/MAURM . . . . myxosarcoma
/MA*URM . . . . metacarpalism
/MAURMT . . . . manometer
/MAURN . . . . moron
/MAURND . . . . mitochondrion
/MAURNT . . . . motonometer
/MAURP . . . . metacarpia
/MA*URP . . . . metacarpalia
/MAURSZ . . . . amaurosis
/MAURT . . . . maturity
/MAURTS . . . . metatarsia

/MAURZ . . . . metatarsus
/MA*UT . . . . mata
/MAUXZ . . . . myoclonus multiplex
/MAUZ . . . . menopause
/MAXL . . . . maxillary
/MAXT . . . . maxillectomy
/MAZ . . . . mazia
/MEB . . . . member
/MEBZ . . . . mesoblast
/MEFKS . . . . meniscus
/MEFLT . . . . myelencephalitis
/MEFLTS . . . . myeloencephalitis
/MEFM . . . . mechanism
/MEFRM . . . . merism
/MEGS . . . . medication
/MEJD . . . . medullary
/MEJS . . . . metagenesis
/MEKD . . . . medic
/MEKL . . . . megalic
/MEKT . . . . mastectomy
/MEL . . . . medical
/MELG . . . . megaly
/M*ELG . . . . melalgia
/MELS . . . . melanosis
/MELSZ . . . . melanosis
/MELZ . . . . mesial
/MENGT . . . . medicant
/MENGTS . . . . meningomyelitis
/MENK . . . . myasthenic
/MENL . . . . mental
/MENLS . . . . mensual
/M*ENT . . . . menthol
/MENTS . . . . meniscitis
/MENZ . . . . myasthenia
/MEPT . . . . metaplastic
/MER . . . . mere
/M*ER . . . . mer
/MERGS . . . . merization
/MERJ . . . . merge
/MERK . . . . meric
/M*ERK . . . . meric
/MERKS . . . . mesenteric
/MERKT . . . . metric
/MERKTS . . . . metrics
/MERL . . . . meral

/MERMD . . . . mesoderm
/MERMS . . . . mesoderm
/M–FBL . . . . missible
/MIFRB . . . . maleficence
/MIFTS . . . . mastitis
/MIGS . . . . mission
/M*IGS . . . . admission
/MIGTS . . . . amygdalitis
/MIKT . . . . myelitic
/M*IM . . . . mimia
/MIMG . . . . mimic
/MIMPT . . . . myelolymphocyte
/MIMT . . . . mimetic
/MIMZ . . . . minimus
/MIND . . . . myodynia
/MIPGS . . . . manipulation
/MIRBL . . . . mandibular
/MIRBLT . . . . mandibularitis
/M*IRK . . . . micria
/MIRKT . . . . metritic
/MIRLGS . . . . mineralization
/MIRMT . . . . imeter
/M*IRMT . . . . mimetry
/MIRMTS . . . . mycodermitis
/MIRN . . . . micron
/MIRNL . . . . mineral
/MIRNLS . . . . minerals
/MIRNS . . . . microns
/M*IRP . . . . manipulator
/MIRT . . . . metria
/MIVT . . . . emotivity
/MIXL . . . . maxilla
/M*IXZ . . . . mixis
/M–KL . . . . mechanical
/M–KS . . . . mechanics
/M–KT . . . . miotic
/MLAEM . . . . melanoma
/MLAING . . . . mesophalangia
/MLAIRL . . . . malarial
/MLA*N . . . . melanin
/MLAOELS . . . . malleolus
/MLAUL . . . . malleal
/MLAURL . . . . malleolar
/M–M . . . . millimeter
/M–N . . . . medicine

/M–NX . . . . immunodetection
/MOBL. . . . . ameloblastoma
/MOEBLT . . . . mobility
/MOEF. . . . . morph
/MOEFN . . . . morphine
/MOEFR. . . . . morph
/MOEFRB . . . . morphophobia
/MOEFRK . . . . morphic
/MOEFRLG . . . . morphology
/MOEFRLT . . . . morphologist
/MOEFRM . . . . morphism
/MOEFRN. . . . . morphine
/MOEFRS . . . . morphosis
/MOEFSZ . . . . morphosis
/MOEGS . . . . motion
/MOEGT . . . . megalogigantism
/MO*EKLS . . . . mucosal
/MOEKS . . . . mucosa
/MOEKT. . . . . metrectomy
/MOEL . . . . molar
/MO*EL. . . . . mole
/MOELD . . . . model
/MOELGD. . . . . modeling
/MO*EM . . . . metrioma
/MOEMP . . . . myolipoma
/MOEMZ . . . . myomatosis
/MOENK . . . . myogenic
/MOENTS . . . . myotonus
/MOEPSZ. . . . . myoliposis
/MOEPX . . . . -omentopexy (*hyphenated*)
/MOERBD . . . . morbid
/MOERBT . . . . immunosorbent
/MOERG . . . . metrogram
/MOERK . . . . morphic
/MOERM . . . . myoneuroma
/MO*ERM. . . . . myosarcoma
/MOERP. . . . . myelopore
/MOERT. . . . . motor
/MO*ERT . . . . motory
/MOERX. . . . . mucormycosis
/MOESZ . . . . mycosis
/MOETD . . . . metapody
/MOEV . . . . motive
/MOEVGS . . . . motivation
/MOEVT. . . . . motivate

/MOEZ. . . . . miosis
/MOFL . . . . macroglossia
/MOFPS . . . . morphopsia
/MOFRB. . . . . morphine
/MOFRJ. . . . . morphogenesis
/MOFRM . . . . morphinism
/MOFRMS . . . . morphinisms
/MOFRT . . . . morphotic
/MOGT . . . . mastigote
/MOIBD . . . . ameboid
/MOID . . . . myoid
/MO*ID . . . . moid
/MOIDZ . . . . mastoiditis
/MOIF . . . . myotrophy
/MOIFL. . . . . mesal
/MOIFM . . . . morphism
/MOIFN . . . . meganephronia
/MOIFR . . . . morphy
/MOIGS . . . . admission
/MOIJS . . . . meninges
/MO*IK . . . . myic
/MOIKD . . . . mucoid
/MOIKT . . . . myomectomy
/MOILD . . . . myeloid
/MO*ILD . . . . myloid
/MOILS. . . . . myelomeningocele
/MOILT . . . . motility
/MOILTS . . . . myeloradiculitis
/MOIM . . . . myoma
/MOIMD . . . . myxoadenoma
/MOIMT . . . . mastoidostomy
/MOINK. . . . . myelinic
/MOINSZ . . . . myelinogenesis
/MOINT . . . . myotonia
/MOIPT . . . . mucoprotein
/MOIRJ. . . . . margarine
/MOIRKL . . . . mercurial
/MOIRKT . . . . mycteria
/MOIRM . . . . myogram
/MOIRP . . . . microscopy
/MOIRTD. . . . . metrioid
/MOISZ. . . . . myosis
/MOIT . . . . myotomy
/MOITD . . . . mastoid
/MOITS . . . . mysiitis

/MO*IX . . . . miction
/MOKT . . . . mycotic
/MOLG. . . . . ophthalmology
/MO*LG. . . . . -ophthalmology (*hyphenated*)
/MOLSZ . . . . myolysis
/MOLT . . . . ophthalmologist
/MO*LT . . . . -ophthalmologist (*hyphenated*)
/MOLTS . . . . ophthalmologists
/MO*PT . . . . myeloneuropathy
/MOPTS . . . . metropsia
/MOPZ . . . . metrocolpos
/MORJ . . . . modulatory
/MORP . . . . metamorphosis
/MOT . . . . myotomy
/MOUFS . . . . morphous
/MOUKL . . . . mucosal
/MOUNS . . . . mucinous
/MOURL . . . . macular
/MOURS. . . . . merous
/MOURTS. . . . . motorius
/MOUT . . . . myomotomy
/MOUTS. . . . . matous
/MRAEJ . . . . menorrhagia
/MRAF . . . . myograph
/MRAFG . . . . myography
/MRA*IJ. . . . . metrorrhagia
/MRAIXT . . . . matrix
/MRAOEN . . . . menorrhea
/MRAOF . . . . micrograph
/MRAOFG . . . . micrography
/MRAOITS . . . . metritis
/MRE . . . . metry
/MR*E . . . . ometry
/MRENGS. . . . . menstruation
/MRENL . . . . menstrual
/M–RKT. . . . . metameric
/MROEB . . . . microbe
/MROEBL. . . . . microbial
/MRO*EFM . . . . metropathism
/MROEK. . . . . microbic
/MROESZ. . . . . metriosis
/–MT . . . . ment
/MUFLZ . . . . musculoskeletal
/MUFRL. . . . . muscular
/MUFS . . . . amorphus

/MUKS . . . . musculoskeletal
/MULTS . . . . medullitis
/MULZ . . . . melus
/MUNT . . . . immunity
/MURBGS . . . . masturbation
/M*UZ . . . . mus
/M–XL . . . . maximal
/MYAL . . . . myal
/MYAOEL . . . . myelia
/MYAOET . . . . mycete
/MYAOETS . . . . mycetes
/MYEKT . . . . mycetic
/MYENG . . . . myosinogen
/MY–L . . . . methyl
/MY–LS . . . . mysial
/MYOEM . . . . myofibroma
/MYOEMD . . . . myxochondroma
/MYOEMT . . . . myomatous
/MY–S . . . . mysia

N

/NAE . . . . pnea
/NAEF . . . . neurography
/NAEFG . . . . neuromyography
/NAEFGS . . . . inactivation
/NAEFK . . . . mnesic
/NAEFP . . . . neurorrhaphy
/NAEFRBGS . . . . innervation
/NAEGT . . . . negativity
/NA*EGT . . . . pneumoplethysmography
/NAEJS . . . . anagenesis
/NAELZ . . . . nasale
/NA*EM . . . . nema
/NAEMG . . . . anatomical
/NAEMGS . . . . animation
/NAEMT . . . . anatomy
/NAEMTS . . . . anatomies
/NAEPT . . . . analeptic
/NAEPTS . . . . pneumohepatitis
/NAERJ . . . . energia
/NA*ERM . . . . numerary
/NAERMS . . . . necrospermia
/NAERSZ . . . . aneresis

/NAERZ . . . . nares
/NAES . . . . mnesia
/NA*ESZ . . . . mnesis
/NAEVGS . . . . inactivation
/NAEVS . . . . invertase
/NAFMT . . . . gnathism
/NAFP . . . . neurorrhaphy
/NAFPD . . . . unsaturated
/NAFRBL . . . . navicular
/NAFRL . . . . navicular
/NAFX . . . . infraction
/NAIFPD . . . . natured
/NAIGS . . . . nation
/NAIGT . . . . negativity
/NA*IJ . . . . neuronophagia
/NAILT . . . . natal
/NAILTS . . . . nasality
/NAILZ . . . . nasal
/NAIMGS . . . . animation
/NAINT . . . . natant
/NAIRJ . . . . neuronophagia
/NA*IRL . . . . narial
/NAIT . . . . nate
/NAITD . . . . nated
/NAJ . . . . neuralgia
/NA*KT . . . . gnathic
/NALTS . . . . analyst
/NALZ . . . . analysis
/NA*LZ . . . . -analysis (*hyphenated*)
/NA*M . . . . nomia
/NAOEFG . . . . nystagmography
/NAOEFMS . . . . cnemism
/NAOEFT . . . . neocystostomy
/NAOEK . . . . technique
/NAO*EK . . . . pneic
/NAOEKZ . . . . techniques
/NAOELD . . . . needle
/NAOEM . . . . ammonemia
/NAO*EM . . . . nemia
/NAOEMD . . . . cnemidion
/NAOEMG . . . . cnemic
/NAOEMS . . . . cnemis
/NAOEMT . . . . nitremia
/NAOEMZ . . . . amnesia
/NAOENT . . . . neurasthenia

/NAOEPT . . . . neopyelostomy
/NAO*ERM . . . . neuromere
/NAOERMG . . . . natremic
/NAOERMT . . . . natremia
/NAOERTS . . . . natriuresis
/NAOEVJ . . . . neovaginorectal
/NAOEVRJ . . . . neovaginorectal
/NAOEVS . . . . nevus
/NAO*EZ . . . . neostomy
/NAOF . . . . anamorph
/NAOFG . . . . pneumoroentgenography
/NAOFM . . . . narcotism
/NAOFT . . . . pneumocyst
/NAOFX . . . . nephropexy
/NAOG . . . . pneumography
/NAOIFL . . . . neutrophile
/NAOIJ . . . . nitrogen
/NAOILG . . . . nigral
/NAOILT . . . . neuromyelitis
/NAOILTS . . . . neuromyelitis
/NAOIMTS . . . . pneumonitis
/NAOIN . . . . nine
/NAOIRL . . . . nitroglycerol
/NAOIRM . . . . neuromyoma
/NAOIRNG . . . . nitroglycerin
/NAOIRT . . . . nitrate
/NAOIRTS . . . . neuritis
/NAO*ITS . . . . nephrolithiasis
/NAOKL . . . . pneumococcal
/NAOLD . . . . nodal
/NAOLG . . . . natology
/NAOLT . . . . natalogist
/NAO*M . . . . noma
/NAOMG . . . . pneumograph
/NAOMSZ . . . . pneumoconiosis
/NAONS . . . . nanosoma
/NAOP . . . . anopia
/NAOPG . . . . anopic
/NAOPS . . . . anopsia
/NAO*PT . . . . anoptic
/NAO*R . . . . neure
/NAORKT . . . . nector
/NAORLT . . . . nodulate
/NAORMT . . . . pneumoperitoneum
/NAORN . . . . neurosurgeon

/NAORNG . . . . . neurosurgery
/NAORNS . . . . . neurosurgeons
/NAORNT . . . . . neutron
/NAORT . . . . . neurite
/NAORTS . . . . . neurositis
/NAOUFGS . . . . . infusion
/NAOUFLT . . . . . neutrophil
/NAOUKL . . . . . nuclear
/NAOUKLD . . . . . nucleoside
/NAOUKLGS . . . . . nucleation
/NAOUKLT . . . . . nucleate
/NAOUKLTD . . . . . nucleated
/NAOUKTD . . . . . nucleated
/NAOULGD . . . . . nucleotide
/NAOULS . . . . . pneumonolysis
/NAOUM . . . . . pneumonia
/NAOUMG . . . . . pneumonic
/NAOUMT . . . . . pneumatic
/NAOUN . . . . . pneumon
/NAOUPG . . . . . nucleoprotein
/NAOUPX . . . . . pneumopexy
/NAO*UR . . . . . ammonuria
/NAOURKT . . . . . neurotic
/NAOURLD . . . . . nodular
/NAOURN . . . . . neuron
/NAOURNL . . . . . neuronal
/NAOURNS . . . . . neurons
/NAOURS . . . . . neurosis
/NAOURSZ . . . . . neuroses
/NAOURX . . . . . pneumothorax
/NAOUSZ . . . . . anacusis
/NAOUX . . . . . nucleus
/NAOUZ . . . . . anacusia
/NAOXZ . . . . . pneumococcic
/NAPZ . . . . . pneumoplasty
/NARKSZ . . . . . narcosis
/NARKT . . . . . narcotic
/NARLS . . . . . analyzer
/NARP . . . . . narcolepsy
/NA*S . . . . . anastomosis
/NAUFK . . . . . gnostic
/NAUFKS . . . . . gnostics
/NAUKL . . . . . neuralgic
/NAULG . . . . . neuralgia
/NA*UM . . . . . onymy

/NAUMG . . . . . nomic
/NA*UMG . . . . . gnomic
/NAUMGS . . . . . nomics
/NAUN . . . . . gnathion
/NAUNK . . . . . gnomonic
/NAUNT . . . . . nauseant
/NAUPT . . . . . anoptic
/NAURKD . . . . . nocardiosis
/NAURLS . . . . . narcoanalysis
/NAURLT . . . . . neuroradiculitis
/NAURMD . . . . . pneumopericardium
/NAUS . . . . . anosmia
/NA*US . . . . . gnostic
/NA*USZ . . . . . gnostics
/NAUT . . . . . neurotomy
/NAXZ . . . . . nystaxis
/NAZ . . . . . neoplasm
/NEB . . . . . nebulous
/NEFGS . . . . . infection
/NEFMG . . . . . nephromegaly
/NEFRBL . . . . . nerval
/NEFRKT . . . . . nephroureterectomy
/NEFRN . . . . . nephrine
/NEFX . . . . . infection
/N*EFX . . . . . -infection (*hyphenated*)
/NEFZ . . . . . nephros
/NEG . . . . . negative
/N*EGS . . . . . ingestion
/NEJSZ . . . . . neogenesis
/N*EKT . . . . . nectomy
/N*EM . . . . . neme
/NENK . . . . . nectin
/NENKS . . . . . nectins
/NENZ . . . . . continence
/NERB . . . . . infectious
/N*ERB . . . . . -infectious (*hyphenated*)
/N*ERJ . . . . . energia
/NERJT . . . . . energetic
/NERJTS . . . . . energetics
/NERKT . . . . . necrectomy
/NERT . . . . . inert
/NEVK . . . . . infective
/NEXZ . . . . . necrosis
/N–FRKT . . . . . infarct
/N*ID . . . . . nodi

/NIFG . . . . nystagmograph
/NILT. . . . . analytic
/N*IM . . . . inoma
/NIMS. . . . . anatomist
/NIMSZ . . . . anatomists
/N*IN. . . . . nin
/N*IR. . . . . neuria
/N*IRKT . . . . neuritic
/N*IRL . . . . neurial
/NIRM . . . . neurium
/NIRN. . . . . neurine
/N*IS . . . . nystagmus
/NIVK . . . . -infective (*hyphenated*)
/NLAIS . . . . neoplasia
/NLAIZ . . . . nuclease
/NLAS . . . . neoplastic
/N–MG . . . . mnemonike
/N–NG. . . . . inic
/NOBLG . . . . anabolic
/NO*D . . . . noid
/NOED. . . . . node
/NOEFB. . . . . engyophobia
/NOEFM . . . . neurofibroma
/NOEFPT . . . . pneumocholecystitis
/NOEKD . . . . nocardiosis
/NOEKLS . . . . nucleolus
/NOELZ . . . . nucleosis
/NOEMS . . . . neuromatosis
/NOEMT . . . . neurotome
/NOEMTS . . . . pneumatosis
/NOERBT . . . . inhibitory
/NOERL . . . . endocardial
/NOERM. . . . . neuroma
/NO*ES. . . . . neuroanastomosis
/NO*ESZ . . . . nosis
/NOFK. . . . . nosic
/NOGS . . . . inoculation
/NO*I. . . . . noia
/NOIFP . . . . pneumoradiography
/NO*IK . . . . anemic
/NOIL . . . . normally
/NOILD . . . . nidal
/NOILT . . . . normality
/NOIM . . . . anemia
/NO*IM . . . . nomy

/NOIMG . . . . pneumogony
/NOIMTS . . . . pneumoperitonitis
/NO*IP . . . . anope
/NOIPD . . . . nephroid
/NOIPGT . . . . anopoietic
/NOIPSZ . . . . anopoiesis
/NOIPT . . . . pneumopathy
/NOIRL . . . . neurial
/NOIRMT . . . . neurocytoma
/NO*IT . . . . gnathia
/NO*ITS . . . . noditis
/NO*IZ . . . . gnosy
/NOJSZ . . . . neogenesis
/NOJT . . . . neogenetic
/NOL . . . . normal
/NOLZ . . . . normalcy
/NOM . . . . nome
/NOMS . . . . nomous
/NOMT . . . . nominate
/NONGT . . . . necronectomy
/NONK . . . . mnemonic
/NONZ . . . . nasion
/NOPG . . . . neurotropic
/NOPS . . . . anopsia
/NORBL . . . . normoblast
/NORBT . . . . inhibitor
/NORMSZ . . . . normocytosis
/NO*RMT . . . . normity
/NOSZ . . . . inosis
/NOUD . . . . noduli
/NOUDZ . . . . nodus
/NOULGS . . . . involution
/NOUM . . . . pneumonium
/NOUMS . . . . nymous
/NOURLG . . . . neuroimmunology
/NOURLS . . . . neurolysis
/NOURM . . . . neuroblastoma
/NOURMTS . . . . neuromyositis
/NOURX . . . . neurotoxin
/NO*UTS . . . . gnathous
/N–RJT . . . . energetic
/N–RJTS . . . . energetics
/NROKT . . . . necrotic
/*NS . . . . ness
/NUGS . . . . nutrition

/NUK . . . . nuclide
/NUKD . . . . nuclide
/NUKDZ . . . . nuclides
/NUKZ . . . . nuclides
/NURK . . . . neurologic
/N*URK . . . . neuric
/NURKT . . . . neurectomy
/N*URKT . . . . necteur
/NURL . . . . neural
/NURLG . . . . neurology
/NURM . . . . aneurysm
/NURMZ . . . . aneurysmorrhaphy
/NURPG . . . . neuropathic
/NURPT . . . . neuropathy
/NURPTS . . . . aneurysmoplasty
/NUSZ . . . . nosus
/N*UTS . . . . gnathus
/NUVL . . . . neovulvar
/NY–M . . . . nymy
/NY*M . . . . nym
/NYON . . . . amnion
/NYOZ . . . . amnios

O

/OD . . . . order
/OEBT . . . . obesity
/O*ED . . . . ode
/OEFD . . . . osed
/OEFK . . . . omphalic
/O*EFK . . . . mphalic
/OEFM . . . . omphalos
/OEFMS . . . . mphalos
/OEFPD . . . . -orchidostomy (*hyphenated*)
/OEFPS . . . . onychosis
/O*EFPS . . . . nychosis
/OEFS . . . . omphalis
/O*EFZ . . . . mphalis
/OEJ . . . . oncogenic
/OEKLS . . . . elcosis
/OEM . . . . oma
/O*EM . . . . ohm
/OEMS . . . . omas
/OEMSZ . . . . onychomycosis

/OEMZ . . . . omatosis
/O*EMZ . . . . matosis
/O*EN . . . . one
/OENGT . . . . ontogenetic
/OENTS . . . . ontogenesis
/O*EP . . . . ope
/OEPG . . . . opening
/O*EPT . . . . optosia
/OEPTS . . . . ptosis
/O*EPTS . . . . optosis
/OEPX . . . . orchidopexy
/O*EPX . . . . rchidopexy
/OERBL . . . . -orbital (*hyphenated*)
/OERD . . . . orad
/OERKD . . . . orchidism
/O*ERKD . . . . -orchidism (*hyphenated*)
/OERKT . . . . orchidectomy
/O*ERKT . . . . rchidectomy
/OERKTD . . . . orchidic
/OERNGS . . . . orientation
/OERNT . . . . orient
/OERX . . . . orexia
/O*ES . . . . ose
/OESZ . . . . osis
/O*ESZ . . . . tosis
/OEVLGS . . . . ovulation
/OEVM . . . . ovum
/OEVRL . . . . ovular
/OEVRLT . . . . ovulatory
/OEVRTS . . . . -ovaritis (*hyphenated*)
/OEVT . . . . -ovariotomy (*hyphenated*)
/OEXZ . . . . oxidosis
/O*EXZ . . . . xidosis
/OFP . . . . onychon
/O*FP . . . . nychon
/OFPD . . . . orchidostomy
/OFRM . . . . orchism
/OID . . . . oid
/O*ID . . . . id
/OIDZ . . . . oids
/O*IDZ . . . . ids
/OIFMD . . . . oidism
/O*IFMD . . . . idism
/O*IFP . . . . archy
/OIFPD . . . . rchidic

/OIFRG . . . . orbitography
/O*IFRG . . . . -orbitography (*hyphenated*)
/OIFRL . . . . orificial
/OIG . . . . ogen
/OIGS . . . . ogens
/OIJ . . . . ergy
/OIKD . . . . orchidia
/O*IKD . . . . -orchidia (*hyphenated*)
/OIKT . . . . amniotic
/OILD . . . . oidal
/O*ILD . . . . idal
/O*IM . . . . -ohm (*hyphenated*)
/O*IMD . . . . omohyoid
/OIND . . . . odontoid
/OINLS . . . . analosis
/OINTD . . . . -odontoid (*hyphenated*)
/OIPS . . . . opsy
/O*IPS . . . . psy
/OIPT . . . . opter
/OIR . . . . ory
/OIRK . . . . orthic
/OIRKD . . . . rchidia
/OIRND . . . . arytenoid
/OIRNDZ . . . . arytenoideus
/OIRT . . . . orthist
/O*IRT . . . . orthic
/OIRTS . . . . orthists
/O*IRTS . . . . orthics
/OIRX . . . . orthics
/OIVL . . . . ovarial
/OIVN . . . . ovarian
/OIVNS . . . . varianism
/OIVRL . . . . ovarial
/OIVT . . . . ovariotomy
/OJ . . . . genous
/O*J . . . . ogenous
/OJD . . . . electrocardiography
/O*KL . . . . cular
/OKLT . . . . cularity
/OKT . . . . otic
/OKTS . . . . otics
/OLG . . . . ology
/O*LG . . . . logy
/OLGS . . . . ologies
/O*LGS . . . . logies

/OLS . . . . olysis
/O*LS . . . . lysis
/OLT . . . . ologist
/O*LT . . . . logist
/OLTS . . . . ologists
/O*LTS . . . . logists
/OLZ . . . . olyses
/OMD . . . . odmia
/OMS . . . . osmia
/O*MS . . . . smia
/ON . . . . on
/ONG . . . . oncus
/O*NG . . . . ncus
/ONGT . . . . ontogenic
/O*NGT . . . . ntogenic
/ONGZ . . . . nyx
/ONX . . . . onyx
/O*NX . . . . nyx
/ONXZ . . . . onyxis
/O*NXZ . . . . nyxis
/OPG . . . . opathic
/O*PT . . . . opathy
/O*PTS . . . . opathies
/OPZ . . . . ops
/ORBL . . . . orbital
/O*RBL . . . . rbital
/ORBLT . . . . orbitale
/ORBT . . . . orbit
/ORGS . . . . organization
/ORKL . . . . orchial
/ORKZ . . . . orchis
/ORL . . . . oral
/O*RL . . . . -oral (*hyphenated*)
/O*S . . . . ostomy
/OSZ . . . . ostasis
/O*SZ . . . . ostomies
/OT . . . . otomy
/O*T . . . . tomy
/OTS . . . . otomies
/O*TS . . . . tomies
/OUFMS . . . . omphalus
/OUFMZ . . . . mphalus
/OUM . . . . onychium
/O*UM . . . . nychium
/OUMS . . . . osmous

/O*UMS . . . . smous
/OUMZ . . . . omphalus
/O*UNG . . . . -oncogene (*hyphenated*)
/OURM . . . . orchium
/O*URM . . . . rchium
/OUS . . . . ous
/OVL . . . . oval
/OVLGS . . . . ovulation
/OVM . . . . vum
/O*X . . . . oxia
/OZ . . . . osmia
/O*Z . . . . smia

P

/PA*E . . . . peia
/PAED . . . . pedia
/PAEDZ . . . . pedics
/PAEFG . . . . perineorrhaphy
/PAEFL . . . . apophyseal
/PAEFLS . . . . epiphyseal
/PAEFM . . . . pinealism
/PAEFT . . . . pedist
/PAEG . . . . opaque
/PAEK . . . . peak
/PAEKT . . . . pietic
/PAELT . . . . petal
/PAEM . . . . lipemia
/PA*EMD . . . . ependymal
/PAEMG . . . . lipemic
/PAENGT . . . . pectineal
/PAENK . . . . pancreas
/PAENL . . . . pineal
/PAENT . . . . patent
/PAEP . . . . apnea
/PAEPG . . . . apneic
/PAERKD . . . . pachyderma
/PAERKT . . . . paretic
/PAERL . . . . parallel
/PA*ERM . . . . pachyderma
/PAERNT . . . . apparent
/PAERPS . . . . piesotherapy
/PAESZ . . . . piesis
/PA*ET . . . . pathy

/PAETS . . . . appendicitis
/PA*ETS . . . . pathies
/PAEX . . . . appendix
/PA*EX. . . . . pexia
/PAEZ . . . . piesia
/PAFBL . . . . pathical
/PAFK . . . . pathic
/PAFKL . . . . pathical
/PA*FM. . . . . pathism
/PAFMT. . . . . pathism
/PAFP. . . . . patch
/PAFT. . . . . pathist
/PAFTS . . . . pathists
/PA*GT. . . . . pathogen
/PAIDZ . . . . peptidase
/PAIFG . . . . pacing
/PAIFR . . . . pacer
/PAIFT . . . . pathist
/PAIFTS. . . . . pathists
/PA*IK . . . . paic
/PAIM. . . . . empyema
/PAIMS . . . . empyesis
/PAIN . . . . pain
/PAINS . . . . pains
/PAIPGS. . . . . palpitation
/PAIRB . . . . patient
/PAIRBT . . . . patient
/PAIRLT . . . . paralytic
/PAIRMD. . . . . pyramidal
/PA*IRMD . . . . pyramidial
/PAIRT . . . . parity
/PAIRZ . . . . parous
/PA*IRZ . . . . iparous
/PA*IT. . . . . pathia
/PALGS . . . . palpation
/PAOD . . . . podia
/PAOEDZ . . . . pedesis
/PAOEF . . . . apophyses
/PAOEFMS . . . . pepsinemia
/PAOEFT. . . . . apostema
/PAO*EK . . . . peic
/PAOEKL . . . . pediculate
/PAOEKS . . . . pedics
/PAOELZ . . . . hypalgesia
/PAO*EM. . . . . pinemia

/PAO*EMD . . . . pedium
/PAOEMG . . . . pyemic
/PAOEN . . . . penia
/PAO*EN . . . . pine
/PAOENG . . . . penic
/PAOENS. . . . . penis
/PAOERB. . . . . alopecia
/PAOERKL . . . . pedicular
/PAOERM . . . . pyremia
/PAOERNT. . . . . perineotomy
/PAO*ES. . . . . apostema
/PAO*ESZ . . . . pyesis
/PAOEVT . . . . pelvioneostomy
/PAOEXZ . . . . pexies
/PAOFK . . . . opathic
/PAOFM . . . . pulmonism
/PAOFR . . . . porphyria
/PAOFT . . . . opacity
/PAO*FT . . . . -opacity (*hyphenated*)
/PAOIDZ . . . . podiasis
/PAOIFM . . . . parathyroidism
/PAOIFT . . . . apophysitis
/PAOIFTS . . . . periphacitis
/PAO*IK . . . . pyic
/PAOIKS . . . . periphakitis
/PAOIKT . . . . pietic
/PAOIL . . . . pile
/PAO*IL . . . . pil
/PAOILT . . . . pyelitis
/PAOILTS . . . . epithelitis
/PAOIMT . . . . pachymeningitis
/PAOIMTS . . . . pachymeningitis
/PAOIN. . . . . pine
/PAOINL. . . . . penile
/PAOINX . . . . pyosalpinx
/PAOIPT . . . . pipette
/PAOIPTD. . . . . peptide
/PAOIRB . . . . piesia
/PAOIRK . . . . pyretic
/PAOIRL . . . . pyrexial
/PAOIRM. . . . . pyopericardium
/PAO*IRN . . . . pinuria
/PAOIRNZ . . . . pyranose
/PAOIRSZ . . . . pyrosis
/PAOIRTS . . . . polyneuritis

/PAOIRX . . . . pyrexia
/PAOIRZ . . . . piezometry
/PAOISZ . . . . pyosis
/PAO*IT . . . . pituicyte
/PAOITS . . . . pancreatitis
/PAO*ITS . . . . posthitis
/PAOIZ . . . . piezometer
/PAOJ . . . . podalgia
/PAOKT . . . . pallidothalamectomy
/PAOLG . . . . opalgia
/PAOLGS . . . . pulsion
/PAOLTD . . . . pallidotomy
/PAON . . . . ponia
/PAONG . . . . phthongia
/PAONK . . . . ponic
/PAONL . . . . penial
/PAO*R . . . . posterior
/PAORJ . . . . purgia
/PAORM . . . . aeroperitoneum
/PAORP . . . . peptonuria
/PAORTS. . . . . parotitis
/PAOS . . . . posia
/PAOUB . . . . pubic
/PAOUBSZ . . . . pubescence
/PAOUBT . . . . puberty
/PAOUBTS . . . . pubescent
/PAOUFL. . . . . pustular
/PAOUFR . . . . porphyrinuria
/PAOUL . . . . pustule
/PAOURBL . . . . puberal
/PAOURBLT . . . . pubertal
/PAOURK . . . . aponeurotic
/PAOURKT . . . . aponeurotic
/PAOURLT. . . . . purulent
/PAOURLTS . . . . purulents
/PAOURN . . . . pepsinuria
/PAOUVKT. . . . . putrefactive
/PARB . . . . partial
/PARKL . . . . pedicular
/PARKT. . . . . paretic
/PARL . . . . particle
/PARMD. . . . . pericardium
/PARNLT . . . . parental
/PARNSZ . . . . parency
/PARNT . . . . parent

/PA*T . . . . path
/PA*TS. . . . . paths
/PAUFK . . . . hypophysectomy
/PAUFP . . . . pachy
/PAUFSZ. . . . . hypophysis
/PAUGT . . . . potassemic
/PAUK . . . . paque
/PAUKT . . . . pexotomy
/PA*UN. . . . . pyon
/PAUNLT. . . . . pontile
/PAUNT . . . . pontine
/PA*UR . . . . para
/PA*URK . . . . paric
/PAURLT . . . . partal
/PAURMD. . . . . pericardium
/PAURMT . . . . partum
/PAURNL . . . . epicondylar
/PA*URT . . . . partite
/PAUS . . . . pause
/PA*US. . . . . apostasis
/PAUT . . . . potassium
/PAUTS . . . . potassemia
/PAUVL . . . . parathyroprival
/PAVLT . . . . pelvioplasty
/PA*X. . . . . pax
/PAXZ . . . . pachynsis
/P–BL . . . . permeable
/P–BLT . . . . permeability
/PEFK. . . . . pelvic
/PEFKT. . . . . pelvectomy
/PEFMT . . . . pelvimetry
/PEFN . . . . pepsin
/PEFRM. . . . . periodism
/PEFRT. . . . . periodicity
/PEFSZ . . . . hypophyses
/PEJ . . . . pathogenicity
/PEJT . . . . pathogenicity
/PEKL . . . . pectoral
/P*EKL . . . . pellic
/PEKLS . . . . pectoralis
/PEKLZ . . . . pelyx
/P*EKT . . . . pectin
/PEKZ . . . . pexic
/PELD . . . . pedal
/PENG . . . . pathogen

/PENGD . . . . appendectomy
/PENGT . . . . pathogenetic
/PENK . . . . pathogenic
/PENSZ . . . . pathogenesis
/PENZ . . . . pepsinia
/PEPGS . . . . pepsinogen
/PEPS . . . . pepsia
/PEPSZ . . . . pepsis
/PEPT . . . . peptic
/P*EPT . . . . peptin
/PEPTD . . . . peptid
/PEPZ . . . . pepsin
/PERD . . . . period
/PERGD . . . . periodic
/PERKL . . . . operculum
/P*ERKT . . . . petrotic
/PERLT . . . . peristaltic
/PERNGS . . . . personification
/PERNL . . . . personal
/PERNLGS . . . . personalization
/PERTS . . . . perineuritis
/PERX . . . . percolation
/PETSZ . . . . pestis
/PEVK . . . . pelvic
/PEVKT . . . . pelvectomy
/PEVLT . . . . pelviperitonitis
/PEVLTS . . . . pelviperitonitis
/PEVMT . . . . pelvimetry
/PEVNL . . . . pelviperitoneal
/PEVRNL . . . . pelviperitoneal
/PEX . . . . pexy
/P*EX . . . . pexin
/PEXZ . . . . pexis
/PID . . . . lipid
/PIDZ . . . . lipids
/PIFLS . . . . epiphysial
/PIFM . . . . pituitarism
/PIFRM . . . . porphyrinism
/PIFSZ . . . . epiphysis
/PILT . . . . epithelium
/PIMGS . . . . pigmentation
/PIMT . . . . pigment
/PINX . . . . pyosalpinx
/PIPT . . . . pipet
/P*IR . . . . pyra

/PIRM . . . . peritoneum
/PIRMD . . . . pyramid
/PIRNL . . . . peritoneal
/PIRNS . . . . perineoplasty
/PIRP . . . . ipara
/P–KD . . . . pedic
/PLA*D . . . . pelade
/PLA*E . . . . epithelia
/PLAEF . . . . pulmonography
/PLAEFG . . . . placentography
/PLAEFNL . . . . placental
/PLAEFNT . . . . placenta
/PLAEGT . . . . plating
/PLA*EGT . . . . plethysmography
/PLA*EL . . . . epithelial
/PLA*EM . . . . proinsulinemia
/PLAEN . . . . plane
/PLAENL . . . . placental
/PLAENSZ . . . . planesis
/PLAENT . . . . placenta
/PLAENZ . . . . planesia
/PLAER . . . . papillary
/PLAERP . . . . appendicular
/PLAESZ . . . . plasis
/PLAET . . . . plate
/PLAEZ . . . . plasia
/PLAFD . . . . plastid
/PLAFK . . . . plastic
/PLAFM . . . . plasm
/PLAFMG . . . . plasmic
/PLAFMS . . . . plasma
/PLAFMT . . . . plasmatic
/PLAFMZ . . . . plasmin
/PLAFN . . . . plastin
/PLAFP . . . . polysaccharide
/PLAFT . . . . plast
/PLAFTS . . . . plasts
/PLAFX . . . . plastics
/PLAIFMT . . . . placement
/PLA*IK . . . . plakia
/PLAIKT . . . . pyelectasia
/PLAIL . . . . pallial
/PLAILT . . . . platelet
/PLA*IN . . . . plania
/PLAIRP . . . . plasmotherapy

/PLAIS . . . . place
/PLAK . . . . plaque
/PLAKD . . . . polysaccharide
/PLAL . . . . epithelial
/PLA*L . . . . palatal
/PLALD . . . . pallidal
/PLALZ . . . . plasmal
/PLAMG . . . . plasmic
/PLANGS . . . . plantation
/PLANGT . . . . planting
/PLANT . . . . plant
/PLAO* . . . . pallesthesia
/PLAOEF . . . . poliodystrophy
/PLAOEFSZ . . . . plasmapheresis
/PLAOEG . . . . plegia
/PLAOEJ. . . . . paraplegia
/PLAOEKT . . . . plectic
/PLAOEL. . . . . epiplocele
/PLAOEMD . . . . papilledema
/PLAOEMG. . . . . prolactinemic
/PLAOEMT . . . . prolactinemia
/PLAOEP . . . . polypnea
/PLAOEPG . . . . polypneic
/PLAOEPT . . . . popliteal
/PLAOEX. . . . . peliopexy
/PLAOEZ . . . . pallesthesia
/PLAOFM . . . . plasmia
/PLAOFN . . . . plastinogen
/PLAOIGS . . . . plication
/PLAO*IK . . . . pylic
/PLAOIKS . . . . apokleisis
/PLAOIKSZ . . . . apocleisis
/PLAOILT . . . . poliomyelitis
/PLAOILTS . . . . poliomyelitis
/PLAOIMG . . . . polycythemic
/PLAOIN . . . . palatine
/PLAOIP . . . . pyeloplasty
/PLAOIRG . . . . polygyria
/PLAOKT . . . . apoplectic
/PLAO*M. . . . . pulmonum
/PLAONK . . . . plankton
/PLAOPS. . . . . palatopharyngoplasty
/PLAORP. . . . . polariscope
/PLAOS . . . . oplasty
/PLAO*S . . . . autoplasty

/PLAOUL . . . . . papule
/PLAOUR . . . . . polyuria
/PLAOURM . . . . . pleuropneumonia
/PLAOURP . . . . . pupillary
/PLAOX . . . . . apoplexy
/PLA*RNT . . . . . plantar
/PLART . . . . . patellar
/PLAS . . . . . plastic
/PLA*S . . . . . plasty
/PLASZ . . . . . plastics
/PLA*T . . . . . plata
/PLAUM . . . . . papilloma
/PLAUNL . . . . . palinal
/PLAUR. . . . . . plantar
/PLAURP . . . . . papular
/PLAURXZ . . . . . parallaxis
/PLAX . . . . . plax
/PLAZ. . . . . . plasma
/PL*EGT. . . . . . plethysmograph
/PLEK. . . . . . plegic
/PLEKT . . . . . pylorectomy
/PL*EKT . . . . . plectic
/PLEKTS . . . . . pyelectasis
/PLEKZ . . . . . plexus
/PLELS . . . . . pellous
/PLENG . . . . . plastigenic
/PLENTS . . . . . pyelonephritis
/PLEPTD . . . . . polypeptidemia
/PLER . . . . . pleura
/PL*ER. . . . . . pleure
/PLERK . . . . . polymeric
/PL*ERK . . . . . pleuric
/PLERL . . . . . pleural
/PLERM. . . . . . polymer
/PLERMGS . . . . . polymerization
/PLERP . . . . . pleuroparietopexy
/PLERTS . . . . . pleuritis
/PLEX . . . . . plex
/PLEXZ . . . . . plexus
/PLIFMZ . . . . . paludism
/PLIFX. . . . . . pompholyx
/PLIJ . . . . . palatodigital
/PLIJT . . . . . palatodigital
/PLIKD . . . . . pallidectomy
/PLILT. . . . . . popliteal

/PLINZ . . . . . proinsulin
/PLIP . . . . . polyp
/PLIPSZ . . . . . polyposis
/PLIVT . . . . . proliferative
/PLIX . . . . . plexis
/PLIXZ . . . . . plexis
/PLO*D . . . . . ploidy
/PLOEF . . . . . lipodystrophy
/PLOEFD . . . . . polydystrophy
/PLOEFK . . . . . lipodystrophic
/PLOEKD . . . . . polysaccharidosis
/PLOEKDZ . . . . . polysaccharidosis
/PLOELS. . . . . poliosis
/PLOEM . . . . . epithelioma
/PLOEMD . . . . . lipochondroma
/PLOEMS . . . . . plasmosis
/PLOEMX . . . . . plaxoma
/PLOERK . . . . . pyloric
/PLOFK . . . . . lipodystrophic
/PLOFT . . . . . pyelonephrostomy
/PLOID. . . . . ploid
/PLO*ID. . . . . ploid
/PLOIF. . . . . plastica
/PLOIFT . . . . . proliferative
/PLOIK. . . . . epiploic
/PLOILD . . . . . polyploidy
/PLOIM . . . . . prolinemia
/PLOIMT . . . . . employment
/PLOIN . . . . . plany
/PLOITS . . . . . papillitis
/PLOIX . . . . . plexy
/PLOIXZ . . . . . plexia
/PLOLD . . . . . polyploidy
/PLOLG . . . . . pyelography
/PLOLS. . . . . plasmolysis
/PLOM . . . . . pulmonary
/PLOMS . . . . . plasmoma
/PLOMT . . . . . polarimeter
/PLOPT. . . . . popliteal
/PLOS . . . . . pyelostomy
/PLO*S . . . . . pyeloneostomy
/PLO*T . . . . . pyelolithotomy
/PLUFM . . . . . paludism
/PLUL. . . . . pallium
/PLULD. . . . . paludal

/PLUNS . . . . palatinus
/PLUPS . . . . polypus
/PLUPZ . . . . polypus
/PLURK . . . . pleuric
/POBT . . . . pubiotomy
/PO*D . . . . pod
/PODZ . . . . pods
/PO*DZ . . . . pods
/POEB . . . . pathophobia
/PO*ED . . . . pody
/POEDZ . . . . lipoidosis
/POEFD . . . . posed
/POEFR . . . . porphyrin
/POEFRG . . . . porphyrinogen
/POEFRM . . . . porphyrinemia
/POEFSZ . . . . pyonephrosis
/POEGD . . . . podic
/POEKSZ . . . . pyknosis
/POEKT . . . . pyknotic
/POEL . . . . pole
/POELGS . . . . polarization
/POELGT . . . . polarizing
/POELS . . . . polesis
/POELT . . . . polarize
/POELTD . . . . polarized
/POEM . . . . pericytoma
/POEMD . . . . podium
/PO*EMD . . . . ependymoma
/POEMT . . . . pericytoma
/PO*EN . . . . openia
/PO*ENT . . . . potent
/PO*ENTS . . . . potency
/POEPT . . . . peptone
/POER . . . . pore
/POERB . . . . potentia
/POERBGS . . . . potentiation
/POERBL . . . . potential
/POERBLT . . . . potentiality
/POERGS . . . . poration
/POERGT . . . . portography
/POERL . . . . polar
/POERTS . . . . poritis
/POERZ . . . . porous
/POES . . . . pose
/PO*ETS . . . . parathyreosis

/POF . . . . apophysis
/POFL . . . . apophysial
/POFM . . . . penniform
/POFMT . . . . apochromatic
/POFPT . . . . apochromat
/POGS . . . . position
/POI . . . . poison
/POID . . . . lipoid
/POIFP . . . . pachia
/POIFR . . . . porphyria
/POIFT . . . . epiphysitis
/PO*IFT . . . . pacity
/POIK . . . . poietic
/PO*IK . . . . poiesic
/POIKLS . . . . poikilosis
/POIKLSZ . . . . poikilocytosis
/POIKLT . . . . poikilotic
/POIKT . . . . pectic
/POILD . . . . polyploid
/POIM . . . . pyemia
/POIMG . . . . pyemic
/PO*IN . . . . pionia
/POIRT . . . . pericyte
/PO*IS . . . . posy
/POISZ . . . . poiesis
/POIT . . . . poietin
/POIX . . . . poikilosis
/POKT . . . . pocket
/POLD . . . . podal
/POLGT . . . . polycyte
/POMP . . . . pompic
/POMPG . . . . pompic
/POMT . . . . potomy
/PONG . . . . ophthongia
/PONGT . . . . ponetic
/PONL . . . . pontile
/PONLD . . . . ponderal
/PONSZ . . . . ponesis
/PO*PG . . . . opsonic
/PO*PS . . . . -opsonin (*hyphenated*)
/POPZ . . . . opsonin
/PO*PZ . . . . psonin
/PO*R . . . . poria
/PORB . . . . pontia
/PORGS . . . . portion

/PORLT . . . . . portal
/PO*RM . . . . . portogram
/PORT . . . . . port
/PORX . . . . . pyothorax
/POS . . . . . positive
/POSZ . . . . . liposis
/POUDZ . . . . . podous
/POUPL . . . . . pulpal
/PO*UR . . . . . aporia
/POUS . . . . . poisonous
/POV . . . . . positive
/PO*X . . . . . pexostomy
/POZ . . . . . positive
/PRAEF . . . . . pancreatography
/PRAEFM . . . . . pancreatism
/PRAEFT . . . . . pancreatography
/PRAEG . . . . . pregnancy
/PRAEKT . . . . . prostatectomy
/PRAENGT . . . . . pancreatectomy
/PRAENK . . . . . pancreatic
/PRAERM . . . . . proaccelerinemia
/PRAERTS . . . . . periarteritis
/PRAET . . . . . prostate
/PRAFM . . . . . parkinsonism
/PRAIBL . . . . . operable
/PRAIBZ . . . . . probasia
/PRAIJ . . . . . pragia
/PRAIKD . . . . . peroxidase
/PRAIKDZ . . . . . peroxidase
/PRAIKTS . . . . . parectasis
/PRAINGS . . . . . penetration
/PRAINZ . . . . . prasin
/PRAIPGS . . . . . precipitation
/PRAIV . . . . . operative
/PRAIVK . . . . . parathyroprivic
/PRAJ . . . . . pragic
/PRA*K . . . . . praxic
/PRALS . . . . . paralysis
/PRALT . . . . . paralytic
/PRAN . . . . . parenchyma
/PRANL . . . . . parenchymal
/PRANLD . . . . . prandial
/PRANT . . . . . protectant
/PRANTS . . . . . protectants
/PRANZ . . . . . penetrance

/PRAOE	pyorrhea
/PRAOEF	periphery
/PRAO*EK	proteic
/PRAOEL	periosteal
/PRAOELT	perithelium
/PRAOELZ	periosteals
/PRAOEMG	proteinemic
/PRAOEMT	proteinemia
/PRAO*EN	purine
/PRAOENGT	proteinic
/PRAOENK	pancreorrhea
/PRAOENL	perineal
/PRAOENT	proteinia
/PRAOENTS	paracentesis
/PRAOES	paresis
/PRAOESZ	pheresis
/PRAOET	prosthesis
/PRAO*ET	prosthesis
/PRAOEVM	proconvertinemia
/PRAOEZ	paresthesia
/PRAOIFM	pyrism
/PRAOIFT	prostatitis
/PRAOIFTS	prostatitis
/PRAOILT	parietal
/PRAOIPX	parietopexy
/PRAOIRSZ	parathyrosis
/PRAOITS	peritonitis
/PRAOIX	peroxide
/PRAOM	periosteum
/PRAONG	prostaglandin
/PRAONGD	prostaglandin
/PRAONL	peritoneoabdominal
/PRAONT	peritonia
/PRAOP	presbyopia
/PRAOUL	preputial
/PRAO*UN	pareunia
/PRAOURB	preputial
/PRAOURK	pruritic
/PRAOURNT	parturient
/PRAOURT	proteinuria
/PRAOVK	peritoneopelvic
/PRAOX	pericardiopexy
/PRAPG	protoplasmic
/PRARD	pericarditis
/PRARL	pericardial

/PRARMD . . . . perimyocarditis
/PRARTS . . . . parasitus
/PRAUM . . . . palmar
/PRAUP . . . . presbyopia
/PRAURK . . . . pericardiac
/PRAVL . . . . prival
/PRAX . . . . apraxia
/PRA*X . . . . praxia
/PRAXZ . . . . praxis
/PREBL . . . . palpebral
/PRED . . . . predator
/PREFD . . . . pressed
/PREFNGS . . . . prevention
/PREFRN . . . . epinephria
/PREFRX . . . . preservation
/PREKLS . . . . parelkysis
/PR*EKT . . . . parathyroidectomy
/PRELSZ . . . . peristalsis
/PRELZ . . . . peristalsis
/PREPTD . . . . peptidorrhachia
/PRERB . . . . pressure
/PRERSZ . . . . pressor
/PRESZ . . . . press
/PREVK . . . . protective
/PREVNGS . . . . prevention
/PREX . . . . protection
/PR*EX . . . . prosexia
/PR-FL . . . . professional
/PRIFG . . . . peritoneography
/PRIFLT . . . . peristole
/PRIFM . . . . prism
/PRILS . . . . pectoralis
/PRINX . . . . parasalpinx
/PRIP . . . . precipitate
/PR*IPGS . . . . precipitation
/PRIPT . . . . precipitin
/PRIT . . . . periostitis
/PRITS . . . . periostitis
/PRIVK . . . . privic
/PRIVL . . . . prival
/PROEB . . . . probe
/PROED . . . . periodynia
/PROEDZ . . . . prosody
/PROEFSZ . . . . perinephrosis
/PROEG . . . . prognosis

/PROEJ . . . . projection
/PROEKT . . . . proctectomy
/PROELG. . . . . prosopalgia
/PROELT . . . . perineoscrotal
/PROELZ . . . . petrosal
/PROEN . . . . prone
/PROENGS. . . . . pronation
/PROENSZ . . . . proteinosis
/PRO*EP . . . . prosope
/PROERBT . . . . potentiator
/PROERM . . . . promontory
/PRO*ES . . . . perineostomy
/PROESZ . . . . porosis
/PROETS . . . . petrosis
/PROETSZ . . . . proteosis
/PROFK . . . . prostatic
/PROFKT. . . . . proctostomy
/PROFKTS. . . . . proctostomies
/PROFMD . . . . parotidism
/PRO*I . . . . proteinia
/PROIFM. . . . . parasitism
/PROIK . . . . parasitic
/PROIKT . . . . porotic
/PROIM . . . . epinephrinemia
/PROIN . . . . protein
/PROING. . . . . proteinic
/PROINSZ . . . . proteinosis
/PRO*IP . . . . panendoscopy
/PROIPG . . . . prosopic
/PROIPS . . . . prosopia
/PROIS . . . . protease
/PROISZ . . . . prisis
/PROIT . . . . parasite
/PROITD . . . . parasiticide
/PROIV . . . . privia
/PROIVS . . . . iprivous
/PROIX . . . . praxy
/PROKD . . . . peroxide
/PROKL. . . . . proctocolectomy
/PRO*KT. . . . . proctic
/PROKTS. . . . . proctitis
/PROKZ. . . . . proctitis
/PRONL . . . . peroneal
/PRONTS. . . . . periodontitis
/PRORB. . . . . proctia

/PRORGS . . . . proportion
/PRORJ . . . . projector
/PRORKL . . . . epitrochlear
/PRORT . . . . porter
/PRO*T . . . . prosthetic
/PRO*TS. . . . . prosthetics
/PROUNTS. . . . . parenchymatous
/PROUPS . . . . prosopous
/PROUVS . . . . privous
/PROUZ. . . . . pyrous
/PRO*X . . . . proximal
/PROXL . . . . paroxysmal
/PRUGS . . . . production
/PR*UM . . . . proctium
/PRUMT . . . . periosteum
/PRUN . . . . proinsulinemia
/PRUPS . . . . prosopus
/PRURB . . . . percussion
/PRURBGS . . . . percussion
/PRURN . . . . purpurin
/PRUSZ . . . . pertussis
/PRUT . . . . product
/PRUX . . . . production
/PUFGS . . . . perfusion
/PUGS . . . . pagus
/PULGS . . . . pulsation
/P*ULGS . . . . pulsion
/PUMZ . . . . palmus
/PUNG . . . . puncture
/PURKL . . . . peduncular
/PUS . . . . pus
/PUVLT . . . . pulvinectomy
/PYAEL . . . . pyelia
/PYAERP. . . . . pyotherapy
/PYAIRP . . . . pyotherapy
/PYAOEL . . . . pial
/PYAOESZ . . . . pyresis
/PYAO*IL . . . . pyle
/PYAOIRM . . . . pyremia
/PYAOR . . . . posterior
/PYAOUR . . . . pyuria
/PYAOURT . . . . pyoureter
/PYAR . . . . pyra
/PYEK . . . . pyretic
/PYEKT . . . . pyetic

/PYENG . . . . pyogenic
/PYERNG . . . . pyrogenic
/PYIJ . . . . pygia
/PYIK. . . . . pylic
/PYINK . . . . pyknic
/PY–J . . . . pyga
/PYOJ . . . . pyogenous
/PYOJS . . . . pyogenous
/PYOK . . . . pyrotic
/PYOKT . . . . pyrotic
/PYOND . . . . pedion
/PYOULT . . . . pyoculture
/PYOUS . . . . pygous

R

/RABLGS . . . . rehabilitation
/RAD . . . . rad
/RAEBS. . . . . ribonuclease
/RAEBZ. . . . . ribonuclease
/RAEF . . . . rrhaphy
/RAEFG. . . . . retinography
/RAEFP . . . . rrhachia
/RAEG . . . . rrhagic
/RA*EGS . . . . radiation
/RAENG. . . . . rrhagenic
/RAENGT. . . . . renalectomy
/RAENL . . . . renal
/RA*ENL . . . . -renal (*hyphenated*)
/RAENLT . . . . retinal
/RAENT . . . . retina
/RAENTS . . . . rachicentesis
/RAEPT . . . . renalopathy
/RA*ERM . . . . erythrodermia
/RAERPG. . . . . radiotherapy
/RAEVX . . . . reactivation
/RAEX . . . . relaxation
/RAFG . . . . retinograph
/RAFP . . . . rachidian
/RAFPD. . . . . arachnoid
/RAIBS. . . . . rabies
/RAIF. . . . . rrhaphe
/RAIFPS . . . . rachis
/RA*IJ . . . . rrhagia

/RAIKS . . . . rrhacis
/RAIKZ . . . . rrhacis
/RAILDZ . . . . radialis
/RAIMPL . . . . ampullary
/RA*ING . . . . ranging
/RAIPZ . . . . radiculodysplasia
/RAIRPG . . . . roentgentherapy
/RA*IT . . . . retinopathia
/RAIVN . . . . riboflavin
/RAIVNS . . . . riboflavinosis
/RAJ . . . . rrhage
/RA*K . . . . rhachidian
/RAL . . . . rational
/RALD . . . . radical
/RAMZ . . . . racemose
/RANGT . . . . reactant
/RANKT . . . . reactant
/RANS . . . . resonance
/RA*NS . . . . resistance
/RA*NT . . . . resistant
/RAOE . . . . rrhea
/RAO*E . . . . orrhea
/RAOEB . . . . rubinemia
/RAO*ED . . . . rrheid
/RAOEFPG . . . . reaching
/RAO*EK . . . . rrheic
/RAO*EKS . . . . rrheics
/RAO*EL . . . . rrheal
/RAO*ELG . . . . rheology
/RAO*ELS . . . . rrheals
/RAO*EM . . . . reninemia
/RAOEMG . . . . reninemic
/RAOENG . . . . renogenic
/RAO*ENT . . . . labyrinthine
/RAOERM . . . . renogram
/RAOERMT . . . . radiometer
/RAO*ET . . . . erythrocythemia
/RAOEX . . . . resection
/RAOFL . . . . rostral
/RAOFP . . . . radiograph
/RAOFPG . . . . radiographic
/RAOIBS . . . . ribosome
/RAOIFPT . . . . rachitis
/RAOIGD . . . . riding
/RAOIKT . . . . rachitis

/RAOIKTS . . . . rachitis
/RAOILG . . . . rhinology
/RAOILTS . . . . radiculitis
/RAO*IN . . . . rrhine
/RAOINL . . . . rhinolaryngology
/RAOINT . . . . retinitis
/RAOINTS . . . . retinitis
/RAOIPTS . . . . retinitis pigmentosa
/RAO*IT . . . . erythrocyte
/RAOLD . . . . radial
/RAOLG . . . . radiology
/RAOLT . . . . radiologist
/RAO*N . . . . rrhinia
/RAONTS . . . . radiculopolyneuronitis
/RAOP . . . . radiculopathy
/RAOPT . . . . radiculopathy
/RAOPX . . . . labyrinthopexy
/RAORBL . . . . rubral
/RAORG . . . . radiogram
/RAORKT . . . . radiometric
/RAORL . . . . areolar
/RAORM . . . . radiogram
/RAO*RT . . . . rotatory
/RAOTD . . . . rooted
/RAOUB . . . . rubin
/RAOUFGS . . . . reinfusion
/RAOUFM . . . . rheumatism
/RAOUGS . . . . reduction
/RAOUMT . . . . rheumatic
/RAOUVK . . . . reductive
/RAPZ . . . . relapse
/RA*R . . . . radicular
/RARKL . . . . radicular
/RAUM . . . . reticuloma
/RAVK . . . . reactive
/RAVKT . . . . reactivity
/RAX . . . . reaction
/REFRJS . . . . refringence
/REFRJT . . . . refringent
/REFRKT . . . . refractometer
/REFX . . . . reflexia
/REGS . . . . regulation
/REKL . . . . rectal
/REKTS . . . . rectitis
/RELT . . . . relate

/RENGTS . . . . . retention
/RENK . . . . . renogenic
/R*EPT . . . . . renopathy
/R*EPX . . . . . rectopexy
/RERBL . . . . . reversible
/RERGS . . . . . reversion
/RERKT . . . . . rector
/RERL . . . . . reversal
/R*ES . . . . . rest
/R*ET . . . . . reticulum
/R*EX . . . . . rhexis
/R-FX . . . . . reflex
/R-FXZ . . . . . reflexes
/R-GT . . . . . regulator
/R-GTS . . . . . regulators
/RIFBT . . . . . erythroblast
/RIFKT . . . . . erythrocytic
/RIFPT . . . . . rachitic
/RIKLT . . . . . reticulate
/RIKLTD . . . . . reticulated
/R*IMT . . . . . rhythmia
/R*IN . . . . . renin
/R*INS . . . . . resistance
/RINT . . . . . resistant
/RIPZ . . . . . erysipelas
/RISZ . . . . . rachischisis
/R*ISZ . . . . . rrhachischisis
/RIVD . . . . . recidive
/RO*EB . . . . . aerobe
/ROEBLS . . . . . erythroblastosis
/ROEFG . . . . . roentgenography
/ROEFMT . . . . . erotism
/ROEKSZ . . . . . reticulosis
/ROENGT . . . . . roentgen
/ROENSZ . . . . . radionecrosis
/ROENZ . . . . . rosein
/ROERJ . . . . . rrhagia
/RO*ERJ . . . . . orrhagia
/ROERM . . . . . retroperitoneum
/RO*ET . . . . . reticuloendothelioma
/ROEZ . . . . . rose
/ROFK . . . . . rectostomy
/ROFKT . . . . . rectostomy
/ROFMT . . . . . eroticism
/ROFT . . . . . erotic

/ROIBT . . . . rubricyte
/ROID . . . . rrhoid
/ROIDZ . . . . rrhoids
/ROIFGS . . . . realization
/ROIFP . . . . radiography
/ROIFPT . . . . arachnoiditis
/ROIKT . . . . rickets
/ROIKTS . . . . rickets
/ROILD . . . . rrhoidal
/ROINT . . . . rhinitis
/RO*INT . . . . labyrinthitis
/ROINTS . . . . rhinitis
/RO*INTS . . . . labyrinthitis
/ROIPG . . . . renoscopy
/ROIPT . . . . radiculoneuropathy
/ROISZ . . . . radiculoneuritis
/ROLT . . . . radiologist
/ROMG . . . . rhombic
/ROMT . . . . radiometry
/RONGT . . . . rectoneostomy
/RONK . . . . rrhoncus
/ROP . . . . renoscope
/ROPG . . . . renotropic
/ROPT . . . . retinopathy
/RO*PT . . . . retinopathy
/ROUB . . . . rubella
/ROULS . . . . arousal
/ROUMS . . . . ramous
/ROUPS . . . . rrhagiparous
/RO*UTS . . . . erythrous
/R–RGT . . . . regulatory
/RUBT . . . . recumbent
/RUKTS . . . . rectus
/RULZ . . . . radialis
/RUM . . . . rectum
/R*UM . . . . rum
/RUMT . . . . rectum
/RUPGS . . . . eruption
/RUPT . . . . rupture
/RURKT . . . . reticular
/RURNZ . . . . recurrence
/RURPT . . . . radiculoneuropathy
/RUS . . . . radius
/RUVK . . . . reductive
/RUVPT . . . . eruptive

S

/S- . . . . . is
/-S . . . . . s
/SA . . . . . sa
/SAEBT . . . . . sorbate
/SAEBTS . . . . . sorbates
/SAEGS . . . . . sation
/SA*EL . . . . . osseal
/SAEMT . . . . . segment
/SA*EN . . . . . xenia
/SAEPS . . . . . antisepsis
/SAEPSZ . . . . . antisepsis
/SAERM . . . . . antiserum
/SAERP . . . . . serotherapy
/SAFK . . . . . sonographic
/SAFP . . . . . saturate
/SAFPGS . . . . . saturation
/SA*I . . . . . assay
/SAIFT . . . . . safety
/SAIGS . . . . . ization
/SAIN . . . . . sane
/SAIRBL . . . . . satiable
/SAIRP . . . . . serotherapy
/SAIRT . . . . . serrate
/SAJT . . . . . sagittal
/SAKLT . . . . . sacculotomy
/SAL . . . . . sal
/SALT . . . . . salt
/SAMZ . . . . . psammus
/SAN . . . . . san
/SANS . . . . . sans
/SANT . . . . . sanity
/SAOEFSZ . . . . . cytapheresis
/SAOEKL . . . . . cecal
/SAOEMTS . . . . . cementosis
/SAO*EN . . . . . sine
/SAOERDZ . . . . . serodiagnosis
/SAO*ERLS . . . . . serosal
/SAOERM . . . . . serum
/SAO*ERS . . . . . serosa
/SAOERSZ . . . . . cerosis
/SAOERTS . . . . . serositis
/SAOETSZ . . . . . cecitis

/SAOFT . . . . esophagostomy
/SAOIBL. . . . . cibal
/SAOID . . . . side
/SAO*ID . . . . cide
/SAOIDZ . . . . sides
/SAOIFSZ. . . . . cyesis
/SAOIKL . . . . cycle
/SAOIKLT . . . . cyclitis
/SAOILD . . . . cidal
/SAOILT . . . . cytal
/SAOILTS . . . . cyclitis
/SAO*IN . . . . sine
/SAOINL. . . . . sinal
/SAOINS . . . . science
/SAOINT . . . . scientist
/SAOINTS . . . . scientists
/SAOIRMT . . . . cytometer
/SAOIRNX . . . . cystosyrinx
/SAOIT . . . . sight
/SAO*IT . . . . site
/SAO*ITS . . . . sites
/SAOLD . . . . sialidosis
/SAOLDZ . . . . sialidosis
/SAOM . . . . soma
/SAONT. . . . . isotonia
/SAOR . . . . superior
/SAORLD . . . . sudoral
/SAOUFP . . . . suture
/SAOUPGS . . . . supination
/SAOURG. . . . . cystourethrogram
/SARKL . . . . sarcocele
/SARKS . . . . sarcokleisis
/SA*RKS . . . . sarcocleisis
/SARKZ . . . . sarcous
/SARS . . . . sarcia
/SA*T . . . . psathyrosis
/SAUFM . . . . sarcotoxism
/SAUMT . . . . cytomata
/SAUNG . . . . sonic
/SAUNGS . . . . sonics
/SAUPS. . . . . xanthopsia
/SAUPT . . . . ccipital
/SAURK . . . . sarca
/SA*URK . . . . sarc
/SAURM . . . . sarcosinemia

/SAURX . . . . sarcotoxin
/SAVL . . . . salivary
/SAVLG. . . . . salivogram
/SBAERB . . . . sebacia
/SBAFL . . . . bacillary
/SBAFLS . . . . bacillosis
/SBAOERB. . . . . sebacea
/SBAOI . . . . bacilli
/SBIL . . . . bacilli
/SBLAOEM . . . . bacillemia
/SBLAOUR . . . . bacilluria
/SBLAR. . . . . cerebellar
/SBLAS . . . . cytoblast
/SBLA*S . . . . cytoblast
/SBLEN. . . . . cystoblennorrhea
/SBLIBL . . . . bacilli
/SBLOEM . . . . cytoblastoma
/SBLOESZ . . . . spongioblastosis
/SBLUM. . . . . cerebellum
/SBLUR . . . . bacilluria
/SBLUS . . . . bacillus
/SBOES . . . . symbiosis
/SBONT. . . . . symbiont
/SBRAEGS . . . . cerebration
/SBRAENL . . . . cerebrorenal
/SBRAENLD. . . . . cerebrorenal syndrome
/SBRAOEK . . . . seborrheic
/SBRAOID. . . . . cerebroside
/SBRAOITS . . . . cerebritis
/SBRUM . . . . cerebrum
/SDAEGS . . . . sedation
/SDAEM. . . . . acidemia
/SDAERP. . . . . sudotherapy
/SDAEV . . . . sedative
/SDAIRP . . . . sudotherapy
/SDAIS . . . . oxidase
/SDAIX. . . . . desiccation
/SDAIZ . . . . -oxidase (*hyphenated*)
/SDAK. . . . . syndactyly
/SDALT. . . . . distal
/SDAOEKL . . . . syndactylia
/SDAOEM . . . . aminoacidemia
/SDAOESZ . . . . syndesis
/SDAOEZ . . . . dysesthesia
/SDAOIF . . . . acidify

/SDAOUR	acidaminuria
/SDAOURM	aminoaciduria
/SDEFT	deficit
/SDEFTS	deficits
/SDER	dysentery
/SDERK	dysenteric
/SDEX	dissection
/SD*ID	acid
/SDIDZ	acids
/SD*IDZ	acids
/SDIFM	sadism
/SDIGS	decision
/SD*IN	cidin
/SDIRK	dysenteric
/SDIRMT	acidimeter
/SDIT	acidity
/SDLAIS	dysplasia
/SDLAS	dysplastic
/SDLA*S	dysplasty
/SDLOK	diastolic
/SDMOFL	desmodial
/SDMOK	desmotic
/SDOED	dysodia
/SDOEL	diastole
/SDOEM	desmosome
/SDOEN	dystonia
/SDOEP	diaphanoscope
/SDOEPG	diaphanoscopy
/SDOERMT	acidometer
/SDOES	acidosis
/SDOESZ	desmosis
/SDOEZ	sidosis
/SDOIK	sodic
/SDOILD	discoidal
/SDOIN	dystony
/SDOKT	desmotic
/SDOPT	sudopathy
/SDOS	dysostosis
/SDOUR	aciduria
/SDPOEFG	disposing
/SDPOGS	disposition
/SDRAEGS	sideration
/SDRAERB	sideratio
/SDRAOEF	dystrophia
/SDRAOUR	siderinuria

/SDRERK	sideric
/SDREX	dextrin
/SDRIN	siderin
/SDROEF	dystrophy
/SDROEFK	dystrophic
/SDROEM	syndrome
/SDROESZ	siderosis
/SDROF	dystrophia
/SDROFK	dystrophic
/SDRUV	destructive
/SDUM	sodium
/SDUMS	desmus
/SDUS	discus
/SDWOESZ	deciduosis
/SDWOS	deciduosis
/SE	se
/S*EFL	self
/SEFLD	cephaloid
/SEFRBT	cervicitis
/SEFRBTS	cervicitis
/S*EGS	cession
/SEJS	somatogenesis
/SEK	second
/SEKT	sect
/S*EKT	cectomy
/SELGS	sexualization
/SENGS	sensation
/SENGT	centetic
/SENS	sense
/SENTS	centesis
/SEPGS	reception
/S*EPGS	ception
/S*EPS	ceps
/SEPSZ	sepsis
/SERKT	sector
/SERPT	ceptor
/SERPTS	ceptors
/SERSZ	serosis
/SERTS	ceratous
/SES	ses
/SESZ	oses
/SEVK	synovectomy
/SEVKT	synovectomy
/SEVP	receptive
/SEVPT	ceptive

/SEX . . . . sex
/SEXL . . . . sexual
/SEXLT . . . . sexuality
/SFAEL . . . . physeal
/SFAELGS . . . . phosphorylation
/SFAEMT . . . . phosphatasemia
/SFA*ET . . . . cephalopathy
/SFAEZ . . . . phosphatasia
/SFAFLS . . . . sphacelus
/SFAFP . . . . cephalorrhachidian
/SFAIG . . . . cytophagic
/SFAIJ . . . . cytophagia
/SFAILGS . . . . phosphorylation
/SFAISZ . . . . phosphatases
/SFAIT . . . . phosphate
/SFAITS . . . . phosphates
/SFAIZ . . . . phosphatase
/SFAKL . . . . cephalalgic
/SFALG . . . . cephalalgia
/SFAOEKL . . . . cephalosyndactylia
/SFAOEL . . . . cephalocele
/SFAOENL . . . . sphenosyndactylia
/SFAOEP . . . . cephalopolysyndactyly
/SFAOER . . . . sphere
/SFAOERK . . . . spheric
/SFAOERM . . . . spherinemia
/SFAOERS . . . . spheres
/SFAOES . . . . pselaphesia
/SFAOIK . . . . cephalogyric
/SFAOILT . . . . sulfite
/SFAOIN . . . . physin
/SFAOIT . . . . cephalitis
/SFAOR . . . . dysphoria
/SFAOURLSZ . . . . spherulosis
/SFAOURLZ . . . . spherulosis
/SFAOURT . . . . phosphaturia
/SFA*T . . . . cephalopathy
/SFAX . . . . asphyxia
/SFEK . . . . cephalic
/SFEKT . . . . physectomy
/SFEKZ . . . . cephalics
/SFELGS . . . . cephalization
/SFEM . . . . phosphatemia
/SFEMG . . . . phosphatemic
/SFERKT . . . . sphincterectomy

/SFERM. . . . . phospheremia
/SFEVMT . . . . cephalpelvimetry
/SFIFL. . . . . symphysial
/SFIFM . . . . cephalism
/SFIFMS . . . . cephalisms
/SFIKL . . . . cephalosyndactyly
/SFILS . . . . physial
/SFIND . . . . cephalodynia
/SF*IX. . . . . sphyxia
/SFLAEGS . . . . sufflation
/SFLAL . . . . cephalia
/SFLAOE . . . . cephaly
/SFLAOEL . . . . sarcomphalocele
/SFLAOES . . . . cephalies
/SFLAOID . . . . syphilide
/SFLAOIS . . . . cephaliasis
/SFLAON . . . . cephalon
/SFLAPT . . . . syphilopathy
/SFLAS. . . . . acephalus
/SFLA*S . . . . esophagoplasty
/SFLIK . . . . syphilitic
/SFLIPD . . . . phospholipid
/SFLIT . . . . spherolith
/SFL*IT . . . . spherolith
/SFLOES . . . . cephalosis
/SFLOLG . . . . syphilology
/SFLURG . . . . cinefluorography
/SFLUS . . . . cephalus
/SFOELGS . . . . exfoliation
/SFOEM. . . . . cephaloma
/SFOEP . . . . cephaloscope
/SFOEPT . . . . physioportal
/SFOERK . . . . phosphoric
/SFOERKD . . . . phosphoric acid
/SFOESZ . . . . spherocytosis
/SFOEZ . . . . cyphosis
/SFOFG. . . . . phosphatemic
/SFOID. . . . . sphenoid
/SFOIDZ. . . . . sphenoiditis
/SFOIG . . . . sphygmia
/SFOIM . . . . sphygmy
/SFOIT . . . . spherocyte
/SFOKT. . . . . sphincterotomy
/SFOM . . . . cephalotome
/SFOPT . . . . physeoportal

/SFOR . . . . esophoria
/SFORMT . . . . cephalometry
/SFOS . . . . phosphorus
/SFOT . . . . cephalotomy
/SFOTS . . . . phosphometer
/SFOUG . . . . cytophagous
/SFOURS . . . . phosphorous
/SFOUS . . . . cephalous
/SFRAEF . . . . cephalography
/SFRAIS . . . . osphrasia
/SFRAIZ . . . . sphrasia
/SFRAOEM . . . . phosphoremia
/SFRAOES . . . . sphresia
/SFRAOESZ . . . . osphresis
/SFRAOEZ . . . . osphresia
/SFRAO*EZ . . . . sphresia
/SFREK . . . . spherectomy
/SFRIFP . . . . cephalorrhachidian
/SFRIVK . . . . physeoprivic
/SFROEPG . . . . physiotropic
/SFROPG . . . . physeotropic
/SFRUM . . . . spherium
/SFUS . . . . cephalus
/SGAUG . . . . sialagogue
/SGEGS . . . . segmentation
/SGEN . . . . carcinogen
/SGENG . . . . carcinogenic
/SGENSZ . . . . carcinogenesis
/SGIKT . . . . stigmatic
/SGLAR . . . . astragalar
/SGLOID . . . . astragaloid
/SGOENS . . . . somatognosis
/SGOENSZ . . . . somatognosis
/SGOT . . . . cystosyringotomy
/SGRAFT . . . . cinematograph
/SGRAM . . . . cytogram
/SGRAOF . . . . sialography
/SGROFT . . . . cystogastrostomy
/SGUBLT . . . . suggestibility
/SHA . . . . tia
/SHAE . . . . otia
/SHAEGS . . . . oxidation
/SHA*EGS . . . . xidation
/SHAES . . . . -oxygenase (*hyphenated*)
/SHAESZ . . . . -oxygenases (*hyphenated*)

/SHAEZ . . . . -oxygenase (*hyphenated*)
/SHAIGS . . . . oxygenation
/SHAIPG . . . . shaping
/SHAIS . . . . oxygenase
/SHAISZ. . . . . oxygenases
/SHAIZ . . . . oxygenase
/SHANG . . . . chancre
/SHAOE . . . . ischia
/SHAOEK . . . . ischiac
/SHAOEKD . . . . ischiadic
/SHAOEKL . . . . ischial
/SHAOEM . . . . ischemia
/SHAOEMG. . . . . ischemic
/SHAO*EMG. -ischemic (*hyphenated*)
/SHAOERBL . . . . -ischial (*hyphenated*)
/SHAOES . . . . seizure
/SHAO*ETD . . . . sheathed
/SHAOEZ . . . . seizure
/SHAOT . . . . shoot
/SHAOUR . . . . sure
/SHAOUT . . . . chute
/SHAOX . . . . sectio
/SHEN . . . . oxygen
/SHEX . . . . sectio
/SHIKL. . . . . ischial
/SHIRBL . . . . cytial
/SHOF . . . . sophy
/SHOIM . . . . cytemia
/SHOIRBL. . . . . -ischial (*hyphenated*)
/SHOK . . . . shock
/SHUG . . . . sugar
/SIBLT . . . . sibilant
/SID . . . . acid
/SIDZ . . . . acids
/SIFLS . . . . syphilis
/SIFM . . . . icism
/SIGS . . . . cision
/SIKT. . . . . cytic
/SILZ . . . . silicosis
/SIMPS . . . . symphysis
/SIN . . . . sin
/S*IN . . . . cin
/SINKSZ . . . . synchysis
/S*INS . . . . cins
/SINZ . . . . sins

/SIPT . . . . occipital
/S*IPT . . . . -occipital (*hyphenated*)
/SIRDZ . . . . siderosis
/SIRJ . . . . syringitis
/SIRKT . . . . circulatory
/SIRN . . . . cinerea
/SIRNGS . . . . incineration
/SIRS . . . . cirrhosis
/SIRT . . . . cyturia
/SIRTSZ . . . . cyrtosis
/SIRZ . . . . cirsocele
/SIVN . . . . sylvian
/S*IZ . . . . sis
/SKA . . . . sac
/SKAE . . . . ischia
/SKAEGS . . . . siccation
/SKAEL . . . . oscheocele
/SKA*EL . . . . scheocele
/SKAELT . . . . skeletal
/SKAEM . . . . coccemia
/SKAFD . . . . scaphoid
/SKAIDZ . . . . saccades
/SKAIK . . . . siccate
/SKAJ . . . . coxalgia
/SKAK . . . . sciatic
/SKAN . . . . scan
/SKAOEB . . . . scabietic
/SKAOEBT . . . . scabietic
/SKAOEK . . . . cecum
/SKAOERMT . . . . viscosimetry
/SKAOETS . . . . skeocytosis
/SKAOFD . . . . scaphoid
/SKAOFL . . . . scaphocephaly
/SKAOIK . . . . psychiatric
/SKAOIKL . . . . psychiatrically
/SKAO*ILD . . . . coccidal
/SKAOIT . . . . psychiatrist
/SKAOITS . . . . psychiatrists
/SKAOIX . . . . coxitis
/SKAO*UR . . . . coccosuria
/SKAOURL . . . . saccular
/SKAOX . . . . coccia
/SKAPT . . . . capsectomy
/SKARLT . . . . scarlatina
/SKARN . . . . scanner

/SKAUK . . . . coccic
/SKAUMT . . . . scotoma
/SKAURM . . . . psychopharmacology
/SKAUX . . . . coccus
/SKBAOUK . . . . scorbutic
/SKEFT . . . . conservative
/SKEKL . . . . skelic
/SKELT . . . . skeleton
/SKENGT . . . . dyskinetic
/SKESZ . . . . schesis
/SKEVP . . . . conceptive
/SKHAK . . . . ischiac
/SKHAL . . . . ischial
/SKHAOE . . . . succorrhea
/SKHAOEM . . . . -ischemia (*hyphenated*)
/SKHAOURL . . . . scapulohumeral
/SKHAOURM . . . . scapulohumeral
/SKHES . . . . oscheos
/SKHIRS . . . . scirrhus
/SKHIZ . . . . schizia
/SKHUM . . . . saccharum
/SKHURL . . . . scapulohumeral
/SKHUS . . . . scirrhus
/SKIFM . . . . schism
/SKIFN . . . . coccolysin
/SKIGS . . . . scission
/SKIJ . . . . coccygeal
/SKIJS . . . . coccygeus
/SK*IK . . . . psychic
/SKIKL . . . . psychical
/SK*IN . . . . coccin
/SKINGT . . . . dyskinetic
/SKIRS . . . . scirrhus
/SKISZ . . . . schisis
/SKIV . . . . siccative
/SK–J . . . . psychologic
/SKLA . . . . sclera
/SKLAER . . . . sclera
/SKLAERL . . . . scleral
/SKLAF . . . . cyclograph
/SKLAGS . . . . osculation
/SKLAGT . . . . osculating
/SKLAIFN . . . . subclavian
/SKLAIVN . . . . subclavian
/SKLAIZ . . . . cementoclasia

/SKLAN . . . . calcin
/SKLAOEM . . . . schlerema
/SKLAOERMT . . . . oscillometer
/SKLAO*ERMT . . . . -oscillometer (*hyphenated*)
/SKLAOGT . . . . osculating
/SKLAOIS . . . . stomatocleisis
/SKLAOISZ . . . . cystocleisis
/SKLAOIT . . . . scleritis
/SKLAOITS . . . . scleritis
/SKLAOR . . . . scleria
/SKLAOT . . . . osculate
/SKLAOUP . . . . scapulum
/SKLAP . . . . scapula
/SKLARLT . . . . scarlatinal
/SKLAT . . . . osculate
/SKLAURP . . . . scapular
/SKLAURPS . . . . scapularis
/SKLE . . . . scelia
/SKLEKL . . . . skellic
/SKL*EKT . . . . cyclectomy
/SKLENT . . . . scleronectomy
/SKLERD . . . . scleroderma
/SKLERL . . . . scleral
/SKLES . . . . scelous
/SKLET . . . . scarlet
/SKLEZ . . . . scelus
/SKLIFM . . . . synclitism
/SKLIK . . . . cyclic
/SKLIM . . . . scapilium
/SKLIP . . . . scapilium
/SKLOERM . . . . scleroma
/SKLOEZ . . . . sclerosis
/SKLOGS . . . . cycloduction
/SKLOIDZ . . . . cyclochoroiditis
/SKLOIK . . . . cycloidal
/SKLOIL . . . . cycloidal
/SKLOIP . . . . cyclotropia
/SKLOIR . . . . cyclophoria
/SKLOITS . . . . sclerotitis
/SKLOK . . . . sclerotic
/SKLOL . . . . scoliosis
/SKLOSZ . . . . cyclosis
/SKLUK . . . . sulcus
/SKLUM . . . . sclerium
/SKMOEM . . . . myosarcoma

/SKMOERT . . . . psychomotor
/SK–NT . . . . siccant
/SKOB . . . . ascorbic
/SKOEFS . . . . cercosis
/SKOEFT. . . . . scopist
/SKOEJ . . . . psychologically
/SKOELZ. . . . . scoliosis
/SKOEM . . . . sarcoma
/SKOEMT . . . . sarcomatosis
/SKOEMTS . . . . sarcomatous
/SKOEP . . . . scope
/SKOEPS. . . . . scopes
/SKOEPT. . . . . cystoscope
/SKOERBL. . . . . psychosocial
/SKOES . . . . psychosis
/SKOESZ. . . . . sarcosis
/SKOETS. . . . . scotosis
/SKOEX . . . . coccicosis
/SKOEZ . . . . psychosis
/SKOFN . . . . coccolysin
/SKOI . . . . cocci
/SKOIDZ . . . . sarcoidosis
/SKOIFD. . . . . scaphoid
/SKOIK . . . . psychic
/SKOIKL . . . . psychical
/SKOIN . . . . coccin
/SKOIP. . . . . scopy
/SKO*IP . . . . oscopy
/SKOIPS. . . . . scopies
/SKO*IPS . . . . oscopies
/SKOIPT . . . . cystoscopy
/SKOIPZ. . . . . oscopies
/SKOJ . . . . psychological
/SKOK . . . . psychotic
/SKOLG . . . . psychology
/SKOLS . . . . coccolysis
/SKOLT. . . . . psychologist
/SKOLTS . . . . psychologists
/SKOP . . . . psychopathy
/SKOPG. . . . . scopic
/SKOPGS . . . . scopics
/SKOS. . . . . cecostomy
/SKO*S. . . . . cecostomy
/SKOX . . . . coccyx
/SKPAFK . . . . psychopathic

Steno	Suffix
/SKPAL	scopical
/SKPEGS	coccypexia
/SKPEX	coccypexy
/SKRA	sac
/SKRAENGS	concentration
/SKRAL	sacral
/SKRALGS	sacralization
/SKRAOE	psychiatry
/SKRAOEF	cineangiocardiography
/SKRAOEGS	secretion
/SKRAOENT	secretin
/SKRAOIB	scribe
/SKRAOID	saccharide
/SKRAOIDZ	saccharides
/SKRAOIT	cytocrit
/SKRAOM	acrosomia
/SKRERT	secretor
/SKROELT	scrotal
/SKROEM	carcinoma
/SKROEP	endoscope
/SKROET	scrotum
/SKROEZ	saccharose
/SKROG	carcinogen
/SKROIFM	synchronism
/SKROIRT	secretory
/SKROM	acrosome
/SKROP	endoscopy
/SKROT	oscheotomy
/SKRO*T	scheotomy
/SKR-PGS	scription
/SKRUM	sacrum
/S-KT	sectomy
/SK*UM	cecum
/SKURT	security
/SKUZ	succus
/SKWAIL	squamosal
/SKWAM	squamous
/SKWAOITS	axitis
/SKWAOLGS	auscultation
/SKWIL	axial
/SKWIS	axis
/SLA	cilia
/SLAE	celia
/SLA*E	coelia
/SLAEK	celiac

/SLAEL . . . . . coelia
/SLAEM . . . . . insulinemia
/SLAER . . . . . sellar
/SLAERT . . . . . cellularity
/SLAINGS . . . . . salination
/SLAL . . . . . sialia
/SLAOB . . . . . salubrious
/SLAOE . . . . . coele
/SLAOEF . . . . . celorraphy
/SLAOEM . . . . . salemia
/SLAOEN . . . . . saline
/SLAOEP . . . . . sleep
/SLAOETS . . . . . celitis
/SLAOID . . . . . slide
/SLAOINTS . . . . . sialadenitis
/SLAOIR . . . . . sialorrhea
/SLAOITS . . . . . cellulitis
/SLAOIVGS . . . . . salivation
/SLAOUGS . . . . . solution
/SLAR . . . . . circular
/SLA*R . . . . . sellar
/SLARKS . . . . . sarcocleisis
/SLAUM . . . . . coeloma
/SL*EM . . . . . celom
/SLEMS . . . . . sialemesis
/SLENTS . . . . . celiocentesis
/SLENZ . . . . . somnolence
/SLER . . . . . cellular
/SL*ERN . . . . . accelerin
/SL*ET . . . . . lecithal
/SLEV . . . . . selective
/SLEVT . . . . . selectivity
/SLEX . . . . . selection
/SL–GS . . . . . circulation
/SLIFM . . . . . insulinism
/SLIFN . . . . . cytolysin
/SL*IL . . . . . celial
/SL*IN . . . . . cillin
/SLIND . . . . . cylinder
/SL*INT . . . . . lecithin
/SLIR . . . . . ciliary
/SLIRN . . . . . insulinar
/SLISZ . . . . . celoschisis
/SLOEDZ . . . . . celidosis
/SLOESZ . . . . . sialosis

/SLOEX . . . . dislocation
/SLOEZ . . . . cellulose
/SLOG . . . . sialagogue
/SLOID . . . . cylindroid
/SLOIK . . . . sialic
/SLOIM . . . . selenium
/SLOINTS . . . . solenitis
/SLOISZ . . . . cyllosis
/SLOM . . . . coelom
/SLOMT . . . . celiotomy
/SLOR . . . . accelerator
/SLORT . . . . circulatory
/SLOUZ . . . . celous
/SL–TS . . . . cellulitis
/SL*UM . . . . cilium
/S–M . . . . system
/SMAEFG . . . . seismography
/SMAEKT . . . . sympathectomy
/SMAENL . . . . cemental
/SMAENLT . . . . segmental
/SMAERB . . . . somatia
/SMAERLT . . . . -osmolarity (*hyphenated*)
/SMAESZ . . . . immunoassay
/SMAF . . . . sphygmograph
/SMAIKT . . . . stigmatic
/SMAIRLT . . . . osmolarity
/SMA*IRLT . . . . smolarity
/SMAKT . . . . asthmatic
/SMALT . . . . osmolality
/SMAOE . . . . somy
/SMAOEL . . . . syringomyelia
/SMAOELG . . . . semiology
/SMAOEN . . . . semia
/SMAOER . . . . smear
/SMAOET . . . . symmetry
/SMAOIMT . . . . desmitis
/SMAOIN . . . . cyamine
/SMAOINTS . . . . cementitis
/SMAO*IT . . . . somite
/SMAOITS . . . . strumitis
/SMAOIZ . . . . somiasis
/SMAOL . . . . somal
/SMAOTD . . . . sternomastoid
/SMAOUFGS . . . . immunodiffusion
/SMAS . . . . asmus

/SMAUG . . . . cinematography
/SMAUK . . . . osmatic
/SMA*UK . . . . smatic
/SMAULG . . . . semeiology
/SMAUMT. . . . . stomatomy
/SMAUS. . . . . osmic
/SMAUX . . . . smallpox
/SMAUZ. . . . . smic
/SMAVK . . . . seminalvesiculectomy
/SMAVKS . . . . seminalvesiculectomies
/SMAZ . . . . asthma
/SMEKT . . . . strumectomy
/SMELZ . . . . mesal
/SMENG . . . . cystomeningocele
/SMEVK . . . . seminalvesiculectomy
/SMEVKS. . . . . seminalvesiculectomies
/SMEZ. . . . . meson
/S–MG. . . . . systemic
/SMIBL . . . . assimilable
/SMIFM. . . . . stigmatism
/SMIK . . . . sphygmic
/SMIKT . . . . osmotic
/SM*IKT . . . . smotic
/SMILGS . . . . assimilation
/SMILT . . . . assimilate
/SMIMT . . . . sympathomimetic
/SMIN . . . . mycin
/SM*INT. . . . . isthmian
/SMIZ . . . . ismic
/SM–L. . . . . ismal
/SM–N . . . . somnia
/SM–NG . . . . somniac
/SM–NS . . . . somnias
/SMOD . . . . spasmodic
/SMOEKT . . . . osmotic
/SMO*EKT . . . . smotic
/SMOEL. . . . . chromosomal
/SMOELS . . . . osmole
/SMOEM. . . . . chromosome
/SMOERT . . . . psychomotor
/SMOES . . . . osmosis
/SMO*ES . . . . smosis
/SMOESZ . . . . -osmosis (*hyphenated*)
/SMOEZ . . . . zymosis
/SMOFT . . . . sigmoidostomy

/SMOID . . . . sigmoid
/SMOIFD . . . . stomized
/SMOIFG . . . . stomizing
/SMOIFS . . . . stomizes
/SMOIKT . . . . sigmoidectomy
/SMOILD . . . . sigmoidal
/SMOIP . . . . sigmoidoscope
/SMOIPG . . . . sigmoidoscopy
/SMOIS . . . . somatize
/SMOISZ . . . . stomizes
/SMOIT . . . . sigmoiditis
/SMOITS . . . . sigmoiditis
/SMOIX . . . . sigmoidopexy
/SMOIZ . . . . stomize
/SMOKL . . . . spasmolytic
/SMOL . . . . stomal
/SMOLS . . . . osmole
/SMORMT . . . . osmometer
/SMO*RMT . . . . smometer
/SMOS . . . . anastomosis
/SMOT . . . . -osmotic (*hyphenated*)
/SMOUTS . . . . somatous
/SMRE . . . . scotometry
/S–MT . . . . systematic
/SMUFGS . . . . emulsification
/SMUM . . . . cementum
/SMUS . . . . ismus
/SNAEF . . . . encephalia
/SNAEFG . . . . encephalography
/SNAEFL . . . . anencephaly
/SNAEK . . . . synechia
/SNAEL . . . . stenomelia
/SNAERB . . . . encephalomalacia
/SNAES . . . . sinase
/SNA*ET . . . . encephalopathy
/SNAFR . . . . encephalograph
/SNAIFG . . . . cineangiography
/SNAIRT . . . . sanitary
/SNA*L . . . . acinal
/SNAM . . . . encephalogram
/SNAMG . . . . encephalomyelogram
/SNAOEF . . . . cineangiocardiography
/SNAOEFL . . . . encephaly
/SNAOEL . . . . encephalomyelia
/SNAO*EL . . . . cnemial

/SNAOEM . . . . inosemia
/SNAO*EM . . . . cnemia
/SNAOEMT . . . . cinesimeter
/SNAOEN . . . . cyanine
/SNAOERN . . . . cinerea
/SNAOES . . . . cinesia
/SNAO*ESZ . . . . cinesis
/SNAOFLS . . . . encephalos
/SNAOFM . . . . encephalomeningocele
/SNAOFT . . . . anastrophe
/SNAOIB . . . . cybernetics
/SNAOIBT . . . . cybernetics
/SNAOIFLG . . . . encephalomyelography
/SNAOIFTS . . . . encephalomeningitis
/SNAOIL . . . . senile
/SNAOILT . . . . encephalomeningomyelitis
/SNAOILTS . . . . encephalomeningomyelitis
/SNAOILZ . . . . incisal
/SNAOIMTS . . . . encephalomyelitis
/SNAOINL . . . . encephalospinal
/SNAOIRZ . . . . incisor
/SNAOPK . . . . encephalotropic
/SNAORJ . . . . synergia
/SNAOS . . . . sinuous
/SNAOUKT . . . . sinusectomy
/SNAOURL . . . . insular
/SNAO*URL . . . . -insular (*hyphenated*)
/SNAOUT . . . . sinuitis
/SNAOUTS . . . . sinuitis
/SNAPT . . . . synaptic
/SNAPZ . . . . synapsis
/SNARJ . . . . asynergia
/SNARM . . . . encephalogram
/SNAUF . . . . sonograph
/SNAUFL . . . . encephalohypophyseal
/SNAUG . . . . cinematography
/SNAUR . . . . acinar
/SNAURL . . . . sinistral
/SNAUSZ . . . . synostosis
/SNAUT . . . . cyanotic
/SNEFK . . . . encephalic
/SNEFL . . . . encephalon
/SNEFLS . . . . encephalus
/SNEFP . . . . synechia
/SNEFTS . . . . encephalitis

/SNEK . . . . cinesthetic
/SNEKTD . . . . insected
/SNEM . . . . sinemia
/SNERGS . . . . insertion
/SNERJ . . . . synergy
/SN*ERJ . . . . synergia
/SNESZ . . . . synizesis
/SNET . . . . cinetic
/SNEVT . . . . centive
/SNEZ . . . . cinesthesia
/SNIBL . . . . sensible
/SNIBLT . . . . sensibility
/SNIFK . . . . encephalitic
/SNIGS . . . . incision
/SNILT . . . . senility
/SNIN . . . . cyanin
/SN*IN . . . . cinin
/SNIR . . . . sinuria
/SNIRN . . . . cineria
/SN*IRS . . . . sinister
/SNIRTS . . . . sinistrous
/SNITS . . . . synovitis
/SNIV . . . . sensitive
/SNIVNS . . . . sensitiveness
/SNIVT . . . . sensitivity
/SNOEFG . . . . sonography
/SNOEFL . . . . encephalocele
/SNOEFR . . . . sonographer
/SNOEFT . . . . cystanastomosis
/SNOEMT . . . . encephalotome
/SNOEP . . . . encephaloscope
/SNO*ES . . . . cystanastomosis
/SNOESZ . . . . stenosis
/SNO*ESZ . . . . ostenosis
/SNOETS . . . . neocytosis
/SNOEV . . . . synovia
/SNOEVL . . . . synovial
/SNOEZ . . . . sinose
/SNO*EZ . . . . cenosis
/SNOFL . . . . encephalomyelopathy
/SNOFM . . . . hypnotism
/SNOFT . . . . encephalotomy
/SNOG . . . . sinogen
/SNOIFL . . . . encephalohypophysial
/SNOILD . . . . sinoidal

/SNO*ILD . . . . sinusoidal
/SNOILDZ . . . . sinusoidal
/SNOIM . . . . senium
/SNOIP. . . . . cyanopia
/SNOIPS . . . . sonoscopy
/SNOIPZ . . . . cyanopsia
/SNOITS . . . . synitis
/SNOKT . . . . cyanotic
/SNOL . . . . inositol
/SNOLG . . . . nosology
/SNOMT . . . . stenotomy
/SNOP . . . . hypnosis
/SNOPG . . . . hypnotic
/SNOPK . . . . hypnotic
/SNOPZ . . . . cytoopsonin
/SNOS . . . . anastomosis
/SNO*S . . . . cystoneostomy
/SNOSZ . . . . cyanosis
/SNOUFLS . . . . encephalous
/SNOUS. . . . . sinous
/SNOUZ . . . . sinuous
/SNOV . . . . synovia
/SNOVL . . . . synovial
/SNUM . . . . centrum
/SNUMS . . . . centrums
/SNUT. . . . . sinusitis
/SNUTS. . . . . sinusitis
/SNUZ . . . . acinous
/SOBL . . . . soluble
/SOEFG . . . . sonography
/SOEFR . . . . sonographer
/SOEM . . . . cytoma
/SOEMS . . . . somus
/SOEMT . . . . cytoma
/SOEMTS . . . . cytomas
/SOEMZ . . . . cytomas
/SOEN . . . . zoon
/SOENG . . . . sonogram
/SOERBGS . . . . association
/SOERKT . . . . psoriatic
/SOERN. . . . . sensor
/SOERNL . . . . sensorial
/SOERNT . . . . sorbent
/SOERPT . . . . receptor
/SOERPTS . . . . receptors

/SOERSZ . . . . psoriasis
/SO*ETS . . . . psathyrosis
/SOF . . . . esophagus
/SOFG . . . . esophagus
/SOFGS . . . . ossification
/SOFL . . . . esophageal
/SOFLG . . . . esophagology
/SOFLT . . . . solvent
/SOFT . . . . soft
/SOFTS . . . . esophagitis
/SOIFJ . . . . cytophagy
/SOIFM . . . . seism
/SOIFMD . . . . pseudohypoparathyroidism
/SO*IFMD . . . . -pseudohypoparathyroidism (*hyphenated*)
/SOIK . . . . zoic
/SOILGS . . . . solization
/SOILT . . . . sitol
/SO*ILT . . . . ositol
/SOIPG . . . . esophagoscopy
/SO*IPT . . . . ccipital
/SOIR . . . . suria
/SOISZ . . . . seisis
/SOIT . . . . cyte
/SO*IT . . . . ocyte
/SOITD . . . . cytoid
/SO*ITS . . . . sitis
/SOKLT . . . . sacculotomy
/SOL . . . . sol
/SOM . . . . some
/SO*M . . . . somia
/SOMG . . . . somic
/SOMS . . . . somes
/SOMT . . . . somatic
/SONT . . . . isotonic
/SORB . . . . absorb
/SORBGS . . . . absorption
/SORBL . . . . social
/SORNL . . . . sensorial
/SORNS . . . . sensor
/SORPGS . . . . sorption
/SORS . . . . source
/SOUN . . . . sound
/SOUS . . . . serous
/SOVL . . . . solve
/SOVLG . . . . solving

/SOVLT . . . . solvent
/SPAED . . . . spadia
/SPAEDZ . . . . spadias
/SPAEF . . . . spinography
/SPAEFM . . . . spermatism
/SPAEGD . . . . spadiac
/SPAELD . . . . spadial
/SPAERBLT . . . . specialty
/SPAERM . . . . spermia
/SPAERMS . . . . spermasia
/SPAERMT . . . . spermatic
/SPAESZ . . . . spasis
/SPAEZ . . . . spasia
/SPAFKT . . . . spastic
/SPAFM . . . . spasm
/SPAIF . . . . spacial
/SPAIFT . . . . spissate
/SPAIL . . . . spatial
/SPAINT . . . . spinatus
/SPAINTS . . . . spinatus
/SPAIS . . . . space
/SPAL . . . . spatial
/SPA*L . . . . cipital
/SPALD . . . . cuspidal
/SPALT . . . . septal
/SPAMS . . . . spasmus
/SPAOELT . . . . spermatocele
/SPAOEM . . . . septicemia
/SPAOEN . . . . cytopenia
/SPAOERM . . . . spermy
/SPAOES . . . . species
/SPAOFM . . . . spasmia
/SPAOG . . . . spongia
/SPAOIFT . . . . salpingo-ovaritis
/SPAOIFTS . . . . salpingo-ovaritis
/SPAOIK . . . . spike
/SPAOIM . . . . spinogram
/SPAOIMT . . . . spermatitis
/SPAOIMTS . . . . spermatitis
/SPAOINL . . . . spinal
/SPAOINLS . . . . spinalis
/SPAOINTS . . . . salpingitis
/SPAO*IR . . . . spire
/SPAOIRDZ . . . . sporidiasis
/SPAOIRL . . . . spiral

/SPAOIRMT . . . . respirometer
/SPAOIRT . . . . respiratory
/SPAOIRX . . . . respiration
/SPAOITS . . . . salpingitis
/SPAOIVT . . . . salpingoovaritis
/SPAOIVTS . . . . salpingoovaritis
/SPAOJZ . . . . spongiosis
/SPAONT . . . . sympathicotonia
/SPAONTS . . . . sympathicotonus
/SPAOPT . . . . septopexy
/SPAOR . . . . spora
/SPAOX . . . . septopexy
/SPARNT . . . . perspirant
/SPAS . . . . spastic
/SPAUNLS . . . . spondylisis
/SPAUT . . . . salpingotomy
/SPEF . . . . specific
/SPEFRM . . . . spermatism
/SP*EGS . . . . spection
/SPEJS . . . . spermatogenesis
/SPEP . . . . septic
/SPEPG . . . . septic
/SPEPGS . . . . perception
/SPEPS . . . . dyspepsia
/SPERJS . . . . spermatogenesis
/SPERM . . . . sperm
/SPERMG . . . . spermic
/SPEVK . . . . spective
/SPID . . . . cuspid
/SPIFM . . . . spermism
/SPINK . . . . salpingectomy
/SPINL . . . . spindle
/SPINX . . . . salpinx
/SPIRLS . . . . spirillosis
/SPIRMD . . . . spermid
/SPITD . . . . cuspidate
/SPIV . . . . perceptive
/SPLAEF . . . . splenography
/SPLAEL . . . . salpingeal
/SPLAEN . . . . splenia
/SPLAENG . . . . splanchnia
/SPLA*ET . . . . splenopathy
/SPLAF . . . . splenograph
/SPLAFMG . . . . cytoplasmic
/SPLAIFMT . . . . displacement

/SPLAIR . . . . disciplinary
/SPLAIRL . . . . spirillary
/SPLANGS . . . . splanchnitis
/SPLANK . . . . splanchnic
/SPLAOE. . . . . spinale
/SPLAOENL . . . . splenial
/SPLAOERB . . . . explexia
/SPLAOESZ . . . . spondylolisthesis
/SPLAOINS . . . . salpingostaphylinus
/SPLAOINTS. . . . . splanchnitis
/SPLAOITS . . . . splenitis
/SPLAOS . . . . septoplasty
/SPLAO*S . . . . septoplasty
/SPLAS . . . . cystoplasty
/SPLA*S. . . . . cystoplasty
/SPLAZ . . . . sternoplasty
/SPLEFM . . . . splenism
/SPLEK . . . . splenectomy
/SPLEKT . . . . splenectomy
/SPLELG . . . . splenomegaly
/SPLEM . . . . splenometry
/SPLENG. . . . . splenic
/SPLENTS . . . . splenitis
/SPLERK . . . . splanchnopleuric
/SPLIFM . . . . spondylism
/SPLIK. . . . . spondylic
/SPLIL . . . . spondylia
/SPLINL . . . . splenial
/SPLIRL. . . . . spirillary
/SPL-N. . . . . splenin
/SPLOERGS . . . . exploration
/SPLOEX. . . . . splenopexy
/SPLOKT . . . . sympatholytic
/SPLOMT . . . . splenotomy
/SPLONT . . . . spondylitis
/SPLONTS . . . . spondylitis
/SPLURK . . . . splanchnopleuric
/SPOEJ . . . . spongiosis
/SPOEJS. . . . . salpingiosis
/SPOEM . . . . salpingoma
/SPO*EM. . . . . spongioma
/SPO*ENTS. . . . . sympathicotonus
/SPOEPT . . . . spectroscope
/SPOER. . . . . spore
/SPO*ER. . . . . sopor

/SPOERDZ . . . . . sporidiosis
/SPOERNG . . . . . sporangia
/SPOERSZ . . . . . sporosis
/SPOERX . . . . . spermotoxin
/SPOETS . . . . . cystopyosis
/SPOG . . . . . salpingography
/SPOGS . . . . . disposition
/SPOIRD . . . . . sporidia
/SPOIRKL . . . . . spirochetal
/SPOIRMT . . . . . spermitis
/SPOIRMTS . . . . . spermitis
/SPOIRS . . . . . sporiasis
/SPOIT . . . . . cuspidate
/SPOIV . . . . . responsive
/SPOIVNS . . . . . responsiveness
/SPOM . . . . . spongioma
/SPONS . . . . . response
/SPORN . . . . . sporin
/SPO*RN . . . . . sporin
/SPOS . . . . . spectroscopy
/SPO*S . . . . . salpingostomy
/SPOURS . . . . . sporous
/SPOUZ . . . . . spermous
/SPRAEF . . . . . spectrography
/SPRAEFG . . . . . spirography
/SPRAEFM . . . . . suprarenalism
/SPRA*EM . . . . . sapremia
/SPRAENL . . . . . suprarenal
/SPRAERT . . . . . spirator
/SPRAFT . . . . . sporoblast
/SPRAI . . . . . spray
/SPRAJ . . . . . sporangium
/SPRAM . . . . . spectrogram
/SPRANK . . . . . sporanic
/SPRAOEMT . . . . . spectrophotometry
/SPRAOERMT . . . . . spirometry
/SPRAOITS . . . . . salpingo-oophoritis
/SPRAOUV . . . . . suppurative
/SPRAUM . . . . . spiroma
/SPREF . . . . . suppressive
/SPREGS . . . . . suppression
/SPREN . . . . . spectrin
/SPRENT . . . . . suppressant
/SPRET . . . . . spectrometry
/SPRID . . . . . sporid

/SPRIFG . . . . . spirography
/SPRIRNT . . . . . perspirant
/SPRIV . . . . . physioprivic
/SPRIVK . . . . . physeoprivic
/SPROEG . . . . . sporogenic
/SPROEL . . . . . spirillosis
/SPROELS . . . . . spirillosis
/SPROEM . . . . . suprarenoma
/SPROEMT . . . . . spectrophotometer
/SPROETS . . . . . spirochetosis
/SPROEZ . . . . . spirosis
/SPROMT . . . . . spirometer
/SPROND . . . . . responder
/SPRUFRB . . . . . suppurative
/SPUJS . . . . . spongiosus
/SPUMG . . . . . spongium
/SPUNS . . . . . suscipiens
/SPURLT . . . . . sepulture
/SPURM . . . . . sporium
/SPUS . . . . . spinous
/SPUT . . . . . occiput
/SP*UT . . . . . ciput
/SPWAD . . . . . entad
/SPWAEGS . . . . . intubation
/SPWAEMT . . . . . integumental
/SPWAERL . . . . . enteral
/SPWAIRGS . . . . . enteration
/SPWAL . . . . . enteralgia
/SPWALG . . . . . enteralgia
/SPWA*M . . . . . intimal
/SPWANT . . . . . intoxicant
/SPWAOEL . . . . . enterocele
/SPWAOIT . . . . . enteritis
/SPWAOITS . . . . . enteritis
/SPWAOPX . . . . . enteriopexy
/SPWAORM . . . . . enteriolum
/SPWAOUS . . . . . induce
/SPWAS . . . . . enteroanastomosis
/SPWA*S . . . . . enteroanastomosis
/SPWEKT . . . . . enterectomy
/SPWEL . . . . . intestinal
/SPWELS . . . . . intestinal
/SPWENS . . . . . intense
/SPWERK . . . . . enteric
/SPWERKZ . . . . . enterics

/SPWERNL . . . . . internal
/SPWERPT . . . . . enteroplasty
/SPW-FRNS . . . . . interference
/SPWIRBL . . . . . interstitial
/SPWLAOIGS . . . . . enteriplication
/SPWLIG . . . . . intraligamentous
/SPWLOIT . . . . . enterocolitis
/SPWLOITS . . . . . enterocolitis
/SPWLOS . . . . . enterocolostomy
/SPWLO*S . . . . . enterocolostomy
/SPWOFL . . . . . intercostal
/SPWOLG . . . . . enterology
/SPWOLT . . . . . enterologist
/SPWOPT . . . . . enteroptosis
/SPWOS . . . . . enterostomy
/SPWO*S . . . . . enterostomy
/SPWOX . . . . . intoxication
/SPWRAEF . . . . . enterorrhaphy
/SPWRAOF . . . . . enteriorrhaphy
/SPWREM . . . . . enterium
/SPWR-FRNS . . . . . interference
/SPWRI . . . . . entry
/SPWROEN . . . . . enterone
/SPWROERP . . . . . entropium
/SPWRON . . . . . enteron
/SPWROP . . . . . enteropathy
/SPWROT . . . . . enterotomy
/SPWUX . . . . . induction
/SP*X . . . . . spection
/SRAFPD . . . . . subarachnoid
/SR-FL . . . . . cervical
/SR-FX . . . . . cervix
/SRINGSZ . . . . . syringosis
/SROERN . . . . . sensory
/SRORNS . . . . . sensory
/SR-VL . . . . . cervical
/SR-VLS . . . . . cervicalis
/SR-VX . . . . . cervix
/STABLT . . . . . stability
/STAD . . . . . cystadenoma
/STAE . . . . . acetate
/STAEF . . . . . staphylorrhaphy
/STAEKZ . . . . . cytotaxia
/STAEL . . . . . steal
/STAELS . . . . . steatolysis

/STAELT . . . . . stealith
/STAENGS . . . . . substantiation
/STAESZ . . . . . stases
/STA*ET . . . . . cytopathy
/STAEXZ . . . . . cytotaxis
/STAEZ . . . . . stasy
/STAFMT . . . . . statism
/STAIBL . . . . . stable
/STA*IBL . . . . . stabile
/STAIBLT . . . . . stability
/STAIDZ . . . . . osteochondrodysplasia
/STA*IDZ . . . . . -osteochondrodysplasia (*hyphenated*)
/STAIFK . . . . . stasic
/STAIJ . . . . . stage
/STAIKT . . . . . cystectasia
/STAIN . . . . . stain
/STAIPD . . . . . stapedial
/STAIPT . . . . . septate
/STAIPX . . . . . stapediopexy
/STAIRB . . . . . eustachian
/STAISZ . . . . . stasis
/STAIT . . . . . state
/STA*IT . . . . . cytopathia
/STAIZ . . . . . stasia
/STAJ . . . . . cystalgia
/STAKT . . . . . static
/STAKTS . . . . . statics
/STALG . . . . . cystalgia
/STANS . . . . . stance
/STAOE . . . . . ecstasy
/STAOEFM . . . . . sterism
/STAOELS . . . . . steatolysis
/STAOEMT . . . . . steatoma
/STAOEN . . . . . osteon
/STAO*EN . . . . . steon
/STAOERMT . . . . . cytometry
/STAOERNS . . . . . cytoadherence
/STAOERP . . . . . stereoscopy
/STAOERT . . . . . stearate
/STAOESZ . . . . . centesis
/STAOEZ . . . . . ostoses
/STAOFT . . . . . staphyloplasty
/STAOFX . . . . . staphylococcic
/STAOIBL . . . . . stabile
/STAOIFD . . . . . sensitized

/STAOIFGS . . . . sensitization
/STAOIFR . . . . sensitizer
/STAOIG . . . . cytogenic
/STAOIK . . . . cytic
/STAOIKT . . . . cytactic
/STAOIL. . . . . style
/STAOIMSZ . . . . stomiasis
/STAOIRN . . . . styrene
/STAOIRS . . . . sensitizer
/STAOIRX . . . . cytorrhexis
/STAOIS. . . . . sensitize
/STAOITS . . . . cystitis
/STAOIX. . . . . cytaxia
/STAOIXZ. . . . . cytaxis
/STAOKT . . . . ostectomy
/STAOLX . . . . staphylococcic
/STAOM . . . . cystoma
/STAOMT . . . . cystotome
/STAOMTS. . . . . cystostomosis
/STAON. . . . . cytozoon
/STAONSZ . . . . cytozoonosis
/STAOPT . . . . stomatoplasty
/STAORMT . . . . cystometry
/STAOSZ. . . . . staphyloschisis
/STAOURS . . . . cystoureterocystotomy
/STAOVJ . . . . ostogavage
/STARN . . . . sternia
/STAT. . . . . stat
/STATS . . . . statistics
/STAUG . . . . cystography
/STAUKT . . . . cytotic
/STAULSZ . . . . stalsis
/STAULT . . . . staltic
/STAUM . . . . stenoma
/STAURMT . . . . cystometer
/STAURT . . . . cystoureterotomy
/STAUS . . . . status
/STAUSZ . . . . ostosis
/STAUT . . . . cystotomy
/STAVJ . . . . stogavage
/STAXZ . . . . staxis
/STAZ . . . . stasis
/ST–D . . . . standard
/STEFK . . . . stenocephalic
/STEGS . . . . stegnosis

/STEGZ . . . . . stegnosia
/STEJS . . . . . cytogenesis
/STEKT . . . . . cystectomy
/STEL . . . . . osteal
/STELG . . . . . ostealgia
/ST*ELG . . . . . stealgia
/STEMT . . . . . osteum
/ST*EMT . . . . . steum
/STEMZ . . . . . cytochemistry
/STEND . . . . . extended
/STENGS . . . . . extension
/ST*ENGS . . . . . distention
/STEP . . . . . step
/STEPGS . . . . . cystopexy
/STEPT . . . . . septum
/STEPTS . . . . . septitis
/STERD . . . . . steroid
/ST*ERK . . . . . steric
/STERKSZ . . . . . cysticercosis
/STERLGS . . . . . sterilization
/STERLT . . . . . sterility
/STERNL . . . . . external
/ST*ERNL . . . . . sternal
/STERNT . . . . . cisternostomy
/ST*ES . . . . . ester
/ST*ESZ . . . . . esters
/STHAOEFG . . . . . esthesiograph
/STHAOEK . . . . . esthesic
/STHAOELS . . . . . thermoesthesia
/STHAOEM . . . . . cythemia
/STHAOEMT . . . . . esthesiometer
/STHAOEN . . . . . sthenia
/STHAOENT . . . . . stheniant
/STHAOERS . . . . . erethesia
/STHAOES . . . . . esthesia
/STHAO*ES . . . . . sthesia
/STHAOESZ . . . . . esthesis
/STHAOEZ . . . . . anesthesia
/STHAOUR . . . . . sthenuria
/STHEK . . . . . synthetic
/STHEKT . . . . . esthetic
/STHENG . . . . . sthenic
/STHENK . . . . . sthenic
/STHERP . . . . . cytotherapy
/STHES . . . . . synthesis

/STHIK . . . . sympathetic
/STHIN . . . . sthenin
/STHOEP . . . . stethoscope
/STHOERM . . . . esthesioneuroma
/STHOERX . . . . serothorax
/STHOMT . . . . sthenometer
/STHORX . . . . serothorax
/STHRAF . . . . stethograph
/STI . . . . city
/ST*I . . . . icity
/STIBL . . . . susceptible
/STIBLT . . . . susceptibility
/STIFK . . . . cystic
/STIKT. . . . . cytic
/STILGS . . . . stillation
/STIMGS . . . . estimation
/STINGS . . . . distention
/STIPSZ . . . . stypsis
/STIPT . . . . styptic
/STIRN . . . . sterin
/STIRNG . . . . cisternography
/STIRNL . . . . cisternal
/ST*IS . . . . cystomy
/STISZ . . . . cystis
/ST*ISZ . . . . cystiasis
/STIVP. . . . . susceptive
/STIVRS . . . . cystivirus
/STIXZ . . . . stixis
/ST–K. . . . . sitic
/STLAIGS . . . . stimulation
/STLAIN . . . . cytoplania
/STLAISZ . . . . cytoclasis
/STLAIZ . . . . cytoclasis
/STLAJ . . . . cytological
/STLAL . . . . crystal
/STLANT . . . . stimulant
/STLAOE . . . . systole
/STLAOEM . . . . sterolemia
/STLAOEN . . . . crystalline
/STLAOFN . . . . staphylolysin
/STLAOIN. . . . . staphyline
/STLAOINS . . . . staphylinus
/STLAO*ITS . . . . cystolithiasis
/STLAUK. . . . . systaltic
/STLIFM . . . . systaltism

/STLIM . . . . . . stimulism
/STLIN . . . . . . crystallin
/STLISZ . . . . . . stenolysis
/STLIT . . . . . . stealith
/STLOK . . . . . . systolic
/STLOS . . . . . . cystocolostomy
/STLO*S . . . . . . cystocolostomy
/STLO*T . . . . . . stolithotomy
/STLUFM . . . . . . stimulism
/STLUS . . . . . . stimulus
/STOEF . . . . . . cystorrhaphy
/STOEFN . . . . . . stethophone
/STOEGS . . . . . . stereognosis
/STOEJ . . . . . . cystojejunostomy
/STOEKT . . . . . . stotic
/STO*EKT . . . . . . ostotic
/STOEL . . . . . . stole
/STOEM . . . . . . stoma
/STO*EM . . . . . . ostoma
/STOEMG . . . . . . cystotomography
/STOEMS . . . . . . cytomatosis
/STOEMTS . . . . . . steatomatous
/STOEMZ . . . . . . stomiasis
/STOENSZ . . . . . . cystostenosis
/STOEPTS . . . . . . cystoptosis
/STOERK . . . . . . stenochoria
/STOERM . . . . . . serotonemia
/STOERMT . . . . . . statometer
/STOERP . . . . . . stereoscope
/STOES . . . . . . cystosis
/STOESZ . . . . . . cytosis
/STOETS . . . . . . steatosis
/STOFT . . . . . . cystostomy
/STOFX . . . . . . cytotoxicity
/STO*I . . . . . . sity
/STOIFL . . . . . . staphylia
/STOIKL . . . . . . cytolytic
/STOIKT . . . . . . cytopoietic
/STOIM . . . . . . stomy
/STO*IM . . . . . . stomia
/STOIMT . . . . . . cytioma
/STOIMZ . . . . . . stomies
/STOIP . . . . . . stereoscopy
/STOIRD . . . . . . steroid
/STOISZ . . . . . . cytopoiesis

/STOIT . . . . . osteitis
/STO*IT . . . . . steitis
/STOITS . . . . . osteitis
/STO*ITS . . . . . steitis
/STOIX . . . . . cytotoxin
/STOIZ . . . . . cytose
/STOJS . . . . . cytogenesis
/STOKL . . . . . stolic
/STOKSZ . . . . . cytoschisis
/STOKT . . . . . stenotic
/STOLG . . . . . cytology
/STOLS . . . . . cytolysis
/STOLSZ . . . . . cytolysis
/STO*M . . . . . stome
/STOMT . . . . . symptomatic
/STOMTS . . . . . stomatitis
/STONL . . . . . stenol
/STORMT . . . . . cytometer
/STO*RT . . . . . orthocytosis
/STO*RTS . . . . . -orthocytosis (*hyphenated*)
/STO*S . . . . . cystostomy
/STOSZ . . . . . stosis
/STOT . . . . . cystotomy
/STOTD . . . . . cystidotomy
/STOUMS . . . . . stomatous
/STPAFK . . . . . cytopathic
/STRABS . . . . . strabismus
/STRAEF . . . . . cystography
/STRAES . . . . . esterase
/STRAF . . . . . scintigraphy
/STRAFD . . . . . stratified
/STRAFTD . . . . . stratified
/STRAIMT . . . . . stratum
/STRAIN . . . . . strain
/STRAL . . . . . central
/STRALT . . . . . stratal
/STRAM . . . . . cystogram
/STRAMG . . . . . scintigram
/STRAMT . . . . . stratum
/STRAOEFS . . . . . cytopheresis
/STRAOEM . . . . . stream
/STRAO*EM . . . . . estrogenemia
/STRAOESZ . . . . . steresis
/STRAOIM . . . . . striatum
/STRAOIT . . . . . striate

/STRAOITD . . . . striated
/STRAOL . . . . sterol
/STRAOLS . . . . sterols
/STRAOMG . . . . scintogram
/STRAOMTS . . . . strumitis
/STRAOUJ . . . . centrifuge
/STRAOUM . . . . struma
/STRAOUMS . . . . strumous
/STRAOUR . . . . citraturia
/STRARK . . . . extractor
/STRAUKS . . . . astronautics
/STRAUL . . . . stromal
/STRAULT . . . . stromatic
/STRAUP . . . . stroboscope
/STRAX . . . . extraction
/STREFNT . . . . centricity
/STREFRNT . . . . centricity
/STREG . . . . estrogen
/STR*EM . . . . estrinemia
/STRENK . . . . centric
/STREPSZ . . . . strepsis
/STRESZ . . . . stress
/STRIFG . . . . systrophy
/STRIFGS . . . . centrifugation
/STRIFM . . . . centrism
/STRIFN . . . . estrinism
/STRIJT . . . . astringent
/STR*IK . . . . citric
/STRIM . . . . citremia
/STRIMG . . . . scintigram
/STRINK . . . . estrogenic
/STRIPSZ . . . . cytotripsis
/STRIRK . . . . constrictor
/STRIRKT . . . . constrictor
/STRIV . . . . constrictive
/STRIVK . . . . constrictive
/STRIX . . . . constriction
/STROEF . . . . strophe
/STRO*EL . . . . centriole
/STROEM . . . . stroma
/STROEMT . . . . astrocytoma
/STROEN . . . . testosterone
/STROEP . . . . isotropy
/STRO*EP . . . . stroboscope
/STROERM . . . . stromuhr

/STROESZ . . . . cystorhinostenosis
/STROFG . . . . systrophy
/STROFM. . . . . somatotropism
/STROFN . . . . streptolysin
/STROG. . . . . stereoradiography
/STROIF. . . . . strophy
/STROIFP. . . . . stereoradiography
/STROIT . . . . striate
/STROITD. . . . . striated
/STROJ . . . . estrogenous
/STROJS. . . . . estrogenosis
/STROK . . . . streptococcic
/STROL. . . . . sterol
/STROLS . . . . sterols
/STRO*M. . . . . stromin
/STRONT. . . . . strontium
/STROPG . . . . cytotropic
/STRO*S. . . . . cystorhinostomy
/STRUFGS. . . . . centrifugation
/STR*UM . . . . centrum
/STRUMS . . . . centrums
/STRUMT . . . . instrument
/STRUR . . . . structure
/STRURL . . . . structural
/STUMT . . . . ostium
/ST*UMT . . . . stium
/STUR . . . . cyturia
/STURM . . . . sternum
/STURNL. . . . . sternal
/STUTD . . . . substituted
/STWAK. . . . . cytotactic
/STWUM . . . . stenium
/STYAOEN . . . . cystine
/STYAOUR . . . . cystinuria
/STYUM . . . . cystium
/SUF . . . . sufficient
/SUFK . . . . sulfuric
/SUFKD . . . . sulfuric acid
/SUFLD . . . . sulfide
/SUFLT . . . . sulfate
/SUFRL. . . . . sulfur
/SUFS . . . . sufficiency
/SUGS. . . . . suggestion
/SUM . . . . sum
/SUPGS . . . . supination

/SURG . . . . surgery
/SURL . . . . surgical
/SUS . . . . sus
/SUSZ. . . . . osseous
/S*USZ . . . . -osseous (*hyphenated*)
/SUX . . . . suction
/SWAE . . . . survey
/SWAELGS . . . . sexualization
/SWAELT . . . . sexuality
/SWAENGT . . . . sanguinate
/SWAINS . . . . surveillance
/SWAL . . . . sexual
/SWALS. . . . . sexualize
/SWANG . . . . sanguine
/SWANGS. . . . . sanguination
/SWAOGS . . . . sudation
/SWAOID . . . . suicide
/SWAOIT . . . . zoite
/SWAOS . . . . psoas
/SWAOT . . . . sudate
/SWAOUP . . . . supine
/SWAS. . . . . psoas
/SWENGS . . . . suspension
/SWEPGS . . . . susception
/SWOEM . . . . schwannoma
/SWOES. . . . . psoas
/SWOESZ. . . . . zoosis
/SWOS. . . . . cystoduodenostomy
/SWO*S. . . . . cystoduodenostomy
/SWRAFPD . . . . subarachnoid
/SWUMT . . . . susceptum
/SWUS . . . . sanguineous
/S–X . . . . section
/SYA*EN. . . . . cyanogen
/SYAENG . . . . cyanogenic
/SYAFM . . . . cyanism
/SYANG . . . . cyanic
/SYANGD . . . . cyanic acid
/SYAOINX . . . . syrinx
/SYIX . . . . sphyxia
/SYOENG . . . . cyanogen
/SYOENK . . . . cyanogenic
/SYOR. . . . . superior

T

/TAD . . . . tad
/TAEBT . . . . tubate
/TAEFT . . . . antagonist
/TAEKL. . . . . tectal
/TAEKT . . . . tecta
/TAEKZ . . . . taxia
/TAENK . . . . tetanic
/TAERK . . . . pteric
/TAERL . . . . terminal
/TAESZ . . . . tasia
/TAEXZ . . . . taxis
/TAEZ . . . . ectasy
/TAFM . . . . atism
/TAFMT . . . . attachment
/TAFP . . . . attach
/TAFT . . . . tast
/TAIBS . . . . tabes
/TAIJ . . . . contagious
/TAIK . . . . take
/TAIKSZ . . . . ectasic
/TAIKT . . . . ectatic
/TAINX. . . . . toxinization
/TAIRT . . . . tegumentary
/TAIS . . . . ectasia
/TA*IS . . . . taste
/TAISZ . . . . ectasis
/TAIZ. . . . . ectases
/TAJ . . . . contamination
/TAM . . . . contaminate
/TAMD . . . . contaminated
/TAMGS . . . . contamination
/TAMPL. . . . . tympanal
/TAOBL . . . . tuberal
/TAOEFK . . . . tocography
/TAOEL. . . . . atelia
/TAOEMSZ . . . . tmesis
/TAOEMZ . . . . toxemia
/TAOENSZ . . . . topokinesia
/TAOENT . . . . tetany
/TAOENX . . . . taxine
/TAOENZ . . . . toxinemia
/TAOERBL . . . . adventitial

/TAOERL . . . . arteriole
/TAOERTS. . . . . tiatrics
/TAOFPG . . . . tachogram
/TAOID . . . . tide
/TAOIDZ . . . . tides
/TAOIFD. . . . . ectomized
/TAOIFG . . . . ectomizing
/TAOIFLT. . . . . typhlitis
/TAOIFLTS. . . . . typhlitis
/TAOIFM . . . . actinomycin
/TAOIFS . . . . ectomizes
/TAOIKL . . . . ptychial
/TAOILSZ . . . . tylosis
/TAOILZ. . . . . tylus
/TAOIP. . . . . type
/TAO*IP. . . . . typy
/TAOIPG . . . . typing
/TAOIPS . . . . types
/TAOIRM . . . . timer
/TAOISZ. . . . . ptysis
/TAO*ISZ . . . . optysis
/TAOITS . . . . titis
/TAOIVT . . . . tenosynovitis
/TAOIVTS . . . . tenosynovitis
/TAOIZ . . . . ectomize
/TAOM . . . . toma
/TAONTS . . . . tenonitis
/TAONX . . . . toxon
/TAOPSZ. . . . . topagnosis
/TAOPZ. . . . . topagnosia
/TAORK . . . . tactor
/TAORL . . . . temporal
/TAORMT . . . . tachometer
/TAO*S . . . . testosterone
/TAOUB . . . . tube
/TAOUBGS . . . . tubation
/TAOUBL . . . . tubule
/TAOUBZ . . . . tuberous
/TAOUFB . . . . tubography
/TAOUKL. . . . . tuberculoma
/TAOUMGS . . . . mutation
/TAOUMS . . . . tumescence
/TAOUMZ. . . . . tumesce
/TAOUR . . . . turia
/TAOURBL . . . . tubular

/TAOURKL . . . . tubercle
/TAOURM . . . . tumor
/TAOURMG . . . . tumorigenic
/TARK . . . . articulate
/TARKT . . . . tarsectomy
/TARL . . . . tarsal
/TA*RL . . . . talar
/TARLG . . . . tarsalgia
/TARMZ . . . . tarsium
/TARNL . . . . tarsophalangeal
/TARSZ . . . . tarsus
/TARX . . . . articulation
/TASZ . . . . tasis
/TAUFT . . . . topicity
/TAUKZ . . . . toxis
/TAULG . . . . otology
/TA*ULG . . . . -otology (*hyphenated*)
/TAUMG . . . . atomic
/TAUMT . . . . tonometer
/TA*UN . . . . tenon
/TAUNG . . . . tonsillectomy
/TAUNK . . . . tonic
/TAUNLG . . . . tonsillectomy
/TAUNLT . . . . tonsillitis
/TAUP . . . . topic
/TA*UP . . . . topia
/TAUPGT . . . . ptotic
/TAUPT . . . . optic
/TA*UPT . . . . -optic (*hyphenated*)
/TAUPTS . . . . optics
/TA*UPTS . . . . ptics
/TAURNL . . . . tonsillar
/TAURSZ . . . . tarsus
/TAURZ . . . . tarsi
/TAUXZ . . . . tomoclasis
/TA*X . . . . ataxia
/TBAET . . . . turbinate
/TBEK . . . . tabetic
/TBEKT . . . . tabetic
/TBLAR . . . . acetabular
/TBLIN . . . . tuberculin
/TBLOEM . . . . endothelioblastoma
/TBLOK . . . . tuberculotic
/TBRIM . . . . timbria
/TBURTS . . . . tendinobursitis

/TEFM . . . . . telism
/TEFRB. . . . . tensive
/T*ELG. . . . . telic
/TELGT. . . . . tegmental
/TELT . . . . . tegumental
/TEMSZ . . . . . temesis
/TEND . . . . . tend
/TENG. . . . . tensinogen
/TENGS . . . . . tension
/TENK . . . . . tenic
/TENTSDZ . . . . . tendency
/TERB . . . . . tertian
/TERK . . . . . teric
/TERL . . . . . material
/TERM . . . . . term
/TERND . . . . . tender
/T*ES . . . . . test
/TETS . . . . . tetanus
/T*ETS . . . . . testis
/TEV . . . . . tensive
/TEXZ . . . . . texis
/THA*EKT . . . . . canthectomy
/THA*EL . . . . . thele
/THAER . . . . . thyrea
/THAERP . . . . . therapy
/THAERPS . . . . . therapies
/THAERPT . . . . . therapist
/THAINS . . . . . thanasia
/THAIRP. . . . . therapy
/THAIRPS . . . . . therapies
/THAIRPT . . . . . therapist
/THALS . . . . . thalamus
/THALT . . . . . pathological
/THAMG . . . . . thalamic
/THAOEBL . . . . . thelioblastoma
/THAOEK . . . . . theca
/THAOEKL . . . . . thecal
/THAOEKS . . . . . thecosis
/THAOEKT . . . . . thetic
/THAOEKTS . . . . . thetics
/THAO*EL . . . . . thelium
/THAOELD . . . . . thelioid
/THAOELGS. . . . . thelialization
/THAOELS . . . . . thermalgesia
/THAOELSZ. . . . . theliosis

/THAOELT . . . . thelitis
/THAOELTS . . . . thelitis
/THAOELZ . . . . theliosis
/THAOEMZ. . . . . thermoanesthesia
/THAOEN . . . . asthenia
/THAOENK . . . . thenic
/THAOERB . . . . anesthesia
/THAOERMT . . . . thermesthesiometer
/THAOERN. . . . . thenar
/THAOERSZ . . . . thyreosis
/THAOERTS . . . . thyreoiditis
/THAOETS . . . . thecitis
/THAOEZ . . . . thesis
/THAOIFM . . . . thymism
/THAOIJ . . . . oothecosalpingitis
/THAOIJS . . . . oothecosalpingitis
/THAOIKS . . . . phthisic
/THAOILTS . . . . epithelitis
/THAOIMG . . . . thymic
/THAOIMGS . . . . thymization
/THAOIMS . . . . thymus
/THAOIN. . . . . thionemia
/THAO*IN. . . . . thionammonemia
/THAOIRD. . . . . thyroid
/THAOIRK . . . . thyrotoxic
/THAOIRLD. . . . . thyroidal
/THAOIRMT . . . . thyrotomy
/THAOIRN . . . . thyrin
/THAOIRP . . . . thyropathy
/THAOIRPT . . . . thyropathy
/THAOIRSZ . . . . thyrosis
/THAOIRT. . . . . thyreotomy
/THAOIRTS . . . . thyreoiditis
/THAOISZ. . . . . phthisis
/THAO*ISZ . . . . ophthisis
/THAOITS. . . . . thyroiditis
/THAOK . . . . thymiac
/THAOLG . . . . pathology
/THAOLGS . . . . pathologies
/THAOLT . . . . pathologist
/THAONG. . . . . thanatology
/THAORK . . . . thoracia
/THAORKT . . . . thoracotomy
/THAORM . . . . thermia
/THAOUP . . . . therapeutic

/THAOUPS . . . . therapeutics
/THAOUPT . . . . therapeutic
/THAOUPTS . . . . therapeutics
/THAOUR . . . . thionuria
/THAUJS . . . . thermomassage
/THAUKL . . . . thermosystaltic
/THAULG . . . . thalamic
/THAUNL . . . . canthal
/THAURKT . . . . cathartic
/THAURS . . . . catharsis
/THAX . . . . thalaxia
/THEFM . . . . catheterism
/THEFRM . . . . thermism
/TH*EKT . . . . pathetic
/THEKTS . . . . thetics
/THELGS . . . . thelization
/TH*EMT . . . . thalamectomy
/THENK . . . . asthenic
/TH*ENK . . . . thenic
/THENKS . . . . thenics
/THERGS . . . . catheterization
/TH*ERL . . . . thermal
/TH*ERM . . . . thermal
/THERMS . . . . thermesthesia
/THERMT . . . . thermometer
/THERT . . . . catheter
/THET . . . . anesthetic
/THEX . . . . ethics
/THIFK . . . . theliolytic
/THIFM . . . . thyroidism
/THIFRT . . . . thecohysterectomy
/TH*IK . . . . canthic
/THILT . . . . theliitis
/THILTS . . . . theliitis
/THIM . . . . rhythm
/THIMG . . . . rhythmic
/THIMS . . . . rhythms
/THINT . . . . authenticity
/THIRM . . . . thermic
/THIRMG . . . . thermic
/THLIPZ . . . . thlipsia
/THOEF . . . . orthography
/THOEG . . . . chthonography
/THOEK . . . . -oothecocele (*hyphenated*)
/THOEKL . . . . -oothecocele (*hyphenated*)

/THOEKTS . . . . canthosis
/THOEL . . . . thioglycerol
/THOEM. . . . . endothelioma
/THO*EM . . . . atheroma
/THOEMT . . . . theliomatosis
/THOEMTS . . . . theliomatosis
/THOEN . . . . thromboplastinemia
/THOEP . . . . stethoscope
/THOERKL . . . . theliosarcoma
/THOERM. . . . . thorium
/THOERX . . . . thorax
/THOESZ . . . . orthosis
/THOGS. . . . . thermognosis
/THOID . . . . athetoid
/THOIFL . . . . thalamohypophysial
/THOIKT . . . . ethmoidectomy
/THOILD . . . . ethmoidal
/THOIM. . . . . thymia
/THOIMD. . . . . ethmoid
/THOIMDZ. . . . . ethmoiditis
/THOIMG . . . . thymic
/THOIMT . . . . thalamectomy
/THOIMTS . . . . endotheliomatosis
/THO*IN . . . . thion
/THOIRDZ . . . . thyroideus
/THOIRLD . . . . thyroideal
/THOIRM . . . . thermy
/THO*IRM . . . . thermia
/THOIRND . . . . thyroidean
/THOIRP. . . . . aerotherapy
/THOITS . . . . theliocytosis
/THOIX . . . . thymopexy
/THOJ . . . . pathologic
/THOKL. . . . . theliochorial
/THOLG . . . . pathology
/THOLGS . . . . pathologies
/THOLT. . . . . pathologist
/THOMT. . . . . thalamotomy
/THON. . . . . thromboplastin
/THONLS . . . . theliolysin
/THOPT . . . . orthopnea
/THORK . . . . thoracic
/THORMT . . . . thermometry
/THORX. . . . . thorax
/THOUMS . . . . thermous

/THOURMS . . . . thermanous
/THOX. . . . . theliotoxin
/THRAIKT. . . . . arthritica
/THRAM . . . . arthrogram
/THRAOEB . . . . prothrombinemia
/THRAOEZ. . . . . athresis
/THRAOIT. . . . . thrombocyte
/THRAOIX. . . . . thricosis
/THRAOIZ. . . . . thyroidectomize
/THRAOPK. . . . . anthropic
/THRAPT . . . . arthroplasty
/THRARK. . . . . arthric
/THRAUB. . . . . prothrombin
/THRAUBT. . . . . thrombotic
/THRAUN . . . . arthron
/THRAURK. . . . . arthric
/THRAUS . . . . arthrus
/THRAVL . . . . thyroprival
/THRAX . . . . anthrax
/THREK . . . . thyroidectomy
/THREKT . . . . thyroidectomy
/THREPS . . . . threpsia
/THREPSZ . . . . threpsy
/THRESZ . . . . arthroses
/THREX . . . . thyropexy
/THREZ . . . . arthroses
/THRIF. . . . . thyroprivia
/THRIFL . . . . thyroprival
/THRIKT . . . . arthritic
/THRIPS . . . . thrypsis
/THRITS. . . . . arthritis
/THRIX. . . . . thrix
/THROBT. . . . . thrombophlebitis
/THROEBS. . . . . thrombosis
/THROED . . . . arthrodia
/THROEFG . . . . thyrotrophic
/THROELD . . . . arthrodial
/THROEMD . . . . thyroidoma
/THROESZ . . . . arthrosis
/THROEX . . . . anthracosis
/THROEXZ . . . . thyrotoxicosis
/THROEZ . . . . arthrosis
/THROG . . . . arthrography
/THROID. . . . . thyroid
/THROIFM . . . . thyroidism

/THROIK . . . . . thyrotoxic
/THROIKT . . . . . -arthritic (*hyphenated*)
/THROIM . . . . . thrombinemia
/THROIMT . . . . . thyrotomy
/THROIMTD . . . . . thyroidotomy
/THROIPG . . . . . thyrotropic
/THROIS . . . . . arthroisis
/THROIT . . . . . theliocyte
/THROITS . . . . . theliocytes
/THROIX . . . . . thyroxin
/THROKZ . . . . . arthrocace
/THROLS . . . . . arthrolysis
/THROM . . . . . thrombin
/THROMP . . . . . thrombia
/THROMS . . . . . thrombosis
/THRONX . . . . . thyroxinemia
/THROPT . . . . . arthropathy
/THRORPT . . . . . -orthopter (*hyphenated*)
/THROT . . . . . arthrotomy
/THROX . . . . . thyroxine
/THRUB . . . . . thrombus
/THUKS . . . . . canthus
/THURG . . . . . atherogenic
/THURM . . . . . therm
/THURMS . . . . . therms
/THURP . . . . . thermotherapy
/TI . . . . . ty
/TIBL . . . . . tibial
/TIBLD . . . . . tibial band
/TID . . . . . tid
/TIF . . . . . active
/TIFK . . . . . typhlic
/TIFM . . . . . tism
/TIFN . . . . . typhlon
/TIFT . . . . . activity
/TIK . . . . . tic
/TIKS . . . . . tics
/TIKZ . . . . . phthisic
/TILSZ . . . . . ptilosis
/TIMPG . . . . . tympanic
/TIMPT . . . . . tympanites
/TIMPTS . . . . . tympanitis
/T*IMS . . . . . tomist
/T*IMSZ . . . . . tomists
/TIN . . . . . tin

/TINK . . . . tinic
/TIRBL . . . . tissular
/TIRD . . . . ectoiridodialysis
/TIRKT . . . . ectoiridectomy
/T*IRN . . . . pterin
/T*IRNS . . . . pterins
/TIRNZ . . . . pterins
/T*IS . . . . tist
/TIV . . . . active
/TIVT . . . . activity
/TIXZ . . . . taxic
/T–J . . . . technology
/TLA . . . . thelia
/TLAEGS . . . . articulation
/TLAEKZ . . . . telectasia
/TLAEL . . . . thelial
/TLAET . . . . articulate
/TLAEX . . . . atelectasis
/TLAING . . . . telephalangia
/TLAIS . . . . telangiectasia
/TLA*IS . . . . -telangiectasia (*hyphenated*)
/TLAIZ . . . . thlasia
/TLAKT . . . . lactic
/TLAKZ . . . . telectasis
/TLAL . . . . thelial
/TLANS . . . . tolerance
/TLANT . . . . tolerant
/TLAOED . . . . triglyceridemia
/TLAOEL . . . . endothelial
/TLAOELS . . . . endotheliosis
/TLAOEM . . . . endothelium
/TLAOENG . . . . telephalangy
/TLAOIFM . . . . ptyalism
/TLAOM . . . . theliomyoma
/TLAOUT . . . . thromboagglutinin
/TLAOVJ . . . . ostolavage
/TLA*RL . . . . talar
/TLATS . . . . atlas
/TLAUR . . . . articular
/TLAURL . . . . talar
/TLAVJ . . . . stolavage
/TLEL . . . . endothelial cell
/TLELS . . . . endothelial cells
/TLEMT . . . . telemetry
/TLIFM . . . . arthritism

/TLIM . . . . thelium
/TLIPSZ . . . . thlipsis
/TLISZ . . . . tolysis
/TLIT . . . . tility
/TLOD . . . . atloid
/TLOEK . . . . lactose
/TLOEM . . . . thelioma
/TLOFM . . . . telorism
/TLO*ID . . . . atloid
/TLOIND . . . . atloidean
/TLOK . . . . teleotic
/TLOKT . . . . tolytic
/TLOND . . . . atloidean
/TLOS . . . . teleosis
/TLOSZ . . . . tylosis
/TLUM . . . . thelium
/TLURM . . . . tellurium
/T–N . . . . technic
/T–NS . . . . technics
/TOE . . . . toe
/TOEFG . . . . tomography
/TOEFK . . . . tocograph
/TOEFLS . . . . typhlosis
/TOEFSZ . . . . typhosis
/TO*EJ . . . . itogen
/TOEKL . . . . toxicology
/TOEKT . . . . toxicologist
/TOELG . . . . otology
/TO*ELG . . . . -otology (*hyphenated*)
/TOELT . . . . total
/TOEM . . . . tome
/TO*EM . . . . otome
/TOEMG . . . . tomogram
/TO*EMS . . . . otomes
/TOEMZ . . . . tomias
/TOEN . . . . tone
/TO*EN . . . . tony
/TOENG . . . . toxinogen
/TO*ENG . . . . tonograph
/TOENK . . . . toxigen
/TOENS . . . . tonus
/TOENTS . . . . tendinosus
/TOENZ . . . . tones
/TOEP . . . . tope
/TOEPG . . . . topography

/TOEPS . . . . otoscope
/TO*EPS . . . . toscope
/TOEPT . . . . ectopia
/TOERB . . . . tocia
/TOERGS . . . . torsion
/TOERMT . . . . tonometry
/TOESZ . . . . ptosis
/TO*ESZ . . . . optosis
/TO*ET . . . . athetosis
/TOEXZ . . . . toxicosis
/TOEZ . . . . ptosia
/TO*EZ . . . . optosia
/TOFK . . . . toxicity
/TOFLT . . . . typhlotomy
/TOFM . . . . toxism
/TOFS . . . . tophagous
/TOFT . . . . tonicity
/TOFX . . . . toxicity
/TOGS . . . . toxication
/TOID . . . . toid
/TO*ID . . . . itide
/TOIDZ . . . . itides
/TOIFD . . . . tized
/TOIFG . . . . tizing
/TOIFK . . . . tomographic
/TOIFS . . . . tizes
/TOIGD . . . . pterygoid
/TOIJ . . . . itogenic
/TO*IJ . . . . togenic
/TOIKD . . . . toxoid
/TOIKT . . . . totic
/TOIMD . . . . tomized
/TOIMG . . . . tomizing
/TOIMS . . . . tomize
/TOIMT . . . . atticotomy
/TOIMZ . . . . tomizes
/TOIN . . . . tendon
/TO*IN . . . . tonin
/TOIND . . . . tonoid
/TOINTS . . . . tendinitis
/TOINZ . . . . tendinous
/TOIP . . . . typical
/TO*IP . . . . topy
/TOIPG . . . . typology
/TOIPK . . . . typic

/TOIPS . . . . tonoscopy
/TOIPT . . . . ectopy
/TOIRL . . . . temporale
/TOISZ . . . . tosis
/TOIT . . . . arthromeningitis
/TOIZ . . . . tize
/TOJ . . . . togenous
/TO*J . . . . itogenous
/TOK . . . . toxic
/TOLG . . . . tology
/TOLGS . . . . tologies
/TOLS . . . . tolysis
/TOLT . . . . tologist
/TOM . . . . tomy
/TOMG . . . . tomic
/TOMS . . . . tomies
/TO*N . . . . tonia
/TONG . . . . tonic
/TONK . . . . toxigenic
/TONS . . . . tonos
/TONTS . . . . tendonitis
/TONX . . . . toxon
/TOPGT . . . . optotic
/TORGS . . . . torsion
/TORNL . . . . tonsillar
/TORNS . . . . tensor
/TO*S . . . . testosterone
/TOUKS . . . . tocous
/TOUM . . . . atom
/TOUMS . . . . tomous
/TOUS . . . . tous
/TOUSZ . . . . tosus
/TOX . . . . toxin
/TOXZ . . . . toxins
/TRAEF . . . . trachelorrhaphy
/TRAEFG . . . . tachygraphy
/TRAEFL . . . . transversalis
/TRAEKL . . . . tracheal
/TRAEKLS . . . . trachelos
/TRAEKT . . . . trachelectomy
/TRAEPGS . . . . trepanation
/TRAEPS . . . . tracheoscopy
/TRAERTS . . . . arteritis
/TRAES . . . . arteriectasia
/TRAEVL . . . . transversalis

/TRAEZ. . . . . tresia
/TRAFG . . . . tachograph
/TRAFP . . . . trichia
/TRAFPG. . . . . tachygraph
/TRAFRB . . . . transverse
/TRAFRT . . . . transversostomy
/TRAIFP. . . . . tarachia
/TRAIFPL. . . . . trichial
/TRAIG . . . . tragus
/TRAIKL . . . . tracheal
/TRAIKLS . . . . trachelectasia
/TRAIKT . . . . tracheotomy
/TRAIN. . . . . train
/TRAIPT . . . . tracheloplasty
/TRAIRS . . . . tracer
/TRAKT . . . . tract
/TRAKTD . . . . tracted
/TRAL . . . . atrial
/TRALS . . . . arteriodialysis
/TRANL . . . . antral
/TRAOEF. . . . . trophia
/TRAOEFN. . . . . atropine
/TRAOEKLS . . . . trachelus
/TRAOEM . . . . electrolytemia
/TRAO*EM . . . . tyrosinemia
/TRAOEMT . . . . treatment
/TRAOENT . . . . nutrient
/TRAOENTS . . . . nutrients
/TRAOEP. . . . . tropy
/TRAOEPS . . . . trypesis
/TRAOEPZ. . . . . trapezial
/TRAOERMT . . . . tropometer
/TRAOESZ. . . . . tresis
/TRAOEZ. . . . . atresia
/TRAOF. . . . . atrophia
/TRAOFG . . . . autotrophic
/TRAOFT. . . . . autotroph
/TRAOGS . . . . trusion
/TRAOIB. . . . . tribe
/TRAOIFPS. . . . . trichiniasis
/TRAO*IG . . . . trigo
/TRAOIKLS . . . . trachelitis
/TRAOIKS . . . . tracheitis
/TRAOIT . . . . trite
/TRAOITS . . . . iritis

/TRAOIVL . . . . . retroviral
/TRAOIXZ . . . . . trichiasis
/TRAOK . . . . . tractor
/TRAOMT . . . . . tachometry
/TRAONT . . . . . antrotomy
/TRAONTS . . . . . antrostomy
/TRAOPT . . . . . ectropia
/TRAORS . . . . . transducer
/TRAOSZ . . . . . toreusis
/TRAOUFGS . . . . . transfusion
/TRAOUR . . . . . natruria
/TRAOURS . . . . . trophoneurosis
/TRAP . . . . . trap
/TRAPGS . . . . . transplantation
/TRAPT . . . . . transplant
/TRAUF . . . . . trophe
/TRAUM . . . . . trauma
/TRAUMS . . . . . traumas
/TRAUMT . . . . . traumatic
/TRAUN . . . . . tropion
/TRAURS . . . . . transversarius
/TRAX . . . . . traction
/TREJ . . . . . pterygium
/TREKT . . . . . transversectomy
/TREMP . . . . . temper
/TREMT . . . . . treatment
/TREN . . . . . trophasthenia
/TRERM . . . . . tremor
/TR–FGS . . . . . transfusion
/TR–FMGS . . . . . transformation
/TR–FRNS . . . . . transference
/TR–GS . . . . . transformation
/TRID . . . . . trichophrydia
/TRIFPD . . . . . trichate
/TRIFPG . . . . . trichic
/TRIFPS . . . . . trichinosis
/TRIFPT . . . . . trichotic
/TRIFPZ . . . . . trichous
/TRIJS . . . . . triginous
/TRIMZ . . . . . trismus
/TRINS . . . . . trypsin
/TR*IPG . . . . . tryptic
/TRIPGT . . . . . triptic
/TRIPS . . . . . tripsy
/TR*IPS . . . . . trypsin

/TRIPSZ . . . . . tripsis
/TRIRPT . . . . . triptor
/TR*IS . . . . . trist
/TR*ISZ . . . . . trists
/TRITS . . . . . antritis
/T-RM . . . . . terma
/TR-MGS . . . . . transmission
/TROEB . . . . . trichophobia
/TROED . . . . . electrode
/TROEF . . . . . trophy
/TROEFB . . . . . trophoblast
/TROEFD . . . . . trophodynia
/TROEFG . . . . . trophic
/TROEFN . . . . . trophin
/TROEGS . . . . . rotation
/TROEJ . . . . . opterygium
/TROEM . . . . . ectromelia
/TRO*EM . . . . . trachoma
/TROEMG . . . . . electronomic
/TROEMP . . . . . ectropium
/TROEN . . . . . ectropion
/TROENK . . . . . trochanterian
/TROENL . . . . . trichomonal
/TROEP . . . . . trope
/TRO*EP . . . . . tropy
/TROEPS . . . . . tropes
/TROEPT . . . . . triptoscope
/TROERK . . . . . trochanteric
/TROERMT . . . . . electrometer
/TROERN . . . . . arteriotony
/TROERZ . . . . . trophoneurosis
/TROESZ . . . . . trosis
/TROET . . . . . rotate
/TROEXZ . . . . . trichosis
/TROF . . . . . atrophy
/TROFG . . . . . trophic
/TROFK . . . . . atrophic
/TROFM . . . . . tropism
/TROFN . . . . . tropin
/TROFNS . . . . . tropins
/TROIF . . . . . troph
/TROIFG . . . . . trophic
/TROIFM . . . . . trichium
/TROIMT . . . . . iritomy
/TROIND . . . . . trigonosigmoidostomy

/TROING . . . . trigonitis
/TROIP . . . . tropia
/TROIPG . . . . tropic
/TROIPS . . . . trypsia
/TROIPT . . . . triptoscopy
/TROIR. . . . . elytrorrhaphy
/TROKL . . . . trochlea
/TROKT . . . . trachelotomy
/TROLT . . . . electrolyte
/TROMT . . . . optometry
/TRO*MT . . . . ptometry
/TRON . . . . electron
/TRO*N . . . . tron
/TRONGT . . . . trigonoenterostomy
/TRONT. . . . . trigonoenterostomy
/TRONTS . . . . tracheobronchitis
/TRO*P . . . . ectropia
/TROPG . . . . tropic
/TROPS . . . . tracheobronchoscopy
/TROPT . . . . tropometer
/TRORKL . . . . trochlear
/TRORT . . . . rotary
/TRO*RT . . . . rotatory
/TRO*S. . . . . transversostomy
/TROUPZ . . . . tropous
/TR–P. . . . . transparent
/TR–PK . . . . tryptic
/TR–PT . . . . transport
/TR–PZ. . . . . transparency
/TR–RMT . . . . transmitter
/TR–RMTS . . . . transmitters
/TRUGS . . . . transduction
/TRUNKZ . . . . truncus
/TRURB . . . . nutrition
/TRUS . . . . tragicus
/TUBL . . . . tubal
/TUMP. . . . . tympanum
/TURNL . . . . turbinal
/TUV . . . . tussive
/TWAEGS . . . . activation
/TWAEPT . . . . osteopathy
/TWAERB . . . . osteomalacia
/TWA*ERB . . . . -osteomalacia (*hyphenated*)
/TWAERK . . . . osteomalacic
/TWA*ERK . . . . -osteomalacic (*hyphenated*)

Steno	Suffix
/TWAERT	activator
/TWAET	activate
/TWAETD	activated
/TWAEX	taxy
/TWAEZ	osteoplasia
/TWAIDZ	osteochondrodysplasia
/TWA*IDZ	-osteochondrodysplasia (*hyphenated*)
/TWAK	tactic
/TWAKT	tatic
/TWAKZ	tactics
/TWANK	tympanic
/TWAOEVR	typhoid fever
/TWAOILTS	osteomyelitis
/TWAON	atonia
/TWAOTS	otitis
/TWAO*TS	-otitis (*hyphenated*)
/TWARPT	osteoarthropathy
/TWAS	osteoplasty
/TWA*S	-osteoplasty (*hyphenated*)
/TWAUT	tympanotomy
/TWAX	ataxia
/TWEJS	osteogenesis
/TWEMP	tympany
/TWEMT	osteum
/TW*EMT	steum
/TWEP	osteophlebitis
/TW*EP	-osteophlebitis (*hyphenated*)
/TWEPT	tenontoplasty
/TWHAOIT	osteophyte
/TWHOIT	steophyte
/TWIM	tendineum
/TWIPG	typic
/TWLAIS	-osteodysplasia (*hyphenated*)
/TWOEFS	osteosis
/TWOEFZ	steosis
/TWOEM	osteoma
/TWO*EM	steoma
/TWO*EN	atony
/TWOERL	tentorial
/TWOID	typhoid
/TWO*ID	osteoid
/TWOIFM	testoidism
/TWOIK	otia
/TWO*IK	tia
/TWOIKT	ataxic

/TWOIP . . . . atypical
/TWOIT . . . . ostitis
/TWO*IT . . . . stitis
/TWOITS . . . . ostitis
/TWO*ITS . . . . stitis
/TWOIX . . . . ataxy
/TWOJ. . . . . osteogeny
/TWOK . . . . tocic
/TWOLG . . . . osteology
/TWOLS . . . . osteolysis
/TWOLSZ . . . . -osteolysis (*hyphenated*)
/TWOM . . . . -osteoma (*hyphenated*)
/TWOMT . . . . tenotomy
/TWONG . . . . architectonic
/TWONGS . . . . architectonics
/TWORPT . . . . osteoarthropathy
/TWOSZ . . . . ostosis
/TWOT . . . . osteotomy
/TWOTS . . . . tenositis
/TWOX . . . . toxicosis
/TWRAEF . . . . osteorrhaphy
/TWROF . . . . osteodystrophy
/TWRO*F . . . . -osteodystrophy (*hyphenated*)
/TWUM . . . . tympanum
/TWUMT. . . . . ostium
/TW*UMT. . . . . stium
/T–X . . . . toxia
/TYAOEL . . . . telia
/TYAOIFM. . . . . ptyalism
/TYOEN . . . . atony
/TYOESZ . . . . actinomycosis
/TYOX . . . . toxy

U

/UM. . . . . um
/*UNG . . . . unguia
/UNK . . . . uncle
/UNKS. . . . . uncles
/UNL . . . . unguial
/UNT . . . . unit
/URGS . . . . neurotization
/URNG. . . . . uranic
/UVLT. . . . . ulcerative

V

/VA . . . . vertebra
/VAEFG. . . . . ventriculography
/VAEFK . . . . vesicoplasty
/VAEFL . . . . vesical
/VA*EGS . . . . invasion
/VAEM . . . . valinemia
/VAENGS . . . . ventilation
/VAERK . . . . valeric
/VAEV . . . . invasive
/VAEX. . . . . evacuation
/VAFL . . . . valve
/VAFR . . . . vascular
/VAFRGS . . . . vascularization
/VAFRL . . . . vascularly
/VAGS . . . . vaccination
/VAIBLT. . . . . availability
/VAIFGS . . . . vivification
/VAIFM . . . . vegetarianism
/VAIFT . . . . varicosity
/VAIJ. . . . . vegetative
/VAINGS . . . . venation
/VAINLS . . . . valence
/VAINLT. . . . . valent
/VAINLZ . . . . valency
/VAINT . . . . valent
/VA*IR . . . . ovaria
/VAIRJ. . . . . vegetarian
/VAIRL . . . . venereal
/VAIRM . . . . ovarium
/VA*IRM . . . . varium
/VA*IRN. . . . . -ovarian (*hyphenated*)
/VAIRNS . . . . variance
/VAIRNT . . . . variant
/VAIRPGS . . . . vaporization
/VAIVGS . . . . vivification
/VAIX. . . . . vaccination
/VA*LG . . . . vagal
/VALGZ . . . . valgus
/VALT . . . . vital
/VA*M . . . . vagogram
/VANK. . . . . ventricular
/VANKS. . . . . ventricularis

/VAOEFG . . . . venography
/VAOEM . . . . volemia
/VAO*EM . . . . volemia
/VAOEMG . . . . volemic
/VAO*EN . . . . vaccine
/VAOENG . . . . venogram
/VAOENTS . . . . venitis
/VAOERMT . . . . viscosimetry
/VAOFLG . . . . vasology
/VAOIBL . . . . viable
/VAOIBTS . . . . vestibulitis
/VAOIFLT . . . . valvulitis
/VAOIFT . . . . visceritis
/VAOIFTS . . . . visceritis
/VAOIJ . . . . vaginitis
/VAOIM . . . . vitamin
/VAOIMT . . . . vitamin
/VAOINL . . . . vinyl
/VAOINLT . . . . vitellin
/VAOIR . . . . virus
/VAOIRK . . . . virotic
/VAOIRL . . . . viral
/VAOIRMT . . . . environment
/VAOIRZ . . . . visor
/VAOIVLT . . . . valvulitis
/VAOIVNS . . . . vivescence
/VAOKL . . . . vacuole
/VAOL . . . . vagino-enterocele
/VAO*L . . . . volia
/VAOMT . . . . valvotomy
/VAONT . . . . venosity
/VAOR . . . . varia
/VAORJ . . . . ovovegetarian
/VAORKL . . . . vacuolar
/VAORM . . . . -ovarium (*hyphenated*)
/VAORNL . . . . venular
/VAO*S . . . . vasostomy
/VAOT . . . . vagotomy
/VAOUFL . . . . volvulus
/VAOUFLS . . . . volvulus
/VAOULGS . . . . evolution
/VAOULT . . . . virulent
/VAOUT . . . . vasculature
/VA*R . . . . var
/VARGS . . . . varication

/VARKT . . . . . vaginorectal
/VARL . . . . . ventral
/VARN . . . . . ovarian
/VA*RN . . . . . -ovarian (*hyphenated*)
/VARS . . . . . varus
/VARSZ . . . . . varicosis
/VART . . . . . variate
/VARTD . . . . . ventrad
/VAUFR . . . . . vascular
/VAUFRGS . . . . . vascularization
/VAUFRL . . . . . vascularly
/VAUFT . . . . . vesicostomy
/VAUL . . . . . vertebral
/VAUNL . . . . . vaccinal
/VAURL . . . . . valvular
/VAUVRL . . . . . valvar
/VAVL . . . . . valve
/VAVLT . . . . . valvulotomy
/VAVRL . . . . . valvar
/VAX . . . . . vaccine
/VAZ . . . . . vasation
/VEBL . . . . . vestibular
/VEFMT . . . . . investment
/VEFN . . . . . versioflexion
/VEFRL . . . . . vesicular
/VEFRN . . . . . versioflexion
/VEFT . . . . . venostomy
/VEFX . . . . . vesicofixation
/VEKL . . . . . vesicle
/VEKLZ . . . . . ventriculus
/VEKT . . . . . vasectomy
/VELS . . . . . vesicle
/VEM . . . . . venom
/VEMS . . . . . venomous
/V*ENGS . . . . . vention
/VENK . . . . . ventricle
/VENZ . . . . . venous
/VERBL . . . . . verbal
/VERG . . . . . vertigo
/VERGS . . . . . version
/VERGT . . . . . vertigo
/VERJS . . . . . vergence
/VERKT . . . . . vector
/VERL . . . . . vertical
/VERLS . . . . . virulence

/V*ERNT	venter
/VERS	verse
/VERT	vert
/V*ERT	verter
/VERTD	verted
/VERZ	versus
/V*ES	vest
/V*EX	vection
/V-FDZ	viscidosis
/VIFRGS	visceration
/VIFRL	visceral
/VIFT	viscosity
/VIGS	vision
/VIJZ	vertiginous
/VIKL	vesiculitis
/VIKLS	vesiculitis
/VILS	villous
/VINLT	vitelline
/VIPS	oviparous
/VIRBL	visual
/VIRK	ventriculi
/VIRMT	environment
/VIRND	verdin
/VIRNLT	vitrinal
/VIT	vitreous
/VIVGS	vivisection
/VLAJ	vaginal
/VLAJT	vaginalitis
/VLAJTS	vaginalitis
/VLAO*I	ventriculi
/VLEKT	vesiculectomy
/VLEKTS	vesiculectomies
/V-LGS	volution
/VLI	villi
/VL*I	ventriculi
/VLOIJ	vaginalitis
/VL*US	villus
/VOELT	volt
/VOEMT	valvulotome
/VOEPX	vesicopexy
/VOERL	variola
/VOERLT	voltmeter
/VOERMT	vasomotor
/VOEXL	vocational
/VOFLGS	evolution

/VOFT . . . . venosity
/VOG . . . . vesiculography
/VOIK . . . . vitaminotic
/VOILGS . . . . volitional
/VO*ILT . . . . violet
/VOIMT . . . . vitaminosis
/VOIMTS . . . . vitaminosis
/VOINL . . . . vaccinial
/VOIRM . . . . vomerine
/VOIRT . . . . vert
/VOIRTD . . . . verted
/VOIS . . . . voice
/VOIT . . . . vasculitis
/VOITS . . . . vasculitis
/VOJ . . . . voltage
/VOKLS . . . . vesiculosis
/VOLT . . . . volt
/VOMG . . . . vomiting
/VOMGT . . . . vomiting
/VONT . . . . vagotony
/VORBL . . . . vocational
/VORJ . . . . -ovovegetarian (*hyphenated*)
/VORLT . . . . voltometer
/VOUFM . . . . evolutionism
/VOUFMT . . . . evolutism
/VOURL . . . . -ovular (*hyphenated*)
/VOURS . . . . vorous
/VUFRL . . . . vulvar
/VURLT . . . . virulent
/VUVRL . . . . vulvar

W

/WAET . . . . weight
/WAEV . . . . wave
/WAEVS . . . . waves
/WAIG . . . . waking
/WAT . . . . watt
/WEL . . . . well
/WELGD . . . . welding
/WHAOEK . . . . rhachidia
/WRAE . . . . rhinorrhea
/WRAEFG . . . . rheography
/WRAEJ . . . . rrhagin

Steno	Suffix
/WRAEJS	rrhagins
/WRAEK	rrhachic
/WRAET	rheostat
/WRAFPD	arachnoid
/WRAIFK	arrhythmic
/WRAIFP	rachia
/WRAIK	rhachia
/WRAIN	rhinia
/WRA*IT	arrhythmia
/WRAIZ	rhizoclasia
/WRA*K	rhachidian
/WRAM	retinogram
/WRAOED	rrheid
/WRAOEL	rrheal
/WRAOELG	rheology
/WRAOELS	rrheals
/WRAOESZ	rrhesis
/WRAOETS	rheostosis
/WRAO*IN	rhine
/WRAOINK	rhinic
/WRAOINL	rhinal
/WRAOISZ	rrhiasis
/WRAOITS	rrhachitis
/WRAOUFM	rheumatism
/WRAOUMT	rheumatic
/WRAPT	rhinoplasty
/WREKT	rrhoidectomy
/WR*EKT	rrhectic
/WRERP	repressor
/WREX	rrhexis
/WRIFK	arrhythmic
/WR*IK	rrhachidian
/WRIMG	rhythmic
/WR*IMT	rrhythmia
/WRISZ	rrhachischisis
/WR*IT	rhythmia
/WRIX	rhexis
/WRIXZ	rhachischisis
/WROEGD	rrhodinogen
/WROEK	rrhoic
/WROELG	rrheology
/WROEND	rrhodin
/WROID	rrhoid
/WROIDZ	rrhoids
/WROILD	rrhoidal

/WROIP . . . . . rhinoscopy
/WROPD . . . . . rhodopsin
/WROT . . . . . rhinocystotomy
/WULGS . . . . . avulsion
/WUN . . . . . one

Y

/YAEFG . . . . . angioadenography
/YAEGS . . . . . radiation
/YAEK . . . . . ileac
/YAEL . . . . . ileal
/YAEM . . . . . ileum
/YAEMG . . . . . amylasemic
/YAEMP . . . . . lymphoplasia
/YAEMPZ . . . . . lymphoplasia
/YAEMS . . . . . amylasemia
/YAENL . . . . . lymphangeal
/YAENTS . . . . . alienitis
/YAERB . . . . . myelomalacia
/YAERKT . . . . . ureteria
/YAES . . . . . amylase
/YAEZ . . . . . erythroplasia
/YAFT . . . . . myeloblast
/YAIGS . . . . . iation
/YAIK . . . . . iac
/YAIMP . . . . . lymphia
/YAIN . . . . . mania
/YAINK . . . . . maniac
/YAINTD . . . . . iodinated
/YAIS . . . . . myelodysplasia
/YAK . . . . . iliac
/YAKL . . . . . ictal
/YAKZ . . . . . iliacs
/YAL . . . . . ial
/YALS . . . . . ials
/YA*LT . . . . . urethral
/YA*LTS . . . . . urethralis
/YAMP . . . . . lympha
/YA*N . . . . . ian
/YAOEFG . . . . . ureteroradiography
/YAOEFL . . . . . eosinophilia
/YAOEKD . . . . . uricacidemia
/YAOEL . . . . . lymphocele

/YAO*EL . . . . ilemmoma
/YAOELS . . . . myelocele
/YAOEMP . . . . lymphemia
/YAOEMS . . . . amyosthenia
/YAOENG . . . . iatrogenic
/YAOENS . . . . amyosthenia
/YAOERK . . . . uricuria
/YAOERKT . . . . ureterocystectomy
/YAOERM . . . . uricemia
/YAOERMG . . . . uricemic
/YAOERT . . . . iatric
/YAO*ERT . . . . urethria
/YAOERTS . . . . iatrics
/YAOERZ . . . . uresia
/YAOES . . . . uresis
/YAOESZ . . . . iosis
/YAOET . . . . iatry
/YAOETS . . . . ureterosis
/YAOFK . . . . urolithic
/YAOFP . . . . urachus
/YAOID . . . . icide
/YAOIFLT . . . . ureteropyelonephritis
/YAOIFT . . . . iatrist
/YAOIFTS . . . . iatrists
/YAOIK . . . . lymphocytic
/YAOIKL . . . . iridocyclitis
/YAOIKLS . . . . iridocyclitis
/YAOIKT . . . . lymphocytic
/YAOILD . . . . icidal
/YAOILT . . . . lyte
/YAOILTS . . . . ureteropyelitis
/YAOIMT . . . . epididymitis
/YAOIMTS . . . . epididymitis
/YAOINTS . . . . lymphangitis
/YAOIRD . . . . uricide
/YAOIRKS . . . . uricaciduria
/YAOIRS . . . . uriasis
/YAOIT . . . . lymphocyte
/YAOITS . . . . ileitis
/YAOR . . . . urea
/YAORKT . . . . uratic
/YAOUFRG . . . . urography
/YAOUGS . . . . eustachian
/YAOUMT . . . . uterotomy
/YAOUNK . . . . urocrinia

/YAOUNTS . . . . ileocutaneous
/YAOUR . . . . uria
/YAO*UR . . . . urea
/YAOURG . . . . urography
/YAOURK . . . . uric
/YAO*URK . . . . uricuria
/YAOURLG . . . . urology
/YAOURM . . . . uremia
/YAOURMS . . . . uricemia
/YAOURP . . . . ureteroscopy
/YAOURT . . . . uterine
/YAOURTS . . . . ureterectasis
/YAOUVL . . . . uvular
/YARLT . . . . urethral
/YARLTS . . . . urethralis
/YA*RS . . . . ureteroplasty
/YART . . . . iatria
/YA*RT . . . . atry
/YATS . . . . atrics
/YAURS . . . . ureterocystotomy
/YAURT . . . . ureterotomy
/YAVL . . . . uterovaginal
/YAX . . . . ataxy
/Y–D . . . . idea
/YEFTS . . . . myeloencephalitis
/YENG . . . . amyosthenic
/YENK . . . . amyosthenic
/YEPD . . . . epididymis
/YERK . . . . uretic
/YERKT . . . . ureteric
/YERLT . . . . ureteral
/YHAL . . . . hyal
/YIFG . . . . lymphoscintigraphy
/YIFK . . . . urolithic
/YIFTS . . . . lymphitis
/YIKT . . . . icteric
/YILS . . . . ileus
/YIMP . . . . lymph
/YIMPG . . . . lymphic
/YIMPT . . . . lymphatic
/YINTS . . . . lymphadenitis
/YIPD . . . . epididymectomy
/Y*IRD . . . . idria
/YIRGS . . . . iatrician
/YIRGSZ . . . . iatricians

/YIRKT . . . . -icteric (*hyphenated*)
/YIRSZ . . . . eurysis
/Y*IRT . . . . erythrin
/YIX . . . . icterus
/YLOIDZ . . . . amyloidosis
/YLOIT . . . . myelocyte
/YOEFL . . . . eosinophil
/YOEFLG . . . . eosinophilic
/YOEFS . . . . lymphomatosis
/YOEFSZ . . . . lymphomatosis
/YOEFT . . . . myeloblastosis
/YOEFZ . . . . ureteronephrosis
/YOEJ . . . . lymphangioma
/YOEM . . . . lymphoma
/YOEMP . . . . lymphocytosis
/YOEMPS . . . . lymphocytosis
/YO*EMT . . . . urethrotome
/YOERG . . . . ureterography
/YOERLS . . . . ureterolysis
/YOES . . . . myelosis
/YOETS . . . . otus
/YO*ETS . . . . tus
/YOFG . . . . epididymography
/YOFT . . . . ileotomy
/YOIFT . . . . ileostomy
/YOILT . . . . myelolymphocyte
/YOINL . . . . lymphangial
/YOIPD . . . . euploidy
/YOIPT . . . . epididymostomy
/YOIRD . . . . hidria
/YOIT . . . . lymphocyte
/YOITS . . . . iliitis
/YOJS . . . . myelogenous
/YOL . . . . myeloma
/YOLD . . . . amyloidosis
/YOLDZ . . . . amyloidosis
/YO*NS . . . . ileoneocystostomy
/YOP . . . . opia
/YO*P . . . . pia
/YOPG . . . . opic
/YO*PG . . . . pic
/YO*PT . . . . myelopathy
/YOULS . . . . ulis
/YOURK . . . . uricuric
/YUFT . . . . ureteroureterostomy

/YURD . . . . . urid
/YURKL . . . . . urachal
/YURPG . . . . . uterotropic
/YUX . . . . . icterus

Z

/--Z . . . . . s
/ZAEM . . . . . zemia
/ZAENG . . . . . xenic
/ZAENT . . . . . xanthine
/ZAIRL . . . . . axillary
/ZANT . . . . . oxanthine
/ZANTS . . . . . xanthose
/ZAOENG . . . . . xenic
/ZAOENTS . . . . . xenitis
/ZAOERZ . . . . . xerasia
/ZAOI . . . . . anxiety
/ZAOIG . . . . . zygote
/ZAOIGT . . . . . zygomatic
/ZAOIM . . . . . enzyme
/ZAOIS . . . . . zoiasis
/ZAOKT . . . . . zootic
/ZAOL . . . . . zoological
/ZAOLG . . . . . zoology
/ZAON . . . . . zoan
/ZAOUR . . . . . azoturia
/ZAUNL . . . . . zonal
/ZAUPZ . . . . . xanthopsia
/ZENT . . . . . xanthene
/ZGEN . . . . . zymogen
/ZGENG . . . . . zymogenic
/ZHA . . . . . amnesia
/ZIFD . . . . . xiphoid
/ZIFR . . . . . xyster
/ZIFRT . . . . . xyster
/ZIM . . . . . izema
/ZINT . . . . . xanthin
/ZKOEM . . . . . xanthosarcoma
/ZMIN . . . . . zymin
/ZMOEZ . . . . . zymosis
/ZMOK . . . . . zymotic
/ZMOKT . . . . . zymotic
/ZNAOE . . . . . xeny

/ZOE . . . . . zoa
/ZOEGT . . . . . zygote
/ZOEL . . . . . zoal
/ZOEM . . . . . chromosome
/ZOEMT . . . . . xanthoma
/ZOEN . . . . . zone
/ZOERNL . . . . . zonular
/ZOESZ . . . . . zygosis
/ZOET . . . . . azotemia
/ZOEZ . . . . . zoosis
/ZOFT . . . . . zygosity
/ZOGT . . . . . zygosity
/ZOID . . . . . zoicide
/ZOIK . . . . . zoic
/ZOIN . . . . . zoin
/ZOIRM . . . . . zoospermia
/ZOIRMT . . . . . zoospermatism
/ZOKT . . . . . zygotic
/ZON . . . . . zoon
/ZONSZ . . . . . zoonosis
/ZUS . . . . . zygous
/ZWAOIT . . . . . zoite
/ZYAOIM . . . . . zyme